CHALLENGING
MULTICULTURALISM

EUROPEAN MODELS OF DIVERSITY

Edited by Raymond Taras

EDINBURGH
University Press

© in this edition Edinburgh University Press, 2013
© in the individual contributions is retained by the authors

Edinburgh University Press Ltd
22 George Square, Edinburgh EH8 9LF
www.euppublishing.com

Typeset in 11/13 Sabon by
Servis Filmsetting Ltd, Stockport, Cheshire, and
printed and bound in Great Britain by
CPI Group (UK) Ltd, Croydon CR0 4YY

A CIP record for this book is available from the British Library

ISBN 978 0 7486 6457 3 (hardback)
ISBN 978 0 7486 6458 0 (paperback)
ISBN 978 0 7486 6459 7 (webready PDF)
ISBN 978 0 7486 6461 0 (epub)
ISBN 978 0 7486 6460 3 (Amazon ebook)

The right of the contributors to be identified as authors of this work has been asserted in
accordance with the Copyright, Designs and Patents Act 1988.

Contents

List of Tables and Figures   v
Notes on the Contributors   vii
Preface   xii
Foreword by Björn Fryklund   xv

PART I Theorizing Multiculturalism

 1 The Twilight of Multiculturalism? Findings from
    across Europe   3
    Pieter Bevelander and Raymond Taras

 2 Contemporary Citizenship and Diversity in Europe:
    The Place of Multiculturalism   25
    Tariq Modood and Nasar Meer

 3 The Challenge of Multiculturalism: Political Philosophy
    and the Question of Diversity   52
    Christian Fernández

PART II Multiculturalism's Pioneers and (Ex-)enthusiasts

 4 The 'Civic Re-balancing' of British Multiculturalism,
    and Beyond . . .   75
    Nasar Meer and Tariq Modood

 5 The Dutch Multicultural Myth   97
    Peter Scholten

 6 Immigrant Integration and Multiculturalism in Belgium   120
    Marco Martiniello

 7 The Political Dynamics of Multiculturalism in Sweden   138
    Karin Borevi

PART III Multicultural Societies without Multiculturalism?

  8 Public Debates and Public Opinion on Multiculturalism
     in Germany   163
     Martina Wasmer

  9 Danish Multiculturalism, Where Art Thou?   190
     Nils Holtug

 10 Multiculturalism Italian Style: Soft or Weak Recognition?   216
     Tiziana Caponio

 11 Redefining a (Mono)cultural Nation: Political Discourse
     against Multiculturalism in Contemporary France   236
     Florent Villard and Pascal-Yan Sayegh

PART IV Multiculturalism's Future Converts?

 12 Poland: Multiculturalism in the Making?   257
     Renata Włoch

 13 Multinationalism, Mononationalism or Transnationalism
     in Russia?   279
     Sergey Akopov

 14 Multiculturalism and Minorities in Turkey   297
     Ayhan Kaya

PART V Conclusion

 15 Multiculturalism: Symptom, Cause or Solution?   319
     Ulf Hedetoft

Index   334

Tables and Figures

TABLES

2.1 The state and citizens' responses to cultural diversity:
five ideal types   34
2.2 Five models of cohesion, equality and difference   37
2.3 Four political responses to diversity   39
2.4 Synthesis of models of state accommodation of
'difference'   42
2.5 Contemporary responses to migration-related
diversity   43
6.1 Number of work permits issued in the three Belgian
regions, 2000–6   123
6.2 Belgian and foreign populations by region, 2008   124
6.3 Number of foreigners acquiring Belgian nationality by
country of origin, 1997–2007   134
8.1 German views on cultural diversity in 1996 and 2006   177
8.2 Public support in Germany for multiculturalism: 2006
compared to 1996   179
8.3 Support for multiculturalism in Germany according to
voting intentions: 2006 compared to 1996   183
9.1 Multicultural Policy scores for selected countries   195
9.2 Danish attitudes to multiculturalism, 2000–11   203
10.1 Attitudes towards migration in Italy: trends from 1999
to 2007   224
13.1 The largest self-identified ethnic groups in Russia and
their language abilities   286

FIGURES

2.1 Four conceptions of citizenship   38
5.1 Policy frames in Dutch immigrant integration policy since
     the 1970s   107
9.1 Conceptions of community: from thick to thin   201

Notes on the Contributors

Sergey Akopov is Associate Professor at the St Petersburg branch of the Russian Presidential Academy of National Economy and Public Administration as well as Senior Fellow Lecturer at St Petersburg State University. His major fields of interest are political philosophy, political anthropology and communication, transnational studies and the political history of Russia. He is the author of over fifty papers, articles and book chapters published in Russian, English and Spanish, as well as two books: *Identichnosti v jepohu global'nyh migracij* ('Identities in the Era of Global Migrations', co-authored with M.Rozanova, Dean, St Petersburg University Centre of Comparative Philosophy 2010); and *Razvitie idej transnacionalizma v rossijskoj politicheskoj filosofii XX veka* ('The Development of the Idea of Transnationalism in Russian Political Philosophy in the 20th century', St Petersburg, RANEPA 2012).

Pieter Bevelander is Professor in International Migration and Ethnic Relations (IMER) and Director of the Malmö Institute for Studies of Migration, Diversity and Welfare. His recent books include *The Economics of Citizenship* (Malmö University 2008) and *Resettled and Included? The Employment Integration of Resettled Refugees in Sweden* (Malmö University 2009). His articles have appeared in leading scholarly journals such as *International Migration Review*, *Journal of International Migration and Integration*, *Journal of Immigrant and Refugee Studies* and *Ethnic and Racial Studies*.

Karin Borevi is Researcher and Lecturer in the Department of Government at Uppsala University. Her research interests include Scandinavian and European comparative perspectives on integration policy, citizenship policy and refugee settlement policy. She has headed a research project titled 'From multiculturalism to assimilation? Swedish integration policy in European comparison'.

Among her publications is the monograph *Välfärdsstaten i det Mångkulturella Samhället* ('The Welfare State in the Multicultural Society', Uppsala University 2002).

Tiziana Caponio is Associate Professor in the Department of Political Science at the University of Turin. Research interests encompass comparative immigration, ethnic minority organizations in Europe, minority political participation and local authorities' policies on minority inclusion. Her scholarly works have appeared in *Rivista italiana di sociologia, Journal of Ethnic and Migration Studies* and *International Migration Review.* She is also the editor of the book *The Local Dimension of Migration Policymaking* (Amsterdam University Press 2010).

Christian Fernández is Postdoctoral Researcher at the Malmö Institute for Studies of Migration, Diversity and Welfare. Before coming to Malmö University he held the position of Senior Lecturer in the Department of Political Science at Lund University. His research and publications address aspects of political philosophy concerned with citizenship, toleration, multicultural societies and normative theory.

Björn Fryklund was the founding Director of the Malmö Institute for Studies of Migration, Diversity and Welfare, which he headed from 2007 until 2012. He has also been Professor in Sociology at Malmö University and served as leader of a major research project titled 'Populism and xenophobia in Europe and Sweden'. Among his many published works on xenophobia is *Populism and a Mistrust of Foreigners* (Swedish Immigration Board 2007).

Ulf Hedetoft is Professor in Nationality and Migration Studies, Director of the SAXO Institute and Dean of the Faculty of Humanities at the University of Copenhagen. He is founding Director of the Academy for Migration Studies in Denmark (AMID). Among his book-length publications are *Signs of Nations: Studies in the Political Semiotics of Self and Other in Contemporary European Nationalism* (Dartmouth 1995); *Political Symbols, Symbolic Politics: European Identities in Transformation* (Ashgate 1998); *The Postnational Self: Belonging and Identity* (University of Minnesota Press 2002); and *The Politics of Multiple Belonging: Ethnicity and Nationalism in Europe and East Asia* (Ashgate 2004).

Nils Holtug is Director of the Centre for the Study of Equality and Multiculturalism (CESEM), and Associate Professor in the Department of Media, Cognition and Communication at the University of Copenhagen. His diverse research interests encompass issues of equality, multiculturalism, migration, secularism, population ethics, global justice, normative ethics and personal identity. Recent books include *Persons, Interests, and Justice* (Oxford University Press 2010); *Nationalism and Multiculturalism in a World of Immigration* (Palgrave 2009); and *Egalitarianism: New Essays on the Nature and Value of Equality* (Oxford University Press 2006).

Ayhan Kaya holds the Jean Monnet Chair for European Politics of Interculturalism and is Professor of Political Science at Istanbul Bilgi University. He has also headed its Centres for Migration Research and European Studies. His research focuses on Euro-Turks in Germany and France, the Circassian diaspora in Turkey and the construction and articulation of modern diasporic identities. Among his many publications on migration is *Islam, Migration and Integration: The Age of Securitization* (Palgrave 2009).

Marco Martiniello has been Research Director at the National Fund for Scientific Research (FNRS) in Brussels as well as Director of the Centre d'Études de l'Ethnicité et des Migrations (CEDEM) and Lecturer in Politics at the Université de Liège. He is the author or editor of many books on this subject including most recently *La démocratie multiculturelle* ('Multicultural Democracy', Paris: Presses de Sciences Po 2011) and *Selected Studies in International Migration and Immigrant Incorporation* (Amsterdam University Press 2010).

Nasar Meer is Senior Lecturer in the School of Arts and Social Sciences at Northumbria University. Recently he has also been a Minda de Gunzberg Fellow at Harvard University and Visiting Fellow with the Institute for Advanced Studies in the Humanities at the University of Edinburgh. He has also held a visiting fellowship with the W. E. B. Du Bois Institute for African and African-American Studies at Harvard. His books include *Citizenship, Identity and the Politics of Multiculturalism* (Palgrave 2010); *European Multiculturalisms: Cultural, Religious and Ethnic Challenges* (Edinburgh University Press 2011); and a forthcoming study, *Race and Ethnicity*, in the Sage Key Concepts Series.

Tariq Modood is Professor of Sociology, Politics and Public Policy and founding Director of the Centre for the Study of Ethnicity and Citizenship at the University of Bristol. A member of the Commission on the Future of Multi-Ethnic Britain, he is a regular contributor to policy and media debates. He headed the EMILIE project titled 'A European approach to multicultural citizenship', and leads a number of current cross-national research teams. Recent books that he has authored or edited include *Ethnicity, Nationalism and Minority Rights* and *Ethnicity, Social Mobility and Public Policy in the US and UK* (both Cambridge University Press 2004); *Multicultural Politics: Racism, Ethnicity and Muslims in Britain* (Edinburgh University Press 2005); *Multiculturalism: A Civic Idea* (Polity 2007); *Secularism, Religion and Multicultural Citizenship* (Cambridge University Press 2009); *Global Migration, Ethnicity and Britishness* (Palgrave 2011); and *European Multiculturalisms: Cultural, Religious and Ethnic Challenges* (Edinburgh University Press 2011).

Pascal-Yan Sayegh has been Associate Researcher at the Institute of Transtextual and Transcultural Studies at Jean Moulin University in Lyon. His doctoral thesis in 2011, titled 'Nationalism as a social imaginary: Negotiations of social signification and (dis)integrating discourses in Britain, France and Poland', was awarded the highest distinction given in France. His published articles have focused on the connection between religion and nationalism in Europe.

Peter Scholten is Associate Professor of Public Policy and Politics at Erasmus University in Rotterdam, and Associate Researcher of the Centre on Migration, Policy and Society (COMPAS) at the University of Oxford. His research, publications and teaching focus on issues of governance in multicultural societies. He is the author of *Framing Immigrant Integration: Dutch Research-policy Dialogues in Comparative Perspective* (Amsterdam University Press 2011). The international journals in which he has published include *Journal of European Public Policy, British Journal of Politics and International Relations, Journal of International Migration and Integration, Journal of Public Policy* and *Nations and Nationalism*.

Raymond Taras has recently served as Willy Brandt Professor at Malmö University, Sweden, and Visiting Fellow at the European University Institute in Florence, Italy. Previously he was Visiting Professor at Aalborg University in Denmark and Lecturer at

Coventry University in England. In the US he is Professor of Political Science at Tulane University in New Orleans, and has been a visiting faculty member at Stanford, Harvard and the University of Michigan. Authored books include *Xenophobia and Islamophobia in Europe* (Edinburgh University Press 2012); *Understanding Ethnic Conflict* (Pearson 2010); *Europe Old and New* (Rowman & Littlefield 2008); and *Liberal and Illiberal Nationalisms* (Palgrave 2002).

Florent Villard is Director of the MC3M Research Centre (Migration and Citizenship – Mutations, Métissage, Multilingualism), Vice-Director of the Institute of Transtextual and Transcultural Studies and Head of the Department of Chinese Studies at Jean Moulin University, Lyon. He also serves as editor of *Transtexts-Transcultures: Journal of Global Cultural Studies*. His major research interests comprise the concepts of interculturalism and Europeanized culture as they apply to China. His recent book is *Global Fences: Literatures, Limits, Borders* (Presses Universitaires de Lyon 2011).

Martina Wasmer is a social scientist in the Department of Monitoring Society and Social Change at GESIS – the Leibniz Institute for the Social Sciences. She has published extensively, including technical reports, using data collected by the German General Social Survey (ALLBUS). Much of her analysis focuses on measuring changing attitudes and values in Germany. She is co-editor of *Germans or Foreigners? Attitudes Towards Ethnic Minorities in Post-Reunification Germany* (Palgrave 2003).

Renata Włoch is a sociologist in the Institute of Sociology at the University of Warsaw. Among her areas of expertise are questions of recognition, discrimination and exclusion of national minorities and migrant communities in Poland. She is the author of the scholarly monograph *Polityka integracji muzulmanów we Francji i Wielkiej Brytanii* ('The Politics of the Integration of Muslims in France and Great Britain', University of Warsaw Press 2011).

Preface

For some years now in France, young people of foreign origin have carried their electoral cards on their persons for an unusual reason. It is believed that brandishing these cards in public reduces the chances that these members of visible minorities will be subject to violence, whether at the hands of 'ethically French' right-wing hooligans or the police. *Une carte électorale* is, then, a talisman – in addition to it constituting a right to vote. The card is an affirmation that the bearer participates in the life of the nation, thereby partially satisfying the French Republican ideal of citizenship.

In 2012 the French Socialist Party captured the presidency and the legislature by gaining the support of the country's multicultural communities. Young people of migrant background used their electoral cards to vote – and to help change the government. The irony is that across the political spectrum in France a consensus exists that the multicultural model of managing diversity is not as effective as the colour-blind Republican approach. At a time when across much of Europe multiculturalism has been discredited as an idea whose time has passed, the purportedly assimilationist French approach has helped infuse cultural diversity with new-found power.

The challenges to multiculturalism in Europe are manifold. Among agents of change are grassroots political movements, whether made up of far-right anti-immigrant – and most of the time also anti-multicultural – movements, or of communities of immigrant or minority backgrounds. But it has been the questioning of multicultural policy by Europe's political elites that has raised the stakes for managing diversity differently: not many politicians today run for election championing the multicultural approach.

This book weighs the many challenges emanating from diverse actors to the model of managing diversity through recognizing distinct cultural communities. These challenges are chronicled in states where multiculturalism has never been official policy, such as in France, as well as in states where it has, or may be in the future.

The writing and editing of this book were carried out in 2012, but its genesis dates back a year earlier. In April 2011 a two-day workshop at Malmö University brought scholars from ten different European universities together to discuss the fate of multiculturalism. It had been a particularly harsh winter for the concept after Europe's leading political figures took turns swiping at the previously politically correct model. The workshop laid the analytical and normative groundwork for the chapters of this book.

First, therefore, I wish to express my gratitude to Björn Fryklund, director of the Malmö Institute for Studies of Migration, Diversity and Welfare (MIM), who provided all the resources needed to bring top specialists to Sweden for this workshop. Fryklund has been a pioneer in the study of multiculturalism and its opponents. The combination of low-key but visionary leadership in the field of migration studies will be his legacy.

Without the attention to detail – and generosity of spirit – of Merja Skaffari-Multala, who assumed responsibility for the logistical planning of the workshop, the intellectually creative atmosphere that emerged would have been hard to forge. Louise Tregert, administrative director at MIM, was also a pillar of strength and support in turning the workshop project into reality. To each I express my sincere thanks.

The authors of working papers presented at the workshop were matched with specialists – mainly drawn from the Malmö-Lund university communities – who served as their discussants. The constructive critiques offered by discussants were critical to launching both a set of reflexive case studies as well as an integrated tested research design. The following workshop participants – migration specialists in their own right – played a key role in exacting a high level of scholarship: Berndt Clavier, Maja Povrzanović Frykman, Katarzyna Gmaj, Anders Hellström, Catarina Kinnvall, Yngve Lithman, Ravi Pendakur, Bo Petersson, Anne Sofie Roald, Karin Sarsenov and Pauline Stoltz.

I wish to single out Mattis Kristoffersson and Ellinor Evain, students at Malmö University at the time, for their conscientious supporting role at the workshop. They also provided warm companionship to all participants.

The process of writing book chapters to fit a common research framework is largely individual. Contributors to this book can be divided into the critical mass that took part in the workshop, and the critical minority that joined the project subsequently. I extend my gratitude to each for conscientious and congenial intellectual exchanges in the preparation of this book. My special thanks go to Nasar Meer for his practical assistance with the publication of this book.

Finally, I wish to acknowledge the flawless professionalism of the editorial team at Edinburgh University Press: Nicola Ramsey, Rebecca Mackenzie, Michelle Houston and Eddie Clark.

Raymond Taras

Foreword

Raymond Taras' period as Willy Brandt Guest Professor in Malmö coincided with the time that leading European politicians were openly claiming that multiculturalism was dead and that it directly counteracted integration. Angela Merkel in Germany was the first to express such sentiments, and she was quickly followed by Nicolas Sarkozy in France and David Cameron in Britain. Against the background of these political developments in Europe and a similar (including scientific) questioning of multiculturalism, Taras strategically intervened by organizing a scientific workshop called 'The Twilight of Multiculturalism: Theory, Empirics and Norms' at MIM in Malmö during the spring of 2011.

Leading scholars from a number of European countries, including Eastern Europe, were invited to the workshop and asked to talk about how multiculturalism and integration were manifested in their own countries. Following the workshop, additional specialists were invited to contribute to the book. A section on theorizing multiculturalism was added in order to give a more holistic picture. Tariq Modood agreed to co-author a chapter on the place of multiculturalism in European diversity. An emphasis on European liberalism and diversity was provided by Christian Fernández. Five additional specialists on multiculturalism – Tiziana Caponio, Ulf Hedetoft, Ayhan Kaya, Pascal-Yan Sayegh and Renata Włoch – who did not attend the workshop agreed to write chapters for the book, adding further richness to the study. Their contributions are absolutely crucial to the book's theme and emphasis.

I regard the publication of this book with Edinburgh University Press as a significant contribution to the current scientific and political debate about the need for improved integration policies. A critical discussion about multiculturalism and integration is both timely and important, especially as right-wing radical populist parties are increasingly gaining ground in Western and Eastern Europe and attracting followers who are opposed to a multicultural society and to those who promote it. The mobilization of right-wing populist parties, whose ideology is based on a mistrust of foreigners and at times pure racism, is mainly directed at the immigrant population as carriers of the multicultural society. This means that important issues about democracy are raised when critical and challenging questions about multiculturalism and who should be included and excluded in both the European and national community are discussed. A useful way of addressing such burning questions would be to carefully read and reflect on the problems highlighted in this publication.

Finally, then, I would like to thank Raymond Taras for masterminding the important workshop during his time as Guest Professor at MIM in Malmö that made this book possible, for his strong interest and engagement and for his ability to identify key issues that migration research needs to address.

Björn Fryklund
Director and Professor
Malmö Institute for Studies of Migration,
Diversity and Welfare
April 2012

Part I

Theorizing Multiculturalism

Chapter One

The Twilight of Multiculturalism? Findings from across Europe

Pieter Bevelander and Raymond Taras

Is there incontrovertible evidence that European publics and elites have become increasingly hostile to multiculturalism? Can the rise in electoral support for anti-immigrant parties be explained as support also for their implied anti-multicultural policies? Just as worrisome, why have most mainstream political leaders in Europe discarded the term 'multiculturalism' in their discursive practices and opted instead for scepticism, critique and rejection of a multicultural model for managing diverse societies?

Following Tariq Modood (2007: 2), we understand the politics of multiculturalism to signify the recognition of group differences within public spheres such as law, policy, democratic discourse, shared citizenship and national identity. In recent decades, global migration – south-north but also south-south – has reached numbers unprecedented in world history. Large-scale immigration into receiving societies creates diversity, even super-diversity, as Britain's demographics are described today.

For a time, immigrant-based multiculturalism – as opposed to one based on a plurality of national minorities and indigenous communities living within a state – was a model that encouraged and enabled ethnic, religious and cultural groups to maintain their distinctiveness in receiving societies. But attacks on multiculturalism became commonplace in Europe, even before the financial crisis hit hard in 2008. They are frequently associated with conservative political actors but, as we describe below, radical theorists have their own disagreements with the premises of multiculturalism.

Only one country seems to have held on firmly to the model and it is not European and therefore not part of our book. A country that pioneered multiculturalism in the 1960s, it is asserted today, sometimes in hyperbolic fashion, that 'You can't kill multiculturalism in Canada' (Anderson 2012). Canadian multiculturalism is 'immortal' because it constitutes political practice which all the country's major political parties accept. Those are its origins and, though skilfully promoted in the theories of liberalism espoused and elaborated by such eminent Canadian philosophers as Will Kymlicka and Charles Taylor, multiculturalism as Canadian political practice and a defining characteristic of Canadian identity give it the semblance of immortal life.

Apart from Canada, the Netherlands has long been considered to be a pioneer of multiculturalism. Dutch scholarship on the subject has been extraordinarily comprehensive and sophisticated. From within it emerged some of the first sceptical assessments of the multicultural model. While early critiques can be found in other European countries, it has been said that 'Blaming multiculturalism for social ills is a Dutch national sport' (Bowen 2011). Has it now become a European sport too, competitive like Champions League football?

Migration and multiculturalism

The financial crisis of 2008 and after awakened millions of citizens around the world to the limitations of the dominant grand ideas of our time. Chief among these was globalization, a policy, process and plausible ideology that was long contested in the world's developing regions such as Africa and Latin America. The economic crises of the US and Europe became global economic crises and many hard-hit victims of them questioned whether globalization had primarily served the interests of transnational economic and political elites. As the economic downturn deepened and unemployment rose, the long-standing and pervasive myth of the inherent value of migration – for migrants and receiving societies alike – was called into question.

In Europe small countries such as Denmark and the Netherlands had developed a sceptical view of immigration some time back so the effects of the most recent economic crisis did not come as a surprise. While unemployment hit many groups of people, higher unemployment among immigrants relative to natives had been a gradual trend that dated back to the mid-1970s (Bevelander 2000). But weaker economic integration was due in large measure to cultural factors and not economic competition, as evidence in this book will indicate.

For the first time in decades, a sharp fall-off in the rate of immigration to Europe was recorded in the naughts. With it came questions about whether multiculturalism was the best model for managing the diversity created by migration. Particularly among right-wing nationalist political entrepreneurs, the conviction hardened that no other aspect of contemporary social life was left as unmanaged and unregulated as immigration policy. The multicultural model of society was, critics of this view believed, a fig leaf concealing how poorly integration of migrants into host societies was taking place. The taboo on crypto-racist, xenophobic, intolerant and exclusionary discourses was unravelling.

The tone of political rhetoric in Europe resonated in harsher tones, evidenced by growing electoral support and political influence of populist parties. Of particular importance was increasing anxiety about Muslims and whether they were integrating – a key explanatory factor for disappointment and disillusion expressed in old-style multiculturalism. Despite this trend, for Modood and Nasar Meer (2012), it was multiculturalism's resilience that was noteworthy: 'despite the turn to a vision of multiculturalism's retreat amongst many European leaders and citizens, a normative conception of multiculturalism remains a resilient means of addressing the challenge of contemporary nation-state citizenship under conditions of diversity'.

Modood and Meer's scepticism about multiculturalism's decline – if not about its fall from grace – was shared by two other leading experts on the model. Keith Banting and Will Kymlicka have highlighted how the supposed alternative type of diversity policy discussed by political leaders and theorists today – civic integration – is not that dissimilar from, and easily compatible with, the multicultural model. It appears to advance 'sharply different premises':

> active integration of immigrants into the economic, social and political mainstream; a muscular defence of liberal democratic principles; insistence on language acquisition and knowledge of the host country's history, norms and institutions; the introduction of written citizenship tests and loyalty oaths. (Banting and Kymlicka 2012: 3)

But the two Canadian authors find that 'In many countries, civic integration programmes are being layered over multicultural initiatives introduced in earlier decades, producing what can be thought of as a multicultural version of civic integration' (ibid.). They categorically conclude, therefore, that liberal forms of civic integration can be combined with multiculturalism.

Not only that: for Banting and Kymlicka few countries (the Netherlands being a clear exception) have actually retreated from multiculturalism. In the 2010 compilation of their Multiculturalism Policy Index (MCP), data indicate that

> While there has been a retreat from multiculturalism policies in a few countries, this is not the dominant pattern. The larger picture in Europe is one of stability and expansion of multicultural policies in the first decade of the 21st century. New language has often emerged to discuss 'diversity policy', but core programs often endure. (Banting and Kymlicka 2012: 3)

They suggest, then, that 'the retreat from multiculturalism in Europe is more complete at the level of discourse than policy'. The majority of case studies in this book provide evidence leading to the same conclusion. But we shall also encounter surprising counterfactuals and counterintuitive findings.

Before there can be immigration-based *multiculturalism*, there must be *immigration*, we have emphasized. Immigration into Europe today overwhelmingly subsumes family unification and labour migration processes and only to a small degree refugees. Immigrants generally, and refugees in particular, have suffered a loss of rights during the global crisis. We should not overlook the fact that nationals and longtime citizens, too, have been adversely affected. For example, there have been flat rates in income growth for the bottom 40 per cent of the employed across most European societies over the last five years.

The way that migration studies – sometimes termed international migration and ethnic relations (IMER) – have been carried out in the last decade leads us to suggest that it subsumes a triad of distinct though interrelated spheres: immigration, integration (in which multiculturalism has been a dominant approach) and citizenship. While not excluding the other parts of the triad, the *explanans* of this book focuses on multiculturalism as outcome. Earlier phases of migration studies centred on immigration flows as outcome. Much of the newest research considers citizenship acquisition as outcome variable.

How multiculturalism has been studied

The trajectory of research on the consequences of international migration is valuable to chart because a longer-term perspective can help us understand the current complicated and contested character of multiculturalism, and immigration generally. In its early stages in the 1960s and 1970s research was generally discipline-oriented, and economic, political, social and cultural angles of immigration were explored by respective disciplinary fields. By the 1980s the integration of labour migrants had become a principal focus. In the 1990s changing immigration policies, as well as the special cases of refugees and family reunification, took on greater importance.

Initially, the trailblazing countries in migration research were those that, significantly, were also pioneering a multicultural model: Britain, the Netherlands and Sweden. Germany, Belgium, Denmark and Norway had active migration research agendas but not on the same scale as the 'pioneers'. France represented a special case: the study of migration was invariably linked to its Republican model of organic unity, and how migrants assimilated into French society was the key research question. Related topics were xenophobia, racism and anti-Semitism, which generated an extensive body of literature. In the 1980s a number of European countries experienced populist mobilization against immigrants, which was the forerunner to strong opposition to the multicultural society organized in right-wing anti-immigrant parties.

Institutionally, a more interdisciplinary approach to studying migration emerged. Research institutes were established in many European countries to study the complexity and interdisciplinary character of the topic. The Institute for Migration and Ethnic Studies (IMES) was founded at the University of Amsterdam in 1993. In Sweden, an institutionalized interdisciplinary study of migration began in the late 1990s at Malmö University, located in the country's most diverse and changing city. Malmö Institute for the Studies of Migration, Diversity and Welfare (MIM) was a response to the pressing need for knowledge on migration in general, the management of diversity in a society, the integration of immigrants and their offspring and the reactions of national populations to a rapidly changing receiving society. The Centre for Migration Policy and Security (COMPAS) at the University of Oxford has a similar mission. Inevitably, key political phenomena have been brought into the research: democracy, citizenship, nationalism, populism and xenophobia. Migration institutes exist today in most countries in Europe including those that are part of the EU's eastern enlargement.

Nothing attests to the growth and significance of migration studies as persuasively as the development and rapid expansion of global organizations. Metropolis is one of these: a broad international network for researchers, policymakers and practitioners engaged in the field of migration, integration and ethnicity. A second is IMISCOE (International Migration, Integration and Social Cohesion), which institutionalizes collaborative research on migration, integration, ethnicity and social unity. NORFACE (New Opportunities for Research Funding Agency Co-operation in Europe) is a third network creating partnership between national research councils so as to promote cooperation in research policy in Europe; migration is one of its key areas. All aim to increase comparative knowledge in the fields of migration, integration and citizenship.

The début-de-siècle *wave of migration research*

In 2000 British political theorist Bhikhu Parekh published *Rethinking Multiculturalism* which represented an early revisionist challenge to multicultural orthodoxy. He reviewed the key ideas shaping multiculturalism: human nature, loyalty to culture, national identity, forms of pluralism, moral monism, structure of authority, collective rights, equality of difference, religion and public life. He came out emphatically in support of a pluralist perspective on cultural diversity in which there would be a 'creative interplay' of three elements: 'the cultural embeddedness of human beings, the inescapability and desirability of cultural diversity and intercultural dialogue, and the internal plurality of each culture'. The implication was that 'From a multicultural perspective, no political doctrine or ideology can represent the full truth of human life' (Parekh 2000: 338).

If our book examines where multiculturalism went off the rails, where it did not and where the rails have been adjusted, this would be no surprise to Parekh. As he forcefully described the context:

> Multicultural societies throw up problems that have no parallel in history. They need to find ways of reconciling the legitimate demands of unity and diversity, achieving political unity without cultural uniformity, being inclusive without being assimilationist, cultivating among their citizens a common sense of belonging while respecting their cultural differences, and cherishing plural cultural identities without weakening the shared and precious identity of shared citizenship. *This is a formidable political task and no multicultural society so far has succeeded in tackling it.* (Parekh 2000: 343, emphasis added)

Five years later, in the aftermath of the London bombings, Modood eloquently set forth the case that British multicultural society was not reducible to a 'black-white dualism'; many other ethnic and religious communities, including Asian, were integral parts of it. In *Multicultural Politics* (2005), he underscored how an integral part of multiculturalism – anti-racism – had registered many successes in Britain. But after the 7/7 bomb attacks in London, Muslims, not blacks, became identified as the most threatening 'other'. This, for Modood, subsumed a cultural racism grounded in the idea that culture is static or 'quasi-natural' and 'cultural racism naturalises culture ... as if culture is automatically reproduced' and 'does not change over time' (2005: 13). The impact of Modood's book was to heighten awareness of the pluralism of cultures in Britain.

A decade after Parekh's book was published, two studies grudgingly recognized that multiculturalism was on the run but nevertheless they refused to offer an obituary for it. *The Multiculturalism Backlash* noted how 'the term has successfully been associated with the idea of misguided policy. Politicians to the right and left of centre prefer to disassociate themselves from multiculturalism' even as 'Policies and programmes once deemed "multicultural" continue everywhere' (Vertovec and Wessendorf 2010: 14, 21). In addition, Alessandro Silj's collection *European Multiculturalism Revisited* (2010) provided an examination of the crisis of the model in six countries (all covered in our volume) but its rootedness as well. Most recently, Anna Triandafyllidou, Tariq Modood and Nasar Meer (2012: 10) framed multiculturalism's 'disappearing act' differently: if there has been an observable retreat from multiculturalism, they write in *European Multiculturalisms* that 'this does not necessarily mean that the desirability of recognizing minority cultural differences as a means of cultivating an inclusive citizenship has been eliminated'.

Back to Canada and its 'immortal' multiculturalism. With firm philosophic foundations cemented by Kymlicka and Taylor, vibrant *début-de-siècle* scholarship on multiculturalism is found in a book examining cross-national case studies and statistical analyses of the relationships among diversity policies, public attitudes and the welfare state (Banting and Kymlicka 2006). The volume examines whether a conflict between the politics of recognition and the politics of redistribution may arise, and it provides data shedding light on the recognition/redistribution linkage. Banting and Kymlicka conclude that there is no inherent tendency for the politics of recognition to undermine redistributive policies.

That is not what other studies of the Canadian experience indicate. Redistribution of power, in particular, may be what the ideology of multiculturalism is cryptically designed to prevent. Left-wing critic Richard Day (2000: 3, 12) suggested that Canada represents a modern-colonial nation state that has embraced a messianic mission:

'while Canadian multiculturalism presents itself as a new solution to an ancient problem of diversity, it is better seen as the most recent mode of *reproduction* and *proliferation* of that problem'. It may be that *failing* to achieve a universal mass of identities is what will inadvertently allow the country to approach its goal of mutual and equal recognition of groups. Put differently, 'Only by *abandoning* the dream of unity, Canada may, after all, lead the way towards a future that will be shared by many other nation-states'.

Around the same time, Eva Mackey indicted pluralist national culture in Canada for facilitating the process in which 'cultural difference has been recognized within the context of the overarching framework of the Western project of nation-building' (Mackey 2002: 165). 'Many cultures, one project', she implies, do not really amount to diversity. Developing Homi Bhabha's critique (1994), she contended that Canadian multiculturalism's 'tolerance actually reproduces dominance (of those with the power to tolerate, because asking for "tolerance" always implies the possibility of intolerance')' (2002: 16). She continued: 'the recognition of difference, in and of itself, is not necessarily the solution, just as the erasure of difference *per se* has not always been the main problem'. The more significant issue was that multiculturalism formed 'an integral part of the project of building and maintaining dominant power, and *reinforcing Western hegemony*' (2002: 163, emphasis added). Even in Canada, then, the multiculturalism model is being challenged.

Key research questions in the study of multiculturalism

Let us consider how economic calculations have come to play a more important role in immigration policy. As part of the IMPALA project (International Migration Policy and Law Analysis) measuring migrant rights, two scholars found evidence supporting the idea that migration involves a zero-sum game or, put differently, the size of the pie to be divided is fixed. Using visa-issuing data for refugee-producing states, Thielemann and Hobolth (2012: 15) described how the cost implications of taking in refugees for receiving states, when combined with more effective measures in restricting their access to states, has meant that when refugees were admitted to a country in larger numbers (as a proportion of the existing population), they received fewer rights and benefits. They analyzed recent asylum data and found some support for the numbers versus rights trade-off in the sphere of forced migration. The authors tentatively concluded that:

Sweden, Norway and Switzerland seem to form a cluster of countries with 'low rights, high numbers' regimes. Here, the number of persons granted protection is relatively large compared with the population size and the status granted to most refugees is of a subsidiary nature. Hence, high numbers goes hand in hand with a less costly protection status. (Thielemann and Hobolth 2012: 19)

Granting refugees full benefits was, by contrast, often accompanied by restricting their overall numbers. The countries in this group were Germany, France, Britain and Belgium. 'Here, admission numbers were relatively low but applicants were instead granted a "costlier" full Geneva protection status'. There was a third category as well: 'A large cluster of mainly Southern and Eastern European states, however, questioned the existence of a trade-off. Here, both numbers and rights were very low'. The argument could also go the other way. By applying the more costly Geneva Convention rights regime, countries could control the influx of migrants more effectively. Paradoxically, they could invoke this regime to keep prospective migrants out.

The importance of economic calculations can be inflated. There is a clearly discernible trend towards old-fashioned *cultural* integration in immigration policy. A good example of this is how naturalization policy has changed; 'naturalization' has become the ultimate integration indicator in immigration policy. Accordingly, whether *citizenship* policy encourages an integration process that entails a naturalization outcome for immigrants has become an important element in recent research; it forms part of the civic integration approach to the study of diversity described above.

As we shall see in our case studies, in many countries across Europe the introduction of language and citizenship tests to spur immigrant integration suggests that 'the celebration of citizenship and integration has replaced talk of multiculturalism' (Bloemraad 2008: 13). Citizenship, not multiculturalism, is becoming the barometer of successful state management of diversity as well as of immigrant integration attainment. However, few studies have actually studied the relationship between citizenship and integration – economic, political or social. One book that compared both 'old world' and 'new world' immigration countries found that 'new world' immigrants seemed to experience a 'citizenship premium'; results for 'old world' countries indicated only a weak positive relationship between economic integration and citizenship acquisition (Bevelander and DeVoretz 2008).

The authors cautioned that citizenship policies of countries included in the study were designed to meet individual countries' self-concepts as ethnic or civic nations and not for 'economic premium' purposes. The results point to a policy trade-off between immigrant and citizenship acquisition policies: if a state applies rigorous screening for immigrant entry, then an economic citizenship premium can be achieved under a liberal citizenship regime. On the other hand, if a country selects its immigrants largely on an individual basis, then only a rigorous citizenship screening policy will yield an economic premium from naturalization. Perhaps most importantly, the study contended that each country, whether in the 'new' or 'old' world, had to recognize that the passive selection of immigrants and of citizenship candidates leads to poor economic integration prospects as adverse selection into citizenship could result. In other words, naturalization should be seen as part of an ongoing immigrant integration process instead of its capstone.

The effects of naturalization on political integration are studied even less often. A project that matched the 2006 Swedish electoral survey to registry data from Statistics Sweden assessed the correlates of voting by Swedish-born and immigrant residents. Instrumental variable regressions provided an estimate of the impact of citizenship acquisition. The chief finding was that acquisition of citizenship makes a real difference to the probability of voting: immigrants who naturalize are generally far more likely to vote than those who do not (Bevelander and Pendakur 2011).

Effective management of diversity, whether through a multicultural policy or some other approach, is dependent, therefore, on a variety of considerations, from hard economic calculations to prospective payoffs from naturalizing. Another factor that can come into play is 'mere' happenstance. Returning to the health of the Canadian multicultural model, there are specific and discrete reasons for it that are not found elsewhere: one is that Canada does not either share a border with Mexico or constitute a majority-Muslim state, thereby making in-migration non-threatening in the view of most Canadians. The 'frontiers of fear', to adapt Chebel d'Appollonia's (2012) frame, do not apply in Canada.

An immigration policy favouring the highly skilled, especially those from South and Southeast Asia, is widely supported in Canada. An 84 per cent naturalization rate – twice that of the US and much higher than the EU average – attests to the integration of foreign-born residents into Canadian society. Multiculturalism also is the way that political leaders and parties gain power in the country; it is a calculated strategy that even includes mathematical formulae used across political party lines (Anderson 2012). This is not to say that it produces egalitarian outcomes: some migrant groups become part of the Canadian core while others remain marginal, so that Canadian multiculturalism has the effect of differentiating between insider and outsider groups. Of course we can find similar processes occurring in European states.

Critiques of multiculturalism originate out of many different normative frameworks; right-wing, nationalist, crypto-racist attacks on the model receive the most publicity, but by no means are they the most piercing. Cultural theorist Slavoj Žižek has imaginatively approached multiculturalism as a way of 'quarantining' 'others' and simultaneously 'decaffeinating' them. As he puts it:

> Socially, what is most toxic is the foreign Neighbor – the strange abyss of his pleasures, beliefs and customs. Consequently, the ultimate aim of all rules of interpersonal relations is to quarantine (or at least neutralize and contain) this toxic dimension, and thereby reduce the foreign Neighbor – by removing his otherness – to an unthreatening fellow man. The end result: today's tolerant liberal multiculturalism is an experience of the Other deprived of its Otherness – the decaffeinated Other. (Žižek 2010)

The feminist critique of multiculturalism is no less incisive or significant. Susan Moller Okin (1997; 1999) was one of the first to suggest that multiculturalism just does not 'see' women in society. She noted how

> most cultures are suffused with practices and ideologies concerning gender. Suppose, then, that a culture endorses and facilitates the control of men over women in various ways . . . Suppose, too, that there are fairly clear disparities of power between the sexes, such that the more powerful, male members are those who are generally in a position to determine and articulate the group's beliefs, practices, and interests. Under such conditions, group rights are potentially, and in many cases actually, antifeminist. They substantially limit the capacities of women and girls of that culture to live with human dignity equal to that of men and boys, and to live as freely chosen lives as they can. (1997)

For Okin, the call for group rights for minorities in liberal states usually ignores the fact that minority cultural groups are themselves gendered, and that they prioritize 'personal law' concerned with marriage, divorce, child custody, control of family property and inheritance. The defence of 'cultural practices' more profoundly impacts 'the lives of women and girls than those of men and boys, since far more of women's time and energy goes into preserving and maintaining the personal, familial, and reproductive side of life'. Okin wraps up her critique of multicultural theory with the assertion that 'most cultures have as one of their principal aims the control of women by men' (1997). Significantly, of the many lines of attack in recent years on the multicultural experience in Europe, very few articulate this feminist perspective.

Both beneficiaries and critics agree that multiculturalism is a way to make claims on the state – justifiable ones for the first group, opportunistic ones for the second. Critics on the left inveigh against the model for failing to address fundamental structural inequalities; some add that it only reproduces the deep structures of power. Migrant communities are sometimes persuaded that neither their integration into a multicultural society nor their complete cultural assimilation is sufficient proof – in the view of the receiving society – of real citizenship integration and undivided loyalty to the receiving society. Indeed, assimilation can still keep the foreign-born fixed as 'others'. One final less commonplace frame on multiculturalism is that it is in essence a postcolonial project: ex-colonizers and colonized negotiate terms of a truce to be upheld on the territory of the metropole. In a relatively recent self-proclaimed multicultural society such as South Korea, multiculturalism is seen as sharing Korean values and culture with the less fortunate – migrants from poor Asian countries. Colonial relations have been reproduced even here.

We acknowledge that critiques of multiculturalism often aim at a moving target: by nature multicultural policies are not static but rather adaptive, malleable, in flux. This is a phenomenon documented across our case studies. Accordingly, the systematic cross-national campaign against the model is all the more remarkable.

Objectives of this study

This book explores the empirical evidence supporting or refuting the end-of-multiculturalism thesis. In the case studies we shall find that our experts are divided among: (1) those who believe that multiculturalism never really existed in their country study; (2) those who are convinced it is now dead; and (3) others who claim that it is more resilient than ever. In theoretical chapters, in turn, we shall discover the importance of multiculturalism and its variants to the managing of diversity. More than that: it is seen as sustaining the Western liberal tradition, the democratic order, even an effective market economy – bedrocks of Europe's values and goals. Part I therefore presents theorizing about the meanings of multiculturalism and about its connection to liberalism.

Why immigrant-based multiculturalism has come under attack in many Western European countries to which it initially appealed is subject to in-depth analysis. Assaying this question can be effectively approached by dividing countries according to where they were located 'upstream', that is, how close they were to the origins of the idea. Accordingly, Part II comprises country studies of the precocious *pioneers and ex-enthusiasts* of multiculturalism. These include Great Britain (England specifically), the Netherlands, Belgium and Sweden. The scepticism – to varying degrees – about multiculturalism discernible in these countries today should not mislead us into concluding that they were not once shaped by the goal of constructing a multicultural society.

Part III encompasses case studies of states that can be described as *multicultural societies without multiculturalism*, that is, societies that are characterized by diversity despite the absence of a policy specifically promoting multiculturalism. These are Germany, Denmark, Italy and France – roughly in the order in which they ever accepted the multicultural model. Indeed, France may be an outlier in this group as it explicitly said *non* to the model and remained shaped by the Republican assimilationist ideal, even as its society became profoundly multiculturalized. In some respects, paradoxically, it is within this group of states located downstream that we find today the bitterest repudiations of multiculturalism.

The three cases in Part IV possibly making up *multiculturalism's future converts* are Poland, Russia and Turkey. Geopolitically, they have been located on Europe's periphery. None of them, significantly, has a historical legacy of Protestantism. Poland's national action script has been labelled *antemurale christianitatis*, a bulwark of Western Christianity – specifically Roman Catholicism – in the East. Russia, in turn, may furnish an example of the proposition that an empire is a failed multinational state. This could also be said, though less convincingly, about the Ottoman Empire but not the modern Turkish Republic. The inclusion of country studies where multiculturalism was never state policy – because immigration-based diversity was practically nonexistent – is explained by our wish to learn about how other types of diversity, especially of ethnic and religious minorities, were managed there. In many respects, Poland, Russia and Turkey are examples of the multicultural road not taken.

Structure of the book: theory and empirics

Multiculturalism has been an elaborately theorized subject as well as having triggered extensive empirical research. The next two chapters approach the concept from differing theoretical perspectives. In Chapter 2 Tariq Modood and Nasar Meer take as a point of departure multiculturalism's resilience. Despite a general retreat from it on the part of many of Europe's leaders, a normative conception of multiculturalism, they argue, offers an effective means of addressing the challenge of nation-state citizenship in conditions of diversity.

The authors chart contemporary responses to migration-related diversity through a cross-tabulation of multicultural attributes and models for promoting liberal citizenship regimes. Attributes include promotion of diversity, recognition of difference, national identity, neutrality of the state, citizen rights, citizens' relationship to the state, promotion of minority or group identities and interaction between groups. The four general models they identify are based on whether priority is assigned to national cohesion, liberal neutrality, limited and localized multiculture or full multicultural citizenship. For Modood and Meer, rebalancing the politics of accommodation and inclusion must be centred on ethno-religious groups, and greater emphasis should be placed on the plural forms of national citizenship and identities than multiculturalist theorists spotlighted in the 1980s and 1990s.

Christian Fernández associates the challenge to multiculturalism with liberal philosophy which, paradoxically, also offers a profound appreciation of diversity. Chapter 3 compares multicultural and liberal approaches to diversity in order to ask how differential treatment on the basis of culture can be justified. Multiculturalism has become synonymous with the politics of identity, the politics of recognition, the politics of difference and the politics of pluralism – each insisting on accommodation rather than suppression of cultural diversity. For Fernández it follows that a just society is conceived as one that recognizes and respects differences between cultural minorities through means of differential treatment.

Tensions between the recognition of the individual and of the group, or between individual liberty and collective autonomy, are products of such differential treatment. Fernández looks at liberal theorists' approaches to these tensions and, while noting differences, underscores their shared concern for cultural minorities and the value of group identities. He concludes that room for genuine cultural diversity is bound to be limited, even in a liberal society. The challenge before multiculturalism becomes how to combat discrimination against minorities that want to lead liberal lives and participate in and belong to mainstream society.

Part II of the book introduces our country studies. The first case is an account of multiculturalism in Britain, perhaps the most celebrated – and notorious – example of the practice of multiculturalism. In Chapter 4 Meer and Modood examine multicultural policies under the last Labour administration and current Conservative–Liberal Democrat coalition government. They argue that the fate of British multiculturalism is far from decided and contest the idea that British multiculturalism has been subject to a wholesale 'retreat'. In fact, Meer and Modood suggest that, if anything, it has been subject to a 'civic thickening'. They document how the ideal of a dynamic political multiculturalism originated in a racial equality paradigm embedded in the 1965 Race Relations Act. This tradition successfully embedded the recognition of difference and also promoted the fact of legal equality of access and opportunity into Britain's self-image. The country's minorities, including Muslim groups, now appeal to this tradition as a means of achieving greater civic inclusion. They also have invoked it to construct new forms of state engagement. These findings lead Meer and Modood to the conclusion that the key features of multiculturalism are being reinvigorated in Britain, rather than withering away.

Chapter 5 by Peter Scholten explodes the Dutch multicultural myth. Widely considered to be an almost ideal-typical example of multiculturalist policies, the so-called Dutch multicultural model has been viewed as facilitating the recognition and institutionalization of cultural pluralism in order for immigrant groups to seamlessly integrate into Dutch society. Scholten emphasizes that Dutch policies of multiculturalism have been dynamic over the past four decades – not characterized by a single national multicultural model; the contrast between Rotterdam and Amsterdam approaches underscores this heterogeneity of approaches. He also documents the persistence of a multiculturalist counter-discourse which juxtaposes the new, more assimilationist policy approach with the alleged Dutch multicultural past, described as a 'multicultural tragedy'. Finally, this chapter discusses the implications of the rise and fall of multiculturalism in the

Netherlands in terms of the growing discrepancy between political norms and empirical facts in integration policies.

Marco Martiniello's analysis of Belgium identifies the federal system as facilitating the emergence of contrasting debates and policies on immigration and integration. He suggests that the politicization of immigration and race has become an important dimension of the domestic conflict between Flemish- and French-speaking Belgians. In Chapter 6 Martiniello concludes that there is virtually no dialogue on immigration and integration issues among the federated entities. He demonstrates these differences in key areas related to migration: admission, socio-economic integration, cultural, political and civic integration, and access to nationality. The perspectives, visions and 'philosophies' of integration and multiculturalism's role in them remain different in the north and south of the country, and in Brussels. Prospects for developing more uniform approaches among federal entities on integration and multiculturalism are poor.

Is it possible that Sweden has witnessed an increase of multiculturalism over the past decade? Karin Borevi in Chapter 7 argues that the answer depends on which aspects of integration policy are considered. If measures to counteract indirect discrimination are viewed as a test of multiculturalism, evidence suggests that Sweden has indeed become *more* multicultural over the last decade. By contrast, already in the 1980s the country backed away from the idea of framing and empowering immigrants as minorities, instead adhering to a policy of integration focusing on individual rights. Sweden has been part of the trend of putting increased emphasis on duties of immigrants, in terms of economic sanctions and incentives. Yet when it comes to cultural requirements, the dominant Swedish approach has been to shy away from applying assimilationist pressures. So if multiculturalism is approached as an absence of prerequisites for immigration integration, Sweden's reticence to adopt such requirements gives cause to characterize it as a multicultural exception bucking anti-multiculturalist trends in Europe.

Part III begins with an account of Germany's diffidence about multiculturalism. Martina Wasmer examines the highly charged debate over the alleged failure of the model but links this to fundamental and conflicting premises about immigration. One is that Germany is not a country of immigration. When it is accepted as one, questions arise about how many immigrants should be admitted and who they should be. The 2005 immigration law highlighted Germany's economic needs, but some politicians contended that accepting immigrants having very different cultures, such as Turks and Arabs, was misguided since integration into German society presented insurmountable obstacles for them. Criticism of Germany having devolved into parallel societies, residential segregation and breeding grounds for youth violence and Islamic fundamentalism characterize public discourse. In addition to a focus on elite perspectives, in Chapter 8 Wasmer provides detailed survey research findings illustrating changing views of migrants and their descendants among German citizens.

Nils Holtug distinguishes between the part played in Denmark by multiculturalism in state policies, which is limited, and that given to it in political debates, which is significant. Chapter 9 explains why debates on immigration have been particularly heated in Denmark and how they have produced restrictive policies. Yet while Denmark is often perceived as being hostile to immigrants, with some of the most restrictive policies in Europe, repeated studies of Danish citizens' attitudes, included in the chapter, reveal that Danes are among the most tolerant people in Europe. Holtug situates this 'Danish paradox' in the wider contemporary European context of a general ambivalence about multiculturalism and suggests that, if anything, the country's anxieties about a multicultural society have eased.

Italy has not adopted a set of coherent integration policies at the national level, argues Tiziana Caponio in Chapter 10. Instead the national government has pursued a mix of both principles of group recognition and universal inclusion. A more multicultural approach, however, has been developed at a local level by some regions and cities, notably Emilia Romagna and Bologna. This 'soft multiculturalism' provides openings to cultural difference but does not constitute a real policy of recognition. Predictably, an ideological cleavage between left and right exists in Italy: left-wing parties have been more favourable to cultural difference than right-wing ones. Consequently left-wing local administrations have usually displayed more openness towards immigrant associations and cultural mediation. Caponio reviews the Roma community and suggests that, as is so often the case in Italy, societal concerns centre on criminality and security rather than cultural recognition or cultural identity. In sum, recognition of cultural difference in the public space, whether it entails Roma camps or mosque building, remains problematic in the country.

France has an incapacity to deal with multiculturalism. This is the conclusion reached by Florent Villard and Pascal-Yan Sayegh in Chapter 11. They contend that multiculturalism represents the absolute antithesis of the French Republican model – the contractual nation formed by a community of citizens in which cultural and linguistic differences are to be erased. These premises have led to non-recognition of culture, race and particularist communities. The chapter examines contemporary assimilationist discourses and policies which increasingly view multiculturalism as a threat to national identity. Former French President Sarkozy's 2011 assertion that 'we have been too concerned about the identity of those who are arriving and not enough about the identity of those who are welcoming' is seen as key to understanding the monocultural turn yet, ironically, also contributed to his electoral defeat in 2012. Far-right nationalism has been revitalized and an assimilationist turn reinforced. Villard and Sayegh conclude that France has witnessed a monocultural redefinition of the nation which highlights differences between the real French and the not yet French or not French enough.

Part IV includes an examination of large eastern states in Europe with little recent history of experiencing immigration and, consequently, managing immigration-based diversity. Renata Włoch asserts that no 'philosophy' or politics of multiculturalism has existed in modern Poland; even multicultural discourse in the media and academic inquiry into multiculturalism is rare. Multiculturalism is generally considered a Western European invention responding to specific Western European problems rooted in its colonial past. The explanation for Poland's blissful dismissal of multiculturalism is straightforward: it remains virtually a homogeneous state. Chapter 12 nevertheless outlines how after 1989 the make-up of Polish society began to change in tandem with processes of democratization and globalization. Cultural difference became more visible with the growing assertiveness of autochthon minorities and growing numbers of legal and illegal immigrants. The Polish state Europeanized its politics towards minorities and immigrants and introduced measures protecting the rights of its culturally different citizens and residents; the Roma community received pride of place in anti-discriminatory legislation. But attitudes of Polish society towards cultural pluralism remain abstract since encounters with cultural, racial, ethnic, national or religious difference are infrequent in Poles' everyday lives.

Sergey Akopov highlights the Russian Federation's extraordinary diversity today: it is home to 158 ethnic groups and indigenous peoples. He enquires into whether the federal system can be viewed as *multicultural* as well as *multinational*. The official Kremlin view has been that multiculturalism leads to particularistic ethnonationalism. The received view of the Western multicultural model is that demands for cultural equality, pluralism and tolerance are largely abstractions: instead of integration of group interests on the basis of universal transnational values and institutions, multiculturalism may cause the diffusion of sovereignty and identity inside and outside the nation state. But Chapter 13 concludes that in recent years a rethinking has taken place in Russia about this critique of Western multiculturalism. Increasingly political actors, particularly in regions close to EU member states, see the value of framing Russia in multicultural terms. Akopov suggests that a transnational approach to identities and rights that transcends multiculturalism may be the best path for Russia to take.

Chapter 14 considers minorities and multiculturalism in Turkey. Ayhan Kaya describes the management of ethnocultural diversity, particularly in the light of significant demographic change in the last decade. He distinguishes between diversity as a phenomenon and diversity as a discourse and suggests that the Turkish state and various ethnic groups in the country have adopted the discourse of diversity in the aftermath of the 1999 Helsinki Summit of the European Union which proclaimed the principle of *unity in diversity*. There has been remarkable progress in the recognition of the ethnocultural and political claims of various minority groups: Kurds, Alevis, Circassians, Lazis, Armenians and Greeks. But Kaya analyses a different trend as well: one of rising Euroscepticism and parochialism as Turkey's EU membership bid has stalled. The political divide within the Turkish political elite, compounded by a social divide between moderate Islamists and secular fundamentalists, creates deep and dangerous cleavages which have the potential to set multiculturalism back.

Ulf Hedetoft's concluding Chapter 15 ascribes to multiculturalism a paradoxical character in the way that 'multicultural' is unproblematic. Whether the 'ism' invokes ideology, policy or discourse, it represents an approach to a culturally diverse social reality that is motivated by the normative consideration to frame, control and steer developments in a particular direction. By contrast, 'multicultural' simply describes a state of affairs commonplace in many European societies. For the author, multiculturalism has had a significant and positive impact across European states over the past thirty-five years. If today it is under siege, it is because multiculturalism has become the straw man standing in for Europe's more profound existential crisis. Like the groundhog, Hedetoft concludes, Europe has become scared of its own shadow, and multiculturalism is a convenient explanation for all its failures.

In summary, this book breaks new ground in a number of ways. It entails an examination of how the premises of European liberalism are being challenged by widespread political opposition to multiculturalism. It offers a cross-national study of European societies' contrasting commitments and efforts to pursue multiculturalism. Related to this, it contains an analysis of how well-intentioned political leaders in Europe once constructed a multicultural model to accommodate diversity, only to observe how opposition to it helped galvanize first radical right, nationalist, populist but – more significantly – then more mainstream anti-multiculturalist political movements. This sequence did not take place in geographically eastern Europe, so this volume also examines demographically and territorially large countries in that region where an immigration-based multiculturalism never took shape.

Multiculturalism lurks in the nooks and crannies of all European states. At a time of a more general crisis and malaise, its relevance – like that of the euro – is being challenged. Is it just multiculturalism – or Europe itself – that may be entering its twilight years? Our volume offers sustained reflection on staking out an appropriate collective identity that can flourish under a set of rapidly changing circumstances.

References

Anderson, Christopher (2012), 'The adaptive qualities of Canadian multiculturalism', paper for presentation at the International Studies Association's Annual Convention 'Power, Principles and Participation in the Global Information Age', San Diego, CA, 1–4 April 2012.

Banting, Keith and Will Kymlicka (eds) (2006), *Multiculturalism and the Welfare State: Recognition and Redistribution in Contemporary Democracies*, Oxford: Oxford University Press.

—— (2012), 'Is there really a backlash against multiculturalism policies? New evidence from the multiculturalism policy index', paper for presentation at the ECSA-C 9th Biennial Conference, Ottawa, 26–8 April 2012.

Bevelander, Pieter (2000), *Immigrant Employment Integration and Structural Change in Sweden, 1970–1995*. Stockholm: Almqvist & Wiksell International.

Bevelander, Pieter and Don DeVoretz (eds) (2008), *The Economics of Citizenship*, Malmö: Malmö University.
Bevelander, Pieter and Ravi Pendakur (2011), 'Voting and social inclusion in Sweden', *International Migration*, 49 (4), pp. 67–92.
Bhabha, Homi K. (1994), *The Location of Culture*, London: Routledge.
Bloemraad, Irene (2008), 'Introduction', in Pieter Bevelander and Don DeVoretz (eds), *The Economics of Citizenship*, Malmö: Malmö University, pp. 13–20.
Bowen, John R. (2011), 'Europeans against multiculturalism', *Boston Review* (July/August).
Chebel d'Appollonia, Ariane (2012), *The Frontiers of Fear*, Ithaca, NY: Cornell University Press.
Day, Richard J. F. (2000), *Multiculturalism and the History of Canadian Diversity*, Toronto: University of Toronto Press.
Mackey, Eva (2002), *The House of Difference: Cultural Politics and National Identity in Canada*, Toronto: University of Toronto Press.
Modood, Tariq (2005), *Multicultural Politics: Racism, Ethnicity and Muslims in Britain*, Edinburgh: Edinburgh University Press.
—— (2007), Multiculturalism, Cambridge: Polity Press.
Modood, Tariq and Nasar Meer (2012), 'Framing contemporary citizenship and diversity in Europe', in Triandafyllidou, Modood and Meer (eds), *European Multiculturalisms: Cultural, Religious and Ethnic Challenges*, Edinburgh: Edinburgh University Press.
Okin, Susan Moller (1997), 'Is multiculturalism bad for women?', *Boston Review* (October/November). Available at http://www.bostonreview.net/BR22.5/okin.html
—— (1999), *Is Multiculturalism Bad for Women?*, Princeton, NJ: Princeton University Press.
Parekh, Bhikhu (2000), *Rethinking Multiculturalism: Cultural Diversity and Political Theory*, Cambridge, MA: Harvard University Press.
Silj, Alessandro (ed.) (2010), *European Multiculturalism Revisited*, London: Zed Books.
Thielemann, Eiko and Mogens Hobolth (2012), 'Numbers vs. rights? On trade-offs in refugee and visa policy', paper for presentation at the International Studies Association's Annual Convention 'Power, Principles and Participation in the Global Information Age', San Diego, CA, 1–4 April 2012.
Triandafyllidou, Anna, Tariq Modood and Nasar Meer (eds) (2012), 'Introduction: diversity, integration, secularism and multiculturalism', in Triandafyllidou, Modood and Meer (eds), *European Multiculturalisms: Cultural, Religious and Ethnic Challenges*, Edinburgh: Edinburgh University Press.
Vertovec, Steven and Susanne Wessendorf (2010), 'Introduction: assessing the backlash against multiculturalism', in Vertovec and Wessendorf, *The*

Multiculturalism Backlash: European Discourses, Policies and Practices, London: Routledge.

Žižek, Slavoj (2010), 'Barbarism with a human face', *In These Times* (23 November). Available at http://www.inthesetimes.com/article/6641/barbarism_with_a_human_face/

Chapter Two

Contemporary Citizenship and Diversity in Europe: The Place of Multiculturalism

Tariq Modood and Nasar Meer[1]

Introduction

This book investigates the nature and extent of multicultural citizenship in European countries. It is a topic that is pursued at a time when the claim that multiculturalism is dying or should be dead has become commonplace. Since 2010 the leaders of three major European states, German Chancellor Angela Merkel, UK Prime Minister David Cameron and former French President Nicolas Sarkozy have all made high-profile speeches which declared respectively that 'multi-kulti has utterly failed', 'multiculturalism is dead' and 'multiculturalism is a defeat' (sic) (Weaver 2010; Cameron 2011). These political obituaries were the culmination of a political discourse that had already gained some traction.

For some, multiculturalism has abetted social fragmentation and deepened social divisions (Policy Exchange 2007; Malik 2007). For others, it has distracted attention from core socio-economic disparities (Barry 2001; Hansen 2006) and encouraged a moral hesitancy amongst native populations (Caldwell 2009; Prins and Salisbury 2008). Some even blame it for international terrorism (Phillips 2006; Gove 2006). Independently of whether or not these criticisms are valid, a consensus has developed amongst scholars and commentators that multiculturalism as a public policy is in retreat (Brubaker 2001; Joppke 2004). What remains less clear, however, is what this retreat of multiculturalism in Europe actually involves. Does it entail the same thing in different countries? What are states actually doing, and not doing, that they were doing or not doing before? And is there a comparative framework for addressing these questions? The key ideas informing the thesis of a retreat from multiculturalism are therefore far from established or well understood.

The answers to some of these questions can be found in the widespread view that a variety of European nation-states today is 're-nationalizing' (Orgad 2009; Mouritsen 2009). That is to say, if in the 1980s and 1990s it was argued that a denationalizing trend was taking place as part of the 'post-national' future, as seen from the vantage point of the second decade of the twenty-first century it appears that many – though not all – central promises contained within ideas of post-national citizenship and post-war cosmopolitanism have *not* come to fruition. This is particularly true of those accounts that saw as the future of citizenship in Europe a retention and administration of citizenship rights in cross-national human rights covenants that would be supported by international law (Soysal 1994).

Others simultaneously anticipated a diminution in the 'particularistic' content of political communities such that the boundaries between nations, states, cultures or indeed societies might become porous and even morally irrelevant (Archibugi et al. 2005; Archibugi et al. 1998). Instead, today we observe a trend in the valorization of national identities in nation-states' citizenship across Western Europe, sometimes characterized as a re-nationalization of citizenship regimes (Kiwan 2008). National identities can encompass a variety of prescribed or remade categories: 'prescribed' would be more exclusive such as a benign or active *Leitkultur*, while 'remade' would be more dialogical or incorporating 'difference'.

In the following section we survey this terrain before critically engaging with a scholarly characterization of it. Then we offer our alternative reading and step back to consider competing normative frameworks before returning to an empirical discussion in the final section of the chapter. We conclude that a *normative* conception of multiculturalism remains a resilient means of explicating empirical developments in nation-state citizenship in Europe. We specifically argue how, in interpreting the new emphasis on national identities, some analysis ignores the fact that particularity is both pragmatically necessary and justifiable within a variety of ideational and empirical political orientations.

The terrain

The chronology of 're-nationalizing' in the context of post-immigration ethno-religious diversity varies between countries. In the case of the UK it came from the centre-left, beginning with New Labour's invocation of an Orwell-type patriotism and proposals to modernize and remake Britishness under the terms of 'Cool Britannia' and 're-branding Britain' (Leonard 1997). Not only was this a strand within what was probably the most multiculturalist government the UK has had (1997–2001), but the ideas of rethinking and remaking Britishness in response to ethnic diversity were stimulated by ethnic minority intellectuals (Gilroy 1987; Modood 1992; CMEB 2000[2]). The concern for making national identities more explicit was widespread across Europe and was evidenced by the European Council agreement in 2004 on 'common basic principles' supporting nation-states in educating immigrants on 'the host society's language, history, and institutions'.[3] The European Union Pact on Immigration and Asylum 'maintains that it is for each Member State to decide on the conditions of admission of legal migrants to its territory and, where necessary, to set their number'.[4] As such, it provides member states with the means to regulate admission criteria. An illustration is Denmark's requirement of Danish language competencies at 'level 3' which effectively 'bars most non-Europeans from ever gaining citizenship' (Mouritsen 2009: 6). It went hand in hand with the introduction of a citizenship test notable for its emphasis on challenging questions concerning historical-national Danish culture. These developments took place in a political context in Denmark in which the very content of popular discourse, particularly around cultural diversity and Islam, had taken a notably nationalistic tone (Meer and Mouritsen 2009).

Similar developments were evident in the debate over a German *Leitkultur* which would promote a German 'leading culture' in a more explicit way than in its traditional conception of ethnic citizenship. After decades of pursuing ethno-national citizenship, Germany since the late 1990s underwent major changes in its management of immigration and integration, as well as in its conception of citizenship. If federal policies had previously focused almost entirely on the control and return of migrants (Schönwälder 2001), in 1998 the Red-Green government characterized Germany as an 'immigration country' and amended the Citizenship Law (2000) to introduce the principle of *jus soli*. These developments have been complemented by others such as the Immigration Law (2005) which encourages the cultivation of 'integration strategies'. Yet the content of this 'integration' has included a nationalist imperative whereby newcomers are expected to undertake 300 to 600 hours of German language classes and lessons on German society and history (Jacobs and Rea 2007).

Simultaneously in the UK, the Nationality, Immigration and Asylum Act (2002) explicitly introduced a test implemented in 2005 for residents seeking British citizenship. Applicants must show 'a sufficient knowledge of English, Welsh or Scottish Gaelic' and also 'a sufficient knowledge about life in the United Kingdom' (Home Office 2004: 11). Those immigrants seeking to settle in the UK – applying for 'indefinite leave to remain' – equally have to pass the test which has been applied since April 2007. If applicants do not have sufficient knowledge of English, they are required to attend English for Speakers of Other Languages (ESOL) and citizenship classes. The government acknowledged, however, that 'it would be unfair for migrants to have to answer questions on British history that many British people would have difficulties with' (McNulty quoted in Kiwan 2008: 69). Accordingly, the emphasis is on the experience of living in the UK rather than an attempt to test Britishness in terms of scholastic knowledge.

What this summary shows is that despite important variations, in north-western Europe there is presently a renewed emphasis and explicitness regarding national identities among countries that have not always prioritized this; the UK, Denmark and increasingly Germany exemplify this. In some cases, the turn to national identities by governments appears to involve a confused means of encouraging forms of social and political unity (cf. Uberoi 2008). In other cases national identities are viewed as a means of engendering a kind of value consensus that may act as a prophylactic against forms of (Muslim) radicalism (McGhee 2008; Uberoi and Modood 2009). In other cases still, the turn to national identities appears as little more than a means of pursuing an assimilationist project. The 'drastic break with multiculturalism' (Entzinger 2007: 201) made by the Dutch has seen the Netherlands discontinue some emblematic multiculturalist policies while introducing others tailored to ignore ethnic minority differences. These include the abandonment of dual-citizenship programmes; a withdrawal of national-level funding for minority group organizations and activities supporting cultural difference; reallocating the small percentage of public broadcasting time dedicated to multicultural issues; and a cessation of ethnic monitoring of labour market participation (Entzinger 2007; 2003; Van De Vijver et al. 2006).

In the 1990s, then, various European states began 're-nationalizing' and reforming access to citizenship and the status of citizens just at the point when some scholars were discerning a trend towards denationalization. This movement accelerated and 'hardened' as states reacted to 9/11, to the threat of international networks recruiting citizens or residents in their country and to an alleged 'failure to integrate' on the part of Muslims, which stood alongside perceptions of Muslims as a cultural and demographic threat (cf. Caldwell 2009; Joppke 2009). The post-national trend has also been deflected by how migrants and subsequent generations have asserted not so much their right to *not* be citizens in the countries in which they have settled, but various kinds of transnational political identities, especially a solidarity with an imagined global Muslim community (the *ummah*) having primacy over civic solidarities (Mandaville 2009).

In this chapter we are only interested in the first of these developments, namely the policies and discourses of European states and opinion-makers on integration. We focus on anxieties over perceived failures in minority, and particularly Muslim, integration (Brubaker 2001; Bauböck et al. 2006; Mouritsen 2009). Here the argument by Christian Joppke (2008) salvages something of the post-national argument in advancing the claim that re-nationalization is not what it appears to be.

Joppke's paradox

Christian Joppke has argued that contemporary discourses of national identity in Europe both normatively and practically strengthen liberalism at the expense of nationalism. In his view, even while some politicians and states talk of national identities as a means of privileging majority cultures as *Leitkultur*, for example in Germany and Denmark, such movements are structurally bound to fail. When states try to formulate language about their national identities, they invariably end up listing universal principles such as liberty, equality, fairness, human rights, tolerance and so on. This means that while many states today appeal to a national identity, the content they give it may be neither ethnic nor cultural (language, history or religion) but rather one comprised of liberal principles. As a result, while the symbolic form may be particularistic, the content is necessarily universal; if it were more particularistic (for example, Christian), it would fail in its purpose to integrate immigrants, especially Muslims. Joppke maintains, therefore, that 'the typical solution to the problem of collective identity across Europe today is the one pioneered by Republican France, according to which to be national is defined in the light of the universalistic precepts of human rights and democracy' (Joppke 2008: 541).

An important feature of Joppke's argument is that where some politicians and states do emphasize particularistic aspects of national identity, such as Lutheranism or Christianity more generally, their own constitutional courts are required to uphold universalist principles. They regularly rule in favour of non-discrimination, which is interpreted as the non-privileging of one culture over another. The result is that these courts strike down particularistic legislation and support appeals of discrimination from minority individuals and groups; for Joppke the European Court of Human Rights (ECHR) furnishes evidence of this.[5]

Joppke acknowledges that a discourse in several countries, typified by Germany and Denmark, employs universalist liberalism in an exclusionary particularistic way: liberalism is 'our culture', it is claimed, and others, such as Muslims, cannot become part of the 'We' because they are not sufficiently liberal (Joppke 2008: 541–2; Mouritsen (2008: 21–2) believes that this may be more widespread than Joppke suggests (cf. Müller 2007). Joppke maintains, however, that these exclusionary uses of liberalism must appeal to the liberal principle of non-discrimination between cultures, and since they do not, they cannot be sustained. Thus, while some liberals may aggressively enforce liberal norms (this is Joppke's reading of the ban on the headscarf in state schools in France), they must do so within liberal constraints (in a non-discriminatory way by not targeting an ethnic group or a religion but by applying universal rules). They end up promoting liberal principles and not a specific national culture. For Joppke, then, 'the decoupling of citizenship and nationhood is the incontrovertible exit position for contemporary state campaigns for unity and integration, especially with respect to immigrants' (Joppke 2008: 543). Joppke sees these developments from the perspective of a 'retreat of multiculturalism' (Joppke 2004; for critiques see Jacobs and Rea 2007; Meer and Modood 2009) and so it is not surprising that, in interpreting the new emphasis on national identities, he ignores the theoretical contribution of multiculturalism.

Our argument is that some degree of particularity is both pragmatically necessary and justifiable within a variety of ideational and empirical political orientations. Where we observe various political projects of remaking and updating national identities, they are not being departicularized. Cases such as Spain and Greece retain a strong orientation toward *jus sanguinis*, but an opposing trend to develop this would not have to drain the historical-cultural character of nationality but instead could include minority ethnicities. The updating of national identities does not have to be blind to minority ethnic groupness but, on the contrary, can seek to pluralize – not drain – cultural content. In other words, for the dominant ethnicity to demonopolize the state and the citizenship by not making cultural assimilation a condition of full citizenship and of full social acceptance is to respect – not wipe out – the varied ethnicities of fellow citizens.

We contend, therefore, that contrary to the view articulated by Joppke (2008: 535), 'neutrality' must not be mistaken for content-lessness. Pure universalism is impossible so equality in citizenship is best pursued as (1) anti-discrimination; (2) recognition of open, mixed and changing ethnicities/identities; (3) multi-logical plural-ity; and (4) inclusivity and the fostering of a sense of belonging. To demonstrate this we need to recognize that citizenship requires some notion of a self-governing political community in which individuals have rights and correlative duties enforced by law. But they are also likely to have a sense of shaping and being shaped by a public space that goes beyond law and politics. Moreover, it is only when we have a conception of citizenship that we can identify who among long-term residents should remain non-citizens, why they should remain so and what rights they should and should not have. We need to ask at least three questions in order to propose a theory of citizenship (Patten 2001, cited in Gagnon and Iacovino 2007: 125):

1. Membership: who is to be granted this status?
2. Entitlement: what rights are implied by this status?
3. Social expectations: what responsibilities, dispositions and identities are expected of someone who holds this status?

With regard to membership, there is indeed a trend in some coun-tries to de-ethnicize citizenship, or at least to dilute the link between citizenship and a single ethnicity. This also means breaking the link between mono-nationality and citizenship, which sees states such as Germany moving towards the British and French example of taking a pragmatic view of dual citizenship (Modood and Meer 2009). By the beginning of the twenty-first century, most EU states were award-ing citizenship to long-term residents and those born to non-citizens, though some states were struggling with the concept of dual nation-ality. In relation to the second question of entitlement, citizenship is fundamentally about equal membership. The EU and its member states have recognized that non-white immigrants and their children and grandchildren do not have effective equality. While some EU states to differing degrees select or deselect by ethnicity those to whom they will grant citizenship, all EU states are now committed to the principle of non-discrimination amongst citizens.

In accordance with the Treaty of Amsterdam (1997), two broad directives were issued to member states to prevent discrimination on the basis of race, ethnicity or religion. The first established a general framework for equal treatment in employment and occupation (the Employment Directive), which would require member states to make discrimination unlawful on grounds of racial or ethnic origin, religion or belief, disability, age or sexual orientation. The second directive implemented the principle of equal treatment irrespective of racial or ethnic origin (the Race Directive). Like the Employment Directive, the Race Directive required member states to make discrimination on grounds of racial or ethnic origin unlawful in employment and training. It went further than the Employment Directive in requiring member states to provide protection against discrimination in non-employment areas, such as education, access to social welfare and the provision of goods and services. While these directives were accompanied by an 'Action Programme' set up by the European Commission and allocated a budget of 100 million euros over six years to fund member state practice promoting non-discrimination, countries that adopted these directives were distinguishable in anti-discrimination policy action ranging from low to high as follows:

- Low: where anti-discrimination laws to promote equality of opportunity are rarely applied in practice, little or no data on ethnicity and race are collected, and no public agency is charged with publicity, coordination and enforcement.
- High: where appropriate data is systematically collected and used, cases are routinely investigated by employers and other institutions, with many reaching the law courts, and are widely publicized by the media and by agencies such as the Belgian or French HALDE (High Authority to Fight Against Discrimination and for Equality) model or the UK EHRC (Equality and Human Rights Commission), which is responsible for policy development and enforcement and reports regularly to a government department or minister.

The issue of non-discrimination is also a question of socio-economic integration and full social citizenship, but it is not merely that. During most of the twentieth century there was a left–right struggle about the extent to which citizenship should entail social welfare and economic rights, illustrated in Marshall's well-known typology (1950). In the 1980s and early 1990s, there was a shift away from citizenship towards post-national membership (Soysal 1994), due to a focus that treated citizenship as identity (Joppke 2008) and citizenship as a common public space for dialogue (Modood 2007; Parekh 2000). These approaches were at the top of the political agendas and raised the fundamental question in relation to post-immigration diversity: what is the identity of citizenship itself and what does it imply for other identities that citizens may have or want to have?

To chart this evolution, we employ six category ranges examining (1) the promotion of equality of opportunity; (2) the extent of the emphasis on national identity; (3) the recognition of 'difference'; (4) the issue of neutrality; (5) the sphere of rights; (6) the relationship to the state. We use these category ranges as they reflect the most salient or core elements across a variety of normative accounts of citizenship in social and political theory. Equally, each of the three questions about citizenship raised by Patten (2001) above, including the question of civic identity, is not about merely vertical (state to citizen) but also horizontal (citizen to citizen) relationships (Gagnon and Iacovino 2007: 125). To address the questions of citizenship, especially the third, concerning social expectations, is also to ask about how the state and citizens should relate to diversity. Let us examine how some scholars, from both European and North American contexts, have typologized these relationships, and what normative and explanatory purchase we can derive from them.

Normative models of citizenship

Modood (1997) has identified five ideal ways in which the state and its citizens can respond to the new cultural diversity that is a consequence of the post-war, large-scale immigration into Europe. Putting aside the default policy of assimilation, the first ideal type is *the decentred state*. Its premise is that because of factors such as migration and the globalization of economics, consumption and communications, societies can no longer be constituted by stable collective purposes and identities organized territorially by the nation-state. Thus the state cannot supply and attach a primary identity to individuals because identities are fluid and multiple as individuals identify with like-minded people across borders in terms of lifestyle, cultural consumption, peripatetic careers, diasporas and other forms of transnational networks. We present this and the other ideal types in summary form in Table 2.1 (see Appendix for an explanation of the categories used).

Table 2.1 The state and citizens' responses to cultural diversity: five ideal types (adaptation of Modood 1997)

Type of state →	Decentred state	Liberal state	Republic	Federation of communities	Plural state
1. Promotion of equality of opportunity	Medium	Low	Low	Medium	High
2. Emphasis on national identity	Low	Low	High (but prescribed)	Low	High (but remade)
3. Recognition of difference	Medium	Low	Low	High	High
4. Seeking neutrality	Not possible	Yes	No	No	No
5. Bearer of rights	Individual	Individual	Individual	Group	Individual and group
6. Relationship to the state	Vertical	Vertical	Vertical	Horizontal	Horizontal and vertical

The second of Modood's types is *the liberal state*, where the state exists to protect the rights of individuals, and where the question of recognizing new ethnic groups does not arise, for the state does not recognize any such groups. Individuals relate to the state as individual citizens, not as members of the group. The ideal liberal state does not promote one or more national cultures, religions, ways of life and so on. These matters remain private to individuals in their voluntary associations with each other. Nor does the state promote any syncretic vision of common living or of fellow feeling between the inhabitants of that territory other than the legal entitlements and duties that define civic membership.

The third type, *the Republic*, refers to the ideal Republic which, like the liberal state, does not recognize groups amongst the citizenry but instead relates to each citizen as an individual. Unlike the liberal state, it is amenable to one collective project – it is itself a collective project which is not reducible to the protection of the rights of individuals or to the maximization of the choices open to individuals. The Republic seeks to enhance the lives of its members by making them part of a way of living that individuals could not create for themselves: its aim is to make the individuals members of a civic community. This community may be based upon subscription to 'universal' principles such as liberty, equality and fraternity; or to the promotion of a national culture; or, as in the case of France, to both. In a Republic, the formation of public ethnicity, by immigration or in other ways, would be discouraged and there would be strong expectation, even pressure, for individuals to assimilate into the national identity.

The federation of communities is Modood's fourth type of categorization. In contrast to the first three responses to multicultural diversity, this one is built upon the assumption that the individual is not the principal unit to which the state must relate. Rather, individuals belong to and are shaped by communities, which are the primary focus of their loyalty and the regulators of their social existence. Far from being confined to the private sphere, communities are rather the primary agents of the public sphere. Public life consists of organized communities relating to each other, and the state is therefore a federation of communities that exists to protect the rights of these communities. The *millet* system of the Ottoman Empire, in which some state powers were delegated to Christian and Jewish communities that had the power to administer personal law within their communities in accordance with their own legal system, is an example of this model of the multicultural state.

The last type is *the plural state*, which can have both strong and weak forms. With it comes a recognition that social existence consists of individuals and groups, and both need to be provided for in the formal and informal distribution of powers, not just in law but in representation – in state offices, public committees, consultative exercises and access to public forums. There may be some rights for all individuals as in the liberal state, but mediating institutions such as trade unions, churches, neighbourhoods and immigrant associations may also be encouraged to be active public players and forums for political discussion, and may even have a formal representative or administrative role to play in the state. The plural state, however, allows for and probably requires an ethical conception of citizenship, not just an instrumental one as in the conception of a federation of communities. The understanding that individuals are partly constituted by the lives of families and communities fits well with the recognition that the moral individual is partly shaped by the social order constituted by citizenship and the public that amplifies and qualifies, sustains, critiques and reforms citizenship. For the plural state, then, multicultural diversity means reforming national identity and citizenship and offering an emotional identity with the whole, to counterbalance the emotional loyalties to ethnic and religious communities (Modood 2007).

This fivefold typology does not assume that all options are equally suitable or feasible in contemporary Europe. Let us briefly compare this typology with a number of later conceptualizations. The Commission on the Future of Multi-Ethnic Britain (CMEB) (2000: 42), chaired by Lord Professor Bhikhu Parekh, advanced the following five possible models of cohesion, equality and difference (see Table 2.2):

1. Procedural: the state is culturally neutral, and leaves individuals and communities to negotiate with each other as they wish, providing they observe certain basic procedures.
2. Nationalist: the state promotes a single national culture and expects all to assimilate to it. People who do not or cannot assimilate are second-class citizens.
3. Liberal: there is a single political culture in the public sphere but substantial diversity in the private lives of individuals and communities.
4. Plural: there is both unity and diversity in public life; communities and identities overlap, are interdependent and develop common features.

Table 2.2 Five models of cohesion, equality and difference (adaptation of Commission for Multi-Ethnic Britain 2000)

Type of state →	Procedural	Nationalist	Liberal	Plural	Separatist
1. Promotion of equality of opportunity	Low	Low	Medium	High	Low
2. Emphasis on national identity	Low	High (but prescribed)	Low	High (but remade)	Low
3. Recognition of difference	Low	Low	Medium	High	High
4. Seeking neutrality	Yes	No	Yes	No	No
5. Bearer of rights	Individual	Individual	Individual	Individual and group	Group
6. Relationship to the state	Vertical	Vertical	Vertical	Horizontal and vertical	Horizontal

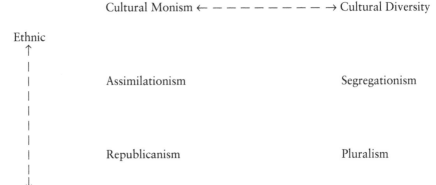

Figure 2.1 Four conceptions of citizenship (adaptation of Koopmans et al. 2005)

5. Separatist: the state expects each community to remain separate from others and to organize and regulate its own affairs, largely confining itself to maintaining order and civility.

Unlike these two five-part models which are based on different positions in political theory, Koopmans et al. (2005: 21) identify two distinct features of citizenship practice; their interactions create four possibilities. Thus, using the following two dimensions

1. The formal basis of citizenship: civic-territorial vs. ethno-cultural (Patten's question 1)
2. The cultural obligations tied to citizenship: cultural monism and cultural pluralism (Patten's question 3)

they produce four conceptions of citizenship (see Figure 2.1):

(a) Ethnic assimilationism (Germany, Switzerland)
(b) Ethnic segrationalism
(c) Civic Republicanism (France; and the UK, qualified by Question 4)
(d) Civic pluralism (Netherlands)

When this model was applied to five countries at three moments in time, two important developments between 1980 and 2002 were perceptible. One was a movement towards cultural pluralism in all countries (though to differing degrees), and the other was a movement towards civic conceptions of citizenship.

The North American context is different and produces four other

Table 2.3 Four political responses to diversity (adaptation of Hartman and Gerteis 2005)

	Basis for cohesion	
Basis for association	Substantive moral bonds	Procedural norms
Individual in society	Assimilation	Cosmopolitanism
Mediating groups	Interactive pluralism	Fragmented pluralism

ways of responding politically to diversity (Hartmann and Gerteis 2005: 224). The two-by-two model is not based on dimensions of citizenship but on social integration:

1. the basis for cohesion: substantive moral bonds versus procedural norms
2. the basis for association: individuals in society versus mediating groups.

Its four possible outcomes are (see Table 2.3):

(a) assimilationism (based on social expectations rather than policy)
(b) cosmopolitanism (multiple hybrid identities based on individual choices)
(c) interactive pluralism or multiculturalism (substantive moral bonds mediated through groups and individuals so that there is unity in diversity)
(d) fragmented pluralism

As with the earlier typologies, civic or interactive pluralism, or multiculturalism, emerges as an attractive option, even the favoured one. Let us then look at a typology expressly aimed at showing the limitations of multiculturalism and the attractions of 'interculturalism'. Alain Gagnon and Raffaele Iacovino (2007) argue that Quebec has developed a distinctive political approach to diversity explicitly in opposition to federal Canadian multiculturalism. Their starting point is that two broad considerations are accepted by a spectrum of political positions ranging across liberal nationalist, Republican and multiculturalist (though not liberal individualism). The first of the two stipulations is that 'full citizenship status requires that all cultural identities be allowed to participate in democratic life equally, without the necessity of reducing conceptions of identity to the level of the individual'. Second, with respect to unity: 'the key element is a sense of common purpose in public matters, a centre which also serves as a marker of identity in the larger society and denotes in itself a pole of allegiance for all citizens' (2007: 96).

For Gagnon and Iacovino, however, Canadian multiculturalism has two fatal flaws that make it de facto liberal individualist. First, it privileges an individualist approach to culture: as individuals or their choices change, the collective culture must change. In contrast, Quebec's policy emphasizes the need to recognize the French language as a collective good that requires protection and encouragement (Gagnon and Iacovino 2007: 99). Second, Canadian multiculturalism does not locate itself in democratic public culture but rather, 'Public space is based on individual participation via a bill of rights' (2007: 110–11); judges and individual choices, not citizens debating and negotiating with each other, constitute the locus of cultural interaction and public multiculturalism.

The argument for interculturalism can, therefore, be summarized as follows:

1. There should be a public space and identity that is not merely about individual constitutional or legal rights.
2. This public space is an important identity for those who share it and so qualifies and counterbalances other identities that citizens value.
3. This public space is created and shared through participation, interaction, debate and common endeavour.
4. This public space is not culture-less but nor is it merely the 'majority culture'; all can participate in its synthesis and evolution and while it has an inescapable historical character, it is always being remade to include new groups.
5. Quebec, and not merely federal Canada, is such a public space and so an object immigrants need to identify with and integrate into; they should therefore seek to maintain Quebec as a nation and not just a federal province.

The same argument may apply to other multinational states even if the 'multinationalisms' they embody may vary.

The resilience of the multicultural framework

What is remarkable about the typologies that we have reviewed is that, despite differences in nomenclature, there is considerable agreement on what the options in relation to diversity are (see Table

2.4). There seems to be virtually no difference between Modood's Plural State, CMEB's Pluralism, Hartmann and Gerteis's Interactive Pluralism and Gagnon and Iacovino's Interculturalism: all represent different ways of stating a preference for a form of multicultural citizenship (Modood 2007). Specifically, there seems to be no difference between Interculturalism and Multiculturalism; Interculturalism is usually framed as a critical alternative to Multiculturalism, but the only difference is an emphasis on the latter's emphasis on multinationalism – significantly, a key feature of Kymlicka's theory of liberal multiculturalism (Kymlicka 1995). In Table 2.4, in order to emphasize the strengths of interculturalism, we have inserted two more categories, one of minority nationalism and another of interaction between groups. Interaction is supposed to be one of the fundamental failings of old-style multiculturalism, reflected in advancing the term 'interculturalism'. This, however, is present in the theoretical conceptualization of multiculturalism we have been considering (for a discussion of interculturalism in relation to multiculturalism, see Meer and Modood 2012).

From the political climate in Europe and the practical proposals that emerge from it, ethno-religious separatism is the most undesirable outcome from diversity; for many, assimilation as policy is also regarded as impractical if not unjust. Anxiety about Muslims and whether they are 'integrating', in the context of expressed disappointment in old-style multicultural arrangements, suggest the following four recommendations (see Table 2.5). Each takes socioeconomic integration (anti-discrimination and countering of social disadvantage) and a certain amount of liberalism (individual rights) as given:

1. National cohesion: civic nationhood and social cohesion are asserted as goals above the recognition of group 'difference'.
2. Liberal neutrality: the state is neutral between all conceptions of good and should administer a uniform set of individual rights and not promote a particular nation, culture or religion.
3. Multiculture: the state recognizes the multicultural experience and hybridity at the level of everyday reality (especially in terms of consumption, entertainment and expressive culture); political emphasis is on the local; scepticism is expressed about collective identities, especially the national and the Islamic; but there is openness to the cosmopolitan.
4. Multicultural citizenship: priority is given to rebalancing the

Table 2.4 Synthesis of models of state accommodation of 'difference'

Type of state →	Plural state (Modood 1997)	Pluralism (CMEB 2000)	Interactive pluralism (Hartman and Gerteis 2005)	Inter-culturalism (Gagnon and Iacovino 2007)
1. Promotion of equality of opportunity	High	High	High	High
2. Emphasis on national identity	High	High	High	High
3. Recognition of difference	High	High	High	High
4. Seeking neutrality	Not possible	Not possible	Not possible	Not possible
5. Bearer of rights	Individual and Group	Individual and Group	Individual and Group	Individual and Group
6. Relationship to the state	Horizontal and Vertical	Horizontal and Vertical	Horizontal and Vertical	Horizontal and Vertical
7. Emphasis on minority nation identity	High	High	High	High
8. Emphasis on interaction between groups	High	High	High	High

Table 2.5 Contemporary responses to migration-related diversity

Political orientation →	National cohesion	Liberal neutrality	Multiculture	Multicultural citizenship
1. Promotion of equality of opportunity	Medium	Medium	High	High
2. Emphasis on national identity	High (but prescribed)	Low	Low	High (but remade)
3. Recognition of difference	Low	Low	Medium	High
4. Seeking neutrality	No	Yes	No	No
5. Bearer of rights	Individual	Individual	Individual	Individual and Group
6. Relationship to the state	Vertical	Horizontal and Vertical	–	Horizontal and Vertical
7. Emphasis on minority nation identity	Low	Low	Low	High
8. Emphasis on interaction between groups	High	Low	High	High

politics of accommodation and inclusion focused on ethno-religious groups, with a greater emphasis on hyphenated and plural forms of national citizenship, plural identities and individual rights than some multiculturalists argued for in the 1980s and 1990s.

From the perspective of multiculturalism, the overriding question becomes whether recommendations 1, 2 or 3 above can fully meet the challenges Europe faces today, normatively and in terms of viability. Or will a notion of group recognition prove necessary?

Conclusions

Our theoretical formulations are not offered as pure models that can seamlessly fit any country; rather, they are a basis for understanding, tabulating and comparing the different perspectives discernible amongst countries examined in this volume. We have argued that, despite the turn to a vision of multiculturalism's retreat amongst many European leaders and citizens, a normative conception of multiculturalism remains a resilient means of addressing the challenge of contemporary nation-state citizenship under conditions of diversity. The new emphasis on 'old' national identities ignores how particularity is both pragmatically necessary and justifiable within a variety of ideational and empirical political orientations. Where various political projects of remaking and updating national identities are carried out at the expense of the particular, a counterbalancing approach would be not to empty out the historical-cultural character of nationality but instead to add to it minority ethnicities. The effort should be to pluralize, not empty, cultural content.

We maintain that for the dominant ethnicity to demonopolize the state and its citizenship by not insisting on cultural assimilation as a condition of full citizenship – and of full social acceptance – is to demonstrate respect for the varied ethnicities of fellow citizens, not to blank them out. We have argued that 'neutrality' must not be mistaken for contentlessness because pure universalism is impossible. So, equality in citizenship is best pursued as (1) anti-discrimination; (2) recognition of open, mixed and changing ethnicities/identities; (3) multi-logical plurality; and (4) inclusivity and the fostering of a sense of belonging. We have detailed a variety of models that remain valid today for promoting liberal citizenship regimes. They draw from the European experience of multiculturalism but also recognize the need for incorporating change reflecting new challenges.

Appendix: criteria for tables

1. Promotion of equality of opportunity
   - Low: where anti-discrimination laws are rarely applied in practice, little or no data on ethnicity and race are collected and no public agency is charged with coordination and enforcement.
   - High: where appropriate data are systematically collected, cases are routinely investigated by employers and other institutions with many reaching the law courts, and they are widely publicized by the media and by agencies responsible for policy development and enforcement that are answerable to a government department or minister.
2. Emphasis on national identity
   - Low: where accounts of nationhood do not feature prominently in characterizations of collective identity and/or are de-emphasized in arenas of public policy and public discourse in favour of local, regional or other scales of identification, or competing notions of collective identity. The state does not promote a vision of common living, of fellow feeling between the inhabitants of that territory, other than the legal entitlements and duties that define civic membership.
   - High: where political and popular discourse promulgates the idea of a collective nationhood through concrete and symbolic means, for instance, educational policy pertaining to the school curricula, particularly with respect to history, naturalization and civic orientation and requirements that have a strong and clear sense of nationhood, as well as public discourse characterizing the collective identity in national terms.
3. Recognition of 'difference'
   - Low: where minorities are expected or required to privatize their cultural differences in taking part in pre-organized public space. This implies that the state will not take into account more than minimal involuntary identities (such as those pertaining to disability) in the construction of the public space, such that policies and practices pertaining to education, discrimination and representation, amongst others, will treat minority difference as invisible and not as a source of legitimate contestation.
   - High: where minority cultural differences and particularities are incorporated into and help fashion the public space so that

there is both unity and diversity in public life; communities and identities overlap, are interdependent and develop common features. Examples can include the adoption of religious symbols as part of school or work uniforms, or targeted socio-economic policies oriented to the specific obstacles disproportionately experienced by some minorities.

4. Seeking neutrality – yes/no and possible/not possible
   Where the state does not promote one or more national cultures, religions or ways of life. They remain private to individuals in their voluntary associations with each other. There is a single political culture in the public sphere.

5. Sphere of rights
   - Private: where although there may be substantial diversity in the private lives of individuals and communities, the state exists to protect the rights of individuals; the issue of recognizing new minority groups does not arise, for the state does not publicly recognize or enfranchise any groups to represent citizens. Individuals therefore relate to the state as individual citizens, not as members of the group.
   - Public: there may be some rights for all individuals but mediating institutions such as immigrant associations are also encouraged to be active public players and forums for political discussion and may even have a formal representative or administrative role to play in the state. Thus, the state recognizes that individuals are partly constituted by the lives of families and communities as well as shaped by the social order constituted by citizenship and by the public that amplifies and qualifies, sustains, critiques and reforms citizenship.

6. Relationship to the state
   - Horizontal: where the state engages and formulates public policy on the understanding that individuals belong to and are shaped by communities which are the primary agents of the public sphere. One outcome is that public life can consist of organized communities relating to each other (which overlaps with the minority nations in Spain and Belgium and with the historical minorities in Greece and Poland). Another outcome is that minority communities would remain intact but outside the public sphere (as in the case of pre-2000 German federal policies oriented towards the return of migrant communities).
   - Vertical: where the state–citizenship relationship is not medi-

ated by groups, communities or third parties, and more directly seeks the protection of the rights of individuals or the maximization of the choices open to individuals.

7. Emphasis on minority nation identity
   - Low: where the very fact of minority or historically autonomous regions does not invite or seek the political capacity to instil or represent its identity in educational and migration policy, and civic or other integrationist measures, such as devolution and regional assemblies in the UK.
   - High: where federal bodies devolve power, including integration policy, to historically autonomous regions and furnish them with the capacity to promote and sustain minority nation identities through such means as regional languages. Thus in some regions, linguistic departments may be established to enforce laws that give the regional language an equal status to a national language.

8. Emphasis on interaction between groups
   - Low: where the state does not pursue strategies to engender 'social mixing' either nationally or locally; this may be because it leaves civil society to serve this function or perhaps does not deem it a policy priority.
   - High: where notions of 'segregation' or other issues of social division are deemed to require concerted efforts and emphases upon social interaction at a variety of levels, and particularly locally. Ideas and emphases upon community cohesion are often illustrative of these sorts of concern, as is the more popular complaint that some minorities 'self-segregate'

Notes

1. This chapter is a revised version of our 'Framing multicultural citizenship in Europe', in A. Triandafyllidou, T. Modood and N. Meer (eds), *European Multiculturalisms: Cultural, Religious and Ethnic Challenges*, Edinburgh: Edinburgh University Press, 2012.
2. The Commission on Multi-Ethnic Britain was chaired by Bhikhu Parekh and included, among others, Stuart Hall, Tariq Modood, Yasmin Alibhai-Brown and Trevor Phillips.
3. See European Council press release, 19 November 2004 (http://ue.eu.int/ueDocs/cms_Data/docs/pressData/en/jha/82745.pdf). Other relevant documents on the issue are the Commission's first response to the Basic Common Principles of the Council (COM/2005/0389 final), the Second Annual Report on Migration and Integration (SEC/2006/892)

and the European Parliament Resolution on Integration of Immigrants (P6_TA(2006)0318).
4. Justice and Home Affairs, 2618th Meeting (Council of the EU, 14615/04, 2004, pp. 17–18).
5. See Orgad (2009: 15) for counter examples showing how even if ECHR verdicts are favourable they are not easily operationalized at the national level.

References

Archibugi, M. K., D. Held and M. Köhler (1998), *Re-imagining Political Community: Studies in Cosmopolitan Democracy*, Stanford, CT: Stanford University Press.

Archibugi, M. K., D. Held and M. Zuran (2005), *Global Governance and Public Accountability*, Hoboken, NJ: Wiley Blackwell.

Barry, B. (2001), *Culture and Equality: An Egalitarian Critique of Equality*, London: Polity Press.

Bauböck, R., E. Ersbøll, C. A. Groenendijk and H. Waldrauch (eds) (2006), *Acquisition and Loss of Nationality. Policies and Trends in 15 European Countries. Vol. 1: Comparative Analyses*, Amsterdam: Amsterdam University Press.

Brubaker, R. (2001), 'The return of assimilation? Changing perspectives on immigration and its sequels in France, Germany, and the United States', *Ethnic and Racial Studies*, 24 (4), pp. 531–48.

Caldwell, C. (2009), *Reflections on the Revolution in Europe: Immigration, Islam and the West*, London: Penguin Books.

Cameron, D. (2011), 'PM's speech at Munich Security Conference', 5 February. Available at www.number10.gov.uk/news/speeches-and-transcripts/2011/02/pms-speech-at-munich-security-conference-60293

Commission on the Future of Multi-Ethnic Britain (CMEB) (2000), *The Future of Multi-Ethnic Britain*, London: Profile Books.

Entzinger, H. (2003), 'The rise and fall of multiculturalism: The case of the Netherlands', in C. Joppke and E. Morawska (eds), *Toward Assimilation and Citizenship*, Basingstoke: Palgrave Macmillan, pp. 59–86.

—— (2007), 'The parallel decline of multiculturalism and the welfare state in the Netherlands', in K. Banting and W. Kymlicka (eds), *Multiculturalism and the Welfare State*, Oxford: Oxford University Press, pp. 177–202.

Gagnon, A. G. and R. Iacovino (2007), *Federalism, Citizenship and Quebec: Debating Multinationalism*, Toronto: University of Toronto Press.

Gilroy, P. (1987), *There Ain't No Black in the Union Jack: The Cultural Politics of Race and Nation*, London: Routledge.

Gove, M. (2006), *Celsius 7/7: How the West's Policy of Appeasement Has Provoked Yet More Fundamentalist Terror – And What Has to be Done About it*, London: Weidenfeld and Nicolson.

Hansen, R. (2006), 'The Danish cartoon controversy: A defense of liberal freedom', *International Migration*, 44 (5), pp. 7–16.

Hartmann, D. and Gerteis, J. (2005), 'Dealing with diversity: Mapping multiculturalism in sociological terms', *Sociological Theory*, 23 (2), pp. 218–40.

Home Office (2004), *Life in the United Kingdom: A Journey to Citizenship*, London: HMSO.

Jacobs, D. and A. Rea (2007), 'The end of national models? Integration courses and citizenship trajectories in Europe', *International Journal on Multicultural Societies*, 9 (2), pp. 264–83.

Joppke, C. (2004), 'The retreat of multiculturalism in the liberal state: Theory and policy', *British Journal of Sociology*, 55 (2), pp. 237–57.

—— (2008), 'Immigration and the identity of citizenship: The paradox of universalism', *Citizenship Studies*, 12 (6), pp. 533–46.

—— (2009), 'Limits of integration policy: Britain and her Muslims', *Journal of Ethnic and Migration Studies*, 35 (3), pp. 453–72.

Kiwan, D. (2008), 'Citizenship education at the cross-roads: four models of citizenship and their implications for ethnic and religious diversity', *Oxford Review of Education*, 34 (1), pp. 39–58.

Koopmans, R., P. Statham, M. Giugni and F. Passy (2005), *Contested Citizenship: Immigration and Cultural Diversity in Europe*, Minneapolis, MN: University of Minnesota Press.

Kymlicka, W. (1995), *Multicultural Citizenship*, Oxford: Oxford University Press.

Leonard, M. (1997), *Britain TM: Renewing Our Identity*, London: Demos.

Malik, K. (2007), 'Thinking outside the box', *CRE: Catalyst*, January–February. Available at www.kenanmalik.com/essays/catalyst_box.html

Mandaville, P. (2009), 'Muslim transnational identity and state responses in Europe and the UK after 9/11', *Journal of Ethnic and Migration Studies*, 35 (3), 491–506.

Marshall, T. H. (1950), *Citizenship and Social Class and other Essays*, Cambridge: Cambridge University Press.

McGhee, D. (2008), *The End of Multiculturalism? Terrorism, Integration and Human Rights*, Milton Keynes: Open University Press & McGraw-Hill Education.

Meer, N. and T. Modood (2009), 'The multicultural state we are in: Muslims, "multiculture" and the "civic re-balancing" of British multiculturalism', *Political Studies*, 57 (3) (October), pp. 473–97.

—— (2012), 'How does interculturalism contrast with multiculturalism?', *Journal of Intercultural Studies, 33 (2), pp. 175–96.*

Meer, N. and P. Mouritsen (2009), 'Political cultures compared: The Muhammad cartoons in the Danish and British press', *Ethnicities*, 9 (3), pp. 334–60.

Modood, T. (1992), *Not Easy Being British: Colour, Culture and Citizenship*, London: Runnymede Trust/Trentham Books.

—— (1997), 'Introduction: The politics of multiculturalism in the new Europe', in T. Modood and P. Werbner (eds), *The Politics of Multiculturalism in the New Europe*, London: Zed Books.

—— (2007), *Multiculturalism*, London: Blackwell.

Modood, T. and N. Meer (2009), 'Multicultural citizenship in Europe: The states we are in', paper for the EMILIE Conference, 'Migration and Diversity Challenges in Europe: Theoretical and Policy Responses', 24 September 2009.

Mouritsen, P. (2008), 'Political responses to cultural conflict: Reflections on the ambiguities of the civic turn', in P. Mouritsen and K. E. Jørgensen (eds), *Constituting Communities. Political Solutions to Cultural Conflict*, London: Palgrave, pp. 1–30.

—— (2009), 'Citizenship versus Islam? Civic integration in Germany, Great Britain and Denmark', draft paper.

Müller, J. W. (2007), 'Is Europe converging on constitutional patriotism? (And if so, is it justified)', *Critical Review of International Social and Political Philosophy*, 10 (3), pp. 377–8.

Orgad, L. (2009), '"Cultural defense" of nations: Cultural citizenship in France, Germany and the Netherlands', *European Law Journal*, 15 (6), pp. 719–37.

Parekh, B. (2000), *Rethinking Multiculturalism: Cultural Diversity and Political Theory*, London: Palgrave.

Patten, Alan (2001), 'Political Theory and Language Policy', *Political Theory*, 29 (5) (October), pp. 683–707.

Phillips, M. (2006), *Londonistan: How Britain Created a Terror State Within*, London: Gibson Square Books.

Policy Exchange (2007), *Living Apart Together: British Muslims and the Paradox of Multiculturalism*, London: Policy Exchange.

Prins, G. and Robert Salisbury (2008), 'Risk, threat and security – the case of the United Kingdom', *RUSI Journal*, 153 (2), pp. 22–7.

Schönwälder, K. (2001), *Einwanderung und ethnische Pluralität. Politische Entscheidungen und öffentliche Debatten in Großbritannien und der Bundesrepublik von den 1950er bis zu den 1970er Jahren*, Essen: Klartext Verlag.

Soysal, Y. (1994), *Limits Of Citizenship: Migrants and Postnational Membership in Europe*. Chicago, IL: Chicago University Press.

Uberoi, V. (2008), 'Do policies of multiculturalism change national identities?', *The Political Quarterly*, 79 (3), pp. 404–17.

Uberoi, V. and T. Modood (2009), 'Who doesn't feel British? Divisions over Muslims', *Parliamentary Affairs*, 63 (2), pp. 1–19.

Van De Vijver, F., S. Schalk-Soekar, J. Arends-Tóth and S. Breugelmans (2006), '"Cracks in the wall of multiculturalism?" A review of attitudinal studies in the Netherlands', *IJMS International Journal on Multicultural Societies*, 8 (1), pp. 102–18.

Weaver, M. (2010), 'Angela Merkel: Multiculturalism has "utterly failed"', 10 October. Available at www.guardian.co.uk/world/2010/oct/17/angela-merkel-german-multiculturalism-failed

The Challenge of Multiculturalism: Political Philosophy and the Question of Diversity

Christian Fernández

Introduction

The word 'challenge' in the title of this chapter refers to the role that multiculturalism has played in political philosophy over the last decades: questioning established norms, criticizing blind spots and neglected areas and reframing central issues and problems. The challenge originates in the conditions of uniformity and assimilation that political membership (often) presupposes. Multiculturalism framed as a challenge serves as a critique of ethnocentricity, discrimination, national chauvinism, cultural repression and more generally intolerance of diversity. But most of all, it is a critique of mainstream political philosophy's inability to offer a proper theory of how to accommodate cultural diversity – conceptually as much as normatively. Hence the name *multiculturalism*.

Multiculturalism's challenge has been successful in the sense of bringing about a greater awareness of problems and injustices related to diversity. It has also been successful inasmuch as multiculturalism now is conceived as *the* diversity-friendly position in politics. As the name implies, the central multicultural claim is that many cultures should live together without being merged into one or subsumed under a superior, overarching culture. It denotes an appreciation of cultural diversity, which compares favourably to all other supposedly monoculturalist views that resist or at least lament the diversification of national cultures.

The case studies comprising this volume focus on the incorporation and rejection of multicultural ideas and policies in countries across Europe. This chapter deals with a corresponding incorporation and rejection in political philosophy. More specifically, I am interested in how the multicultural challenge has been met by proponents of another theory that is associated with a strong appreciation of diversity, namely liberalism. The liberal entry point is both a delimitation of the subject and a conscious choice. It is motivated by the fact that liberalism is a dominating theoretical perspective and key reference point in contemporary philosophy, which means that mainstream liberal philosophy has been and remains the main target of the multicultural critique.

To this end, the chapter will compare the multicultural and the liberal approaches to diversity, and examine how the former has affected the latter. The main purpose is to examine three attempts to incorporate the multicultural critique into liberal philosophy, and to discuss the normative implications thereof. In so doing, the analysis revolves around one central question: *How can differential treatment on the basis of culture be justified?*

The chapter is divided into three sections. In the first I sketch the main themes of the multicultural challenge. The second describes and discusses three different liberal arguments relating to differential treatment on the basis of culture. The third and last section offers some final reflections on the contributions of multiculturalism and its possible decline in political philosophy and political practice.

The multicultural challenge

Multiculturalism comes in different packages with diverse labels: 'the politics of identity', 'the politics of recognition', 'the politics of difference', 'the politics of pluralism', among others. What they all have in common is an insistence on the accommodation rather than the suppression of cultural diversity. A just society, according to this view, is a society that recognizes and respects the differences between the various cultural minorities of society through means of differential treatment.

The multicultural critique of assimilation targets the ways in which mainstream societies strive to preserve and disseminate one culture. It is focused on the various norms, rules and laws that favour mainstream culture and/or impose it on minorities: state-subsidized churches, morning prayers in public schools, mandatory Sunday closing, dress code in public schools, prohibition against the building of minarets and so on. Multiculturalists resist these overt forms of assimilation because cultural homogeneity should not be a precondition for political inclusion.

Most liberals share this view – the liberal insistence on religious liberty and the separation of state and church is a case in point – which means that the difference between the multicultural and the liberal approach to cultural diversity lies elsewhere. It has less to do with attitudes towards assimilation and diversity, and more to do with conceptions of culture and equality. Essentially, the difference can be reduced to two themes. The first relates to the 'multi' of multiculturalism, namely the protection of diversity through *differential treatment* of groups, and the second refers to the 'culturalism', namely the belief that *cultural belonging* is essential to human flourishing and self-fulfilment. Both clash with the conventional conception of diversity and equality in liberal thought. In order to clearly discern the divergence, a brief comparison is presented.

DIFFERENTIALISM

The liberal norm of equal treatment commands the state to treat all citizens equally regardless of gender, sexual orientation, age, religion and other personal characteristics and affiliations. It can be described as a deliberate indifference, commonly referred to as 'benign neglect', of all the small and big differences that make people different from one another despite their being citizens of the same state. The purpose of such neglect is on the one hand to protect everyone's right to be different (private freedom) and on the other hand to assure that all citizens *qua* citizens are equal. To these ends, the norm of equal treatment is guarded by universal individual rights that protect the private lives of individuals and groups from state intervention. The norm is also guarded by laws designed to protect citizens from varying forms of discrimination in education, on the job market, in politics and so on. Such rights and laws are especially important for minorities, liberals believe, since they protect them from the 'tyranny of the majority', to borrow John Stuart Mill's well-known expression.

The norm of equal treatment is based on several assumptions or approximations. One is the assumption of a *common public interest* that supposedly unites all citizens and creates an equal relation between them and the state. This common public interest is based on norms and values that are shared by all citizens. In his later works John Rawls (1987, 1993) refers to this common interest as an 'overlapping consensus', emphasizing its constitution through the convergence of particular ways of life and beliefs – 'comprehensive doctrines' in Rawlsian terminology – and not from some inherently free-floating conception of good citizenship. The unifying bond of liberal citizenship ideally derives from nothing more, and nothing less, than this overlapping consensus and, more concretely, the rights and liberties that confer on citizens the power to negotiate and renegotiate it. (How negotiable the overlapping consensus really is can be questioned since it is constricted by and derived from various principles that specify the fundamental terms of a just, liberal order (cf. Rawls 1993: 144ff).)

Within the boundaries of the overlapping consensus, citizens are regarded as an abstract mass of equals, the diversity of which the state benignly neglects for egalitarian reasons. Outside these boundaries, however, they are all unique individuals and groups who should be left alone to pursue, maintain and reproduce the different comprehensive doctrines that endow their private lives with a sense of meaning and purpose. According to a common phrase, the state should be *neutral* vis-à-vis these doctrines. This means two things: on the one hand, that the state should refrain from favouring or disfavouring certain ways of life – say, Catholicism over Calvinism, or heterosexuality over homosexuality – and, on the other hand, that the state should disregard and be insusceptible to demands that derive from comprehensive doctrines and particular conceptions of the good. The boundaries of the overlapping consensus ideally limit the authority of the state to actions that can be justified by public reasons.

The liberal norm of equal treatment through benign neglect and state neutrality is closely related to a presumption of *separateness*, that is, to the view that different spheres of society can and should be separated and contained from one another. These separations are defining elements of liberal societies, for example, the separation of state and church, of civil society and political community, of democracy and the market, and of office and property (cf. Walzer 1984: 315). This idea of separateness is a way of enabling both liberty and equality. As Michael Walzer explains:

> we can say that a [. . .] society enjoys both freedom and equality when success in one institutional setting isn't convertible into success in another, that is, when the separations hold, when political power doesn't shape the church or religious zeal the state. (Walzer 1984: 321, cf. Walzer 1983: 6–17)

The realization of the common public interest and state neutrality presuppose this separation of spheres, then, as it protects the 'purity' and autonomy of each sphere from the distorting influences of other spheres. In culturally diverse societies, it supposedly ensures both the common bond of citizenship and a flourishing diversity of ethnic and religious identities.

The multicultural critique departs from these liberal assumptions. Just as socialists and feminists have done before, multiculturalists question the liberal separation of spheres although in slightly different ways and with different consequences. A number of objections are raised that allegedly disqualify the liberal notion of the neutral state and the viability of equal treatment. One of them is that personal identities cannot be switched on and off as citizens enter and exit the public sphere in the way that liberals assume or hope. Identities are deeply rooted and pervasive social affiliations. They define for people who they are, configure their interests and aspirations and inform the choices people make and why they make them. Therefore it is misleading, multiculturalists argue, to assume that one's identity as a woman, homosexual, devout Christian or parent can be separated or 'bracketed off' from the role of the citizen. Such identities influence citizenship, not just with respect to how individuals exercise their rights, for example how they vote, but with respect to the very institution of citizenship itself and how that institution is shaped by the experiences and interests of people. It is therefore inevitable, multiculturalists claim, that the institution of citizenship and the common public interests more generally come to reflect the needs and interests of the majority rather than the minorities. The fictitious neutral liberal state functions as a cover-up for a mainstream culture that systematically benefits the majority (Taylor 1994; Galeotti 2002; Parekh 2000).

The liberal state is an assimilationist state in yet another sense, according to multiculturalists. Despite its purported neutrality, liberalism and liberal societies consistently favour some ways of life over others, namely the ones that reflect the liberal ideal of personal autonomy (Galston 1995; Macedo 1995 and 2000). The public culture and its institutions are based on this ideal, which implies a preference for some values over others: individualism and self-fulfilment over collective loyalty and solidarity, secularism and moral relativism over religious devotion and deep faith, social mobility and self-sufficiency over familial ties and obedience. A society based on the ideal of autonomy, multiculturalists insist, is from the very outset a society that encourages and sponsors a certain way of life at the expense of others.

Multiculturalism is not a denunciation of the liberal aims of equality and freedom but a differing view on how these aims should be pursued in diverse societies – a view that proposes *differential treatment* of groups as a complement and sometimes replacement of equal treatment of individuals. Justifications of differential treatment come in various guises (as we see in the following sections); the general aim is to dissolve the connection between equality and assimilation so that the latter ceases to be a precondition for the former. The ethos of differential treatment is equal respect for and recognition of all members of society, not just as individual members of the state (citizens) but as members of groups within the state. The recognition of group membership, multiculturalists claim, is an affirmation of the differences that make people into what they are. It enables them to maintain their way of life and collective identity without being marginalized, and to be equal without being assimilated.

CULTURALISM

Differential treatment is a means by which groups are singled out and granted rights, freedoms and resources not offered to other citizens. This is not a new idea in political theory and practice: the redistribution of material resources through progressive taxation and social welfare programmes is a well-established system of differential treatment, whereby low-income groups are given preference over high-income groups. Preferential treatment of women (sometimes) at the expense of men is also a form of differential treatment, whereby women are compensated for gender discrimination in society. Egalitarian liberals tend to support both forms, but especially the first.

Differential treatment on the basis of culture is a more difficult and controversial matter, however. While money and sex are fairly straightforward categories, cultures are notoriously subjective and amorphous. There is no simple way of delineating cultures, no simple way of deciding how culture and identity inform and constrain individual choice and, most importantly, no simple way of deciding who belongs to which culture – as opposed to income group and sex. Because of these difficulties, most modern political philosophers (not just liberals) have been reluctant to defend culture as a reason for differential treatment.

The typically liberal approach to cultures is to conceive of them as voluntary associations, which means emphasizing the subjective and self-ascriptive nature of cultural identity. This is how John Locke (2003: 219f) once described congregations and this is how liberals have tended to think of all other groups that mediate the relation between state and citizen. The reasons are obvious. If cultures are voluntary associations between individuals, they are no business of the state. And, if cultures are analogous to voluntary associations, they are compatible with the liberal insistence on personal autonomy and can be assessed accordingly. Indeed, the existence of a rich diversity of such cultures facilitates social mobility and free choice since it offers a large variety of lifestyles to choose and (perhaps) combine (Raz 1986: 369ff).

While this may be a valid approximation of some lifestyle cultures – veganism, goth, Falun Gong, and so on – it misrepresents the deeper cultural diversity that also characterizes plural societies. We do not *choose* in the proper meaning of the term to be raised as Muslims, Turkish-Germans or Basques. It is a choice that is made for us, not by us. Such cultures are better conceived as involuntary organizations that we enter by birth, not choice, and that to varying degrees shape and mould us into what we grow up to be (Walzer 2004: 44ff; Jones 2006). A more serious attempt to unpack the black box of culture is noticeable from the 1980s. This 'cultural turn' was initiated by the so-called communitarians in the late 1970s and 1980s, many of whom became influential multiculturalists in the 1990s and after. Simplified, the communitarian thesis emphasizes the social and cultural contingency of personal identity, and the ontological (and normative) priority of the community over the individual (cf. Taylor 1985; Sandel 1982). Communitarians rarely concretized what the term community refers to, but it was mostly assumed to be a *national* community with a fairly homogeneous culture.

The multicultural challenge echoes and builds on the communitarian conception of culture and its implications for personal identity and politics, although from a much more pluralist viewpoint. While the communitarian critique targeted a liberal ignorance of the importance of community and cultural homogeneity, the multicultural critique uses similar ontological premises for very different normative purposes – diversification, pluralism and protection of minorities. Differential treatment is an empirical recognition of the importance of culture and the diversity of cultures in modern societies, and it is a normative prescription in favour of state-sanctioned protection of such diversity. If the wearing of religious symbols is vital to cultural identity, then exemptions should be made to secular dress codes. If official bilingualism is fundamental to the cultural preservation of a minority nation, then public education should be provided in two languages. If group representation is crucial to cater to the special needs of minorities, then preferential treatment should be applied to marginalized, powerless groups. Such recommendations presuppose a replacement of equal treatment for differential treatment.

Questions remain, however: What is a culture? Which fundamental human values are contingent on cultural belonging? And how should individuals be matched with cultures? The following section examines three attempts to answer these questions.

The justification of culture

The early debate on multiculturalism was a more or less direct confrontation between communitarian insights on culture and identity on the one hand, and liberal principles of individual autonomy and state neutrality on the other. Initially, the multicultural challenge took the shape of an external critique of liberalism. Gradually, however, the focus shifted from the question 'what's wrong with liberalism?' to 'how and why should liberalism accommodate cultural diversity?' The shift of focus marks a steady convergence of multicultural and liberal agendas, but also a relative relocation of the debate from the boundaries to the heart of liberal theory (cf. Kymlicka 2002: 336ff).

This section examines liberalism's internal struggle with the multicultural challenge. On the one hand liberals have come to recognize that cultures constitute part of the framework of ideals and norms that help define people's conception of the good, of what it means to lead a meaningful and prosperous life. On the other hand liberals worry that protection of cultures works as a collectivist restraint on individual freedom that imposes limits on social mobility and free choice. The following three arguments represent different attempts to alleviate this tension.

IN DEFENCE OF AUTONOMY

The first argument in support of incorporating culture into the liberal equation of freedom and equality is filtered through the traditional liberal emphasis on personal autonomy. Cultural embeddedness is a precondition for autonomy, according to this thesis, because it confers meaning to the choices people make. The development and practice of autonomy is endogenous to cultures and anyone who values the former must also be concerned with the latter (see

Kymlicka 1989 and 1995; Miller 1995; Raz 1994 and 1998; Tamir 1993).

Among the best-known proponents of this position is Will Kymlicka (1989, 1995) who has sought to reconcile mainstream liberalism with a theory of cultural rights. Kymlicka departs from the conception of 'societal culture', by which he means a 'vocabulary' of traditions and conventions as well as the language that perpetuates them. These vocabularies make up the context within which passions and interests, convictions and goals, develop and become worthwhile pursuing (cf. Dworkin 1985: 228ff). They include common memories, values, institutions and customs that permeate most areas of human interaction, for instance schools, the media, the economy and public administration. Due to the comprehensive character of these cultures it is virtually impossible for anyone to fully take part in public and social life without sharing the key tenets of the culture (Kymlicka 1995: 84ff).

Kymlicka's justification of societal cultures is based on their instrumental value for autonomy. It is not the culture as such that should be protected and preserved but the functions it fulfils for the realization of autonomy. He describes societal cultures as 'contexts of choice' that enable autonomous lives. It follows that the state should protect societal cultures from decay. In the case of national majority cultures, no special means are required and the principle of state neutrality should prevail. But in the case of minority cultures preservation often requires specific, group-based cultural (that is, differential) rights. Just like social rights serve to compensate for economic inequality and keep the latter from engendering political inequality, cultural rights serve to compensate for inequalities between majority and minorities by assuring the latter some degree of protection through specific cultural resources.

This means that the ultimate purpose of differential rights is to achieve greater equality between cultures which supposedly leads to greater equality of opportunities for individuals of different cultures; the purpose is not to preserve any particular culture for the sake of its uniqueness and inherent value. In Kymlicka's opinion, there is no contradiction between the protection of endangered societal cultures and the endorsement of liberal rights because most minorities seek empowerment and liberal emancipation through their culture, not seclusion from mainstream society. He contends that it is important to ensure that the external protection of cultures through differential rights does not entail internal restrictions of individual rights.

Accordingly, internal unity and homogeneity must not be achieved at the expense of basic liberal rights such as freedom of belief and expression (Kymlicka 1995: Ch. 3). Again, the value of societal cultures is contingent on their significance for personal autonomy and free choice, not the other way around. This means that rights protecting internal dissent must trump those protecting the integrity of the culture.

Because of its entrenchment in the concept of societal culture, Kymlicka's theory of cultural rights provides a strong defence for some groups and virtually no defence for others. It applies primarily to minority nations, such as Quebec, Scotland, Catalonia and the Basque Country, and to indigenous populations, such as the Indians and Inuits of North America, the Maori of New Zealand, the Aborigines of Australia and the Sami of Scandinavia. Both types of minorities have (rightful) claims to a particular territory and tend to be geographically concentrated, which of course facilitates cultural reproduction. The existence and widespread use of a minority language is an especially salient and persuasive manifestation of cultural distinctness.

Conversely, Kymlicka's theory offers few if any cultural rights to immigrated (ethnic) minorities. His justification for this combines normative and empirical reasons. Unlike minority nations and indigenous groups, the position of immigrant minorities is not the result of colonization and forced annihilation but of voluntary choice – more or less – which makes any claim to self-determination or cultural protection weaker. Furthermore, and more importantly, since ethnic minorities do not have and are unlikely to establish societal cultures, their members' safest way to personal autonomy goes via access to (assimilation into) the mainstream national culture. Such assimilation is not to be lamented as long as ethnic minorities are allowed and able to maintain bits and pieces of their original culture in the form of hyphenated, hybrid identities (Kymlicka 1995: 96ff).

An additional and possibly more profound restriction derives from the emphasis placed on autonomy as a justifying condition for cultural protection. This emphasis implies that only minorities that embrace personal autonomy and its associated values – individualism, self-sufficiency, independence – are eligible for differential group rights. Only minorities that are internally liberal in a way similar to mainstream society deserve external protection. On this view, several indigenous groups may be ruled out since cultural protection would imply preservation of traditional ways of life in which patriarchy, monotheism and subordination to authoritarian leaders are key elements. For the same reason it may rule out deeply religious minorities that live in seclusion from mainstream society, for instance Hasidic Jews, Amish and Mennonite Christians, and Salafist Muslims (Kymlicka 1995: Ch. 8).

Given these caveats, Kymlicka's theory of cultural rights offers significantly less protection for minorities than he claims. His cultural rights are premised on conditions that seem to have a much more assimilating influence on minorities than he is willing to admit (cf. Patten 1999). The equality between societal cultures, which is the ultimate aim of differential treatment in Kymlicka's theory, presupposes internal liberalization/modernization of conservative and traditional groups. What are preserved, then, are the boundaries of the group, not its distinctiveness and authenticity. Put differently, while the group maintains a considerable degree of autonomy, it is likely to wind up losing its defining cultural traits.

IN DEFENCE OF DIGNITY

The second argument for the protection of minority cultures is based on the connection between culture and dignity. It stresses the comprehensive nature of societal cultures and their importance for personal identity. Public recognition of such cultures is essential for people's dignity and self-esteem, according to this thesis, because it is an affirmation of the beliefs, values, customs and traditions that define people for themselves and others. Cultural protection, then, is both a question of preserving cultures through differential rights and of affirming their equal value through public visibility and recognition (Galeotti 2002; Margalit and Halbertal 1994; Margalit and Raz 1990; Taylor 1994; Tully 1995; Young 1990).

My reconstruction of this position focuses mainly on two articles (Taylor 1994; Margalit and Halbertal 1994). Both depart from a conception of culture which is more explicitly communitarian than Kymlicka's. The right to culture, Margalit and Halbertal argue, is not a right to just any culture that can release the individual's potential for autonomous action. It is the right to one's own culture; a culture which is intertwined with self-perception, personal identity, self-esteem and dignity. The philosophical underpinnings of this position can be traced to Herder and Hegel, and have in contemporary philosophy been applied to multiculturalism by Charles Taylor and Axel Honneth. Taylor's influential essay 'The politics of recognition'

(1994) examined the connection between personal identity and culture. It conceived of culture as an expression of authenticity and originality that reflects the unique experiences and history of a group of people. The culture is a source of identification that helps members define who they are in relation to one another and the world. Cultures develop dialogically in a complex interplay with 'significant others', by which distinct notions of difference emerge and are maintained. Such dialogue is a constantly ongoing although historically contingent process. It presupposes interaction with other cultures because without it there can be no contrast and distinction, no reflection of originality and authenticity, indeed no sense of a *We* (Taylor 1994: 31ff).

Taylor's main concern is not the preservation of cultures but the recognition of personal identities. Unlike Kymlicka, however, Taylor's theory builds on a holistic approach that does not lend itself to instrumentalism. Culture is inextricably linked to personal identity, which means that recognition of the person requires recognition of his or her culture. Conversely, the withholding of recognition amounts to a form of oppression because it constitutes a denial or rejection of the defining traits that make people into who they are – a deprivation of their authenticity (Taylor 1994: 36). In a similar way, Margalit and Raz (1990: 447ff) declare that cultural belonging is important because it has a 'high social profile'. It affects how people perceive and treat one another, and as such it plays an important role in how personal identities are shaped. This signifies that a people's self-respect is contingent on how their culture is esteemed by others. Therefore, 'the right to culture' is synonymous with 'the right to secure one's own personal identity' (Margalit and Raz 1990: 502).

Securing the cultural survival of minorities requires a non-neutral state that actively supports vulnerable cultures. The purpose of such support, however, is not just to provide minorities with secure access to a culture but to secure the survival of minority cultures 'as they are'. Unlike Kymlicka, proponents of this position are not indifferent to the internal transformation (liberalization) of such cultures because survival implies preservation of authentic cultural traits rather than just the cohesion of its adherents. Arguably this enhances the state's responsibility for restoring and conserving endangered cultures, approximating what might somewhat provocatively be described as the role of the curator. It is a role that markedly supersedes that of merely protecting groups from the external forces of assimilation.

Does this mean that recognition of cultural authenticity is a conservative enterprise? Not necessarily. Conservation or progression is of secondary importance to the recognition of cultural identities. Taylor's defence of recognition is couched in emancipatory terms. His main focus is public visibility and the inclusion of marginalized, discriminated or ostracized groups – say, homosexuals and the Roma. But the argument lends itself just as easily to the claims of conservative minorities which seek isolation from mainstream society in order to be able to preserve their traditional customs and beliefs. For instance, Margalit and Halbertal defend public protection through seclusion of Ultra-Orthodox Jews in Israel because of the need to preserve personal identities. Their way of life is not sustainable in mainstream Israeli society and everything they do is dictated by a stern religious doctrine that derives from the Torah. The state's recognition of this way of life means assisting the group in its self-inflicted isolation (Margalit and Halbertal 1994).

Justifying culture in the interests of securing personal identity and dignity constitutes a challenge to the liberal emphasis on the primacy of the individual before the collective. In Kymlicka's theory of cultural rights, the collective serves individual ends, or at least collective ends compatible with individual ends. In the communitarian approach of Taylor and others, the order of priorities is less clear cut since individual and collective ends are entangled in a way that makes them indistinguishable from one another. This has problematic normative implications for a liberal theory of cultural rights. Is every practice that contributes to the preservation of an authentic cultural identity legitimate? If not, where should the line between tolerable and intolerable practices be drawn? And how should such a line be justified if the criterion of personal autonomy is ruled out?

Neither Taylor nor Margalit and Halbertal offer answers to such questions, although the latter makes a passing reference to the Millian harm principle (Margalit and Halbertal 1994: 498). Other liberals have suggested a softer conception of personal autonomy: if a particular way of life is endorsed by members of the group, it does not constitute a violation of individual rights even if it presupposes gender inequality, strict obedience of internal authorities and other illiberal norms (Spinner 1994; Spinner-Halev 2000). The criterion of voluntary endorsement seems insufficient in enclosed and secluded communities where contact with the outside world is limited and the social costs of dissent may be unbearable or insurmountable, especially for women and children (cf. Arneson and Shapiro 1996; Okin 2005; Fernández 2010).

The recognition argument for cultural rights supports a wide array of potential claims. From a liberal viewpoint the most compelling are ones subsuming the discriminated and marginalized minorities where recognition means inclusion and empowerment without assimilation. The most difficult cases, on the other hand, are ones implicating the deeply conservative groups which overtly reject basic liberal values. At the same time, it is precisely to the latter that Taylor's and Margalit and Halbertal's communitarian conception of culture is most applicable. Not many people in modern societies are as reliant on a comprehensive culture for personal identification as Ultra-Orthodox Jews. In most cases, to be properly recognized as an authentic subject involves a more individualized process in which minorities and majorities alike combine and revise their cultural attachments rather than compete to maintain just one of them. In such cases, recognition of groups employing Taylor's conception – to dig out and affirm the cultural identity that makes people into what they really are – is an inadequate strategy. It applies an implicitly monolithic, essentialist notion of culture to individuals who have several cultural attachments and multiple identities (cf. Appiah 1994: 155f; Benhabib 2002: 61–4).

IN DEFENCE OF VOLUNTARISM

The third argument for the protection of cultural minorities is libertarian and probably the most permissive of cultural diversity. Its point of departure is a minimalist conception of the state, whose role is to intervene as little as possible in the private lives of citizens, and to impose as few conditions as possible on people's ways of organizing themselves. It defends cultural diversity on the basis of voluntarism and anti-paternalism, not of an assumed right to culture (Kukhatas 1992; cf. Galston 1995 and 2002; Gray 2000; Stolzenberg 1993).

My account of the voluntarist position relies primarily on an influential article by Chandran Kukhatas (1992). It does not advocate group rights or state-sanctioned protection of endangered or marginalized cultures but instead is grounded on a neutral conception of the state. In this sense, Kukhatas is not a multicultural theorist. Nonetheless, his minimalist state and laissez-faire liberal society offer more leeway for deep-seated cultural diversity than any of the previous positions we have reviewed. This is not a mere side-effect of his libertarian agenda but a principled defence of toleration in the widest possible sense. Although Kukhatas repudiates the need for group rights, his primary concern is the ability of cultural minorities to preserve their ways of life to the best of their abilities. In this respect he is a multicultural theorist, or at least a liberal with far-reaching multicultural concerns.

Kukhatas emphasizes the fluid and contingent character of cultural groups. 'Groups are constantly forming and dissolving in response to political and institutional circumstances,' he argues, which means that they 'do not exist prior to or independently of legal and political institutions but are themselves given shape by those institutions' (Kukhatas 1992: 110). This makes for a less rigid and essentialist understanding of culture than Taylor or Margalit and Halbertal. Kukhatas stresses the fundamental importance of external incentives and constraints that influence which particular group traits become salient and defining in particular contexts, as well as internal heterogeneity that often creates tensions within the group. This does not mean that cultures are unimportant but that they cannot be treated as given, homogeneous entities with coherent, uniform interests. The problem with cultural rights, then, is that they help construct and reconstruct what they are supposed to preserve; they forge homogeneity where there is heterogeneity.

Kukhatas' conception of the relation between individuals, cultures and legal-political contexts leads to a defence of the classical liberal view of cultures as voluntary associations. The protection of cultures is best achieved through a strong right to *freedom of association*. Kukhatas avoids making primordialist assumptions about cultures and group identities – for him, cultures are whatever their adherents want them to be. This position appears to offer little protection to minorities since the preservation of cultures becomes a private enterprise without support from public authorities. In Kukhatas' view, however, this privatization is a form of protection because it liberates the group from the assimilating conditions that accompany public support and differential treatment. Thus conceived, the individual right to free association 'gives a great deal of authority to cultural communities' because it 'does not require them to be communities of any particular kind' (Kukhatas 1992: 117). It confers on members of the group the right to protect whatever practices and beliefs they deem necessary for the preservation of their way of life and identity, regardless of whether they are compatible with the liberal values of mainstream society.

Viewing cultural groups as private and voluntary associations implies a default understanding of membership as freely consented by individual members. While this allows for a less deterministic conception of culture, it implies other problems for liberal theory. The voluntariness of cultural membership is best interpreted as a metaphor, according to Kukhatas, because it is rarely freely chosen and rarely granted to outsiders. It is voluntary, however, in so far as every member is free to leave the group – to terminate membership; as long as members do not leave they are presumed to be content with their membership (Kukhatas 1992: 116). This is the default understanding upon which Kukhatas' accommodation of cultural diversity rests. It is not difficult to see how this private freedom of cultural groups may lead to grave limitations on the rights of members, limitations that the state would have to interpret as freely consented and therefore it would be obliged to tolerate. It may command the state to tolerate deeply illiberal practices such as clitoridectomy and denial of basic education to children, or just girls. In the case of children, individual protection seems non-existent; in Kukhatas' society of 'voluntary associations' their fate is entirely in the hands of parents. This parental right is only restricted by a (vaguely formulated) prohibition against direct physical harm.

Kukhatas' vision of the liberal society is a society of semi-autonomous cultural communities. What is legally recognized in such a society is the individual right to free association (Kukhatas 1992: 126), although this right amounts to a de facto recognition of groups. The only thing that guards individual liberty in this society and protects individuals against the cultural community's potential abuse of power and repression is the exit option (cf. Kukhatas 1992: 133). Kukhatas recognizes the importance of the right to exit, but he devotes little attention to what the necessary conditions for exit should be. The formal right and actual ability to exit may be very different in the secluded, non-transparent communities that his tolerant libertarian state must permit. According to him, the 'most important condition which makes possible a substantive freedom to exit from a community is the existence of a wider society that is open to individuals wishing to leave their local groups' (Kukhatas 1992: 134). But if the existence of an open yet passive mainstream society is the only barrier standing in the way of cultural communities turning into radical sects, there seem to be good reasons for liberals to be sceptical of Kukhatas' theory. In sum, it offers much freedom of manoeuvre to elites and political leaders of illiberal minorities, but little to the ordinary people who for one reason or another might wish to exit (see Barry 2002; Fernández 2010; Okin 2005; Spinner-Halev 2000).

Conclusion

Is there a place in liberal societies for extending differential treatment on the basis of culture? It depends on who you ask. In this chapter I have focused on two affirmative answers and one negative, although all three of them share a concern for cultural minorities and the value of group identities. It should be noted that not all liberals share this concern. The three positions I have reviewed are noteworthy in that each struggles with the tensions between recognition of the individual and the group, between individual liberty and collective autonomy, and between social mobility and the preservation of different ways of life. These are tensions that characterize a typically liberal take on differential treatment.

Kymlicka's solution builds on the belief that the tensions are exaggerated, that the two sides can be reconciled and that most claims for differential treatment are claims for personal autonomy. Taylor's solution has a more communitarian bent and builds on the belief that the tensions themselves are deceptive since all values – even personal autonomy – reflect and reproduce a certain conception of culture and community. Kukhatas' solution, finally, recognizes the tensions but rejects the idea that liberal societies have to consist of people who cherish individual liberty and other basic liberal values.

My assessment of the three positions has dealt with the normative implications of differential treatment on the basis of culture. My focus on liberal philosophy is motivated by liberalism's central place in contemporary political philosophy. But this centrality is not limited to philosophy; it applies to politics and society as well. People across the West live in capitalist, liberal-democratic, post-industrial, diverse, hybrid and highly individualized societies that are imbued with liberal values and liberal culture. To a large extent people throughout the West lead 'liberal lives' which revolve around the pursuit of personal autonomy, self-realization, voluntary affiliations and relations, and upward social mobility. Liberalism, then, is as much a reflection of an existing society as it is a normative theory about how that society should be organized and governed (cf. Taylor 1985; Walzer 1990). To reject liberalism implies much more than merely voting for a socialist or conservative party; it means rejecting a standard and mainstream way of life altogether. Multiculturalism's most valuable contributions to political philosophy, I believe, have to do with this realization.

The multicultural challenge has successfully exposed the conflation of mainstream culture with liberal culture, of state neutrality with liberal values and of diversity with individualism. It has revealed the pervasive and assimilating effects of liberal culture. It has also made political theorists aware of the costs associated with denouncing or resisting liberalism for the sake of alternative, non-liberal ways of life. It is obvious that the principle of equal treatment can sometimes disadvantage minorities in deeply divided societies and, conversely, that measures of differential treatment can protect such minorities from being acculturated, assimilated or marginalized. But the extent to which such measures can be justified on liberal grounds remains contested. Is a society that permits arranged marriages and religious indoctrination through home schooling still a liberal society? Is a society that defends the individual liberties of most but not all of its citizens still a liberal society? Such questions have no simple answers. We may have to accept that the room for genuine cultural diversity is bound to be limited in the liberal society – just like in any other society – and that some ways of life are bound to be favoured over others, notwithstanding the intended neutrality of the state.

The 'easy' cases of diversity, on the other hand, are ones in which differential rights are a temporary means to overcome discrimination or past injustices. That is, they represent cases where the end goal is integration into mainstream, liberal society rather than protection from it. The challenge of multiculturalism in such cases is not how to establish a *modus vivendi* among alternative ways of life, but how to combat discrimination against minorities which want to lead liberal lives, participate in mainstream society and want to belong. These cases are 'easy' inasmuch as they do not contest the idea of liberal society as such, 'only' its imperfect political realization. Does this distinction between difficult and easy cases tell us anything about the alleged demise of multiculturalism? To answer this question I wish to propose a somewhat provocative and tentative thesis.

The early European multicultural policies of the 1970s and 1980s – which were not multicultural in any elaborated sense – were modelled on the easy cases of diversity. They departed from the benign and slightly naïve assumption that most if not all minorities want integration, and from the implicit assumption that cultural differences represent minor, private differences. Whatever problems arose from increasing (immigrant) diversity, such as discrimination, marginalization and social inequality, could be solved through more effective means of integration and tolerance.

From the 1990s on conceptions of diversity have drastically changed. Policies on cultural diversity are increasingly modelled on the difficult cases, as evidenced by debates on parallel societies, enclavization and ghettoization. These debates, which focus on minorities that allegedly do not want to be a part of society, have changed the conceptual frame of policy as well as understandings of multiculturalism. Even though most minorities continue to be 'easy' cases, they tend now to be perceived as 'difficult' ones, especially Muslims and immigrants from the Middle East. This is noticeable in political philosophy as the focus has shifted to the relation between individual liberty and cultural diversity, the necessary limits of liberal toleration and the distinctions between liberal and illiberal values. It is also discernible in political practice, evidenced in the conflation of liberal with Western society.

This shift is partly a consequence of the multicultural challenge, I suggest, because the challenge has brought about a greater awareness of the importance of cultural identity, the pervasiveness of such identities, and the religious and ethnic undertones of Western liberalism. Indirectly it has pointed out the difficulties of integration and the fallacy of assuming that people are more or less 'all the same'. The success of multiculturalism has been to show that what is normally called integration really means assimilation, and that assimilation is an unjust demand that causes real harm. This is also one of the reasons for the disenchantment with multiculturalism in Europe, I believe: it has led decision-makers and opinion-makers to think of cultural diversity as a threat to public unity and the liberal way of life. Although liberalism was always based on the accommodation of religious and other forms of diversity, it is nowadays conceived as incompatible with the beliefs and practices of many minorities. In this sense – but only in this sense – the *twilight* of multiculturalism derives from the *success* of multiculturalism.

References

Appiah, K. (1994), 'Identity, authenticity, survival: Multicultural societies and social reproduction', in A. Gutmann (ed.), *Multiculturalism: Examining the Politics of Recognition*, Princeton, NJ: Princeton University Press.

Arneson, R. and I. Shapiro (1996), 'Democratic autonomy and religious freedom: A critique of *Wisconsin v. Yoder*', in I. Shapiro and R. Hardin (eds), *NOMOS 38: Political Order*, New York: New York University Press.

Barry, B. (2002), *Culture and Equality*, Cambridge: Polity Press.

Benhabib, S. (2002), *The Claims of Culture: Equality and Diversity in the Global Era*, Princeton, NJ: Princeton University Press.

Dworkin, R. (1985), *A Matter of Principle*, Cambridge, MA: Harvard University Press.

Fernández, C. (2010), 'Education and diversity: Two stories of a liberal dilemma', *Public Affairs Quarterly*, 24 (4), pp. 279–96.

Galeotti, A. E. (2002), *Toleration as Recognition*, Cambridge: Cambridge University Press.

Galston, W. (1995), 'Two concepts of liberalism', *Ethics*, 105 (April), pp. 516–34.

—— (2002), *Liberal Pluralism: The Implications of Value Pluralism for Political Theory and Practice*, Cambridge: Cambridge University Press.

Gray, J. (2000), *Two Faces of Liberalism*, Oxford: Blackwell.

Jones, P. (2006), 'Bearing the consequences of belief', in R. E. Goodin and P. Pettit (eds), *Contemporary Political Philosophy* (2nd edn), Oxford: Blackwell.

Kukhatas, C. (1992), 'Are there any cultural rights?', *Political Theory*, 20 (1), pp. 105–39.

Kymlicka, W. (1989), *Liberalism, Community and Culture*, Oxford: Oxford University Press.

—— (1995), *Multicultural Citizenship*, Oxford: Oxford University Press.

—— (2002), *Contemporary Political Philosophy: An Introduction* (2nd edn), Oxford: Oxford University Press.

Locke, J. (2003/1689), 'A letter concerning toleration', in I. Shapiro (ed.), *Two Treatises of Government and A Letter Concerning Toleration. John Locke*, New Haven, CT and London: Yale University Press.

Macedo, S. (1995), 'Liberal civic education and religious fundamentalism: The case of God v. John Rawls?', *Ethics*, 105 (April), pp. 468–96.

—— (2000), *Diversity and Distrust: Civic Education in a Multicultural Democracy*, Cambridge, MA: Harvard University Press.

Margalit, A. and M. Halbertal (1994), 'Liberalism and the right to culture', *Social Research*, 61 (3), pp. 491–510.

Margalit, A. and J. Raz (1990), 'National self-determination', *Journal of Philosophy*, 87 (9), pp. 439–61.

Miller, D. (1995), *On Nationality*, Oxford: Oxford University Press.

Okin, S. Moller (2005), '"Mistresses of their own destiny": Group rights, gender and realistic rights of exit', in K. McDonough and W. Feinberg (eds), *Citizenship and Education in Liberal Democratic Societies*, Oxford: Oxford University Press.

Parekh, B. (2000), *Rethinking Multiculturalism*, Cambridge, MA: Harvard University Press.

Patten, A. (1999), 'The autonomy argument for liberal nationalism', *Nations and Nationalism*, 5 (1), pp. 1–17.

Rawls, J. (1987), 'The idea of an overlapping consensus', *Oxford Journal of Legal Studies*, 7 (1), pp. 1–25.

—— (1993), *Political Liberalism*, New York: Columbia University Press.

Raz, J. (1986), *The Morality of Freedom*, Oxford: Oxford University Press.

—— (1994), 'Multiculturalism: A liberal perspective', *Dissent*, 41 (1) (winter), pp. 67–79.

—— (1998), 'Multiculturalism', *Ratio Juris*, 11 (3), pp. 193–205.

Sandel, M. (1982), *Liberalism and the Limits of Justice*, Cambridge: Cambridge University Press.

Spinner, J. (1994), *The Boundaries of Citizenship. Race, Ethnicity, and Nationality in the Liberal State*, Baltimore, MD: The Johns Hopkins University Press.

Spinner-Halev, J. (2000), *Surviving Diversity. Religion and Democratic Citizenship*, Baltimore, MD: The Johns Hopkins University Press.

Stolzenberg, N. M. (1993), '"He drew a circle that shut me out": assimilation, indoctrination, and the paradox of liberal education', *Harvard Law Review*, 106, pp. 581–667.

Tamir, Y. (1993), *Liberal Nationalism*, Princeton, NJ: Princeton University Press.

Taylor, C. (1985), 'Atomism', *Philosophical Papers 2*, Cambridge: Cambridge University Press.

—— (1994), 'The politics of recognition', in A. Gutmann (ed.), *Multiculturalism: Examining the Politics of Recognition*, Princeton, NJ: Princeton University Press.

Tully, J. (1995), *Strange Multiplicity. Constitutionalism in an Age of Diversity*, Cambridge: Cambridge University Press.

Walzer, M. (1983), *Spheres of Justice: A Defense of Pluralism and Equality*, New York: Basic Books.

—— (1984), 'Liberalism and the art of separation', *Political Theory*, 12 (3), pp. 315–30.

—— (1990), 'The communitarian critique of liberalism', *Political Theory*, 18 (1), pp. 6–23.

—— (2004), *Politics and Passion. Towards a More Egalitarian Liberalism*, New Haven, CT: Yale University Press.

Young, I. M. (1990), *Justice and the Politics of Difference*, Princeton, NJ: Princeton University Press.

Part II

Multiculturalism's Pioneers and (Ex-)enthusiasts

The 'Civic Re-balancing' of British Multiculturalism, and Beyond . . .

Nasar Meer and Tariq Modood

I used to believe that multiculturalism was bound sooner or later to sink under the weight of its intellectual weaknesses . . . There is no sign of any collapses so far. (Barry 2001: 6)

To be quite honest, living through this period of organized mendacity has been one of the least agreeable ordeals that we conservatives have had to undergo. (Scruton 2010: 50)

Like all family quarrels the tone of some interested commentators is predictably angry and self-righteous. (Parekh 2006: 169)

Introduction

In an earlier study of citizenship and multiculturalism in Britain, we came to the conclusion that contemporary revisions of British multiculturalism were evidence of a 'civic re-balancing' (Meer and Modood 2009; and described below). In retrospect, it may have been more appropriate to term what we were describing as a 'civic thickening', given the steady incorporation of diversity into British practices and institutional life. The argument over the change in the character of British multiculturalism was subsequently taken up by Banting and Kymlicka (2010); Faas (2011); Rodriguez-Garcia (2010); Mansouri and Pietsch (2011) and Kivisto (2012), among others.

Our reading stood in marked contrast to an emerging thesis proposed by some commentators pointing to a 'post-multicultural' era, or at least to a 'retreat' from multiculturalism (Joppke 2004). While we agree that the *term* has become politically damaged, we also recognize that the policies and discourses that make up the strands of British multiculturalism remain in place (see also Meer and Modood, in process). A number of intellectual and political developments (sometimes competing, sometimes complementary) have been shaping British multiculturalism over the medium to long term, in which current changes need to be located and interpreted.

As a result, we believe that it is a mistake to view British multiculturalism as a completed or closed project, not least because the identities it seeks to take account of are dynamic even when they are coherent. So a *political* multiculturalism will always need to be open to renewal, though not of course without contestation amongst advocates, as much as between them and opponents. Re-balancing is one way to renewal though, as we caution in this chapter, it can be a double-edged sword.

Our argument is that it is short-sighted to view the new emphasis on previously underemphasized features such as civic engagement and national identity as an abandonment of British multiculturalism. Such developments need no more lead to the abandonment of British multiculturalism than such features would lead to the abandonment of other public policy approaches concerned with promoting equality of access, participation and public recognition, for example gender mainstreaming and the disability rights agenda. On the contrary, in the case of a multiculturalism sensitivity to ethnic, racial and religious differences, a degree of 'civic thickening' and the promotion of an inclusive national identity have appeared to reconcile themselves to what had earlier been promoted (perhaps to the disappointment and frustration of its critics) (Modood 2012).

Our 2009 article, entitled 'The multicultural states we are in', covered the period from the mid-1960s on, with particular attention to the period between 2000 and Prime Minister Tony Blair's departure in 2007. British multiculturalism in the period of Prime Minister Gordon Brown has been studied by McGhee (2009), but as yet little scholarly attention has focused on the Conservative–Liberal Democrat coalition's approach, a government that was formed in May 2010. In this chapter we first review the core features of British multiculturalism before turning to the present government's strategy, deemed by some to be forging a new path (Goodman 2012). This is a strategy that is allied – indeed twinned – with changes taking place both in immigration and settlement policies: these are widely touted as being more restrictive and perhaps even leading to something like a British guest worker model (Travis 2012). The new strategy is also interpreted as an anti-terrorism approach that identifies 'integration' as one of the primary objectives of counter-radicalism.

One note of caution is that we cannot account for the potential significance of centrifugal tendencies in Britain for questions of 'integration'. These tendencies include the galvanized movement for the 'break up of Britain' evident in the proposed referendum for Scottish independence (timetabled for 2014); the potential fracturing of the European project and the prospect of splintering states therein (or formal tiering of membership); and the rise of popular English nationalisms in the form of either relatively benign, though ultra conservative, forms (for example, the English democrats) or, more menacingly, far right articulations (such as the English Defence League) which explicitly trade on an anti-Muslim instead of anti-minority platform (Allen 2011).

Contextualizing the terrain[1]

It may be said that multiculturalism in Britain has for some time been perceived to have been creaking under the Muslim weight of allegedly 'culturally unreasonable or theologically alien demands' (Modood 2006: 34). Governmental and other non-right-wing criticism of multiculturalism took off after riots in some cities in the north of England in 2001. By 2004 a swathe of civil society institutions and fora comprising the centre left and the liberal produced reports with titles such as 'Is multiculturalism dead?', 'Is multiculturalism over?' and 'Beyond multiculturalism'. These views could be found in *Prospect* magazine, *The Observer*, *The Guardian*, the Commission for Racial Equality (CRE), Open Democracy, Channel 4 and the British Council.

A chorus of commentators has declared that multiculturalism was killed off by the London bombings of 7/7. Examples include William Pfaff 's (2005) certainty that 'these British bombers are a consequence of a misguided and catastrophic pursuit of multiculturalism'; Gilles Kepel's (2005) observation that the bombers 'were the children of Britain's own multicultural society' and that the bombings have 'smashed' the implicit social consensus that produced multiculturalism 'to smithereens'; Martin Wolf 's (2005) conclusion that multiculturalism's departure from the core political values that must underpin Britain's community 'is dangerous because it destroys political community . . . [and] demeaning because it devalues citizenship. In this sense, at least, multiculturalism must be discarded as nonsense'. These views have also been elaborated in Anthony (2007), Cohen (2007), Gove (2006) and Phillips (2006), suggesting a large degree of convergence between 'left' and 'right' commentators on the topic of multiculturalism.

It is not surprising, then, to encounter the view that British multi-culturalism is in 'retreat' (Appleyard 2006; Joppke 2004; Kepel 2005; Liddle 2004). To assess the validity of multiculturalism's retreat, it is important to distinguish between those pointing to a normative or factual tendency and others who have political motives in rejecting Britain's multiculturalism. The latter camp includes the influential centre-left commentator David Goodhart (2004), who sympathizes with the position of those he perhaps unfairly calls 'Burkeans'. They assert that 'we feel more comfortable with, and are readier to share with and sacrifice for, those with whom we have shared histories and similar values. To put it bluntly – most of us prefer our own kind'. In this group is also Trevor Phillips, former Chair of the CRE and subsequently head of the Equality and Human Rights Commission (EHRC). He stated that Britain should 'kill off multiculturalism' because it 'suggests separateness' (quoted in Baldwin 2004).

While in opposition David Cameron (2007) characterized British multiculturalism as a 'barrier' that divides British society. Once in office, he argued that 'the doctrine of "state multiculturalism" has encouraged culturally different people to live apart from one another and apart from the mainstream' (Cameron 5 February 2011). Perhaps seeking to stake out a British *Leitkultur*, Cameron complained that multiculturalism has led to the minimization of Christianity as a guiding public ethos, and has 'allowed segregated communities to behave in ways that run completely counter to our values and has not contained that extremism but allowed it to grow and prosper' (quoted in Butt 16 December 2011).

While vitriolic critique is not unusual from a centre right in Britain that has historically lamented governmental interventions that endorse the diversity of minority populations, opposition to the recognition of minority cultural practices has been strengthened by the addition of a new actor – 'the pluralistic centre-left [and] articu-lated by people who previously rejected polar models of race and class and were sympathetic to the "rainbow", coalitional politics of identity' (Modood 2005a).

The impact has been that the British approach to the inclusion of ethnic minorities is now increasingly premised upon their having higher qualifications. This is epitomized by the introduction of citizenship tests, the swearing of oaths during citizenship ceremonies and language proficiency requirements for new migrants, as well as repeated calls for an unambiguous disavowal of 'radicalism' or 'extremism' from Muslims in particular.

Joppke (2004: 253) interpreted these changes as evidence of a 'retreat' from multiculturalism and a 'turn to civic integration' that is 'most visible in Britain and the Netherlands, the two societies in Europe ... that had so far been most committed to official multiculturalism'. But we contend that Joppke incorrectly assumes a dichotomy between 'civic integration' and 'multiculturalism', or at least places them in a zero-sum equation. In fact they could just as plausibly be synthesized in a potential outgrowth of one another.

If it is the case that Britain has been engaged in a 'retreat' from multiculturalism, thereby signalling a victory for liberal or Republican universalism, would it not follow that Britain should 'also have rejected the claims of substate national groups and indigenous peoples *as well as* immigrants? After all, the claims of national groups and indigenous peoples typically involve a much more dramatic insertion of ethnocultural diversity into the public sphere, and more dramatic degrees of differentiated citizenship (Banting and Kymlicka 2007: 7). This does not appear to be the case in Britain – indeed, with the scheduling of a referendum on Scotland's independence the opposite seems to be true.

One explanation of the 'widely divergent assessments of the short history and potential future of multiculturalism' (Kivisto and Faist 2007: 35) pertains to the meaning and usage of the term itself. This 'highly contested and chameleon-like neologism whose colours change to suit the complexion of local conditions' (Pearson, quoted in Kivisto and Faist 2007: 35) seems to have a 'chameleon' quality (Smith 2010) that is adopted to support different projects. In relation to post-immigration multiculturalism, the critiques advanced by intellectuals, commentators and politicians have revealed the diverging ways in which multiculturalism has been conceived. We believe that there are at least three distinct positions:

1. an integration and social cohesion perspective that seeks to include minorities through a process of greater assimilation to majority norms and customs;
2. an alternative, explicitly secular 'multiculture' or 'conviviality' approach (see Chapter 2 of this book) that welcomes the 'fact' of difference, and stresses anti-essentialist, lifestyle- and consumption-based behavioural identities which invalidate 'group' identities;
3. a political multiculturalism that incorporates the goals of either or both of these positions while accommodating 'groupings', including subjectively conceived ethno-religious minority ones.

Since the early 1990s it is political multiculturalism that has increasingly taken institutional forms, mainly by elaborating racial equality discourses and policies in response to minority ethnic and religious assertiveness (Modood 2005b). This has taken legal form in the outlawing of religious discrimination and incitement to religious hatred (Meer 2008), and an educational form in the inclusion of some non-Christian, non-Jewish faith schools within the state-maintained sector (Meer 2009).

It is this multiculturalism that has been the principal target of recent critiques. But rather than having been defeated, the fate of this peculiarly British multiculturalism remains undecided. It may equally be characterized as subject to 're-balancing' rather than 'retreat'. One way to explore this possibility is to focus on the most robust and coherent public policy advocacy of multiculturalism that Britain has experienced.

Has the multicultural moment passed?

In the course of ushering in an era 'after multiculturalism', journalist and intellectual Yasmin Alibhai-Brown (2001: 47) proposed that 'all societies and communities need to take stock periodically to assess whether existing cultural and political edifices are keeping up with the people and the evolving habitat'. Such an exercise was conducted by the much maligned report produced by the Commission on the Future of Multi-Ethnic Britain (CMEB) (2000), sponsored by the Runnymede Trust and chaired by political philosopher Bhikhu Parekh.[2] This report made over 140 policy recommendations to assist 'a confident and vibrant multicultural society' to take advantage of 'its rich diversity' in order that Britain should realize its full potential (CMEB 2000: viii). Entitled *The Future of Multi-Ethnic Britain*, it strongly endorsed both the possibility and desirability of forging a meta-membership of 'Britishness' under which diversity could be sustained.

To this end its recommendations sought not only to prevent discrimination and to eradicate its effects, but also simultaneously championed an approach that could move *beyond* conceptions of formal equality by recognizing the 'real differences of experience, background and perception' (ibid. 296). For example, the CMEB acknowledged that while high-profile statements of ideals by senior politicians and civil servants are important, 'they remain mere paper commitments or rhetoric'. It therefore advocated an ethnic monitoring that would 'go beyond racism and culture blind strategies' (ibid. 297), and enable public institutions to promote an awareness of cultural diversity in general, and unwitting discrimination in particular (ibid. 296–7).

The report represented a 'multicultural moment' after the inquiry into the racist-motivated murder in 1993 of Stephen Lawrence, a black teenager in south London. The New Labour government declared its commitment to creating a country where 'every colour is a good colour', where 'everyone is treated according to their needs and rights' and where 'racial diversity is celebrated' (Home Office 2000: 1). Individual politicians boasted that 'Britain's pluralism is not a burden we must reluctantly accept. It is an immense asset that contributes to the cultural and economic vitality of our nation' (Cook 2001). As Prime Minister Blair insisted:

> This nation has been formed by a particularly rich complex of experiences ... How can we separate out the Celtic, the Roman, the Saxon, the Norman, the Huguenot, the Jewish, the Asian and the Caribbean and all the other nations [sic] that have come and settled here? Why should we want to? It is precisely this rich mix that has made all of us what we are today. (Blair 2000)

In a similar vein, but rather uncharacteristically, Tory leader William Hague was moved to assert that 'Britain is a nation of immigrants' while attending the Caribbean-influenced Notting Hill Carnival (*Daily Telegraph* 13 October 2000, quoted in Fortier 2005: 560). This 'time of reflection' upon Britain's ethnic diversity coincided with policy recognition of the country's historical multinational diversity, exemplified by devolution in Scotland, Wales and Northern Ireland. It was logical, then, that post-migrant ethnic minorities too were seeking recognition of particularities arising from their previously disregarded identities, not in the form of self-governance but through an endorsement of the pluralizing of the mainstream which their own distinctive differences, derived from ethnic, religious or cultural diversity, could be a part of.

This high-water mark of multiculturalism was the cumulative product of a political movement subsuming the migrations of parents and grandparents of many of Britain's post-immigrant ethnic minorities. They had exercised their Commonwealth citizenship to move to its metropole from South Asia, the Caribbean and elsewhere. This is why the CMEB recommended that central government take steps to formally declare Britain 'a multicultural society'; it was hoped that such an approach would more effectively address the social and political inequalities derived from minority cultural differences (CMEB 2000: 296).

The report was subject to an unrelenting critique by the right (McLaughlin and Neal 2004). But it also incurred the wrath of some prominent liberals who considered its approach a grave contravention of universalistic principles, not least those recommendations that promoted diversity as a means to facilitate equality (cf. Barry 2001). Indeed, even Lord Anthony Lester, one of the founders of the Runnymede Trust and a key architect of Britain's race equality legislation, said of the report that 'much of the more theoretical sections is written entirely from the perspective of victims, with little to challenge attitudes and practices prevalent among some minorities and their leaders that are difficult to reconcile with the ideals of a liberal democratic society based upon the rule of law' (Lester 2003).

In his assessment of the CMEB recommendations Kenan Malik (2007) underscored the principles that should be promoted:

> Political equality only becomes possible with the creation of a ring-fenced public sphere, which everyone can enter as political equals, whatever their cultural, economic or ethnic backgrounds. [. . .] Only by establishing a distinction between the public and the private can we forge a relationship between diversity and equality, allowing citizens to have full freedom to pursue their different values or practices in private, while ensuring that in the public sphere all citizens are treated as political equals whatever the differences in their private lives.

What this view underestimates, however, is the influence of negative or demeaned differences that serve as an obstacle to political equality in the public sphere, a key problematic for the CMEB, as well as the substantive elements of a British approach that historically, if inconsistently, has intertwined equality and diversity agendas.

Equality and diversity in British multiculturalism

Multiculturalism in Britain originates in the group of post-war migrants who arrived as Citizens of the United Kingdom and Commonwealth (CUKC). Together with subsequent British-born generations, they have been recognized as ethnic and racial minorities who merit state support and differential treatment in order to overcome distinctive barriers in their exercise of citizenship. The 1948 British Nationality Act had granted freedom of movement to people living in British Commonwealth territories – irrespective of whether their passports were issued by colonial or independent states – by creating this category of CUKC. Until they acquired national citizenships in their post-colonial countries, these former British subjects continued to retain their British status. This is one of the reasons why Kymlicka's distinction between national minority rights and ethno-cultural minority rights is not easily transposed onto Britain (Modood 2005b, 2007).

Under the remit of several Race Relations Acts (RRAs), the state has sought to integrate minorities into the labour market and other key arenas of British society through an approach that promotes equal access, in effect, equality of opportunity. The passage of the 1976 Race Relations Act (RRA 1976) cemented state sponsorship of race equality by consolidating two earlier, weaker legislative instruments. The Act spanned public and private institutions, recognized *indirect* discrimination and imposed a statutory public duty to promote good 'race relations'. It also created the CRE to assist individual complainants and monitor the implementation of the Act (Dhami et al. 2006: 19–25).

The Equality Act of 2006 extended the prohibition on religious forms of discrimination to the provision of goods, services and facilities and to the public functions of public bodies. It amalgamated various monitoring bodies into one: the EHRC. The Equality Act of 2010 extended the duty on public bodies to tackle discrimination on all grounds: age; race and ethnicity; gender; disability; sexuality; and religion and belief. The latter sphere now received the same protection as racial discrimination (see Meer 2010). This Act came with the additional provision that the government 'initiate specific projects to work with communities to identify solutions' (Department for Communities and Local Government (DCLG) 2010: 13). The current DCLG strategy (2012: 3) for integration complements 'the wider Government commitments to equalities and social mobility, including the Equality Act 2010, Equality Strategy, and Social Mobility Strategy'. In Joppke's (1999: 642) terms, this is an example of a citizenship that strikes a 'precarious balance between citizenship universalism and racial group particularism [that] stops short of giving special group rights to immigrants'. We recall that the Race Relations Acts do not allow positive discrimination or affirmative action favouring a particular racial group; this would represent discrimination on racial grounds and would therefore be unlawful (Karim 2004/5).

These Acts represent a defining characteristic in the British approach to integrating minorities: the institutionalization of redress against racially structured barriers to participation. But does this amount to multiculturalism? It can be argued that it does add up to a *British* multiculturalism which, although lacking an official 'Multicultural Act' or 'Charter' in the way of Australia or Canada (CMEB 2000), has rejected the idea of integration based upon unity achieved through uncompromising cultural 'assimilation'. This view was supported by Labour Home Secretary Roy Jenkins (1966), who defined integration as 'not a flattening process of assimilation but equal opportunity accompanied by cultural diversity in an atmosphere of mutual tolerance'.

Alongside this state-centred and national focus, there is also a tradition of what we might characterize as 'municipal drift' where multicultural discourses and policies have been pursued through local councils and municipal authorities, making up a patchwork of British multicultural public policies (Singh 2005: 170). To be sure, the high point of local authority multicultural innovation has passed. In 1986 the cornerstone of multiculturalist municipal authorities, the Greater London Council (GLC), was abolished because Prime Minister Margaret Thatcher found it too left-wing. But this did not prevent the subsequent development of a multiculturalist London. Moreover, the New Labour government's response to the threat both of 'ghettos' and of terrorism was to seek local solutions.

The Cameron government's Localism Act (2011) has also devolved significant powers to local authorities. While this should be seen as an 'anti-statist' instrument conceived as a means of helping different groups to run local services, the Act's goal to establish what the government calls a 'community right to challenge' allows minorities – especially faith groups and social enterprises – to compete for the delivery of service provision (DCLG 2011). Nonetheless, this comprises a different activity from earlier examples of local multiculturalism reflected in programmes of anti-racist education (Mullard 1985; Troyna 1987) and multicultural education (Swann 1985).

Policies promoting social cohesion and anti-radicalization have strengthened the 'race relations' practice of seeking local solutions based on partnerships between local authorities and communities. To be sure, local education authorities (LEA) – a source of anti-racism and multiculturalism in an earlier period – have lost considerable power to the national government. A national education curriculum and semi-independent 'academies' have also chipped away at LEA influence. Nevertheless, English schools remain one of the principal sites of multiculturalist sensibility today.

Multicultural sensibility is a notion central to Banting and Kymlicka's (2007: 6) conclusion that 'multiculturalism has become deeply embedded in the legislation, jurisprudence, and institutions of many Western countries and indeed their very self image'. It is not difficult to find evidence of the continuing presence of this Swann sensibility, even from a Home Secretary not known for his sympathy toward the promotion of ethnic minority cultural differences. In summer 2001 civil unrest and 'rioting' took place in some northern towns with sizeable Muslim communities. Home Secretary David Blunkett (2001: 3) announced that 'one of this government's central aims is to achieve a society that celebrates its ethnic diversity and cultural richness; where there is respect for all, regardless of race, colour or creed'. In the same statement he gave notice of Home Office-funded teams which would review all relevant community issues. But such multicultural sensibility was lacking in a contemporaneous local report from Bradford which set the pattern for official questioning of multiculturalism. It emphasized that particular communities, widely understood as Muslim ones, were self-segregating (Ouseley Report 2001). This purported tendency was also noted in another report as the phenomenon of leading 'parallel lives' (Cantle 2001).

In our earlier article (Meer and Modood 2009) we concluded that such developments could not accurately be called a 'retreat' of multiculturalism. The revised multiculturalism of the 1990s that was attempting to accommodate Muslim communities was critiqued in two ways, each a reaction against emergent ethno-religious communitarianism. One emphasized the importance of commonality, cohesion and integration. The other was alive to fluidity, multiplicity and hybridity, especially in relation to expressive culture, entertainment and consumption. We suggested that 'it is better to see these newly asserted emphases and the interaction between these three positions, as a re-balancing of multiculturalism rather than its erasure' (Meer and Modood 2009: 490).

Immigration, integration and security

A key piece of legislation in the Blair period was the 2002 Nationality, Immigration and Asylum Act, which mandated tests for applicants seeking British citizenship requiring them to show 'a sufficient knowledge of English, Welsh or Scottish Gaelic' and also 'a sufficient knowledge about life in the United Kingdom' (Jacobs and Rea 2007). Immigrants seeking to settle in the UK (applying for an 'indefinite leave to remain') were also required to pass the test. If they did not have sufficient knowledge of English, applicants were required to attend English for Speakers of Other Languages (ESOL) and citizenship classes. In explanatory documents, the Home Office has stressed that the tests aim at 'integration', but without this term meaning 'complete assimilation' (Home Office 2004: 14).

The Immigration, Asylum and Nationality Act 2006 provided the springboard to a post-Blair migration and integration strategy adopted by Prime Minister Brown and Home Secretary Jacqui Smith in 2008. For the Labour leader (Brown 2008), becoming a British citizen should not just be a matter of the applicant's choice but ought to reflect their entry into a contract whereby they accept the responsibilities of *becoming* British and thus 'earn' the right to citizenship. Accordingly, a status of 'probationary citizenship' was created as a pathway from temporary immigration status to either naturalization or the right to abode. The length of probation was elastic:

> Crucially, the length of this period could be reduced by two years in cases where a person demonstrated that they were contributing to the community through 'active citizenship'. This could be achieved through 'formal volunteering' or 'civic activism'. The idea of taking this further and developing a points based system of citizenship was put forward in 2009. This included the prospect of 'deducting points or applying penalties for not integrating into the British way of life, for criminal or anti-social behaviour, or in circumstances where an active disregard for UK values is demonstrated'. (Choudury 2011: 124)

A study of the new selectivity under the managed migration points system (McGhee 2009: 52) reduced more than eighty possible work and study routes to obtaining permission to remain into five main 'tiers':

- tier 1: highly skilled, e.g. scientists or entrepreneurs;
- tier 2: skilled workers with a job offer, e.g. nurses, teachers, engineers;
- tier 3: low-skilled workers filling specific temporary labour shortages, e.g. construction workers for a particular project;
- tier 4: students;
- tier 5: youth mobility and temporary workers, e.g. working holidaymakers or musicians coming to perform.

The Cameron-led coalition government announced its intention to narrow these tiers further, mainly by eliminating tier 3 (Green 2012). More significantly, however, and perhaps as evidence of an emerging guest worker approach for new non-European Economic Area (EEA) migrants, the Home Secretary indicated her intention to break the link for the first time between migration and settlement, by taking away the right to remain in Britain for more than five years from any migrant worker earning less than £35,000 a year (Home Office 2012; Travis 2012).

In addition, compared to earlier periods when slippage between initially *implicit* integration and security agendas was discernible, these agendas now are more *explicitly* coupled. Indeed, a striking development – one that could not have been anticipated by proponents of multiculturalism in the 1990s – has been how the assemblage of citizenship strategies has been reorganized to give a central role to counterterrorism strategies.

Multiculturalism and securitization: 'Preventing Extremism Together'

The Labour governments (1997–2010) responded to the London transport attacks and to several aborted bombings blamed on a 'leaderless Jihad' (Sageman 2008) by devising a strategy under the banner 'Preventing Extremism Together' (PET). Seven working groups were convened that comprised representatives of Muslim communities: (1) engaging with young people; (2) providing a full range of educational services that met the needs of the Muslim community; (3) engaging with Muslim women; (4) supporting regional and local initiatives and community actions; (5) facilitating Imam training and accreditation and enhancing the role of Mosques as a resource for the whole community; (6) ensuring security and combating Islamophobia by protecting Muslims from extremism and building community confidence in policing; and (7) tackling extremism and radicalization.

Initiated by the Home Office, this PET strategy was subsequently transferred to the Department for Communities and Local Government. The seven working groups devised a series of proposals to develop 'practical means' of tackling violent extremism. Sixty-four recommendations were put forward in a report published in November 2005; particular emphasis was given to three recommendations that would serve as central planks in government strategies on preventing violent extremism.

The first was to be the development of a 'Scholars Roadshow' coordinated by British Muslim organizations to facilitate 'influential mainstream' Muslim thinkers to address audiences of young British Muslims. The rationale was that these speakers would undermine extremists' justification for terrorism by denouncing it as un-Islamic. This would 'counter the ideological and theological underpinnings of the terrorist narrative' (Foreign and Commonwealth Office).

A second proposed plank focused on the creation of Muslim forums against extremism and Islamophobia. These were to be led by key individuals and would bring together members of local Muslim communities, law enforcement and public service agencies to discuss how to tackle extremism and Islamophobia in their area.

The third and perhaps most substantive recommendation in terms of structural capacity building within British Muslim communities was the formation of a Mosques and Imams National Advisory Board (MINAB). To this end, a steering group of Muslim leaders undertook extensive national consultation on matters such as the accreditation of imams, better governance of mosques and interfaith activity. Alongside this professional development programme or 'upskilling' of imams and mosque officials, recommendations were also made for a national campaign and coalition to increase the visibility of Muslim women, and to empower and equip them in the course of becoming 'active citizens'.

Preventing Extremism Together inevitably included security-related work. It was criticized for a variety of reasons 'ranging from targeting the wrong people to stigmatizing Muslim communities by treating them all as potential terrorists' (Bartlett and Birdwell 2010: 8). Two recurring issues were that, first, intelligence agencies were using the softer cohesion aspects of PET 'to spy and illicitly collect intelligence, which has dramatically harmed the programme as a whole' (ibid.: 8). Second, PET was oriented to address wider social policy within Muslim communities, implying that this policy was only valuable because it contributed to counter-terrorism. This criticism was substantiated by the fact that PET funding was directly linked to the size of the Muslim population in a local authority, not on the basis of known risk.

It is not surprising that a strategy premised upon entering, and to some extent reformulating, the life worlds of British Muslim communities has been the subject of critical debate in the study of ethnic relations generally (Spalek and Imoual 2007; Lambert 2008; McGhee 2009). This is not a fortuitous development: after the

London bombings the Home Office signalled that it would establish a Commission on Integration and Cohesion (COIC 2007) 'to advise on how, consistent with their own religion and culture, there is better integration of those parts of the community inadequately integrated'.[3]

The incorporation of faith-based groups into the practices and models of representation, stakeholders and advocacy is a relatively novel approach (DeHanas et al. 2010). It may be part of the emergence of a multicultural 'municipal drift' described earlier (Meer and Modood 2009). In constituting part of the broad counter-terrorism strategy, PET appears to be simultaneously subject to two broader dynamics comprising:

> [first] the implementation of anti-terrorist laws that can be used disproportionately against Muslims leading to the potential for their increased surveillance and control and thereby serving to reduce Muslims' trust of state institutions, while [second] at the same time pursuing approaches that acknowledge, and stress the importance of, the involvement of British . . . Muslim communities in helping to combat extremism. (Spalek and Imoual 2007: 191)

Indeed, Spalek and Imoual frame these dynamics relationally in terms of 'harder' and 'softer' strategies of engagement; the former may be understood as consisting of various means of surveillance, policing and intelligence gathering, the latter as including dialogue, participation and community feedback between Muslim communities, state agencies and voluntary organizations in a way that increases trust in 'the battle for hearts and minds'. The PET strategy also sought to extend to Muslims long-established equality traditions historically orientated towards ethnic and racial minorities:

> we must make the most of the links with wider community work to reduce inequalities, tackle racism and other forms of extremism (e.g. extreme far right), build cohesion and empower communities [. . .] Likewise, it is recognised that the arguments of violent extremists, which rely on creating a 'them' and an 'us', are less likely to find traction in cohesive communities. (DCLG 2008: 6–7)

This was an extension of a recognition within government policies and legislation of Muslim religious difference that has been manifested in other ways, including measures against religious discrimination set out in the Equality Act 2006 and 2010. The tensions centre, then, on the extent to which the prevailing British citizenship being extended to Muslims – through social and community cohesion agendas – are twinned with or placed within the same register as anti-/counter-terrorism strategies that import or rely upon certain securitized 'hard' aspects of state–Muslim engagement.

The securitization and citizenship dyad of Muslims

The risk has always been that 'active citizenship' for Muslims will be framed in terms of demonstrable counter-terrorism activities on their part. The unstated assumption is that Muslim communities remain the 'locus of the issue of extremism' (Spalek and Imoual 2007: 194). While it may not be the case, as Fekete (2004: 25) has suggested, that public policy engaging with Muslims amounts to being 'tough on mosques, tough on the causes of mosques', it certainly is common to find statements such as that made by former Communities Secretary Ruth Kelly that it is a requirement for Muslim organizations to take 'a proactive leadership role in tackling extremism and defending our shared values' (11 October 2006).

This role is now a stated policy ambition of the new PET strategy. One finds in it the concern that insufficient attention has been paid to whether organizations comprehensively subscribe to what are considered to be mainstream British values. As Home Secretary Theresa May stated in her Foreword to the renewed Prevent strategy:

> [W]e will respond to the ideological challenge of terrorism and the threat from those who promote it. In doing so, we must be clear: the ideology of extremism and terrorism is the problem; legitimate religious belief emphatically is not. But we will not work with extremist organisations that oppose our values of universal human rights, equality before the law, democracy and full participation in our society. If organisations do not accept these fundamental values, we will not work with them and we will not fund them. (Home Office 2011: 1)

The new Prevent strategy takes a much more interventionist line on the constellation of British Muslim politics, openly insisting that the government will not fund organizations 'that hold extremist views or support terrorist-related activity of any kind' (ibid. 35). The current DCLG integration strategy explicitly asserts what was implicit before, that 'Prevent remains distinct from but linked to integration, tackling non-violent extremism where it creates an environment conducive to terrorism and popularizes ideas which are espoused by terrorist groups' (DCLG 2012: 16–17).

Few British Muslim organizations support violent activity in

Britain, though many are committed to armed self-defence against Israeli occupation of Palestine in ways that supporters of Israel interpret as 'terrorism'. Having British Muslims in mind, the Coalition government has launched a 'Near Neighbours' strategy, a three-year project that seeks to 'bring people together in diverse communities, helping them build relationships and collaborate to improve the local community they live in'. The Prevent agenda, a policy that New Labour pursued for a while but distanced itself from, remains the Cameron government's most significant investment in Muslim civil society organizations. It is a policy that divides mainstream Muslim organizations and, counterproductively, makes credible partners unavailable to the government. This is clearly not without risks in relation to effective community cooperation against terrorism, but also in relation to the aspiration for a plausible integration.

Notes

1. The following sections revise and update Meer and Modood (2009). We gratefully acknowledge *Political Studies* and Blackwell Publishers.
2. Interest disclosure: Modood too was involved in the CMEB report.
3. Outlined by Tony Blair himself; see the Prime Minister's press conference, 5 August 2005. Available at http://www.pm.gov.uk/output/Page8041.asp

References

Alibhai-Brown,Y. (2001), 'After multiculturalism', *Political Quarterly*, 72 (1), pp. 47–56.

Allen, C. (2011), 'Opposing Islamification or promoting Islamophobia? Understanding the English Defence League', *Patterns of Prejudice*, 45 (4), pp. 279–94.

Anthony, A. (2007), *The Fallout: How a Guilty Liberal Lost His Innocence*, London: Jonathan Cape.

Appleyard, B. (2006), 'Eureka', *The Sunday Times*, 17 December.

Baldwin, T. (2004), 'I want an integrated society with a difference', Interview with Trevor Phillips, *The Times*, 3 April.

Banting, K. and W. Kymlicka (eds) (2007), *Multiculturalism and the Welfare State. Recognition and Redistribution in Contemporary Democracies*, Oxford: Oxford University Press.

Banting, K. and W. Kymlicka (2010), 'Canadian multiculturalism: Global anxieties and local debates', *British Journal of Canadian Studies*, 23, pp. 43–72.

Barry, B. (2001), *Culture & Equality: An Egalitarian Critique*, Cambridge: Polity Press.

Bartlett, J. and J. Birdwell (2010), 'On the edge of violence?', *Demos*. Available at http://www.demos.co.uk/projects/fromthreattoopportunity

Blair, T. (2000), 'Tony Blair's Britain speech', *The Guardian*, 28 March. Available at http://www.guardian.co.uk/uk/2000/mar/28/britishidentity.tonyblair

Blunkett, D. (2001), 'Respect for all', *Connections Magazine* (summer), p. 2.

Brown, G. (2008), 'Prime Minister Speaks on Managed Migration and Earned Citizenship', 20 February. Available at http://www.ippr.org/events/54/6463/prime-minister-speaks-on-managed-migration-and-earned-citizenship

Butt, R. (2011), 'Cameron calls for return to Christian values as King James Bible turns 400', *The Guardian*, 16 December. Available at http://www.guardian.co.uk/world/2011/dec/16/cameron-king-james-bible-anniversary

Cameron, D. (2007), 'Address to Handsworth Mosque', Birmingham, 30 January 2007.

Cameron, D. (2011), 'PM's speech at Munich Security Conference', 5 February 2011. Available at http://www.number10.gov.uk/news/pms-speech-at-munich-security-conference/

Cantle, T. (2001), *Community Cohesion: A Report of the Independent Review Team*, London: HMSO.

Choudhury, T. (2011), 'Evolving models of multiculturalism in the United Kingdom', in M. Emerson (ed.), *Interculturalism: Europe and its Muslims, In Search Of Sound Societal Models*, Brussels: Centre For Europe and Policy Studies.

Cohen, N. (2007), *What's Left? How Liberals Lost Their Way*, London: HarperPerennial.

Commission on the Future of Multi-Ethnic Britain (CMEB) (2000), *The Future of Multi-Ethnic Britain*, London: Profile Books.

Commission on Integration and Cohesion (COIC) (2007), *Our Shared Future: Themes, Messages and Challenges: A Final Analysis of the Key Themes from the Commission on Integration and Cohesion Consultation*, London: HMSO.

Cook, R. (2001), Speech by the Foreign Secretary to the Social Market Foundation in London, 19 April 2001. Available at http://www.guardian.co.uk/racism/Story/0,,477023,00.html

DeHanas, D., T. O'Toole, T. Modood and N. Meer (2010), *Muslim Participation in Contemporary Governance: Literature Review Summary*. Available at http://www.bris.ac.uk/ethnicity/projects/muslimparticipation/documents/literature.pdf

Department for Communities and Local Government (2008), *Preventing Violent Extremism: A Strategy for Delivery*, London: HMSO. Available at http://webarchive.nationalarchives.gov.uk/20080305134410/http://dfes.gov.uk/publications/violentextremism/downloads/Preventing%20Violent%20Extremism%20A%20Strategy%20for%20Delivery%203%20June%202008.pdf

—— (2010), *Tackling Race Inequality: A Statement on Race*, London: DCLG. Available at http://www.communities.gov.uk/documents/communities/pdf/1432344.pdf

—— (2011), *Proposals to introduce a Community Right to Challenge*, London: DCLG. Available at http://www.communities.gov.uk/documents/localgovernment/pdf/1835810.pdf

—— (2012), *Creating the Conditions for Integration*, London: DCLG. Available at http://www.communities.gov.uk/documents/communities/pdf/2092103.pdf

Dhami, R. S., J. Squires and T. Modood (2006), *Developing Positive Action Policies: Learning from the Experiences of Europe and North America*, Department for Work and Pensions Research Report no. 406. Available at http://research.dwp.gov.uk/asd/asd5/rports2005-2006/rrep406.pdf

Faas, D. (2011), 'A civic rebalancing of British multiculturalism? An analysis of geography, history and citizenship education curricula', *Educational Review*, 63 (2), pp. 143–58.

Fekete, L. (2004), 'Anti-Muslim racism and the European security state', *Race and Class*, 46 (1), pp. 4–29.

Foreign and Commonwealth Office (undated), 'EIWG fact sheet'. Available at http://www.fco.gov.uk/servlet/Front?pagename=OpenMarket/Xcelerate/ShowPage&c=Page&cid= 1153388310360

Fortier, A.-M. (2005), 'Pride, politics and multiculturalist citizenship', *Ethnic and Racial Studies*, 28 (3), pp. 559–78.

Goodhart, D. (2004), 'Too diverse?', *Prospect* (February). Available at http://www.carnegiecouncil.org/media/goodhart.pdf

Goodman, P. (2012), 'At last, an integration strategy. But no full plan to "outflank extremism" yet', Conservative Home. Available at http://conservativehome.blogs.com/thetorydiary/2012/02/draft-integration-td.html

Gove, M. (2006), *Celsius 7/7*, London: Weidenfeld and Nicolson.

Green, D. (2012), Speech by Immigration Minister. Available at http://www.homeoffice.gov.uk/media-centre/speeches/making-immigration-work

Home Office (2000), *Race Equality in Public Services: Driving Up Standards and Accounting for Progress*, London: HMSO.

—— (2004), *Life in the United Kingdom: A Journey to Citizenship*, London: HMSO.

—— (2011), *Prevent Strategy*, London: HMSO.

—— (2012), *Statement of Intent and Transitional Measures*.

Jacobs, D. and A. Rea (2007), 'The end of national models? Integration courses and citizenship trajectories in Europe', paper presented at the EUSA-conference, Montréal (17–19 May).

Jenkins, R. (1966), Address given by the Home Secretary to a meeting of voluntary liaison committees, 23 May 1966, London: National Committee for Commonwealth Immigrants.

Joppke, C. (1999), 'How immigration is changing citizenship: A comparative view', *Ethnic and Racial Studies*, 22 (4), pp. 629–52.

Joppke, C. (2004), 'The retreat of multiculturalism in the liberal state: Theory and policy', *British Journal of Sociology*, 55 (2), pp. 237–57.

Karim, R. (2004/5), 'Take care when being positive', *Connections* (winter), p. 17.

Kelly, R. (2006), Speech by Communities Secretary Ruth Kelly to Muslim organizations on working together to tackle extremism. Local Government House, London, 11 October 2006. Available at http://bradfordmuslim. blogspot.com/2007/03/preventing-extremism-strategy-going.html

Kepel, G. (2005), 'Europe's answer to Londonistan', *Open Democracy*, 24 August. Available at http://www.opendemocracy.net/conflict-terrorism/ londonistan_2775.jsp

Kivisto, P. (2012), 'We really are all multiculturalists now', *The Sociological Quarterly*, 53 (1), pp. 1–24.

Kivisto, P. and T. Faist (2007), *Citizenship: Discourse, Theory, and Transnational Prospects*, London: Blackwell.

Lambert, R. (2008) 'Empowering Salafis and Islamists against Al-Qaeda: A London counter-terrorism case study', *Political Science (PS) Online* (January).

Lester, A. (2003), 'Nailing the lie and promoting equality – The Jim Rose Lecture', Runnymede Trust, 15 October 2003. Available at http://www. runnymedetrust.org/uploads/events/aLesterSpeech.pdf

Liddle, R. (2004), 'How Islam killed multiculturalism', *The Spectator* (May). Available at http://www.lewrockwell.com/spectator/spec289.html

Malik, K. (2007), 'Thinking outside the box', *Catalyst*, January–February 2007. Available at http://www.kenanmalik.com/essays/catalyst_box.html

Mansouri, F. and J. Pietsch (2011), 'Local governance and the challenge of religious pluralism in liberal democracies: An Australian perspective', *Journal of Intercultural Studies*, 32 (3), pp. 279–92.

McGhee, D. (2009), 'The paths to citizenship: A critical examination of immigration policy in Britain since 2001', *Patterns of Prejudice*, 43 (1), pp. 41–64.

McLaughlin, E. and S. Neal (2004), 'Misrepresenting the multicultural nation, the policy-making process, news media management and the Parekh Report', *Policy Studies*, 25 (3), pp. 155–74.

Meer, N. (2008), 'The politics of voluntary and involuntary identities: Are Muslims in Britain an ethnic, racial or religious minority?', *Patterns of Prejudice*, 42 (1), pp. 61–81.

—— (2009), 'Identity articulations, mobilisation and autonomy in the movement for Muslim schools in Britain', *Race, Ethnicity and Education*, 12 (3), pp. 379–98.

—— (2010), 'The impact of European equality directives upon British anti-discrimination legislation', *Policy and Politics*, 38 (1), pp. 197–216.

Meer, N. and T. Modood (2009), 'The multicultural state we are in: Muslims, "multiculture" and the "civic re-balancing" of British multiculturalism', *Political Studies*, 57 (3), pp. 473–97.

—— (in process) 'Revisiting the "un-dead" – have Muslims made British multiculturalism a "zombie category"?'.

Modood, T. (2005a), 'Remaking multiculturalism after 7/7'. Available at http://www.opendemocracy.net/conflict-terrorism/multiculturalism_2879.jsp

—— (2005b), *Multicultural Politics: Racism, Ethnicity and Muslims in Britain*, Edinburgh: Edinburgh University Press.

—— (2006), 'British Muslims and the politics of multiculturalism', in T. Modood, A. Triandafyllidou and R. Zapata-Barrero (eds), *Multiculturalism, Muslims and Citizenship: A European Approach*, London: Routledge, pp. 37–56.

—— (2007), *Multiculturalism, a Civic Idea*, Cambridge: Polity Press.

—— (2012), *Post-Immigration 'Difference' and Integration*, London: British Academy.

Mullard, C. (1985), *Anti-racist Education: The Three O's*, Cardiff: National Association for Multicultural Education.

Ouseley Report (2001), *Community Pride Not Prejudice: Making Diversity Work in Bradford*, Bradford: Bradford Vision.

Parekh, B. (2006), *Re-thinking Multiculturalism* (2nd edn), Basingstoke: Palgrave Macmillan.

Pfaff, W. (2005), 'A monster of our own making', *The Observer*, 21 August 2005. Available at http://www.guardian.co.uk/uk/2005/aug/21/july7.terrorism

Phillips, M. (2006), *Londonistan: How Britain Created a Terror State Within*, London: Gibson Square Books.

Rodriguez-Garcia, D. (2010), 'Beyond assimilation and multiculturalism: A critical review of the debate on managing diversity', *International Journal of Migration and Integration*, 11, pp. 251–71.

RRA (Race Relations Act) 1976, Available at http://www.legislation.gov.uk/ukpga/1976/74

Sageman, M. (2008), *Leaderless Jihad: Terror Networks in the 21st Century*, Philadelphia, PA: University of Pennsylvania Press.

Scruton, R. (2010), 'Multiculturalism R.I.P.', *The American Spectator* (December 2010–January 2011), pp. 50–1. Available at http://spectator.org/archives/2010/12/07/multiculturalism-rip

Singh, G. (2005), 'British multiculturalism and Sikhs', *Sikhs Formations*, 1 (2), pp. 157–73.

Smith, K. E. (2010), 'Research, policy and funding – Academic treadmills and the squeeze on intellectual spaces', *The British Journal of Sociology*, 61 (1), pp. 176–95.

Spalek, B. and A. Imoual (2007), 'Muslim communities and counter-terror responses: "Hard" approaches to community engagement in the UK and Australia', *Journal of Muslim Minority Affairs*, 27 (2), pp. 185–202.

Swann, M. (1985), *Education for All: The Report of the Inquiry into the Education of Pupils of Children from Ethnic Minority Groups*. London: HMSO.

Thomas, P. (2011), *Youth, Multiculturalism and Community Cohesion*, Basingstoke: Palgrave.

Travis, A. (2012), 'Skilled migrants to lose right to settle in UK', *The Guardian*, 29 February 2012. Available at http://www.guardian.co.uk/uk/2012/feb/29/skilled-migrants-lose-right-settle

Troyna, B. (1987), 'Beyond multiculturalism: Towards the enactment of anti-racist education in policy provision and pedagogy', *Oxford Review of Education*, 13 (3), pp. 307–20.

Wolf, M. (2005), 'When multiculturalism is a nonsense', *Financial Times*, 31 August 2005. Available at http:// www.ft.com/cms/s/0/4c751acc-19bc-11da-804e-00000e2511c8.html

Chapter Five

The Dutch Multicultural Myth

Peter Scholten

Introduction

The Dutch case has been widely considered an almost ideal-typical example of multiculturalist policies. This applies both to national and international literature as well as in public discourse in the Netherlands. The so-called Dutch multicultural model has been widely used as an example of how to develop immigrant integration policies in other European countries. The basic premise of this national multicultural model is that the recognition and institutionalization of cultural pluralism is an important condition for the emancipation and integration of immigrant groups into Dutch society. Moreover, the multicultural model would match the very specific Dutch history of pillarism (Lijphart 1976) that extended into the 1950s and 1960s, when many facets of everyday social life in the Netherlands were institutionalized in distinct Protestant, Catholic, Socialist and Liberal pillars. In this respect, immigration meant that the Dutch social structure of pillars for national minorities was simply extended to incorporate ethnic minorities too.

Today this Dutch multicultural model is broadly disowned as a failure in public as well as in political debate. Public intellectual Paul Scheffer (2000) even refers to the Dutch multicultural 'tragedy'. Critics claim that, under the banner of benevolent multiculturalism, many integration problems have been ignored, such as urban segregation, criminality, radicalization and alienation of significant groups within Dutch society. Populist politicians who have risen on the Dutch political stage since 2002 blame the multiculturalist beliefs of the past for the failure of immigrant integration in the Netherlands. In the realm of social scientific research, too, the Dutch multicultural model has become contested. Sociologists like Koopmans and Statham, and Sniderman and Hagendoorn have drawn attention to the discontents of Dutch multiculturalist policies

(Sniderman and Hagendoorn 2007; Koopmans et al. 2005). In particular, the critique points to how the recognition of cultural groups has reified ethno-cultural cleavages in society and contributed to the alienation of these groups.

Others have contended that there has never really been a multicultural model in the Netherlands, or at least that the role of multiculturalism in Dutch policies has been very limited (Duyvendak and Scholten 2011). The era in which Dutch policies resembled the ideal-typical multicultural model was confined largely to the 1980s; since then, the Dutch have framed immigrant integration policies in very different ways (see Scholten 2011). However, in spite of the assimilationist turn in national policies, on the local level there are more resilient practices in accommodating cultural differences, such as coopting and cooperating with migrant organizations (Uitermark et al. 2005). Rather than being driven by multiculturalist policy beliefs, these local practices are derived more from policy routines and pragmatic ways of coping with problems (see Poppelaars and Scholten 2008). Furthermore, the Dutch multicultural model remains vivid in Dutch political and media discourse (Roggeband and Vliegenthart 2007), revealing it may serve as a counter-discourse against which current policy developments are juxtaposed.

This chapter critically examines the Dutch multicultural model that has become nationally and internationally famous – and infamous. First of all, I locate the multicultural model in Dutch policies as well as in public and academic discourse. Resisting the tendency to construct Dutch policies *ex-post* as multiculturalist, the key objective is to pin down the specific elements of Dutch policies that are or at least have been multiculturalist. Second, I deconstruct the Dutch multicultural model by studying shifts in policy discourse, media discourse and public attitudes. Finally, I assess the implications that the rise and fall of multiculturalism has had, both for policies and for actual integration trajectories.

The rise and fall of multiculturalism in the Netherlands

Let me begin by defining multiculturalism in the Netherlands. It is important to distinguish between what can be labelled as multiculturalist based on an ideal type of multiculturalism derived from the literature, and what is identified as multiculturalist in societal discourses. Analyzing the latter is important for pinning down multiculturalism as a mode of discourse in the Netherlands, but it does not resolve the extent to which there has actually been a Dutch multicultural model. Therefore, I adopt an ideal type of multiculturalism deduced from the social scientific literature, focusing in particular on: (1) how ideal-type multiculturalism names and frames immigrant integration; (2) how it socially constructs the involved target groups; (3) what causal theory it assumes or communicates to explain integration problems; and (4) what normative perspective it employs for interpreting the implications of migration for society at large (Scholten 2011). Subsequently, I confront this ideal type with evidence from Dutch policy discourses over the past decades to establish what elements of Dutch policies have actually been multiculturalist.

As an ideal type, multiculturalism is generally posited as the opposite of assimilationism, as it stresses cultural pluralism and a more culturally neutral, open form of citizenship (Koopmans and Statham 2000). However, an important point of convergence between assimilationism and multiculturalism lies in their focus on the nation state. In multiculturalist theory, the nation state is redefined in terms of the recognition of being a multiculturalist state (Vertovec 2001). Multiculturalism describes immigrant integration in terms of cultural diversity and the need for emancipation of groups of varying cultural backgrounds. Where adaptation involves finding commonalities between individuals in society, multiculturalism searches for compatibilities between groups and for tolerance of those facets of social life that groups do not have in common. Groups are socially constructed based on their cultural, ethnic, religious or racial traits, to name a few.

Political theorists Kymlicka (1995) and Parekh (2002) have argued that accommodation of cultural differences between groups may even require the diversification of social and political rights for distinct groups. The causal theory underlying multiculturalist thinking is that the only way to accommodate cultural pluralism is to recognize cultural diversity and to differentiate policies for particular cultural groups (Taylor and Guttman 1992). As an example, group-specific policies have to be developed in various spheres, including general policy spheres such as education and labour. Finally, multiculturalism contains a normative perspective that cultural diversity is a value in itself – a facet of the ongoing process of modernization – and that government interference with cultures should be limited (that is, tolerance should be the rule) as it will determine the identities of members of cultural groups.

The rise of multiculturalism in the 1970s and 1980s

Until well into the 1970s, a firm belief that the Netherlands was not and should not be a country of immigration voided the need for an immigrant integration policy.[1] The migration that had taken place in the 1960s and 1970s was seen as an inadvertent consequence of economic and political developments, and most immigrants were expected to eventually return to their home countries. Policies developed in this period rarely corresponded to what has been described as a differentialist model (Koopmans and Statham 2005). So-called 'two-track' policies were developed: they implied that although migrants were to be active in the socio-economic sphere, in other respects they were to be differentiated from Dutch society. This approach was manifest in policy and political discourse, summarized in the slogan 'integration with retention of identity' (*integratie met behoud van eigen identiteit*).

Initially, this slogan referred only to the social and economic integration of migrants during their stay in the Netherlands. Migrant groups were not 'named and framed' as a single category but described in terms of their different foreign origins – Surinamese, Antilleans, Moluccans, foreign workers. Emphasis was placed on the fact that they were not from the Netherlands. A key premise of this policy was that policies aimed at permanent integration could hamper return to the home countries: to facilitate return migration, migrants would have to be able to preserve as well as possible their cultural identities and internal group structures.

This differentialist image of migrants' position in Dutch society started to change in the late 1970s. A series of developments had occurred that challenged the prevailing policy beliefs: the oil crises of the 1970s that brought labour recruitment to a halt; the decolonization of Surinam in 1975 that caused large immigration flows; ethnic riots in Rotterdam and Schiedeman in 1972 and 1976; and a series of terrorist acts carried out during the 1970s by Moluccan migrants. Simultaneously, the emergence of several anti-immigrant parties in city councils in the early 1970s caused great concern. In response to these developments, various actors claimed a growing 'tension between norm and fact', of being or not being a country of immigration (Entzinger 1975). These developments revealed what can happen if government does not actively support the integration of immigrants who intend to settle permanently.

The first official immigrant integration policy in the Netherlands was developed in the early 1980s with the draft Minorities Memorandum in 1981 and its final version in 1983. This new policy was based on the 'assumption that ethnic minorities will remain permanently in the Netherlands [. . .] thereby distancing itself from the idea that their presence would have been of temporary order'. [2] Migrants were also 'named and framed' as permanent settlers, or as 'cultural' or 'ethnic minorities' within Dutch society.

Assimilationism and differentialism as policies to manage diversity were explicitly rejected.[3] Assimilationism would be at odds with the freedom of minorities to experience their own cultures, and differentialism would have served as an excuse for government not to create a policy on integration. This Ethnic Minorities Policy was a mixture of elements that match the multiculturalist ideal-type, together with elements from a more liberal-egalitarianist (or 'universalist') approach. On the one hand, policy discourse stressed 'mutual adaptation' in the context of the Netherlands as a 'multi-ethnic' or 'multicultural' society.[4] On the other, this mutual adaptation not only involved social-cultural emancipation of minorities and measures to combat discrimination, but also enhanced the socio-economic participation of members of minorities. The mixture also reflected combining group and individualistic features in the official policy aim: 'to achieve a society in which the members of minority groups that reside in the Netherlands can, *each individually as well as group-wise*, enjoy an equal position and full opportunities for development'.[5]

The strong focus on 'ethnic minorities' in all policy documents since 1979 represents a more multiculturalist trait of the Ethnic Minorities Policy. Migrant groups were no longer categorized according to foreign origin but as permanent populations within Dutch society. The notion of ethnic minorities also introduced a common frame of reference for the migrant groups that had thus far been treated separately. Government, however, did not provide a definition of 'ethnic minorities' but instead selected a number of 'minorities' for which it felt a special and historic responsibility: Moluccans, Surinamese, Antilleans, foreign workers, gypsies, caravan dwellers and refugees.

A central premise of the Ethnic Minorities Policy was that social-cultural emancipation of minority groups would also favour socio-economic participation of individual members of these groups. For instance, it was believed that by maintaining group-specific facilities for Immigrant Minority Language and Culture classes, the social-cultural emancipation of these groups could be furthered, expanding individual participation. Mother-tongue learning, according to this logic, would support identity development amongst minorities and would as such contribute to multicultural richness. In addition, the democratic voice of migrants would be strengthened by developing consultative structures between the national government and immigrant self-organizations. Thus, liberal-egalitarian features emerge in this emphasis on the accessibility of institutions and on proportionality governing socio-economic participation.

Finally, the Ethnic Minorities Policy expressed the vision that Dutch society at large had become a multi-ethnic or multicultural society, even though the word 'multicultural' is only used a few times in the 1983 Minorities Memorandum. This did not, however, involve strong cultural relativism; the slogan 'integration with retention of identity' was now abandoned, at least in official policy discourse, in favour of a more dynamic conception of immigrant cultures. This shift was also manifest in the stress on mutual adaptation. Because of the asymmetrical relationship between minorities and the majority, the integration of minorities would inevitably require some degree of adaptation to Dutch society. This followed 'When the values and norms that minorities embrace in their culture of origin clash with the established norms of our own plural society, considered fundamental to Dutch society'.[6]

The liberal turn in Dutch immigrant integration policies

Rarely recognized by contemporary Dutch politicians is the fact that the Ethnic Minorities Policy of the 1980s changed substantively long before 2001. Already in the late 1980s, the Dutch government began to express concerns about progress in integration, especially in material domains such as housing, education and labour.[7] A government-commissioned report by the Scientific Council for Government Policy (WRR 1989) called for a more socially, economically and individually focused policy approach. It argued that 'the institutionalization of ethnic pluralism must not be regarded as an independent policy objective' (ibid.: 61), and that labelling migrant groups in terms of an accumulation of socio-economic deprivation and social-cultural differences would have made minorities too dependent on the state (ibid.: 9).

Furthermore, in 1991–2 the climate changed significantly when the issue of immigrant integration emerged on the political agenda.

The leader of the main opposition party in this period, Frits Bolkestein of the Liberal Party, triggered a first broad national debate in politics and the media when he called for a stricter and more 'courageous' approach toward immigrant integration that would have to be founded on the basic principles of a liberal society, such as the separation of church and state, freedom of expression, tolerance and non-discrimination.[8] It is here, according to Bolkestein, that 'the multicultural society meets its limits, that is, when above-mentioned political principles come into play'.[9]

An important policy shift took place in the years following the 1989 WRR report and the 1991 National Minorities Debate. This involved an important change in policy discourse from the 'Minorities Policy' to the 'Integration Policy', and the emergence of the 'citizenship' concept. The focus on integration instead of emancipation (Fermin 1997: 211) had put immigrant integration into the framework of participation in central societal institutions (education, labour, welfare state, politics). Instead of group emancipation, individual immigrants now became the unit of integration into Dutch society. This more liberal-egalitarianist (or universalist) character of the Integration Policy is best illustrated by the social categorization of migrants as 'citizens'. The 'primary goal' was formulated as 'real active citizenship of persons from ethnic minorities'.[10] This means that the rights as well as the duties of members of minorities became more central as they were reframed as citizens.

The view of the Netherlands as a multi-ethnic or multicultural society now moved into the background. Government no longer regarded the active promotion of such a society as integral to public policy. This perspective was articulated in terms of 'the changing role of the government', and recognition that 'more parties than just government are responsible for the dilemmas of the multicultural society'.[11] Instead, government policy was to be restricted to the sphere of socio-economic participation, also because of rising concerns about the viability of the welfare state given the scale of immigration. 'A deteriorated economic climate and the permanent immigration of new immigrants and too little attention for the problems of native citizens in a position of socio-economic deprivation has made mutual adaptation and the support for an integration policy less obvious'.[12]

The assimilationist turn in Dutch policies

The focus of government policy shifted significantly once more with the turn of the millennium. In 2000, a second national minorities debate emerged – the so-called Scheffer debate – which focused attention on an alleged 'multicultural tragedy'. A series of events widely discussed in Dutch politics and the media drew further attention to the supposed 'clash of civilizations'. This included violence that involved immigrants, as well as moral events that focused attention on the dilemmas of cultural and religious diversity: imams made radical statements about homosexuals, or refused to cooperate with the female Minister for Integration. Especially path-breaking was 'the long year of 2002' when the populist politician Pim Fortuyn made immigrant integration the centre of public and political attention. He called for 'zero-immigration' as the Netherlands was 'full', and called for a 'cold war against Islam', dismissing Islam as 'an idiotic culture'.[13] While campaigning in the 2002 parliamentary elections, Fortuyn was assassinated by an animal rights activist on the very day that polls indicated his party would come out first in the elections.

The 'long year of 2002' set the stage for a third turning point in Dutch immigrant integration policies. In 2003 a parliamentary investigative committee was established to examine why the integration policy had been so unsuccessful.[14] In addition, the centre-right governments from 2002 on carried through strong political leadership in the domain of immigrant integration. In particular the Minister of Immigration and Integration from 2002 to 2007, Rita Verdonk, was a key policy entrepreneur for a more assimilationist policy approach. In one of her first policy memoranda, Minister Verdonk described the contours of a so-called 'Integration Policy New Style'.[15] Whereas the Integration Policy had focused primarily on socio-economic participation, the emphasis now shifted towards the social and cultural distance between migrants and Dutch society.[16]

In order to support 'the continuity of society', concern was directed at bridging differences rather than 'the cultivation of their own cultural identities'. Cultural differences were now framed as problematic cultural distances.[17] It was argued that 'too large a proportion of minority groups live at too great a distance from Dutch society'. In this context, the goal became to 'diminish the distance between minorities and the native population in social, cultural and economic respects'.

Under this new policy, all newcomers as well as long-term resident migrants – so-called 'oldcomers' – were to be target groups of the integration policy. All newcomers were obliged to follow 'civic integration programmes' after their arrival in the Netherlands. Citizenship remained the primary means for categorizing minorities, but the focus shifted from 'active' citizenship to 'common' or 'shared' citizenship, with a more assimilationist meaning. Common citizenship involves a sort of citizenship based on common values and norms; it involves 'speaking Dutch and complying with basic Dutch norms, [such as] doing your best to support yourself and observing laws and regulations'. It brings with it a willingness to 'take care of the social environment, respect the physical integrity of others, including within marriage, accept everyone's right to express their opinion, accept the sexual preferences of others and the equality of man and woman'. Also, it retains some of its liberal-egalitarian premises that citizens are individually responsible for their participation in society.

Rather than social-cultural emancipation being a condition for socio-economic participation (as in the Minorities Policy) or socio-economic participation being a condition for social-cultural emancipation (as in the Integration Policy), the new causal story was that social-cultural differences could form an obstacle to socio-economic participation. Diminishing the social and cultural distance between migrants and natives would support the participation of migrants in society and would eliminate problems such as criminality and rising social tensions in neighbourhoods with high concentrations of immigrants. Just as with the Integration Policy, the individual migrant remained the main unit of analysis. Much would depend on the efforts made by immigrants themselves.[18]

This 'assimilationist turn' in Dutch integration policies seemed to be on its way back with the new government coming to power in 2006. Rather than 'Integration Policy New Style', immigrant integration now became connected to Urban Policy and Neighbourhood Policies, that is, removed from the more symbolic facets of national integration policies and issues of national identity. However, the centre-right coalition led by Prime Minister Rutte that came to power in 2010 returned discursively to the ideas of assimilation, national unity and 'Dutchness'. It did not actually pursue corresponding policies in these areas, predictably given the political composition of this coalition (with key support for it extended by the anti-immigrant Freedom Party).

Indeed, this government seemed reticent to pursue integration policies and preferred to focus on limiting immigration. For instance, pre- and post-admission integration tests now create a nexus between migration and integration, and integration into society is primarily considered the individual responsibility of migrants. In short, government policies seem to have drifted further away from a multicultural 'model' with which Dutch policies have been and sometimes continue to be associated.

Accordingly, this analysis of Dutch policy discourse reveals that rather than there being one Dutch multicultural model, Dutch integration policies have been characterized by the rise and fall of various 'models'. They are characterized by strong discontinuity over the past four decades (see the summary in Figure 5.1); at least once every decade or so, a new policy 'model' has emerged while another one is declared a 'failure.' Furthermore, this discontinuity also seems to involve strong inconsistencies in policies conducted in various periods, especially on the social-cultural dimension (see Figure 5.1; also Duyvendak and Scholten 2011). Whereas the Ethnic Minorities Policy of the 1980s clearly assumed a positive relationship between socio-cultural emancipation and integration, this relationship is nowadays framed more negatively. Under Integration Policy New Style, socio-cultural distinctiveness is assumed to be primarily an obstacle to integration.

Deconstructing the Dutch multicultural model

Policy is not the only sphere in which multiculturalism can be situated. This section looks at multiculturalism in several other spheres, including political and media discourses (which are distinguishable from formal policy discourses), academic discourses and actual everyday policy practices in which formal policies are often not only implemented but also tend to be translated to a 'street-bureaucrat' level.

THE MULTICULTURAL MODEL AS A COUNTER-DISCOURSE IN MEDIA AND POLITICS

The image of a Dutch multicultural model appears to have been most persistent in political and media discourses. Though the Ethnic Minorities Policy of the 1980s contained many elements that resembled the multiculturalist ideal type as deduced from the migration

	No integration policy <1978	Ethnic Minorities Policy 1978–94	Integration Policy 1994–2003	Integration Policy New Style >2003
Terminology	– Integration with retention of identity	– Mutual adaptation in a multicultural society	– Integration, active citizenship	– Adaptation, 'Common citizenship'
Social classification	– Immigrant groups defined by national origin and framed as temporary guests	– Ethnic or cultural minorities characterized by social-economic and social-cultural problems	– 'Citizens' or 'Allochthonous', individual members of specific minority groups	– Immigrants defined as policy targets because of social-cultural differences
Causal stories	– Social-economic participation and retention of social-cultural identity	– Social-cultural emancipation as a condition for social-economic participation	– Social-economic participation as a condition for social-cultural emancipation	– Social-cultural differences as obstacle to integration
Normative perspective	– The Netherlands should not be a country of immigration	– The Netherlands as an open, multicultural society	– Civic participation in a de facto multicultural society	– Preservation of national identity and social cohesion

Figure 5.1 Policy frames in Dutch immigrant integration policy since the 1970s (adapted from Scholten 2011)

literature, in formal policy documents little reference was made to 'multiculturalism'. In contrast, political and media discourses used the concept of 'multiculturalism' more frequently. It seems that the image of Dutch multiculturalism originates more from these broader public discourses than from actual policy discourses.

Why did this image remain so powerful even after multicultural-ism was largely removed from formal policies? An important factor was the role of the Dutch multicultural model as a *counter-discourse*. Counter-discourses can play an important role in the formation of discursive coalitions by articulating a new mode of discourse. Such counter-discourse then involves a definition (often *ex-post*) of a spe-cific problem area, or a specific policy approach, that must convince actors not to adopt that definition or approach.

Focusing on the early 1990s, Dutch social scientist Baukje Prins (1997) observed how the multiculturalist elements of Dutch poli-cies were over-emphasized in order to signal the need for a different approach (and tone) toward immigrant integration. In that period, a different 'tone' was set in discourses on immigrant integration, not just with studies like the 1989 WRR report but also in political discourse making up the first National Minorities Debate in 1991 and 1992. It was triggered by public statements from opposition leader Frederik Bolkestein who was sceptical about the relationship between Islam and integration. He described the rise of a new mode of discourse, which he defined as 'new realism'. New realist dis-courses sought to address immigrant integration problems 'head on', and called upon immigrants to live up to their civic responsibilities.

This new realist discourse established multiculturalism as a counter-discourse, for instance by associating multiculturalism with political correctness, taboos and being 'too soft' on migrants. This discourse played an important role in the policy shift from the Ethnic Minorities Policy to the (more liberal-egalitarian) Integration Policy of the 1990s. However, the discourse of a Dutch multicultural model persisted well beyond the early 1990s. Indeed, a defining moment ushering in more recent policy changes was the second national minorities debate triggered in 2000 by Paul Scheffer's article enti-tled 'The Multicultural Tragedy'. In this article, the author referred to Dutch multicultural policies as being responsible for the failure to address pressing integration problems, such as weakening cohe-sion, an eroding sense of national belonging and criminality. He constructed an image of a 'multicultural house of cards' that would now be collapsing. Populist politicians like Fortuyn and Wilders also depicted Dutch policies as being too multiculturalist. Wilders coined the term 'multiculti-nonsense', and sought to pin the multicultural label on his opponents.

A key argument used by the critics of multiculturalism has been that under its banner the 'voice on the street' has been ignored. Immigrant integration became a powerful issue for populist politicians to use against the established political elite: it came to symbolize the technocratic and elitist character of the consensual Dutch type of policymaking.

In response to the steady rise in support for these populist parties in national elections since 2002, the incumbent government's immigrant integration policies became more responsive to public opinion. Duyvendak et al. (2004: 201) cited an emergent 'articulation logic' in Dutch politics: politics was engaged in naming the problems and feelings of society and articulating them so as to ensure that the 'voice on the street' was taken seriously. Prins described this process as a 'hyperrealism' in which politics aims to eradicate taboos and speak freely about problems of integration, but 'in which the courage of speaking freely about specific problems and solutions became simply the courage to speak freely in itself' (Prins 2002: 252). Hyperrealism wished to replace the old 'political correctness' with a new political correctness where 'saying something positive about the integration of immigrants would be naïve and would mean ignoring the problems'.[19]

Political and media discourses on immigrant integration have, therefore, been characterized by multiplicity. Beyond the dominant discourse or 'model' of the 1980s, there are now various discourses competing for political and media attention. Dutch mass communications scholar Rens Vliegenthart has delved deeper into this multiplicity of frames, in the spheres of both media and politics (Vliegenthart 2007; see also Roggeband and Vliegenthart 2007). His analysis shows that already in the 1990s, the multicultural frame was just one among several, including one that stressed emancipation of migrants (in particular migrant women); another that underscored the need for limiting migration; a frame that viewed migrants as victims; and one that focused primarily on Islam as a threat to Dutch society (ibid.: 13).

It is noteworthy that in media debates, the 'Islam as a threat' frame came into use much earlier than it did in parliamentary debate (ibid.: 21). Roggeband and Vliegenthart explained this delayed effect by pointing to the formation of more centre-right governments after

2002 (though one was briefly in coalition with the Labour party, which maintained a silence on issues relating to immigrant integration) (ibid.: 14). Also remarkable is that the multiculturalist frame today appears more frequently in both parliamentary and media debates than it did a decade ago. This lends support to the thesis that the multicultural 'model' of integration is becoming more important as a counter-discourse against which new policy developments are to be juxtaposed.

THE MULTICULTURAL MODEL IN ACADEMIC DISCOURSE

The idea of a Dutch multicultural model has also persisted in academic discourse. Especially in the 1970s and 1980s, social scientists played a key role in formulating the Ethnic Minorities Policy. Rath (2001) described the strong technocratic symbiosis on the national level between researchers and policymakers. When minority policy was challenged in the late 1980s and early 1990s, established researchers, particularly from the strategically positioned Advisory Committee on Minorities Research (ACOM), denounced such challenges as unscientific and potentially damaging to migrants.

However, as with political discourses, the idea of a Dutch multicultural model persisted well beyond this period. For example, a study by Sniderman and Hagendoorn (2007), *When Ways of Life Collide: Multiculturalism and its Discontents in the Netherlands*, still described the Dutch approach in terms of a multiculturalist model. The authors argued that the labelling of collective identities inadvertently deepened social-cultural cleavages in society. In addition, they rooted the Dutch approach in the history of pillarization: 'The Netherlands has always been a country of minorities thanks to the power of religion to divide as well as unite' (2007: 13). This pillarist legacy was tenacious because the 'collective trauma of World War II where the Dutch failed to resist the massive deportation of Jews would have contributed to the fact that immigrant minorities have been seen in the light of the Holocaust [. . .] or that critical views of immigrants are labelled racist and xenophobic'. Accordingly, well after the demise of multiculturalism in formal policy discourses, academics still invoked it, often to blame multiculturalist policies for the alleged failure of immigrant integration in the Netherlands. Dutch sociologist Ruud Koopmans (2006: 5) also drew attention to the discontents of multiculturalism in the Netherlands. He too directly linked Dutch multiculturalism to pillarism and argued that pillarist policies were unsuitable for application to immigrant integration.

These scholars assumed a direct link between pillarism, Ethnic Minorities Policies and integration policies. However, Maussen (2009) and Duyvendak and Scholten (2011) *inter alia* have called into question the assumed direct link between minorities policies and the history of pillarization. First of all, Dutch society had been de-pillarizing in many sectors as early as the 1960s and particularly in the 1970s. Pillarization was considered as belonging to the past. Yet Dutch governments responded to the arrival of newcomers with what Vink (2007) has called a 'pillarization reflex': Dutch policy makers resorted to the traditional frame of pillarization for providing meaning to the new issue of immigrant integration.

Others have contended that it was not so much integration policy itself that was inspired by pillarization (Maussen 2009). Rather, it was the influence of more generic institutions that were still to some extent pillarized, such as the Dutch tradition of state-sponsored special (religious) education, a pillarized broadcasting system and a health service. Integration policy itself has never explicitly constructed minority groups as pillars. Minorities never achieved the level of organization (and separation) that national minorities had achieved in the early twentieth century. According to Rath et al. (1999: 59): 'in terms of institutional arrangements, there is no question of an Islamic pillar in the Netherlands, or at least one that is in any way comparable to the Roman Catholic or Protestant pillars in the past'. Indeed, Duyvendak and Scholten (2009) have emphasized how neither pillarization nor multiculturalism were ever embraced as normative ideals; multiculturalist assertions refer only in a descriptive way to an increase of diversity in society.

MULTICULTURAL PATH-DEPENDENCY IN POLICY PRACTICES

A final key argument found in Dutch debates on multiculturalism today is that even though multiculturalism has been abandoned in formal policies, it has survived in policy practices, especially at the local level. Beyond the Dutch case, a thesis has emerged in migration studies that local policies are generally more accommodative towards ethnic differences and group-specific measures than national policies. Local opportunity structures are more open for migrant groups than national opportunity structures, for example, because policymaking takes place primarily 'behind closed doors' (Guiraudon 1997), relatively insulated from broader (national) public and political debates. It is also in greater proximity to local governments and local migrant organizations.

Given the rise of assimilationist or citizenship-oriented ('colour-blind') policies throughout Europe, De Zwart (2005) drew attention to replacement strategies on the local level. Traditional target group constructions and group-specific policies that characterized earlier (multiculturalist) policies are formally abandoned, but they re-emerge in actual policy practices where the selection of formal target groups is carried out through other means with the same result – the same groups are targeted without being mentioned explicitly. For instance, the shift in Dutch policies from integration policies to urban or neighbourhood policies are interpreted as such replacement policies since the selected neighbourhoods are generally populated by the same target groups as before. Furthermore, various scholars (Poppelaars and Scholten 2008; Vermeulen and Stotijn 2010; Uitermark 2010) found that many local governments, in spite of their formal colour-blind discourses, still tend to cooperate with migrant organizations, often for pragmatic reasons.

Koopmans, therefore, referred to the strong tendency to path-dependency in Dutch integration policies at the local level, as well as to many change-resistant policy measures on the national level. Although formal policy as well as public discourse appear to have changed, Koopmans argued that in their actual way of dealing with ethno-cultural diversity the Dutch have remained accommodative: 'Outside the limited world of op-eds in highbrow newspapers, the relation between Dutch society and its immigrants is still firmly rooted in its tradition of pillarization' (2007: 4). Indeed, there seem to be many instances of pragmatic accommodation on the local level in cities such as Amsterdam and Rotterdam. De Zwart and Poppelaars (2007) found that Amsterdam's city government as well as many district governments continued to cooperate with migrant organizations or to accommodate ethno-cultural differences for various pragmatic reasons. For street-level bureaucrats, cooperation with these groups was a primary way of staying in touch with policy target groups, gaining information about them and eliciting their assistance. Similarly, Vermeulen and Stotijn (2010) found that local policies aimed at reducing unemployment amongst immigrant youth still took the ethno-cultural factor into account in street-level bureaucratic processes.

For Uitermark and his co-authors (2005), accordingly, whereas

Amsterdam's diversity policy was post-multiculturalist in seeking to negate ethnic differences, paradoxically the ethnic factor continued to play a central role in local political discourse. Social problems such as criminality, radicalization, social isolation, lack of respect for women's rights and school dropout rates, are often directly associated with specific migrant groups. Amsterdam alderman Rob Oudkerk was unwittingly caught by a TV camera in 2002 complaining he was fed up with the problems of *kut-marokkaanen* (a difficult-to-translate insult to Moroccans along the lines of 'damned Moroccans'). Or, in response to migrant delinquency and 'street-terror' linked to Moroccan youth, a Moroccan neighbourhood fathers' project was conceived under which Moroccan fathers would patrol the streets to enforce control of Moroccan youngsters. The city of Rotterdam has adopted more assimilationist policies which are not directed at specific groups, but it does associate social problems with specific groups: 'the colour is not the problem, but the problem has a colour' (Uitermark and Duyvendak 2008).

Such policies should not be mistaken for normatively driven multiculturalist policies. Instead, Poppelaars and Scholten (2008) argue, based primarily on the Rotterdam case, that these measures are meant to address concrete integration problems that local governments face. They are forms of coping with problems pragmatically, especially by street-level bureaucrats, rather than instances of group accommodation. In such pragmatic problem-coping practices, the need to acquire information as well as cooperation from members of immigrant groups played an important role, and adopting bureaucratic routines from past policies provide elaborate networks of contacts with migrant organizations.

Conclusions: implications of the rise and fall of the Dutch cultural model

This chapter has exposed the myth of the famous, or infamous, Dutch multicultural model, in at least two different ways. First, it has shown that Dutch policies have been dynamic and fluid over the past four decades. Rather than being characterized by a singular, consistent and coherent national multicultural model, a new policy discourse has emerged about once in every decade. Some scholars even question whether there has been a multicultural model at all. Besides this national-level pattern, some experts have pointed at resilient multiculturalist practices existing on the local level. Indeed, path-dependency seems to involve policy routines that, in spite of formal policy changes on the national level, still persist in local policy practices, in particular through the pragmatic accommodation of ethnic differences and cooperation with migrant organizations. These practices cannot simply be regarded as consequences of multiculturalist policy beliefs: instead of being normatively driven, they are shaped more by routines and pragmatic concerns produced by reaching out to relevant target groups.

The second mythic aspect of Dutch multiculturalism is exposed by distinguishing multiculturalist discourse that has persisted over the past decades (though increasingly the term 'multiculturalism' has become politically incorrect) from the multiculturalist counter-discourse that is mobilized primarily by the critics and opponents of multiculturalism. This counter-discourse is employed to juxtapose the new, more assimilationist policy discourse with the so-called Dutch multicultural past or, as Scheffer put it, 'multicultural tragedy'. This multiculturalist counter-discourse seems primarily an *ex-post* construction of Dutch policies. Perhaps more importantly, counter-discourse may explain why the image of a single Dutch multicultural model persists.

What are the implications of the rise and fall of multiculturalism in the Netherlands, both for immigrant integration and for Dutch politics and society? First, various scholars (Prins 2002: Entzinger 2010) have drawn attention to the performative effects of the tougher tone on immigrant integration and of rejection of multiculturalism on the integration trajectories of individual migrants. On the one hand, public attitudes toward the presence of migrants in Dutch society have worsened since the turn of the millennium (Gijsberts and Lubbers 2009: 284). Natives have become more negative towards the presence of migrants, in particular in social-cultural and religious terms, and they feel more threatened by their presence. On the other hand, migrants feel less accepted (ibid.: 285), and their subjective perception of their degree of integration has also declined (Entzinger 2010). The tough tone on immigrant integration seems to have contributed to self-perceptions of less integration.

This performative effect has contributed to what has been described as 'the integration paradox' (Entzinger 2010). The subjective self-perception of degree of integration has been declining even as, at the same time, integration has deepened on a number of 'objective' indicators. Thus, Duyvendak et al. (2004) concluded that the position of migrants improved significantly in the sphere of education, which is considered a strong predictor of successful integration for this and subsequent generations. In terms of labour market participation, language proficiency and housing, signs of progress can be found. However, the culturalization of discourses on immigrant integration, in terms of both multiculturalism and assimilationism, has diverted attention away from indicators of integration successes.

A second consequence of the changed status of Dutch multiculturalism lies in the important consequences it has had for developments in Dutch society and politics at large, especially after 9/11 and major events in the Netherlands. The rise of the populist parties of Pim Fortuyn and Geert Wilders reflected how immigrant integration had become one of the most salient political topics of the time. Populists turned immigrant integration into a key symbol to evoke not just anti-immigrant sentiments but also broader public resentment against the technocratic and elitist policymaking style of Dutch national politics. Immigrant integration policies became a symbol for how the voice on the street had been ignored.

In response to the populist challenge, Dutch politicians have developed an exceptionally broad consensus that a new approach to immigrant integration is required. It reflects Duyvendak et al.'s (2004) notion of the 'articulation function' of Dutch politics in which the articulation of public sentiments concerning multiculturalism and immigration plays a central role in government policymaking. Some writers believe that the logic of immigrant integration policymaking became increasingly divorced from the actual concerns and objective indicators of integration (Scholten 2011), or that immigrant integration was increasingly transformed into an issue of symbolic politics (Entzinger 2003). These arguments may explain the paradox regarding why integration policies are broadly discarded as a failure at the same time as many indicators are showing that integration is progressing slowly but steadily.

NOTES

1. Foreign Workers Memorandum, Memorandum of Understanding, Parliamentary Document TK 1973–1974, 10504, no. 9.
2. Minorities Memorandum, Parliamentary Document, TK 1982–1983, 16102, no. 21: 10.
3. Reply Memorandum to WRR report Ethnic Minorities (1979), Parliamentary Document, TK 1980–1981, 16102, no. 6.

4. Minorities Memorandum, Parliamentary Document, TK 1982–1983, 16102, no. 21: 107.
5. Ibid.: 12.
6. Ibid.: 107.
7. Action Programme 1988, Parliamentary Document, TK 1987–1988, 20260, no. 2.
8. Bolkestein gave his speech at the International Liberal Conference in Luzern on 6 September 1991. A summary appeared in 'Islamitische immigranten moeten integreren', *NRC Handelsblad*, 10 September 1991. Bolkestein then published an article for another newspaper: 'Integratie van minderheden moet met lef worden aangepakt', *De Volkskrant*, 12 September 1991.
9. *NRC Handelsblad*, 10 September 1991.
10. Minorities Memorandum, Parliamentary Document, TK 1982–1983, 16102, no. 21: 24.
11. Ibid.: 4.
12. Ibid.: 21.
13. *Elsevier Magazine*, 25 August 2001; *De Volkskrant*, 2 November 2001; *De Volkskrant*, 9 February 2002.
14. Parliamentary Documents, TK 2002–2003, 28689, no. 1.
15. Parliamentary Document, TK 2003–2004, 29203, no. 1.
16. Ibid.: 7.
17. Ibid.: 7.
18. Ibid.: 10.
19. Parliamentary Treaties, 6 April 2004, 63-4112.

REFERENCES

Alexander, M. (2007), *Cities and Labour Immigration: Comparing Policy Responses in Amsterdam, Paris, Rome and Tel Aviv*, London: Ashgate.
Bertossi, C. and J. W. Duyvendak (2009), 'Modèles d'intégration et intégration des modèles ? Une étude comparative entre la France et les Pays-Bas', *Migrations Société*, 21 (122), pp. 25–276.
De Zwart, F. (2005), 'The dilemma of recognition: Administrative categories and cultural diversity', *Theory and Society*, 34 (2), pp. 137–69.
De Zwart, F. and C. Poppelaars (2007), 'Redistribution and ethnic diversity in the Netherlands: Accommodation, denial and replacement', *Acta Sociologica*, 50 (4), pp. 387–99.
Duyvendak, J. W., R. Rijkschroeff, M. de Gruijter, H. J. Daal and G. Weijers (2004), 'Zelforganisaties van migranten', *Aanvullend bronnenonderzoek Verwey-Jonker Instituut*, 12 (2003–4), pp. 108–63.
Duyvendak, J. W., T. Pels and R. Rijkschroeff (2009), 'A multicultural paradise? The cultural factor in Dutch integration policy', in J. L. Hochschild

and J. Mollenkopf (eds), *Bringing Outsiders In*, Ithaca, NY: Cornell University Press.

Duyvendak, J. W. and P. Scholten (2009), 'Questioning the Dutch multicultural model of immigrant integration', *Migrations Société*, special issue entitled 'Beyond models of integration: France, the Netherlands and the crisis of national models', edited by C. Bertossi and J. W. Duyvendak.

Duyvendak, W. G. J. and P. W. A. Scholten (2011), 'Beyond national models of integration: The coproduction of integration policy frames in the Netherlands', *Journal of International Migration and Integration*, 12, pp. 331–48.

Entzinger, H. (1975), 'Nederland immigratieland?', *Beleid en Maatschappij*, 2/12, pp. 326–36.

Entzinger, H. (2003), 'The rise and fall of multiculturalism: The case of the Netherlands', in C. Joppke and E. Morawska (eds), *Toward Assimilation and Citizenship: Immigrants in Liberal Nation-States*. Basingstoke: Palgrave.

Entzinger, H. (2010), 'Immigration: open borders, closing minds', in E. Besamusca and J. Verheul (eds), *Discovering the Dutch. On Culture and Society of the Netherlands*, Amsterdam: Amsterdam University Press, pp. 231–41.

Fermin, A. (1997), 'Dutch political parties on minority policy 1977–1995: English summary', Rijksuniversiteit, Utrecht. Amsterdam: Thesis Publishers.

Gijsberts, M. and M. Lubbers (2009), 'Wederzijdse beeldvorming', in *Jaarrapport Integratie 2009*, ed. M. Gijsberts and J. Dagevos, The Hague: SCP.

Guiraudon, V. (1997). 'Policy change behind gilded doors: Explaining the evolution of aliens' rights in France, Germany and the Netherlands, 1974–94', PhD thesis, Harvard University.

Joppke, C. (2007), 'Beyond national models: Civic integration policies for immigrants in Western Europe'. *West European Politics*, 30 (1), pp. 1–22.

Koopmans, R., and P. Statham (2000), 'Migration, Ethnic Relations, and Xenophobia as a Field of Political Contention: An Opportunity Structure Approach', in Koopmans and Statham (eds.), *Challenging Immigration and Ethnic Relations Politics: Comparative European Perspectives*. Oxford: Oxford University Press, pp.13–56.

Koopmans, R. (2006), 'Trade-offs between equality and difference: The crisis of Dutch multiculturalism in cross-national perspective', Copenhagen: Danish Institute for International Affairs Brief.

Koopmans, R. (2007), 'Good intentions sometimes make bad policy: A comparison of Dutch and German integration policies', in *Migration, Multiculturalism, and Civil Society*, Berlin: Friedrich Ebert Stiftung, pp. 163–8.

Koopmans, R., P. Statham, M. Giugni and F. Passy (2005), *Contested Citizenship: Immigration and Cultural Diversity in Europe*, Minneapolis, MN: University of Minnesota Press.

Kymlicka, W. (1995), *Multicultural Citizenship: A Liberal Theory of Minority Rights*, Oxford: Oxford University Press.

Lijphart, A. (1976), *The Politics of Accommodation: Pluralism and Democracy in The Netherlands*, Berkeley, CA: University of California Press.

Maussen, M. (2006), *Ruimte voor de Islam, stedelijk beleid, voorzieningen, organisaties*, Utrecht: Forum.

Parekh, B. (2002), *Rethinking Multiculturalism: Cultural Diversity and Political Theory*, Cambridge, MA: Harvard University Press.

Poppelaars, C. and P. Scholten (2008), 'Two worlds apart. The divergence of national and local integration policies in the Netherlands', *Administration & Society*, 40 (4), pp. 335–7.

Prins, B. (2002), 'Het lef om taboes te doorbreken: Nieuw realisme in het Nederlandse discourse over multiculturalisme', *Migrantenstudies*, 4, pp. 241–54.

Prins, B. (2005), *Voorbij de Onschuld: het debat over de multiculturele samenleving*. Amsterdam: Van Gennep.

Rath, J., R. Penninx, K. Groenendijk and A. Meijer (1999), 'The politics of recognizing religious diversity in Europe', *Netherlands Journal of Social Sciences*, 35, pp. 53–67.

Rath, J. (2001), 'Research on immigrant ethnic minorities in the Netherlands', in P. Ratcliffe (ed.), *The Politics of Social Science Research. Race, Ethnicity and Social Change*, New York: Palgrave.

Roggeband, C. and R. Vliegenthart (2007), 'Divergent framing: The evolution of the public debate on migration and integration in the Dutch parliament and media, 1995–2004', *West European Politics*, 30 (3), pp. 524–48.

Scheffer, P. (2000), 'Het multiculturele drama', *NRC Handelsblad*, 29 January.

Scholten, P. (2011), *Framing Immigrant Integration: Dutch Research-Policy Dialogues in Comparative Perspective*, Amsterdam: Amsterdam University Press.

Scholten, P. and F. Van Nispen (2008), 'Building bridges across frames? A meta-evaluation of Dutch immigrant integration policy', *Journal of Public Policy*, 28 (2), pp. 181–205.

Sniderman, P. M. and L. Hagendoorn (2007), *When Ways of Life Collide: Multiculturalism and Its Discontents in the Netherlands*, Princeton, NJ: Princeton University Press.

Taylor, C. and A. Gutmann (2002), *Multiculturalism and the Politics of Recognition: An Essay*, Princeton, NJ: Princeton University Press.

Uitermark, J. (2010), *Dynamics of Power in Dutch Integration Politics:*

From Accommodation to Confrontation, Amsterdam: University of Amsterdam Press.

Uitermark, J. and J. W. Duyvendak (2008), 'Citizen participation in a mediated age: Neighbourhood governance in The Netherlands', *International Journal of Urban and Regional Research*, 32 (1) (March), pp. 114–34.

Uitermark, J., U. Rossi and H. Van Houtum (2005), 'Reinventing multiculturalism: Urban citizenship and the negotiation of ethnic diversity in Amsterdam', *International Journal of Urban and Regional Research*, 29 (3), pp. 622–40.

Vermeulen, F. and R. Stotijn (2010), 'Local policies concerning unemployment among immigrant youth in Amsterdam and Berlin: Towards strategic replacement and pragmatic accommodation', in T. Caponio and M. Borkert (eds), *The Local Dimension of Migration Policymaking*, Amsterdam: Amsterdam University Press.

Vertovec, S. (ed.) (2001), *Journal of Ethnic and Migration Studies*, 27 (4), special issue entitled 'Transnationalism and identity'.

Vink, M. (2007), 'Dutch multiculturalism: Beyond the pillarisation myth', *Political Studies Review*, 5, pp. 337–50.

Vliegenthart, R. (2007), 'Immigratie en Integratie. Relaties tussen Maatschappelijke Ontwikkelingen, Parlement, Media en Steun voor Anti-Immigratiepartijen in Nederland', *Tijdschrift voor de Communicatiewetenschap*, 35 (4), pp. 369–84.

Wetenschappelijke Raad voor het regeringsbeleid (WRR) (1989), *Minderhedenbeleid*, The Hague: Staatsuitgeverij.

Chapter Six

Immigrant Integration and Multiculturalism in Belgium

Marco Martiniello

Belgium's immigration policy, together with the integration policies of the units of the federal state, have been the subject of extensive academic research (Martiniello 1996). But the link between the process of federalization and immigration/integration policy change has been largely understudied. This chapter seeks to fill this gap. In contrast to other cases examined in this book, Belgium's federal structure was itself a response to centrifugal forces that claimed subnational autonomy or even independence. It is therefore a federalism of disunion and, to make matters more complex, Belgium is both a multinational and a polyethnic state in Kymlicka's (1995) terms. My focus will be on the interconnection between new phases in the federalization process and immigrant integration policies. I examine policies in three key areas: immigration admission; their socio-economic, cultural, political and civic integration; and access to citizenship.

The federal context

Théo Lefèvre, a former Prime Minister, used to say that 'Belgium is a happy country composed of three oppressed minorities' (Covell 1985). Since its creation in 1830, it has always been a divided country in which national unity has been problematic. The opposition between the Flemings and the Walloons has been the principal source of disunity. But there was also an implicit consensus between the major political forces in the country to keep the Belgian unitary state functioning. Institutional devices were constructed to control centrifugal forces and even to produce what is usually called *un pacte à la belge*. In summary, Belgium was 'sufficiently concerned with its potentiality for internal conflicts and with its intrinsic risk of self-demolition to establish and maintain permanent pacts between the various actors about social issues considered to be critical' (Martiniello 1993: 251).

Claims for autonomy have existed for a long time in both Flanders and Wallonia. These led to the 'linguistic laws' of 1962 which divided the country into two monolingual areas: a Flemish-speaking zone in the north and a French-speaking counterpart in the south. In the late 1960s other threats to the unitary state linked to the Fleming-Walloon divide emerged, leading to constitutional amendments in 1970 that initiated the protracted process of federalization (Witte and Craeybeckx 1990). This 'top-down' acknowledgment of regional and communitarian autonomies took more than twenty years to be converted into further constitutional amendments. Coincidentally, the federalization process began at the time that the Belgian government decided to stop the recruitment of migrant workers from abroad. In the early 1970s, consensus had developed to apply a zero-immigration doctrine.

Belgium has been a federation since the adoption of the 1993 revision of the constitution. Article 1 states that Belgium is a federal state composed of communities and regions. The federal state, the regions and the communities are placed on the same footing. The federal level is responsible for policy concerning all Belgian citizens independently of any linguistic, cultural or territorial considerations. The list of federal competences includes European Union policy, external relations, defence, justice, finances, home affairs, social security and parts of public health. The three regions – Wallonia, Flanders and the Brussels-Capital Region – are socio-economic entities. In contrast, the three communities – French-speaking, Flemish and German-speaking – are linguistic and cultural entities. In Flanders, the region and the community overlap perfectly and the distinction between the Flemish region and the Flemish-speaking community is consequently merely notional. Such isomorphism of region and community does not exist in the south. At a local level, Belgium also comprises ten provinces (five French-speaking and five Flemish-speaking) and 589 *communes* (cities and towns).

Four levels of power share responsibilities for immigration and integration matters: the EU level (for immigration, asylum and anti-discrimination policies); the federal, community and regional level; the provinces; and the communes. Multi-level governance is not always organized efficiently and recurring conflicts of competences result from this complex structure.

Furthermore, nobody in Belgium believes that the federalization process is complete. In Flanders, the process of nation-building is well under way. For Flemish radical nationalists, the aim is to end the Belgian experience as soon as possible and attain independence for Flanders. For moderate, or patient, Flemish nationalists, whilst independence is the final goal, they favour a multiple-steps strategy and advocate a reform of the state to ensure greater efficiency for all the federated entities. On the francophone side, the refusal to engage in further reform of the state was the dominant approach until 2010. Since then, there has been a recognition of the need to delegate more competences to the federated entities and consequently to reduce the powers of the federal state. In Brussels, in turn, many citizens feel treated like hostages by both the Flemings and the Walloons. Immigration and the integration of migrants are discussed, therefore, in the context of the formation of a new Belgian state or of new post-Belgium states.

Belgium's immigrant-origin population

Some time back it became clear that Belgium found itself in both a migration and post-migration situation. On the one hand, the official halt to new labour immigration decided by the Belgian government in 1974 in response to growing unemployment in the wake of the first oil crisis was in name only. In practice, various types of migration flows – labour migration, freedom of circulation of European citizens, asylum seekers, family reunification, foreign students, and so on – continued after that and have become increasingly diversified. Therefore, Belgium is an immigrant-receiving society even though there is no proactive federal immigration policy. On the other hand, the migration waves of the past have led to the settlement of migrants and their descendants. For them, the migration cycle is complete.

How can we characterize the migration patterns to Belgium over the past decade? Contrary to what is often assumed, contemporary immigration remains largely European. In 2007 62 per cent of new immigrants came from EU member states (CECLCR and GéDap 2008: 25). France and the Netherlands are the top source countries for migrants to Belgium. Poland and Romania have also become significant source countries. Even though Morocco and Turkey remain the most important countries of origin for new migrants to Belgium through family reunification, diversification of origins is highlighted by migrant flows from China and India (Martiniello et al. 2010: 41–91).

Historically, Wallonia represented the main region of immigration.

Table 6.1 Number of work permits issued in the three Belgian regions, 2000–6

Year	Regions		
	Brussels	Wallonia	Flanders
2000	3,811	2,006	15,662
2001	3,956	2,092	16,313
2002	3,784	1,935	12,742
2003	11,765	6,308	17,450
2004	13,165	7,352	18,784
2005	12,044	7,416	20,337
2006	12,381	7,703	27,522

Source: GERME-ULB, in Martiniello et al. (2010), p. 89.

But contemporary migration flows affect primarily Flanders, then Brussels and only then Wallonia (CECLCR 2010). The main reason is that the economic situation of Flanders is better than that of Wallonia. A secondary reason is that many highly qualified EU citizens who work in Brussels choose to live in the green belt around Brussels, which is largely part of the Flemish region. Striking differences appear in the regional profiles of immigration. For example, Polish and Romanian immigration settlement is high in the Brussels region, while Chinese and Indian immigration to Flanders occurs on a larger scale (Mariniello et al. 2010). But even the economically depressed parts of the Walloon region attract new, mostly non-European migrants.

Generally, new migrants possess a higher level of formal education compared to previous migrants: more than 30 per cent are educated to university level. Some evidence also supports in part the thesis of the feminization of migration. This is particularly true for migration from Eastern European countries such as Ukraine or Russia and for migration from certain Asian countries such as Thailand and the Philippines (CECLCR and GéDap 2008: 50, 54).

Motives for immigrating to Belgium are complex. EU citizens come mainly for well-paid work demanding highly qualified people. Migrants who need a visa to enter Belgium are motivated by reasons relating to family reunion and family formation. Table 6.1 provides data on the total number of work permits delivered in the three regions between 2000 and 2006. The difference between Flanders and the other two regions is striking: the number of permits issued

Table 6.2 Belgian and foreign populations by region, 2008

	EU citizens	non-EU citizens	Total foreign pop.	Belgians	Total pop.	% of foreigners
Belgium	658,589	312,859	971,448	9,695,418	10,666,866	9.1
Flanders	225,242	129,128	354,370	5,807,230	6,161,600	5.8
Wallonia	251,692	70,343	322,035	3,134,740	3,456,775	9.3
Brussels-Cap.	181,655	113,388	295,043	753,448	1,048,491	28.1

Source: Adapted from Registre National Calculus (2009), Direction Générale Statistique et Information Economique (DG SIE), 2009, data compiled by Nathalie Perrin and Marco Martiniello.

almost doubled over this short period, with Flanders consistently accounting for as many as the greater Brussels Region and Wallonia combined and, by 2006, considerably more than the other two regions.

If the number of applications for work permits has steadily increased since the beginning of the century, that of applications for asylum has declined. The total number of applications for 2009 was 17,186, which represented 22,785 people (one application can include several family members). This marked a dramatic fall of more than 50 per cent from the peak year of 2000, when 42,691 applications subsuming 54,220 people were made (Fedasil 2010). The pattern in Belgium is consistent with overall EU trends: asylum seeking as a way of obtaining residence in Europe has become less commonplace as EU rules and directives have become more restrictive.

In 2008 the total foreign population in Belgium represented 9.1 per cent of the country's total (see Table 6.2). In Flanders, the total was nearly 6 per cent, although it reached 28 per cent in Brussels. These data do not take into account people with a migrant background who have acquired Belgian citizenship. If we included the latter, the percentage of the population with a migration background would approach 40 per cent in Brussels. Europeans are better represented in Wallonia than in Flanders, whilst non-Europeans live in greater numbers in Flanders than Wallonia. The regions of Belgium have, in fact, rapidly become multicultural. Have they developed different 'philosophies of integration', to employ Adrian Favell's (2001) term?

'Philosophies' of immigration integration in a fragmented state

Two long-standing assumptions on immigration and integration require re-evaluation (see Martiniello 1993). The first is that the terms of debate on immigration and integration in each federal entity of Belgium have been shaped by the dominant form of nationalist discourse in it, which posits an ideal national society. The second is that the politicization of immigration and multiculturalism has developed into an important dimension of the domestic conflict between Flemish-speaking and French-speaking Belgians.

Already in the 1990s in Flanders, public discourse on a Flemish *Kulturnation* in political life became dominant. It opposed multiculturalism and its defenders to monoculturalism and its partisans. Other approaches became socially and politically marginalized. In contrast, the predominance of a public discourse on a *Staatnation* in Wallonia facilitated the imposition of a Walloon version of assimilation and rendered other approaches irrelevant.

A definition of integration proposed in 1991 that still has currency today was intentionally broad and general enough to accommodate divergent approaches in the three regions. The *Commissariat Royal à la Politique des Immigrés* (CRPI), later to become the Centre for Equal Opportunities and Opposition to Racism, understood integration as a form of 'insertion'. The main criteria are: (1) assimilation where it is required; (2) acceptance of the fundamental social principles ('modernity', 'emancipation' and 'pluralism') of the host society; and (3) unequivocal respect for cultural diversity as an opportunity for reciprocal enrichment. The CRPI report concluded that 'The host society must offer opportunities for this integration, by promoting the structural conditions for the participation of the migrants in the goals and activities of society' (Vranken and Martiniello 1992: 247).

According to Blommaert and Verschueren (1993: 49–63), two Flemish researchers whose work was contested in Flanders in the early 1990s and unknown in Wallonia, there was in Flanders 'a collective psyche profoundly troubled by the very idea of diversity in society (linguistic or otherwise)' (Blommaert and Verschueren 1991: 503). Thus, ethnic and cultural diversity was regarded as a problem. Two major sides emerged to analyze and solve this problem of diversity. Defenders of the *cultural homogeneity* of Flanders sought either repatriation of immigrants or their total assimilation into Flemish society. By contrast, a relatively 'progressive' side wished to promote a kind of multicultural society based on the rhetoric of tolerance (Blommaert and Verschueren 1993). Assimilationist tendencies were not completely absent from these 'multicultural' approaches, but they nevertheless constituted an attempt to manage cultural diversity and make it compatible with the collective psyche of homogeneism. At the policy level, the Dutch approach to ethnic minorities was seen as a model which, if applied to Belgium, could reduce the risks of social and political disruptions posed by cultural diversity while simultaneously supporting human rights and democracy.

In Wallonia, conditions were different. Consciousness of a history of immigration and assimilation was more deeply ingrained. Since the end of the nineteenth century, poor, low-skilled Flemish workers had been recruited to work in the coalmines of rich Wallonia and, later, in metallurgy. These Flemish immigrants were forced to assimilate (Quairiaux 1990). As a result, politicians 'of Flemish descent' are recognizable in the contemporary Walloon socialist movement which still plays an important political role. These two features – a subjective history of assimilation and the salience of socialist rhetoric – help explain the relative lack of attention paid to the cultural and ethnic dimensions of immigration in Wallonia. As the Minister-President of the Walloon Region put it in 1993:

> There are far more foreigners here than in Flanders, and this situation has never created any major problem: there is no discrimination, either towards those who come from Italy, Portugal and from more distant countries or towards those who come from Flanders. (Spitaels 1993)

Put bluntly, racism and ethnic problems were seen in official Walloon rhetoric as Flemish problems. Such a perspective could only be understood in the framework of the Belgian domestic ethnic conflict between the Flemings and the Walloons. This also explains why the emphasis was placed on social and economic issues in academic and political circles. In academic discussions, an approach centred on ethnicity was almost automatically rejected because it was seen to be linked to racial theories of the nineteenth century. The very use of 'ethnic' vocabulary was often condemned as politically dangerous and scientifically invalid (Rea 1993).

Politically, any singling out of immigration and ethnic issues was rejected – and with it specific policies for immigrants. Integration policies were generally included in broader social policies aimed at constructing equilibrium in the employment, housing and health sectors, in this way following the French Republican model.

The two contrasting 'philosophies' of integration developed in a social context characterized by the wide acceptance of the zero-immigration option. After the end of the 1990s, and particularly after September 11th, anti-multiculturalist discourse became more commonplace in Belgium as elsewhere in Europe. Greater attention was paid to security issues, the struggle against irregular migration and the presence of Muslims in the cities. Diversity was increasingly problematized but a new version of an old discourse also started to emerge: interculturalism.

Until the financial crash of 2008, Flanders was more open to new labour migration on a temporary basis for economic reasons. Many jobs were not filled in different sectors of the Flemish economy. Some politicians called for the introduction of an autonomous Flemish immigration policy. By contrast the Walloon economy suffered from high levels of unemployment and the wisdom of recruiting migrant workers from abroad was challenged.

In terms of 'philosophies' of integration, Flanders, like the Netherlands at the end of the 1980s, made an assimilationist U-turn and endorsed cultural homogeneity over deep cultural diversity. Wallonia, like France, gradually opened up to limited cultural diversity but often discussed it as 'transitional interculturalism': the ultimate objective was that migrants would conform to the majority culture and identity. In Brussels, diversity, not just superficial but deep, was regarded as a structural component of the region; few here defend a vision of a monocultural capital region. Indeed, it is increasingly difficult to identify a majority to which newcomers should conform. The urban region has become a multicultural, multiethnic, multiracial and multifaith society in a more profound way than the other regions of the country. How to combine this structural diversity with enough unity is the question at the core of debates in the city. In other words, the challenge is not to plan effective assimilation while allowing for superficial diversity as in the other regions. It is more about building a new multicultural Brussels citizenship based on a shared local identification.

After the 2010 elections

How does this federally structured politics of difference affect immigration and integration policies in an increasingly disunited state? The 2010 legislative elections underlined the complexity of policy-making of any kind in Belgium, and especially in an area as divisive as immigration. The results in Flanders were favourable to the nationalist and independentist party (NVA), which led the field with about 30 per cent of the vote. In Wallonia, the elections confirmed the historical leadership of the francophone socialist party (PS). How could a federal government be formed out of these disparate pieces?

Coalition building has always been a daunting exercise in a fragmented society such as Belgium. This time, the challenge was how to form a coalition in which the key parties were so far apart. The nationalist NVA's political objective is the independence of Flanders. In turn the PS acknowledged the importance of deep reforms to the federal state but, until recently, its aim was to ensure the continuity of the Belgian state. On social and economic issues the NVA's agenda was conservative whereas the PS had a social democratic programme. The issue of the end of Belgium also formed part of discussions on a coalition government. It was prompted by the Flemish nationalists' call for complete autonomy in the making of immigration and integration policies. The very idea of negotiating on these allegedly non-negotiable issues at the federal level was abhorrent to many Flemish nationalists. Perhaps without knowing it, parties disagreeing on these policies were, in effect, negotiating the dissolution of Belgium and were on the road to creating new states in the heart of the European Union.

Formally, as I have pointed out, competences in the areas of immigration and integration are shared by different levels of government according to complex formulas. In practice, Flanders claims exclusive powers in these domains. Given the decisive character of these topics, let us examine three sets of issues shaping diversity in Belgium.

1. ADMISSIONS OF IMMIGRANTS

In contrast to countries like Canada and Australia, the federal government in Belgium has no coherent proactive labour immigration policy, whether for the short, medium or long term. However becoming fortress Belgium is an impossibility and the country is de facto a country of immigration, emigration and transit. The 1980 Admission Law, which has been revised several times, outlines five grounds for being admitted to and allowed to reside in Belgium: freedom of circulation for EU citizens; asylum; family unification; course of studies; and employment. Each category requires a specific residence permit. The law was passed six years after the government announced an end to new unskilled labour migration in 1974. The 1980 Admission Law appeared to contradict the earlier decision in that it explicitly recognizes employment as a reason to come to Belgium. In effect, this law revealed how the official halt to immigration was a symbolic measure aimed at convincing the population that migration was under control in a period of severe economic crisis.

The Belgian federal law is consistent with EU immigration policies. In that respect double governance (EU–Belgium) is not problematic. The main difficulty is the lack of cooperation between the Belgian regions in terms of the delivery of work permits. Admission authorization and residence permits are delivered at the federal level but work permits are issued at the regional level. The separate regions follow different directives and contrasting administrative practices, and most importantly they do not work with each other. Because of their different economic structures and labour needs, they have different lists of 'critical functions', that is the list of economic sectors and functions in which there are job openings and needs.

To complicate the process further, most working permits delivered by each region are also valid in the other regions of the country. Critically, therefore, the policy of work permits issued by one region has an impact on the arrival of 'unwanted' migrants in the other regions. Organizational cultures differ across Belgium too. In Flanders the administrative process is highly standardized and quick: it can take as few as five days to obtain a work permit there, especially for the most wanted, highly skilled workers. By contrast, in Brussels and even more so in Wallonia, the same procedure often takes more than six weeks (Martiniello et al. 2010: 85–115). In the case of Flanders, then, the call for a devolution of admission policies and residence permits grows louder as the region sees itself and acts in this sphere more like a nation state in the making than a partner in a federation. The Brussels region, which would like to develop its own distinct solutions to the challenge of large-scale immigration and integration, for example in the area of public education, is held hostage to the policies of Flanders and the French community.

2. SOCIO-ECONOMIC AND CIVIL-CULTURAL INTEGRATION

A second contested area subsumes policies on the socio-economic and civil-cultural integration of immigrants, which are crucial to determining the multicultural status of Belgium. Except for political rights on access to nationality, all other dimensions of immigrant and integration policies were devolved to the communities and the regions in two steps, in 1980 and in 1994 (Martiniello and Perrin 2009). Formally, socio-economic issues affecting immigrant integration should be managed by the regions, and education and cultural dimensions by the communities. This separation of competences has no practical relevance to Flanders since, as mentioned earlier, the Flemish region and community overlap. But it is highly relevant in the Walloon and Brussels cases. As an example, immigrant children living in Brussels have in theory the choice between complying with Flemish integration policy or the French community immigration policy in the area of education; immigrant children living in Flanders or Wallonia must follow their respective region's policies.

As in many other fields, little cooperation occurs in immigration integration between the communities and the regions. This is not due to any institutional deficiencies but rather is caused by a lack of political willingness. Flanders' vision of immigrant integration is shaped by a nation-building project and it does see the added value of collaboration with Wallonia. Wallonia does not have a clear vision of immigration integration but neither does it see what it could gain from cooperation with Flanders, at least in official discourse. As for Brussels, it resists what it perceives is internal colonialism from Flanders and Wallonia through non-cooperation.

The federal government tried several times early in the new century to organize a debate on integration and multiculturalism in order to reconcile the various philosophies of diversity management in the country. In 2004 it launched the Commission for Intercultural Dialogue, whose aim was to redefine integration and citizenship policies through an expansive consultative process subsuming experts and civil society. The final report, published in 2005, presented an assessment of the key issues linked to cultural diversity, equality and citizenship in the country. It offered specific policy recommendations to the regions and communities on managing diversity and adopting anti-discrimination measures. However, none of the main recommendations were implemented.

A few years later, in 2009, a different federal government initiated a process to revive the conclusions of the Commission. The Interculturality Sessions (*Assises de l'Interculturalité* in French, *Rondetafels van de Interculturaliteit* in Flemish) were launched under the auspices of the Francophone federal Minister of Equal Opportunities and Social Integration. The regions and communities were not represented in the steering committee which had been appointed by the Minister and represented various groups in civil society. To make matters worse, the federal government collapsed during the process and it became unclear who would ever make use of the conclusions of these sessions, the final report of which was published in November 2010. These two institutionalized attempts to debate diversity in Belgium proved ineffective and revealed how potentially irreconcilable differences exist not only in the philosophies of integration but also in the policy priorities and budgetary make-up of integration programmes.

In Flanders, socio-economic and civic-cultural immigrant integration policies are mainly contained in two laws. The first, on civic integration for newcomers and for first-generation immigrants, envisages a process of 'citizenization' (the approximate meaning of the Flemish term *inburgering* which is difficult to translate succinctly) under which a non-Flemish newcomer (or 'primo-migrant') would be turned into a Flemish citizen. The second law on ethnocultural minorities targets succeeding generations of immigrants, often called *allochtones* in Flanders. The original meaning of the term refers to species of fauna and flora that are not native to the regions in which they are found. It is surprising, therefore, that the term *allochtone* has come to be used in public policies to distinguish between populations of immigrant and non-immigrant origin, first in the Netherlands and then in Flanders.

These laws propose integration courses that cover both socio-economic and civic-cultural dimensions. These courses are obligatory for newcomers and only encouraged for the established first generation. The introductory stage consists of Dutch-language classes: Flanders and the Netherlands share the same official and standardized Dutch language, though in daily life they reflect a variety of local accents and dialects.

This stage also includes a social orientation class in which newcomers are taught the basics about the functioning of society, its norms and values. These integration courses also contain a vocational element. Newcomers who successfully complete the introductory integration programme receive a certificate that allows them to move to the second stage. Here they receive career training and attend classes in advanced Dutch. At the end of this stage, the newcomer is considered to have become a good active Flemish citizen – not so much a Belgian one.

The 1998 law on ethnocultural minorities concerns the

descendants of immigrants. Revised in 2009, the legislation was inspired by the multiculturalist discourse of the Dutch ethnic minority policies of the 1980s which focused on residents who were disadvantaged because of their ethnic origin and needed to be emancipated in order to integrate into Flemish society. The anti-multiculturalist U-turn across much of Europe in the first decade of the new century was reflected in terminological changes introduced by 2009 modifications to the legislation. The law was renamed the 'Flemish integration policy'; the term 'ethnocultural minorities' disappeared and the word 'integration' survives as the main objective of the revised law.

A very different trajectory of diversity management was followed in Wallonia. The 1996 law on integration of foreigners and persons of foreign origin referred to 'positive discrimination' though it was not defined. Regional integration courses were not proposed and migrants have no obligation to attend integration programmes. Certainly, French-language classes are available, as are ones on labour-market integration and social orientation. The law leaves considerable autonomy to sub-regional integration centres: for example, the one in Namur stresses culture while its Liège counterpart highlights socio-economic issues. The law was revised in 2009 and replaced the concept of positive discrimination with that of positive action. It also introduced the idea of an intercultural society, though the meaning of this was not developed.

In the Brussels region, the integration of immigrants is the responsibility of both the French-speaking and Flemish part of the Brussels government. The former passed legislation on social cohesion in 2006 which described the integration of newcomers in different areas: social assistance, housing, health and French-language acquisition by immigrant children. Not surprisingly, the Flemish part of the Brussels government has organized immigrant integration courses along the lines found in Flanders. One crucial difference, however, is that there is no obligation for newcomers in Brussels to register for them. The nineteen city councils representing the nineteen communes of the Brussels region are also key actors in formulating immigrant and ethnic communities' integration. In some of the central communes of Brussels (Molenbeek, Schaerbeek, Saint-Josse, Brussels-City) the immigrant-origin population now represents the majority of the total population and its electoral power has led to 'softer' integration policies that have no counterpart elsewhere in Belgium.

3. POLITICAL INTEGRATION AND ACCESS TO NATIONALITY

The Belgian Nationality Law – a federal competence – identifies three principal ways of becoming a Belgian citizen: regular naturalization, *jus soli* (birth on Belgian territory) and marriage to a Belgian citizen. After three years of legal residence (two years for recognized refugees) in the country, the foreigner can apply for naturalization. The law sets no requirement in terms of integration of the migrant during this relatively short period of residence. No language or civic knowledge test is required by law.

Naturalization applications are submitted to the Naturalization Service of the Chamber of Representatives. After review, the Service submits applications to the Commission of Naturalization of the Chamber of Representatives, which makes the official decision whether to grant Belgian citizenship to the applicant. Since naturalization is seen as a favour granted by Belgium to the foreigner, Parliament can and does reject applications. Between 48 per cent and 65 per cent of applications have been rejected every year since at least as far back as 1997. Data on the total number of people who acquired Belgian nationality between 1997 and 2007 are presented in Table 6.3.

The Nationality Law allows dual citizenship. It also converts naturalization into an entitlement after seven years of residence, unless the person has a criminal record. Again no language or civic knowledge test is required. *Jus soli* applies to third-generation immigrant children who were registered by parents living in Belgium for a minimum of five of the ten years preceding the birth of the child. Finally, acquisition of Belgian citizenship through marriage requires a minimum of six months' marriage and three years of legal residence, which are not onerous requirements.

Table 6.3 presents data on the total number of foreigners who acquired Belgian citizenship between 1997 and 2007. For a small country like Belgium, the figures are quite significant: more than 430,000 foreigners acquired Belgian citizenship over the ten-year period. Furthermore, most of them were previously citizens of a non-EU state.

This liberal law has been contested, especially in Flanders. The main argument against it is that it conflicts with the obligatory integration courses. In 2010 a new, more restrictive draft law was adopted by the government: the minimum length of residence in Belgium before one could apply for citizenship was raised to five

Table 6.3 Number of foreigners acquiring Belgian nationality by country of origin, 1997–2007

From	1997	1998	1999	2000	2001	2002	2003	2004	2005	2006	2007	Total
EU-15	3,367	2,987	2,353	6,297	6,605	5,173	5,019	4,864	4,622	5,081	4,956	51,324
Non-EU	28,311	31,047	21,843	55,683	56,377	41,244	28,690	29,890	26,890	27,585	32,157	37,971
Total	31,678	34,034	24,196	61,980	62,982	46,417	33,709	34,754	31,512	32,666	37,113	431,041
Country of origin												
Turkey	7,835	6,932	4,402	17,282	14,401	7,805	5,186	4,467	3,602	3,279	3,113	88,373
Algeria/Tunisia	1,187	1,298	821	1,930	2,010	1,444	1,205	1,232	1,036	1,079	1,121	14,363
Morocco	11,078	13,486	9,133	21,917	24,018	15,832	10,565	8,704	7,977	7,753	8,722	163,749
Congo	1,059	1,753	1,890	2,933	2,830	2,564	1,651	2,406	1,917	1,751	2,020	22,774

Source: Institut National de Statistique: Brussels, 2008, adapted by Marco Martiniello and Andrea Rea.

years. A second change was that the applicant is now required to demonstrate knowledge of the language of the part of the country in which he or she is established. Finally, the bill introduced the condition of willingness to integrate that the application would be required to prove. The absence of a functioning government for 541 days (from April 2010 to December 2011) meant that Parliament could not vote the bill into law. The downgrading of Belgium's credit rating triggered the formation of a new coalition government, led by Elio Di Rupo, both the first Socialist and the first French-speaking Prime Minister since the 1970s.

Conclusion

What can we conclude from this overview of immigrant integration policies in the Belgian federation? Belgium is generally seen as a unique federal system because it consists of an attempt to counter centrifugal forces more than an attempt to assemble separate units into a new federal system. My argument goes beyond that statement. I have claimed that there is virtually no dialogue, let alone cooperation, on immigration and integration issues between the federated entities. I have also shown that the perspectives, the visions and the 'philosophies' of integration remain very different in the north, the south and Brussels, even though differences have tended to diminish over time, especially between Flanders and Wallonia. The policies and programmes also differ, such as the obligatory integration course that exists in Flanders but not in the other two regions. This policy variation has become a political issue: Flemish authorities would like the other regions to have their own obligatory programmes, but Wallonia and Brussels resist in the name of regional autonomy.

The Belgian federal government is often considered to be either a constraint on the development of specific policies at the level of the federated entities or an irrelevant level of policymaking and governance. Especially in Flanders, federal 'interference' is seen as highly problematic and unacceptable given the commitment to regional autonomy. The enormous complexity of institutional arrangements appears to be an excuse for rather than a cause of the lack of cooperation and for efforts to keep the federal government from taking a more active role in managing diversity.

Even though Belgium is still formally a federation, it is moving away from a federal structure, mainly because Flanders is engaged in a concerted nation-building process that is forcing the other entities to adopt a defensive strategy. Is there a way to really reconstruct a federal Belgium in which autonomous federated entities would cooperate on, among other issues, immigration and integration issues? It is difficult to be optimistic given the political developments of the past two decades. The left–centre-right national coalition government formed in December 2011 and led by Walloon socialist Elio Di Rupo faces enormous challenges, above all addressing Belgium's economic and social crisis and implementing the reform of state structures and institutions that was agreed as one of the main prerequisites for forming a government.

In addition, local elections, in which many foreign-born residents can vote, are highly politicized and polarized in many towns and cities. Flemish nationalist and independentist parties in opposition at the federal level have strong electoral support; the NVA alone accounts for close to 40 per cent of Flemish voting intentions. In these conditions, meaningful dialogue and cooperation between federal entities is improbable. This is especially the case on the issues closely linked to national sovereignty, such as the integration of immigrants and the multiculturalism of Belgian society. The 2012 local elections furnish an assessment, therefore, of 'the state of the Belgian federation' as well as the state of public opinion on immigration, integration and multiculturalism.

In the specific area of access to citizenship, political agreement exists at the federal level to make Belgian nationality more difficult to get. To be granted naturalization after five or ten years' residency in the country, a condition of integration may soon have to be met; successfully taking integration courses, for example, could become a requirement. In Wallonia, a new regional law is expected in 2013 which may introduce regional integration courses. A new-found resolve to address immigration and integration issues has emerged.

References

Blommaert, Jan and Jef Verschueren (1991), 'The pragmatics of minority politics in Belgium', *Language in Society*, 20 (4) (December), pp. 503–31.
—— (1993), 'The rhetoric of tolerance or, what police officers are taught about migrants', *Journal of Intercultural Studies*, 14 (1), pp. 49–63.
CECLCR (2010), *Migration: Rapport annuel 2009*, Brussels: CECLCR.
CECLCR and GéDap (2008), *Migrations et Populations issues de l'immigration en Belgique: Rapport statistique et démographique 2008*, Brussels: CECLCR.

Covell, Maureen (1985), 'Ethnic conflict, representation and the state in Belgium', in Paul Brass (ed.), *Ethnic Groups and the State*, London: Croom Helm, pp. 228–61.

Favell, Adrian (2001), *Philosophies of Integration: Immigration and the Idea of Citizenship in France and Britain* (2nd edn), New York: Palgrave.

Fedasil (2010), *Annual Report 2010*. Brussels: Federal Agency for the Reception of Asylum Seekers. Available at http://www.emnbelgium.be/publication/fedasil-annual-report-2010

Kymlicka, Will (1995), *Multicultural Citizenship*, Oxford: Clarendon Press, pp. 11–26.

Martiniello, Marco (1993), '"Ethnic leadership, ethnic communities": political powerlessness and the state in Belgium', *Ethnic and Racial Studies*, 16 (2), pp. 236–55.

—— (1996), 'La question nationale belge à l'épreuve de l'immigration', in Alain Dieckhoff (ed.), *Belgique. La force de la désunion*, Brussels: Éditions Complexe, Espace international, pp. 85–104.

Martiniello, Marco, Andrea Rea, Christiane Timmerman and Johan Wets (2010), *Nouvelles migrations et nouveaux migrants en Belgique*, Gand: Academia Press.

Martiniello, Marco and Nathalie Perrin (2009), 'Immigration et diversité en Belgique', in Jean Beaufays and Geoffroy Matagne Geoffroy (eds), *La Belgique en mutation. Systèmes politiques et politiques publiques (1968–2008)*, Brussels: Bruylant, pp. 217–51.

Quairiaux, Yves (1990), 'L'immigration flammande en Wallonie (1880–1914): Problèmes d'intégration – l'exemple de la région du centre', paper presented at the Conference on Second Generation Immigrants in Europe, Florence, European University Institute, April.

Rea, Andrea (1993), 'La politique d'intégration des populations d'origine étrangère', in Marco Martiniello and Marc Poncelet (eds), *Migrations et minorités ethniques dans l'espace européen*, Brussels: De Boeck Université, pp. 143–66.

Spitaels, Guy (1993), 'Interview', in *La Wallonie* (28 January).

Vranken, Jan and Marco Martiniello (1992), 'Migrants, guest workers and ethnic minorities. Historical patterns, recent trends and social implications of migration in Belgium', in Dietrich Thränhardt (ed.), *Europe: A New Immigration Continent*, Münster: Lit Verlag.

Witte, Els and Jan Craeybeckx (1990), *La Belgique politique de 1830 à nos jours*, Brussels: Labor.

Chapter Seven

The Political Dynamics of Multiculturalism in Sweden

Karin Borevi

Introduction

There seems to be a broad consensus across Europe today that multiculturalism is on the retreat. Political leaders in various countries seek to outdo each other in declaring that multiculturalism has constituted a misguided approach which should not be allowed to shape future policies. In the academic debate, multiculturalism has been subject to a massive attack; it is depicted as an ideology rooted in a relativist rejection of liberalism where the maintenance of collective group identities is prioritized over the protection of individual civil rights (Barry 2001; Okin 1999; cf. Phillips 2007; Kymlicka 2007: 108). Given this widespread critique it appears difficult to understand how countries up until quite recently celebrated and supported the multicultural approach. How could a political project the subject of a devastating critique today ever have been introduced? Indeed, the adoption of multicultural policies is often treated as a mystery by its current critics – 'as if gremlins snuck into national parliaments and drafted multicultural policies while no one was watching' (Kymlicka 2007: 103).

Sweden is internationally renowned as one of the most prominent representatives of an officially declared multicultural policy. It was often mentioned, together with the UK and the Netherlands, as one of the European countries that in the post-war period most explicitly adopted a multicultural policy approach (Castles and Miller 1993; Freeman 2004; Koopmans et al. 2005). But what were the political dynamics that made it possible for this approach to be established in Sweden in the mid-1970s? And what changes has Swedish multiculturalism undergone since then? These are the questions that are addressed in this chapter.

One important feature of the current debate on multiculturalism is the considerable confusion surrounding the meaning of the concept. More often than not the critique lacks specificity about what is actually implied by the concept. Or it takes as its point of departure a biased perception – even a caricature – of what specific political norms and strategies constitute the multicultural approach (for example Kymlicka 2010: 35). The traditional understanding whereby multiculturalism means that collective cultures take priority over individual rights is commonly (explicitly or implicitly) the natural point of departure. Contrary to this, Will Kymlicka maintains that multiculturalism should be regarded as one specific phase (starting from the 1960s across Western countries) in a series of political movements which together form part of a wider process involving the spread of civil rights liberalism. The claim that multiculturalism is rooted in liberalism does not itself explain, however, why it received considerable support across Western democracies. Instead, Kymlicka argues that there is a need to 'bring politics back in' to identify the framework of power relations in various national and historical contexts, and to consider what the perceived costs and benefits were of accepting various multicultural demands (Kymlicka 2007).

Given these considerations, we should not expect multiculturalism to be able to attract the active and wholehearted support of the majority. The hypothesis should be instead that multiculturalism may receive 'the passive acquiescence' of the majority as long as it is not associated with considerable costs and risks. Kymlicka argues that a gradual process of 'desecuritization' of ethnic relations, together with the emergence of a consensus concerning human rights, helped to reduce the risk to dominant groups of accepting multicultural claims. This also helps to explain the decline in salience and legitimacy that multiculturalism is currently experiencing:

> [T]he fact that liberal multiculturalism receives the passive acquiescence rather than active support of most members of dominant groups means that it is vulnerable to backlash and retreat, particularly if critics are able to raise fears that it may after all be a threat to human rights or to state security. (Kymlicka 2007: 121)

Inspired by Kymlicka's reasoning, my aim is to examine what the normative principles and political coalitions were that underpinned the multicultural approach in Sweden, and how they have subsequently come to change. First, attention will be paid to the question of *who* (i.e. what political actors) have been pushing for multiculturalism and who have been opposed to or sceptical of it. Second, what has been the *content* of the multicultural approach in the Swedish context, and how has this changed over time?

The emergence of multiculturalism in Sweden

Multicultural ideas were brought to the fore for the first time in Sweden in the mid-1960s, in the context of labour immigration. At that point in time Sweden had already received large groups of post-war immigrants. The end of World War II marked an important change in Swedish attitude towards immigration. The previous strict immigration regulations introduced in the 1930s were liberalized. This meant that assumptions that had informed former policies – that the Swedish labour market had to be protected from foreign competition and that there was a need to preserve the purity of 'the Swedish race' – were also abandoned (for example Svanberg and Tydén 1992).

Likewise, there were relaxations in wartime regulations that had limited foreign citizens' rights to influence Swedish politics, motivated by the interest to protect security and law and order (Hammar 1964). Industrial expansion led to a huge demand for foreign labour and Sweden removed previous barriers so as to make it easy for immigrants to enter the country. Additionally, Sweden actively recruited foreign labour via a system of organized recruitment from other European countries (Lundh and Ohlsson 1994).

In the early 1960s the situation of practically free immigration started to be questioned. The Swedish Trade Union Confederation (*Landsorganisationen* – LO) in particular demanded that the government introduce immigration regulations. The demands were not made because immigration had suddenly become unprofitable; instead they reflected a growing concern that unregulated immigration could lead to a socially stratified society where foreign workers suffered from socio-economic marginalization. Simultaneously representatives of employers' associations argued for a continuation of the liberal immigration rules (Johansson 2005). It was, however, the opinion of the LO that had an impact on the Social Democratic government. In 1968 it officially declared the principle of equality: 'immigrants shall have the opportunity to live under the same conditions as the rest of the population, i.e. have the same standard of living'. It also emphasized how this goal presupposed a regulation of immigration: 'guarantees for the demand that equal standards must be able to be maintained cannot be created without a relatively in-depth examination of immigration' (Government Bill 1968).

Adopting Kymlicka's reasoning, by the 1960s the immigrant issue – and more generally issues concerning national minorities – had long ago been taken out of the 'security box' where it had belonged before and during the war. It was now put in the 'democratic politics box' (cf. Kymlicka 2007: 120). Hence the goal – officially declared in 1968 – was to enable immigrants to achieve a situation of equal political and socio-economic standing in relation to the native population. The question was *how* this goal should be reached. From the perspective of the prevailing Social Democratic welfare state ideology, the default answer had been that any efforts to achieve equality presupposed a certain level of cultural homogeneity (Borevi 2012). The fundamental idea behind the welfare state project was that a feeling of solidarity or integration would be achieved by reducing the gaps between various strata in society, and the goal was therefore to *eliminate* differences between various social classes.

Indeed, assimilation had been the progressive answer to the question of how the process of democratic 'citizenization' (to borrow Kymlicka's expression) of various marginalized groups should be brought about. This logic was particularly evident in relation to the Roma minority whose 'unsuitable' way of life was regarded as an obstacle to its becoming emancipated and integrated into mainstream society and achieving living conditions equal to the rest of the population. The official goal of Sweden's 'Gypsy policies' (applied from 1954 to 1969) was therefore to help the Roma *abandon* their cultural practices and distinct way of life, so that they could integrate into the Swedish welfare state (Roth 2001: 219; Román 1993).

From the mid-1960s some voices began to challenge this assimilationist logic of the welfare state project. It was now argued that state authorities should make active efforts to integrate immigrants into the Swedish welfare state system, but that they could not demand of immigrants that they abandon their original cultural identities or practices. Importantly, some political actors now argued that this had the implication that Swedish authorities must not only *tolerate* cultural pluralism but also *actively promote* immigrants' preservation of their distinct cultural identities in Swedish society. Who were formulating these new ideas and demands, and what was the response they received?

Among the most active lobbyists for the new ideas of cultural pluralism were activists with immigrant backgrounds who could be said to represent an 'ethnic elite' (Wickström 2012; Román 1994; Schwarz 1971). In 1964 the most prominent of these activists, the sociology student and concentration camp survivor David Schwarz, published an article in Sweden's largest daily newspaper, *Dagens Nyheter*, in which he criticized the Swedish attitude of neglect and assimilation involving the social and cultural situation of immigrants. Instead he urged adoption of an active policy of cultural pluralism. A wider debate followed revolving around the crucial question: should the state encourage cultural assimilation or cultural pluralism?

Advocates of cultural pluralism demanded that the government establish a new 'minority policy' where immigrants' and national minorities' distinctive collective identities were clearly recognized and actively promoted. The opposite standpoint was represented by those who saw 'assimilation' as the only possible solution if immigrants were to become full members of society (Román 1994).

It is noteworthy that in Sweden it was the Conservative party (*Högerpartiet*) that most clearly and enthusiastically embraced cultural pluralism. In the minority and immigrant programme launched in 1968 (the first of its kind in Sweden), the party declared as its aim freedom for every member of a minority group 'to choose the degree of assimilation into the native population' (Högerpartiet 1968). In a number of Conservative parliamentary motions the party advanced various efforts to promote immigrants' rights to maintain their distinct cultures, while criticizing the Social Democratic government for its 'assimilationism' (Schwarz 1971).

The Social Democrats, on the other hand, were initially negative about expanded minority rights for immigrants. A statement adopted by its party congress in 1968 declared that 'a pluralist society should not be the object of our efforts. Immigrants should not be seen as minority groups but rather as interest groups'. Moreover efforts were to be made 'to foster a natural sense of belonging to the Swedish community and the Swedish people' and to ensure that immigrant groups must not be allowed to form isolated islands in Swedish society (Socialdemokratiska arbetarpartiet 1968: 300). Some individual Social Democratic party members, however, embraced the demands for cultural pluralism (Schwarz 1971).

In 1967 the LO took the side of the cultural pluralists, launching a 'minority programme' and demanding that the Social Democratic government take action consistent with this programme and recognize the cultural aspirations of minority groups

(Landsorganisationen 1967; Ahlvarsson 1967). Arguably, this helped explain why the Social Democratic government, despite its sceptical approach to cultural pluralism, in the 1968 Bill on immigration highlighted the need to make special efforts 'to cater for the wish of immigrants to maintain contact with their original country's language and culture' (Government Bill 1968). The task was given to the parliamentary Commission on Immigration which worked for six years to formulate a new comprehensive immigrant and minority policy.

Unlike the situation today, but similar to what used to be the case in other Western European countries, immigration was not a salient political issue in Sweden during the 1960s and 1970s. The result was that other actors got the opportunity to shape immigrant policy. As argued by Tomas Hammar, 'the major determinants of the immigrant policy were not the political parties, but rather the bureaucracy and interest groups' (Hammar 1985: 45). Political activists representing an ethnic elite, academics engaged in the emerging field of immigrant and minority studies, and the leadership of the Immigration Board (personified by Kjell Öberg who was general director from 1969 to 1980) among others could therefore influence the policymaking process. One illustration of this is given in a study by Bengt Jacobsson; he argued that reform of mother tongue instruction in public schools was profoundly influenced by a collection of minority legal experts, immigrant teachers, parents, psychologists and researchers:

> as late as six weeks prior to the commission's final meeting, active supporters were brought together with the members of Parliament in the commission. It was at this point that the MPs became convinced that supporting mother tongue instruction made good sense, after which the main paragraphs were formulated. (Jacobsson 1984: 78)

In addition, it should be mentioned that the Finnish government exerted direct pressure on the Swedish government to enable Finnish-speaking children in Swedish schools to receive mother tongue instruction in Finnish, and also to have Finnish as a teaching language (Jacobsson 1984: 75).

In 1975 the Swedish Parliament unanimously supported the new immigrant and minority policy. Paraphrasing the French revolution's *liberté, égalité et fraternité*, the goals were formulated as 'equality, freedom of choice and partnership'. The aim of *equality* was to ensure that immigrants were provided with conditions equal to those of the native population. The *freedom of choice* objective meant

> that members of linguistic minorities living in Sweden must, via efforts taken by society, be given the opportunity to choose for themselves the extent to which they are to retain and develop their original cultural and linguistic identity, and the extent to which they are to become part of a Swedish cultural identity. (SOU 1974: 69, 95)

Additionally, the cultural rights of immigrants were protected in a new formulation in the constitution (SFS 1974: 152). The third policy goal of *partnership* implied that immigrant and minority groups should work together as partners in the development of society, which presupposed that immigrants received public support to build and maintain their own associations (Government Bill 1975; Hammar 1985: 35).

To summarize, when first formulated in the mid-1960s multicultural demands were met with scepticism by the Social Democrats but embraced by the Conservatives. This revealed a distinctive feature of the Swedish variant of multiculturalism. The immigrant policy launched in 1975 had been carefully adapted to the ideology of the Social Democratic welfare state, which was embraced by the vast political majority. This meant that the positive approach to cultural pluralism had to be combined with a strong commitment to the integrative logics of the Swedish welfare state, advocating standardized institutional arrangements and rules that applied equally to all recipients. Hence Swedish multiculturalism did *not* imply the promotion of special institutions designed for ethnic groups, and it should therefore be distinguished from, for example, multicultural policies in the Netherlands where such institutions comprised an important feature (for example Entzinger 2003). In contrast to the Dutch case, there was widespread Swedish opposition particularly against minority schools, since they challenged the idea that pupils with different backgrounds should get the chance to meet in a public school system common to all.

In this light, the introduction of mother tongue instruction in public schools was an effort to combine recognition of cultural pluralism with the conviction about the importance of institutional integration. To the Conservatives – the only party at the time favouring private schools – this approach was insufficient. Consequently, Conservative MP Ingrid Diesen declared in a parliamentary debate that the 'freedom of choice' objective was little more than 'simply paying lip service' so long as immigrants and minorities were denied the right to run separate pre-schools, homes for the elderly and minority schools (Parliamentary records 1975: 80, 21).

Finally, another factor helping to explain why Sweden decided to embrace the cultural pluralistic approach in the 1970s is that it fitted in well with the national self-image developed in the post-war period of Sweden as a pioneer in human rights issues (cf. Demker and Malmström 1999; Johansson 2008). In the era of decolonization Sweden had acted as a champion of the rights of minorities internationally. However, as long as the country was unable to improve the situation for its own minorities, it was difficult 'to boast about its international commitment' (Hansen 2001). The minority political goals of the new immigrant and minority policy therefore constituted an effort to dissociate from the history of assimilatory and 'Swedifying' policies directed, for example, at the Sámi minority in the northern part of the country (Mörkenstam 1999). Hence, in line with what Kymlicka holds to be the general frame of multiculturalism, Sweden's introduction of a multicultural approach in the 1970s was considered to be part of a general endeavour to spread human rights, which in turn reinforced the Swedish conception of itself as a moral superpower (Johansson 2008). In the 1975 parliamentary debate the Social Democratic Minister of the Interior, Anna-Greta Leijon, noted with satisfaction that a political consensus had emerged on the new immigrant policy approach, stating that 'this bodes well for our efforts to turn Sweden step by step into something of a pioneer country within the field of immigrant policy' (Government Bill 1975).

The Swedish retreat from multiculturalism in the mid-1980s

Despite the restrictive immigration regulations introduced in the late 1960s, immigration to Sweden continued. From the mid-1970s the main change was that former labour migration was replaced by asylum seekers and family members of earlier immigrants. The composition of immigrants also changed: if previously they had consisted largely of people from the Nordic countries (above all Finland) and from countries in southern and Eastern Europe, now they were made up of people arriving from Latin America, Asia and the Middle East. In this context, questions arose concerning the multicultural direction of the policy. What did the goal of 'cultural freedom of choice', formulated in 1975, actually mean? Did it imply that immigrants were not obliged to follow laws and norms that applied to the rest of the population? And what responsibility did the state have for the long-term preservation of minority groups? In the early 1980s the Social Democratic government empanelled a number of commissions to take on these questions.

These commissions undertook a critical assessment of the multicultural approach that bears strong similarities to the arguments put forward today across Europe commonly characterized in terms of a 'retreat from multiculturalism' (Joppke 2004). Thus the critical discussion on multiculturalism in Sweden had started in the mid-1980s – at least a decade before corresponding debates occurred in other countries, for example in the Netherlands in the mid-1990s (Entzinger 2003). In the Swedish debate it was argued that the multicultural goal introduced in 1975 to support the safeguarding of minority identities was unrealistic, and that it might even compete with the goal of promoting social integration. The Commission on Discrimination, for example, argued that there was a risk that 'measures of a minority-supportive character compete in terms of time and money with measures to promote a long-term cautious and natural adaptation' (SOU 1984: 55, 263). Moreover, it was pointed out that the multicultural approach tended to *misdiagnose* the problems that immigrants were facing, so that economic marginalization or ethnic discrimination was narrowly understood in terms of 'multicultural questions', which therefore hindered an effective solution to the problem (SOU 1984: 58, 55).

As when multiculturalism had been established in the 1970s, the commissions of the 1980s were highly influenced by researchers and experts on immigration and ethnic relations. The research, however, now represented a more 'problematizing' attitude towards the minority-politics approach. For example, cultural anthropologist Ulf Hannerz pointed out that multiculturalism ran the risk of reinforcing an essentialist view of culture, arguing that 'a static view of culture is, at worst, not much better than racism – it could also be used to legitimize various kinds of apartheid systems' (Hannerz 1981: 41).

Only ten years after it had been introduced, in 1986 the multicultural approach was abandoned. Reiterating arguments put forward in commission reports (referred to above), the government now declared that ethnic groups consisting of immigrants who had arrived after World War II should *not* be considered to constitute linguistic or national minorities. The government emphasized that the goal was to meet the needs of individuals and not to promote the existence of 'immigrants as collective entities' (Government Bill 1985/6: 98).

Consequently, the policy area was renamed from 'immigrant and minority policy' to simply 'immigrant policy'. Most policy measures, however, remained more or less intact; the fundamental change was in how they were justified (Borevi 2002; 2012; cf. Dahlström 2004). The 1986 decision put an end to the former process of equalizing immigrants and national minorities. For example, mother tongue instruction in public schools was no longer seen as part of a long-term endeavour to protect immigrant languages. In practice this meant stricter conditions for immigrant children to be eligible for mother tongue instruction when compared to those belonging to one of Sweden's officially recognized national minorities (Hyltenstam and Tuomela 1996).

The 1986 change fundamentally dismantled the multicultural approach adopted in 1975. Interestingly, the government down-played the depth of this ideological change, arguing that it only represented a 'clarification' of what had been the actual intentions back in the 1970s (Government Bill 1985/6: 98). In Parliament, the Left Party and the Centre Party independently expressed res-ervations against the proposal and insisted that the previous label 'immigrant and minority policy' should be retained since 'it is important to emphasize that the immigrants are national minorities' (Parliamentary Committee on Social Insurance 1985/6: 20, 8). The other parties, however, supported the new direction.

A decade later, in 1997, the Social Democratic government presented a new 'integration policy' in which the former minority-political ambitions were again criticized, this time for having hindered integration: they stigmatized immigrants as being 'different' from the rest of the population (Government Bill 1997/8). The 1997 integration policy Bill can be regarded as confirmation of the 1986 multicultural retreat rather than as a new policy shift (see Borevi 2002; 2012). One interesting difference is, however, the manner in which it was presented. While the retreat from multiculturalism in 1986 had been said to merely constitute a 'clarification' of existing policy goals, the government in 1997 explicitly rejected previous policies for having done more damage than good:

Immigrant policy, along with the particular administration that has been established to implement it, has unfortunately come to reinforce a division of the population into 'us' and 'them' and thus reinforced the emergence of the 'outsider feeling' [*utanförskap*] that many immigrants and their children experience in Swedish society. (Government Bill 1997/8: 16, 17)

Moreover, the new integration policy proposed in 1997 was held to be a *paradigm shift* suggested by the very title of the bill: 'From immigrant policy to integration policy'. Previous targeting of immigrants as a group was restructured so that measures now selectively targeted at 'immigrants' would only be justified during the initial period (of approximately two years) after their arrival in Sweden; after that point they would be eligible for the same social programmes as the population at large. Neither idea was really new. The principle that migrants should, as far as possible, be included in the same social programmes as the population at large had been a principal element in Swedish immigration policy since the 1960s (see Borevi 2002; 2012; cf. Dahlström 2004).

To review our account, the particular variant of multiculturalism that had been adopted in the 1970s was abandoned twice: first substantively but discreetly in 1986, then more vocally but with less substantive change in 1997. How should this difference in reformulating multiculturalism be understood? One answer is to point to the changing political context between the two decisions. Even though unemployment among immigrants had started to become a problem in the 1980s, it had not reached the alarming situation that prevailed in the 1990s, which was caused by Sweden's most serious budgetary crisis since the 1930s. This crisis coincided with mass immigration from the former Yugoslavia. Thus, a search for effective political solutions became urgent. The 1997 framing of integration policy in terms of a paradigmatic policy shift was therefore a logical result.

Furthermore, immigration issues in general had become significantly more politicized in the 1990s than they had been in the mid-1980s. This also helps explain the government's self-critical rejection of earlier immigrant policy efforts. Interestingly, the apolitical nature of the immigrant policy area in the 1980s had been highlighted as a problem in itself. Thus, in its final report from 1984 the Commission on Discrimination argued that:

apparent unity regarding the aims of immigrant and minority policy has certainly had its advantages. The disadvantage is that these aims have thereby not become political in a true sense. People have not seriously taken a stance on the actual content of immigration and immigrant policy, because their political representatives have only on rare occasion promoted dialogue or debate about it. (SOU 1984: 55, 253)

As numbers of asylum seekers increased from the mid-1980s onwards, issues related to immigration appeared more frequently on the political agenda. They also displayed a diminished degree of party political unity (Green-Pedersen and Krogstrup 2008). An event that heralded an increase in political salience was a local referendum in 1988 on refugee reception (in the Skane municipality of Sjöbo) where the majority voted against the idea (Fryklund and Petersson 1989). In the election campaign three years later a right-wing populist party called New Democracy (*Ny Demokrati*) for the first time managed to gain seats in the Swedish Parliament, with a political programme based on anti-immigration. Although the success of New Democracy proved short-lived (in the next general election it disappeared from Parliament with only 1.2 per cent of the vote), its presence in the Swedish Parliament from 1991 to1994 contributed to an increase in the political salience of issues connected to immigration (Rydgren 2005).

The debate on multiculturalism in the 2000s

Two issues in the present Swedish debate on multiculturalism are also at the heart of current multicultural debates across Europe. The first concerns whether or not it is legitimate to make group-specific exemptions or accommodations to meet the wishes and interests of various cultural and religious groups. The second has to do with how national identity is defined and whether more robust efforts should be made to ensure that minority members stay loyal to it. As I shall suggest, a certain Swedish scepticism is discernible surrounding both these issues insofar as they entail group-specific measures solely targeting new arrivals or cultural minorities.

MULTICULTURALISM AS ALLOWANCE OF CULTURAL EXEMPTIONS

In contrast to the multicultural policy adopted in the UK (Favell 1998), Sweden has generally taken a negative view of cultural or religious demands for exemptions from common rules and regulations. There are no signs that this attitude is about to change, at least not when it comes to the 'stronger' forms of cultural exemptions. This

149

category can encompass legal recognition of marriage, divorce and inheritance traditions that differ from common law; acceptance of slaughtering methods that are otherwise prohibited if they involve 'ritual slaughter'; or other exemptions from regulations such as the famous UK example of Sikhs being exempt from wearing a helmet when driving a motorcycle even though that is generally the rule (for example Phillips 2007; Vertovec and Wessendorf 2010).

Sweden does not generally allow the legal exercise of 'cultural defence'. Thus, it does not offer legal recognition of other marriage, divorce and inheritance traditions (Sayed 2009), and ritual slaughter is explicitly prohibited (Nilsson and Svanberg 1997). Political demands for the introduction of these stronger types of cultural exemptions from common law are rare. The call by representatives of the Church of Sweden during the 2010 election campaign to do away with the prohibition of ritual slaughter since it was said to place unreasonable limits on religious freedom (Fast et al. 2010) should therefore be regarded as exceptional. This is not to say that in practice minority members in Sweden have never achieved differential treatment justified on the grounds of showing respect for other people's cultures. Indeed, it has been argued that the celebration in Swedish politics of 'a multicultural ideal' has had the effect of having society turn a blind eye to abuses of women and children (Wikan 2004), or that it fails to observe and combat aspects of fundamentalist Islamism (Carlbom 2003). Honour crimes, however, also occur in societies where a multicultural approach is absent.

When it comes to 'softer' forms of allowance of cultural exemptions, the Swedish approach has traditionally been negative too. Examples that might belong to this category include time off work for worship; adaptions of dress codes in workplaces where uniforms are worn; provision of proscribed foods (halal, kosher, vegetarian) in public institutions; and dress codes, gender-specific practices and other issues in public schools showing sensitivity to the values of specific ethnic and religious minorities (list inspired by Vertovec and Wessendorf 2010). Particularly as concerns dress-code policies in the workplace, a shift towards a significantly more permissive attitude seems to have emerged in Sweden (Borevi in press).

The crucial change came with the introduction of the 2008 Discrimination Act where not only direct but also indirect discrimination was made illegal. Indirect discrimination is defined as when:

someone is disadvantaged by the application of a provision, a criterion or a procedure that appears neutral but that may put people of a certain sex, a certain transgender identity or expression, a certain ethnicity, a certain religion or other belief, a certain disability, a certain sexual orientation or a certain age at a particular disadvantage, unless the provision, criterion or procedure has a legitimate purpose and the means that are used are appropriate and necessary to achieve that purpose. (SFS 2008: 567, 1:4)

This definition means that the Act applies when someone is denied the right to wear religious clothing (a Muslim headscarf, Jewish skull-cap or Sikh turban) in the workplace. The act furthermore makes employers responsible for ensuring 'that the working conditions are suitable for all employees regardless of sex, ethnicity, religion or other belief' (SFS 2008: 567, 3:4). Accordingly, several official workplaces where uniforms are worn have adjusted their dress-code policy to include religious garments. The right to wear turbans, headscarves and skullcaps in place of the standard-issue cap is explicitly acknowledged by both the Swedish police and the Swedish armed forces (Rikspolisstyrelsen 2011; Försvarsmakten 2011).

Critical voices have been raised against the new regulation allowing the wearing of religious garments in the workplace. In one polemical book, for example, it is argued that this represents a form of 'normative multiculturalism' that threatens both individual human rights and the general safety of citizens. According to the authors the idea that professions such as the police, the military, the fire brigade or the rescue services should allow employees to wear religious garments when on duty constitutes a potential security problem since it becomes unclear whether such employees are more loyal to their religion than to their public function. Instead, the authors advocate the introduction of the French *laïcité* principle, where religious symbols are prohibited in the public sphere (Bauhn and Demirbag-Sten 2010). Another issue in the debate has been whether the 'extreme' Muslim headscarf, the burka and niqab, should be allowed in, for example, public schools. Since 2003 there have been guidelines, formulated by the Swedish National Agency for Education, that give school headteachers the right to prohibit both pupils and teachers from wearing the burka and niqab in the school (Skolverket 2012). In the 2010 election campaign the Liberal Party demanded that this principle should be made part of the Education Act also (*Svenska Dagbladet* 2010).

MULTICULTURALISM AS ABSENCE OF INTEGRATION REQUIREMENTS

The debate on exemptions is naturally linked to how the common Swedish national identity is perceived and formulated. In 1986 the government underlined that the positive approach towards cultural pluralism should *not* be interpreted 'so that it involves a rejection of the Swedish language and the common interests shared by all of Swedish society' (Government Bill 1985/6: 98). In fact, a similar statement, although one that was more vague, had also been made in the 1970s when the government declared that support for minority cultures must take place within the societal and legal framework of 'the common interests shared by all of Swedish society' (Government Bill 1975). Hence references have repeatedly been made to a common core of norms and interests that are perceived to constitute the 'glue' that unites the Swedish citizen community.

The 1997 Government Bill on new integration policy suggested a formulation of common national identity that differed from earlier ones. It was formulated in a more explicitly multicultural manner since the goal was now the promotion of 'a notion of societal community that is based on social diversity' (Government Bill 1997/8: 16). The policy goal was unanimously supported by Parliament, and it still applies. Thus, even though the word 'multiculturalism' is avoided in Swedish political debate today, there is a widespread political support for multiculturalism, understood as recognition of Swedish society as being inherently culturally diverse in character. In September 2010 the prevailing political consensus on this issue was broken when the Sweden Democrats (*Sverigedemokraterna*) won parliamentary seats. This party prioritizes instead a distinct Swedish majority culture, demands that immigration be restricted (particularly from countries with cultures and value systems perceived to diverge from the Swedish) and calls for decisive efforts to make immigrants assimilate into Swedish culture (Sverigedemokraterna 2011).

A question explicitly linked to multiculturalism is whether special efforts targeting new arrivals and cultural minorities should be undertaken to guarantee that they stay loyal to the national community. Since the turn of the millennium a 'seismic shift' in integration policies has occurred across Europe, marked by different measures promoting mandatory integration requirements and tests targeted at non-European immigrants (for example Joppke 2004, 2007; Entzinger 2003). Significantly, this shift is conceived as a 'retreat from multiculturalism' (Joppke 2004), pointing to an understanding of multiculturalism as meaning the *absence* of such demands. That such integration requirements have been conspicuous by their absence has made commentators conclude that Sweden, in contrast to most other countries, continues to pursue a 'multicultural' policy approach (for example Koopmans 2010).

Sweden constitutes something of an exception to the European integration policy trend described above. The country has introduced neither formal language requirements nor other tests of knowledge as conditions for naturalization. Even though economic incentives have recently been introduced to encourage new arrivals to follow integration courses, participation in the programmes is not linked to the individual's chances of achieving residency or citizenship (Djuve and Kavli 2007). In short, Sweden's approach could be said to represent a distrust of any type of 'cultural' prerequisites that effectively target new arrivals or other non-citizens (Borevi 2012).

This sceptical attitude has been expressed repeatedly in various policy documents. In 1999 the Swedish Citizenship Committee rejected the suggestion to introduce a language requirement to achieve Swedish citizenship this way:

> Such demands could result in longer qualification periods for certain categories of applicants before they can become Swedish citizens. Furthermore it could exclude certain people from ever becoming Swedish citizens. The committee regards citizenship as a path to societal cohesion and as an essential part of the integration process. Increasing the qualification demands would instead have the counterproductive result of decreasing cohesion in the nation as a whole. (SOU 1999: 34, 318)

In a government inquiry in 2010 the proposal to make participation in civic education compulsory to obtain citizenship was rejected in a similar fashion:

> It is not for the state to lay down conditions for citizenship which require completing a civic education course. A democratic state should treat all citizens, indiscriminately and equally, without testing their level of civic knowledge. Anything else would be a historic breach of the enabling, solidarity-based inclusive idea of the Swedish people's home and welfare state. (SOU 2010: 16, 25)

Since the turn of the new century, a number of political actors – most notably the Liberal Party (*Folkpartiet*) and the Moderate Party (*Moderata samlingspartiet*) – have advocated an official language requirement. The Liberal Party has also proposed that a completed civic education course should become a condition for receiving Swedish citizenship (*Svenska Dagbladet* 2008). Such proposals have usually been shot down as representing a 'flirtation' with the xenophobic parts of the electorate (Parliamentary records 2002/3: 79; cf. Milani 2008). The Sweden Democrats, however, have taken up the case and insist that naturalization should entail proficiency in the Swedish language and knowledge about Swedish society and history (Sverigedemokraterna 2011). All the other parliamentary parties wish to dissociate themselves from the Sweden Democrats, and their entry into Parliament has had the effect (in the short term at least) of other parties softening their earlier calls for raising integration requirements. For example, the Liberal Party no longer champions an official language requirement for citizenship (Severin 2011).

Concluding remarks

In this chapter I have analyzed immigrant-based multicultural-ism in Sweden from the mid-1960s up to the present. The findings are consistent with Kymlicka's thesis that multiculturalism could receive the passive acquiescence of the majority as long as it was not associated with any significant costs and risks. So, what were the cost-benefit analyses that informed the introduction of multicul-turalism in Sweden in the 1970s? And what particular drawbacks or dangers regarding the multicultural approach have subsequently been identified by critics of Sweden's multiculturalism?

When demands for the cultural rights of minorities were first made in the mid-1960s, the minorities were indeed regarded as a potential threat, not so much to national security or respect for human rights, but instead to the integrative logics of the Swedish welfare state. Consequently, the Conservatives – at the time rep-resenting the only political party that opposed Social Democratic welfare state ideology – were among the most enthusiastic supporters of minority rights, while the Social Democrats were the most scepti-cal. Other political actors who had gained influence in the policy process, however, presented convincing evidence that recognition of immigrants' specific cultural needs involved significant benefits; it would, for example, ease integration, promote harmonious social relations and enhance Sweden's international reputation as a cham-pion of human rights. In 1975 the Swedish Parliament adopted its immigrant and minority policy which gave the state the responsibility for group-targeted support that would help immigrants maintain their status as minorities.

Yet in 1986, Sweden retreated from this minority-political approach. The change of course was based upon concerns that efforts to help immigrants maintain their cultures might conflict with the goal of promoting immigrants' equal integration into mainstream society. The consensus was that future policies should focus solely on assisting *individuals* attain status as equal citizens, and not on promoting the maintenance of their ethnic collectivities. A 1997 policy document confirmed that the previous 'multicultural' focus on immigrants' ethnic groups had obstructed the integration goal since immigrants were stigmatized as being inherently 'different' from the rest of the population, reinforcing a division of the population between 'us' and 'them'.

Similar to what is the case in other European countries, 'multiculturalism' in Sweden today is often depicted as a misguided or even dangerous policy approach. This chapter, however, underlines the argument that we must pay attention to what particular multiculturalism the critique is concerned with. When Sweden retreated from multiculturalism in the mid-1980s, this meant a backing away from previous group-targeted efforts to help minorities maintain their cultural distinctiveness, since such an approach was regarded as having serious drawbacks.

Policy developments since the late 1990s could, however, simultaneously be said to represent a strengthened multicultural approach, if 'multiculturalism' is understood as active efforts to make public institutions more inclusive and hospitable to ethnic and religious diversity. Furthermore, the overwhelming majority of Swedish parliamentary parties, with the right-wing populist Sweden Democrats being the only exception, recognize the 'multicultural' description of Sweden as a culturally diverse society. And finally, if 'multiculturalism' is defined in a negative manner as the *absence* of specific integration requirements targeted at new arrivals and other non-citizens, the noteworthy Swedish reluctance to adopt such prerequisites makes it appropriate to characterize the country as 'a multicultural exception'.

References

Ahlvarsson, Lars (1967), 'Vi behöver en klar målsättning för svensk minoritetspolitik', *Fackföreningsrörelsen*, 47 (14–15).

Barry, Brian (2001), *Culture and Equality. An Egalitarian Critique of Multiculturalism*, Cambridge: Polity Press.

Bauhn, Per and Dilsa Demirbag-Sten (2010), *Till frihetens försvar. En kritik av den normativa multikulturalismen*, Stockholm: Norstedts.

Borevi, Karin (2002), *Välfärdsstaten i det mångkulturella samhället.* Uppsala: Acta Universitatis Upsaliensis.

Borevi, Karin (2010), 'Dimensions of citizenship: European integration policies from a Scandinavian perspective', in Bo Bengtsson, Per Strömblad and Ann-Helén Bay (eds), *Diversity, Inclusion and Citizenship in Scandinavia*, Newcastle-upon-Tyne: Cambridge Scholars Publishing.

Borevi, Karin (2012), 'Sweden: The Flagship of Multiculturalism', in Grete Brochmann and Anniken Hagelund, *Immigration Policy and the Scandinavian Welfare State*, Basingstoke: Palgrave Macmillan, pp. 25–96.

Borevi, Karin (in press), 'Understanding multiculturalism in Sweden', in Peter Kivisto and Östen Wahlbeck (eds), *Debating Nordic Multiculturalism*, Basingstoke: Palgrave Macmillan.

Carlbom, Aje (2003), *The Imagined versus the Real Other. Multiculturalism and the Representation of Muslims in Sweden*, Lund: Lund Monographs in Social Anthropology.

Castles, Stephen and Mark J. Miller (1993), *The Age of Migration. International Population Movements in the Modern World*, Basingstoke: Palgrave Macmillan.

Dahlström, Carl (2004), *Nästan välkomna. Invandrarpolitikens retorik och praktik*, Gothenburg: Statsvetenskapliga Institutionen.

Demker, Marie and Cecilia Malmström (1999), *Ingenmansland? Svensk immigrationspolitik i utrikespolitisk belysning*, Lund: Studentlitteratur.

Djuve, Anne Britt and Hanne Cecilie Kavli (2007), *Integrering i Danmark, Sverige og Norge. Felles utfordringer – like løsninger?*, Copenhagen: Nordiska ministerrådet.

Entzinger, Han (2003), 'The rise and fall of multiculturalism: The case of the Netherlands', in Christian Joppke and Ewa Morawska (eds), *Toward Assimilation and Citizenship: Immigrants in Liberal Nation-States*, Basingstoke: Palgrave Macmillan.

Fast, Sven-Bernhard, Caroline Krook, Peter Weiderud and Karin Wiborn (2010), 'Är vi beredda att älska juden och muslimen?', *Dagens Nyheter*, 11 September.

Favell, Adrian (1998), *Philosophies of Integration: Immigration and the Idea of Citizenship in France and Britain*, Basingstoke: Palgrave Macmillan.

Försvarsmakten (2011), *Instruktion för försvarsmakten. Uniformsbestämmelser 2009*. Available at http://www.forsvarsmakten.se/sv/Om-Forsvarsmakten/Dokument/Uniformsbestammelser/

Freeman, Gary P. (2004), 'Immigrant incorporation in Western democracies', *International Migration Review*, 38 (3), pp. 945–69.

Fryklund, Björn and Tomas Petersson (1989), '*Vi mot dom*'. *Det dubbla främlingsskapet i Sjöbo*, Lund: Lund University Press.

Government Bill 1968:142, *Angående riktlinjer för utlänningspolitiken m.m.*

Government Bill 1975/6:26, *Om riktlinjer för invandrar- och minoritetspolitiken m.m.*

Government Bill 1985/6:98, *Om invandrarpolitiken*.

Government Bill 1997/8, *Från invandrarpolitik till integrationspolitik*.

Green-Pedersen, Christoffer and Jesper Krogstrup (2008), 'Immigration as a political issue in Denmark and Sweden', *European Journal of Political Research*, 47 (5) (August), pp. 610–34.

Hammar, Tomas (1964), *Sverige åt svenskarna: invandringspolitik, utlänningskontroll och asylrätt 1900–1932* doctoral thesis, Stockholm University, Faculty of Social Sciences, Department of Political Science.

Hammar, Tomas (ed.) (1985), *European Immigration Policy: A Comparative Study*, Cambridge: Cambridge University Press.

Hannerz, Ulf (1981), 'Leva med mångfalden', in Kjell Öberg, Erland Bergman and Bo Swedin (eds), *Att leva med mångfalden. En antologi från Diskrimineringsutredningen*, Stockholm: Liber Förlag.

Hansen, Lars-Erik (2001), *Jämlikhet och valfrihet. En studie av den svenska invandrarpolitikens framväxt*, Stockholm: Almqvist & Wiksell International.

Högerpartiet (1968), *Minoritets- och invandringspolitik*, Stockholm: Högerpartiets kommitté för minoritets- och invandringsfrågor.

Hyltenstam, Kenneth and Veli Tuomela (1996), 'Hemspråksundervisningen', in Kenneth Hyltenstam (ed.), *Tvåspråkighet med förhinder? Invandrar- och minoritetsundervisning i Sverige*, Lund: Studentlitteratur.

Jacobsson, Bengt (1984), *Hur styrs förvaltningen? Myt och verklighet kring departementens styrning av ämbetsverken*, Lund: Studentlitteratur.

Johansson, Christina (2005), *Välkomna till Sverige? Svenska migrationspolitiska diskurser under 1900-talets andra hälft*, Malmö: Bokbox Förlag.

Johansson, Christina (2008), 'Svenska flyktingpolitiska visioner. Självbild eller verklighet?', in Urban Lundberg and Mattias Tydén (eds), *Sverigebilder. Det nationellas betydelse i politik och vardag*. Stockholm: Institutet för framtidsstudier.

Joppke, Christian (2004), 'The retreat of multiculturalism in the liberal state: theory and policy', *The British Journal of Sociology*, 55 (2), pp. 235–57.

—— (2007), 'Transformation of immigrant integration in Western Europe: Civic integration and antidiscrimination policies in the Netherlands, France, and Germany', *World Politics*, 59 (2) (January), pp. 243–73.

Koopmans, Ruud (2010), 'Trade-offs between equality and difference: Immigrant integration, multiculturalism and the welfare state in crossnational perspective', *Journal of Ethnic and Migration Studies*, 36, pp. 1–26.

Koopmans, Ruud, Paul Statham, Marco Giugni and Florence Passy (2005), *Contested Citizenship. Immigration and Cultural Diversity in Europe*, Minneapolis, MN: University of Minnesota Press.

Kymlicka, Will (2007), *Multicultural Odysseys: Navigating the New International Politics of Diversity*, Oxford: Oxford University Press.

Kymlicka, Will (2010), 'The rise and fall of multiculturalism? New debates on inclusion and accommodation in diverse societies', in Steven Vertovec and Susanne Wessendorf (eds), *The Multiculturalism Backlash: European Discourses, Policies and Practices*, London: Routledge.

Landsorganisationen (LO) [Swedish Trade Union Confederation] (1967), *PM angående LO:s syn på minoritetsfrågorna*. LO. Arbetsmarknadspolitiska enheten, vol. F 02:3, ARAB.

Lundh, Christer and Rolf Ohlsson (1994), *Från arbetskraftsimport till flyktinginvandring*, Stockholm: SNS.

Milani, Tommaso (2008), 'Language testing and citizenship: A language ideological debate in Sweden', *Language in Society* 37 (1), pp. 27–59.

Mörkenstam, Ulf (1999), *'Om Lapparnes privilegier'. Föreställningar om samiskhet i svensk samepolitik 1883–1997*, Stockholm: Stockholm Studies in Politics.

Nilsson, Åsa and Ingvar Svanberg (1997), 'Religiös slakt', in Pia Karlsson and Ingvar Svanberg (eds), *Religionsfrihet i Sverige. Om möjligheten att leva som troende*. Lund: Studentlitteratur.

Okin, Susan Moller (1999), 'Is multiculturalism bad for women?' in Joshua Cohen, Matthew Howard and Martha C. Nussbaum (eds), *Is Multiculturalism Bad for Women?*, Princeton, NJ: Princeton University Press.

Parliamentary Committee on Social Insurance 1985/6:20. *Om invandrarpolitiken*. Available at http://www.riksdagen.se/sv/Dokument-Lagar/Utskottens-dokument/Yttranden/om-invandrarpolitiken-prop-1_G905KrU5/

Parliamentary records 1975:80. *Riktlinjer för invandrar- och minoritetspolitiken, m. m.* Available at http://www.riksdagen.se/sv/Dokument-Lagar/Kammaren/Protokoll/Riksdagens-protokoll-197580_FY0980/

Parliamentary records 2002/03:79. *Integrationspolitik*. Available at http://www.riksdagen.se/sv/Dokument-Lagar/Utskottens-dokument/Betankanden/Arenden/200203/SFU7/

Phillips, Anne (2007), *Multiculturalism without Culture*, Princeton, NJ: Princeton University Press.

Rikspolisstyrelsen (2011), *Rikspolisstyrelsens föreskrifter och allmänna råd om Polisens uniformer*. FAP 798-1. Available at http://www.polisen.se/Global/www%20och%20Intrapolis/FAP/FAP798_1_RPSFS2011_1.pdf

Román, Henrik (1993), *Folkhemmet och det hemlösa folket. Om svensk zigenarpolitik 1954–1969*, Uppsala: Centrum för multietnisk forskning.

Román, Henrik (1994), *En invandrarpolitisk oppositionell. Debattören David Schwarz syn på svensk invandrarpolitik åren 1964–1993*, Uppsala: Centrum för multietnisk forskning.

Roth, Hans-Ingvar (2001), 'Det multikulturella Sverige', in Kurt Almqvist and Kay Glans (eds), *Den svenska framgångssagan?*, Stockholm: Fischer & Co.

Rydgren, Jens (2005), *Från skattemissnöje till etnisk nationalism: högerpopulism och parlamentarisk högerextremism i Sverige*, Lund: Studentlitteratur.

Sayed, Mosa (2009), *Islam och arvsrätt i det mångkulturella Sverige: en internationellt privaträttslig och jämförande studie*, doctoral thesis, Uppsala University, Humanities and Social Sciences, Faculty of Law, Department of Law.

Schwarz, David (1971), *Svensk invandrar- och minoritetspolitik 1945–68*, Stockholm: Prisma.

Severin, Malin (2011), *Språkkravet som kom av sig. En studie om integrationspolitiska strategier och splittringar inom Folkpartiet Liberalerna*, Master's thesis, Uppsala University, Statsvetenskapliga institutionen.

Skolverket (2012), *Elever med heltäckande slöja i skolan.* Available at http://www.skolverket.se/lagar-och-regler/juridisk-vagledning/elever-med-heltackande-sloja-i-skolan-1.165928

Socialdemokratiska arbetarpartiet [Social Democratic Party] (1968), Proceedings from the 1968 Party Congress. Available at Labour Movement Archives and Library, http://www.abark.se/

SOU [Statens offentliga utredningar] 1974: 69. *Invandrarutredningen 3. Invandrarna och minoriteterna: huvudbetänkande.* Stockholm: LiberFörlag/Allmänna förl.

SOU 1984: 55. *I rätt riktning. Etniska relationer i Sverige. Slutbetänkande av diskrimineringsutredningen*, Stockholm: Fritzes.

SOU 1984: 58. *Invandrar- och minoritetspolitiken. Slutbetänkande av Invandrarpolitiska kommittén*, Stockholm: Fritzes.

SOU 1999: 34. *Svenskt medborgarskap. Slutbetänkande av 1997 års medborgarskapskommitté*, Stockholm: Fritzes.

SOU 2010: 16. *Sverige för nyanlända. Värden, välfärdsstat, vardagsliv. Delbetänkande av Utredningen om samhällsorientering för nyanlända invandrare*, Stockholm: Fritzes.

Svanberg, Ingvar and Mattias Tydén (1992), *Tusen år av invandring: en svensk kulturhistoria*, Stockholm: Gidlund.

Svensk författningssamling (SFS) 1974:152. *Regeringsformen.*

Svensk författningssamling (SFS) 2008:567. *Diskrimineringslag.*

Svenska Dagbladet (2008), *Fp kräver kurs för medborgarskap*, 11 March.

Svenska Dagbladet (2010), *Björklund vill förbjuda burka och niqab i skolan*, 4 August.

Sverigedemokraterna (2011), *Sverigedemokraternas principprogram 2011*. Available at https://sverigedemokraterna.se/vara-asikter/principprogram/

Vertovec, Steven and Susanne Wessendorf (2010), 'Introduction', in Steven Vertovec and Susanne Wessendorf, *The Multiculturalism Backlash: European Discourses, Policies and Practices*, London: Routledge.

Wickström, Mats (2012), 'The difference white ethnics made: The multiculturalist turn of Sweden in comparison to the cases of Canada and Denmark', in Heidi Vad Jønsson, Elizabeth Onasch, Saara Pellander and Mats Wickström (eds), *Migrations and Welfare States: Policies, Discourses and Institutions*, Helsinki: Nordwel Studies in Historical Welfare State Research, 3.

Wikan, Unni (2004), 'Deadly distrust: honor killings and Swedish multiculturalism', in Russell Hardin (ed.), *Distrust*, New York: Russell Sage Foundation, pp. 192–204.

Part III

Multicultural Societies without Multiculturalism?

Public Debates and Public Opinion on Multiculturalism in Germany

Martina Wasmer

Introduction

Germany has never stood as the prototype of a multicultural society and it does not do so now. But empirical assessments of the political practice of cultural diversity management indicate that, over time, Germany has adopted more multicultural policies. In 2010 Germany's score in the multiculturalism policy index (MIPEX; see Banting and Kymlicka 2012), measuring the presence (or absence) of a range of policies intended to recognize, support or accommodate diversity, is 2.5 out of a maximum of 8 – a still low score albeit higher than in 2000. Koopmans et al. (2005) see Germany's position in their two-dimensional model of citizenship (presented in Chapter 2 of this book) as no longer close to the ethnic-assimilationist pole where it had been until the mid-1990s but, on both axes – individual citizenship rights and differential group rights – as near the middle.

At the same time, in Germany as well as in other European states with long-established commitments to multiculturalism, in public and political debate, the controversy about the right way to deal with ethnic and cultural diversity in society was growing more intense. In Germany it culminated in 2010 with German Chancellor Angela Merkel's declaration that attempts to build a multicultural society had 'utterly failed'. A bestselling book appeared that same year, Thilo Sarrazin's *Germany Does Away with Itself* (*Deutschland schafft sich ab*) which blamed Muslims for dragging Germany down. Its provocative argument divided the nation. So is there a common 'sceptical turn' against policies recognizing cultural diversity? Is Germany turning away from multiculturalism before actually having reached it?

This chapter examines recent trends in different areas – policies, public debate and public opinion – and looks for hints as to whether this is the case or not. After providing background information on immigration to Germany, I review the laws and policies related to diversity that have recently been introduced. In order to ascertain the degree of public and political support for the multicultural model, I consider the public debates of the last decades as well as changes in attitudes since the mid-1990s.

Public opinion on multiculturalism is chosen as the main focus of this chapter for several reasons. Although policy, laws and formal regulations are of major relevance, much depends on the views held by the majority. In everyday life prejudices and xenophobic attitudes may manifest themselves in subtle signs of disrespect, in overt discriminatory practices or even in aggressive behaviour. Additionally, interaction effects may follow, for example when public support is needed to put formally adopted measures into practice.

From a theoretical perspective, a degree of congruency between public policy change and public opinion change should be expected, since in a liberal democratic system policy should be responsive to public opinion, and public opinion should react to changes in policy and political debates. Finally, there is a more pragmatic reason for the focus on public opinion: the availability of time series data from replicative surveys to identify time trends in support for or opposition to multiculturalism. This stands in contrast to the monitoring of policies and debates regarding multiculturalism which has to contend with more ambiguity. For this reason, repeated attitude measurements from the German General Social Survey (ALLBUS; see p. 176) can help us obtain a clearer picture of developments in Germany with regard to multiculturalism. If the empirical results reveal widespread opposition against multicultural policies then, as Crepaz (2006: 97) puts it, public opinion would be 'like the proverbial canary in the coalmines', indicating danger.

Foreigners and immigrants in Germany

On a descriptive level, Germany is obviously a 'polyethnic society' (Kymlicka 1995) characterized by cultural diversity that is predominantly immigration-induced. There have been several waves of foreign immigration (Münz and Ulrich 2003). In 1955 the first recruitment agreement with Italy marked the starting point of a large wave of labour migration to West Germany. Foreigners from the Mediterranean were recruited as *Gastarbeiter* (guestworkers) for particular workplaces, predominantly low-skilled jobs in the industrial sector. The intention was to implement a 'rotation model' of temporary migration, with migrants working in Germany for a period of one to two years and then returning home. After labour recruitment stopped in 1973, foreign immigration continued at a lower rate; it comprised mainly family reunifications. In the late 1980s and early 1990s the number of asylum seekers and refugees rose significantly, reaching a peak in 1992 when – all types of immigration taken together – a record high of more than 1.5 million immigrants came to Germany. In the following years the number of immigrants declined, mainly due to more restrictions on asylum and ethnic Germans. The result was even negative net migration in 2008 and 2009. Since then it has again increased, primarily because of rising numbers of migrants from Eastern European countries (Federal Statistical Office 2011a; Bundesministerium des Innern 2011).

A feature unique to Germany is the large-scale immigration of ethnic Germans. Their migration was initially privileged but, since 1990, has been more carefully screened (Zimmermann 1999) as the stakes were high: German citizenship was extended to ethnic Germans upon their arrival. This special case that entails an understanding of German identity (Joppke and Rosenhek 2002) is not the subject of this chapter on German multiculturalism.

Several factors account for the proportion of foreign nationals in Germany increasing from about 1 per cent in 1960 to 9 per cent of the total population in 2010 (Federal Statistical Office 2011b). Immigration rates are among the highest in the world; return migration is well below the originally intended level; *jus sanguinis* (up to 2000) meant that children born in Germany of foreign parents had difficulties naturalizing; low naturalization rates generally created a statistically high number of 'foreigners'. Today nearly 20 per cent of the population (Federal Statistical Office 2011b) has a 'migration background', that is, made up of those who (1) immigrated to Germany after 1950; (2) were born in Germany as foreigners; and (3) have at least one parent who immigrated to Germany after 1950 or was born in Germany as a foreigner. In the eastern part of Germany (the former East Germany state) the share of foreigners is much lower, below 2.5 per cent in most regions. The large majority of immigrants live today in the urban areas of western Germany (Münz and Ulrich 2003; Bundesministerium des Innern 2011).

By far the largest group of foreigners in Germany are Turks (about 24 per cent of the foreign population). Other important regions of origin are the former Yugoslavia, Italy and, increasingly in recent years, Poland. The vast majority of the population with a migration background, however, is made up of former guestworkers and their families and descendants. The mean time of residence in Germany of this group is nearly twenty-five years. Nevertheless, they overall still have a lower educational and occupational status than the native German population, but to a lesser degree in the second and third generation (Bender and Seifert 2003). A disproportionate number of those with a migration background are unemployed and dependent on welfare benefits. Particularly important for the issue of multiculturalism is the fact that, owing to the high share of Muslim immigrants, Islam has become an essential part of the new cultural diversity in Germany.

Multicultural policy in Germany

Up until now, there has never been an explicit multicultural agenda in Germany. Generally, immigration-related policy in Germany is, as O'Brien (2011: 1) has stated, 'controversial, contended and therefore highly fluid' and consequently it 'defies easy categorization into neat typologies'. This incoherency in multiculturalism during the past decade may be attributed in part to the complicated balance of political power during this period. The absence of a broad consensus about the best way to deal with immigration-induced diversity made it necessary to reach compromises, especially during the Grand Coalition from 2005 to 2009, and to half-heartedly accept 'path dependence' after the changes of government in 2005 and 2009. In short, pragmatic policies became inescapable. In addition, the federal structure of Germany – with states at the subnational level being responsible for educational and cultural affairs – hampered the elaboration of a comprehensive policy programme.

Even in the absence of a coherent, explicitly multicultural policy approach, the management of migration-related ethnic diversity may include elements of a de facto multicultural policy. According to Castles (2004: 429), multiculturalism as public policy has two key dimensions: recognition of cultural diversity and social equality for members of minorities. Koopmans et al. (2005) developed a set of empirical indicators for these two dimensions and compared five Western European countries, among them Germany, at three points in time; 1980, 1990 and 2002. As already noted, they concluded that between 1990 and 2002 Germany moved away from an assimilationist conception, 'trailing behind' Britain and the Netherlands 'on the path of multiculturalism' (Koopmans 2007: 72). My interest is, then, to focus on recent temporal trends that shed light on the question of whether Germany is still moving in this direction.

Laws and regulations on nationality acquisition are a crucial dimension of multicultural policies. For the individual migrant, citizenship means access to civil rights. Additionally, the concepts of nationhood underlying citizenship laws are of extraordinary symbolic importance, shaping national identity, definitions of 'we' and 'us'. Thus, the new Citizenship Law of 2000, supplementing the traditional principle of descent (bloodlines) with the *jus soli* principle, was a remarkable change of political practice in Germany. All children born in Germany now automatically receive German citizenship if at least one of their parents has lived in Germany for at least eight years. They are entitled to dual citizenship but have to decide whether to retain German nationality or the nationality of their parents between the ages of eighteen and twenty-three. Also, the number of years of residence in Germany required before immigrants can request naturalization was reduced. With this liberalization of citizenship regulations Germany has moved away from the former ethnic conception of citizenship towards a more civic-territorial one.

No additional progress has been made since then on citizenship regulations. The naturalization rate in Germany remains very low compared to other European countries. A key impediment to higher numbers is the fact that dual citizenship is still not officially recognized and is only a transitional status. In general, those applying for German citizenship are not allowed to retain their old nationality. Although there are exceptions to this rule, they do not apply to the important group of applicants of Turkish descent. In 2007 stricter language requirements for naturalization were introduced and since 2008 applicants have had to prove knowledge of the German legal and social system and cultural background by passing a standardized citizenship test.

These changes point to a notion of citizenship not as a *means* of integration but as the *end point* of a completed integration process (Van Oers 2010). With the coming into force of the Immigration Act in 2005, integration courses comprising 600 hours of German language lessons and 45 hours of civic instruction were introduced. Attendance is obligatory for people applying for a residence permit who do not show minimal proficiency in German. Moreover, settled migrants dependent on welfare may be required to register for these courses (Bundesministerium des Innern 2012). The stated purpose of integration courses is 'helping immigrants ... in their efforts to become integrated', thus ensuring 'that immigrants have equal opportunities and the chance to participate in all areas, especially social, economic and cultural life' (BMI 2012a). According to Joppke and Morawska (2003), the rise of civic integration programmes indicates a shift towards the logic of assimilation and away from the multicultural paradigm.

A steadily more restrictive approach to migration was also exemplified in the tougher rules for family reunification introduced in 2007. Their intention was to promote integration from the outset and to combat forced marriages. Immigrating spouses now must be at least eighteen and pass a compulsory language test abroad before they can join their partner in Germany. Exemptions are made for other EU citizens, citizens of other privileged Western nations and highly qualified immigrants. They raise doubts about the non-discriminatory character of this regulation. Because of its 'pursuing liberal goals with illiberal means', it may deserve the label 'repressive liberalism' (Joppke 2007).

Apart from the right to citizenship, little has changed since 2002 with respect to policies aiming to promote equal individual rights. EU Anti-discrimination Directives were subsumed into national legislation in 2006 but the number of lawsuits has remained modest and is mainly related to discrimination based on disabilities, gender or age (Peucker 2010). On the other hand, foreign residents still largely enjoy the same social benefits as Germans. Reliance on welfare, however, still endangers their legal status (residence permit, naturalization) and jeopardizes prospects for immigration of family members. As for political rights, voting for foreign residents is restricted only to EU nationals and only at the local level. But progress has been made on the political representation of immigrants: 'Integration Summits' and 'Islam Conferences' have been organized by the federal government with participants from immigrant and Muslim organizations.

Measures have been taken to improve immigrants' prospects in the educational system and labour market, for example through special training programmes. Different dimensions of multiculturalism are combined in such policies, which strive for equality and to accommodate group differences. But these measures often imply a 'deficit perspective' on immigrants, in contrast to the positive view of diversity that would be characteristic for a multicultural approach. German language acquisition as a means to resolving problems with education and employment is regarded as the cornerstone of integration. Accordingly, in some cases coercive measures have been taken requiring pupils to speak only German at school and not merely in the classroom but also during breaks. Affirmative action programmes such as quotas or preferential hiring schemes are not part of German integration policy. However, projects to recruit young people from migrant backgrounds for careers in public administration and efforts to enhance the transferability of educational qualifications acquired abroad have been intensified in the last few years.

Over the last decades, the integration of immigrants has been understood primarily as structural integration while the issues of cultural and religious diversity have received less attention. Yet notable changes are apparent regarding the accommodation of religious differences. The recurring Islam Conference has served as a basis for helping integrate the Muslim community into the German system of church-state relations. Islamic religious instruction in German schools has been introduced. In 2011 the first centre for Islamic theology started to train teachers for Islamic religious education and imam responsibilities.

On the other hand, in recent years one half of the states of Germany (among them the most populous and those with the largest Muslim populations) have enacted legislation that bans the Islamic headscarf for teachers – a reflection of the 'principle of neutrality' that has to be observed at schools. Only legislation in Lower Saxony and the city states of Bremen and Berlin treat all religions in the same way, in accordance with a Federal Constitutional Court decision. Other states' bodies of law privilege Judaeo-Christian religions (Berghahn 2009).

To sum up, the overall view of recent 'multicultural' policies shows an unclear picture with no identifiable comprehensive multicultural policy. Policies at the core of the multiculturalist approach – recognizing and supporting immigrants in maintaining and expressing their distinct identities and practices (Banting and Kymlicka 2006) – are not key elements of German integration policy. Phil Triadafilopoulos (2012) worries that the undesired side effects of Germany's integration policy (the 'preoccupation with "problem" groups, above all undereducated, unemployed and potentially threatening young men and putatively embattled immigrant women') might foster an atmosphere of distrust and disrespect towards immigrants. The policy may also lead to a negative definition of integration as a 'prophylactic' process that seeks to pre-empt problems and to guard the majority of society against dangers caused by immigration. Finally, Germany's integration policy increasingly gives the impression that the responsibility for successful integration lies with the immigrants themselves. Despite official rhetoric that integration is a 'two-way process' that 'requires acceptance by the majority popula- tion' (BMI 2012b), little is done to increase the majority's acceptance of culturally different groups. This would entail a positive recogni- tion of diversity that would be a clear sign of multiculturalism.

Public debate on multiculturalism

The term 'multiculturalism' is rarely used in German public debates. 'Multicultural society' usually refers to the existence of a multiplicity of cultures, and not a particular public policy approach. In Germany, the term 'multicultural' during the late 1970s and the 1980s circu- lated in church, union, social workers' and teachers' circles. The Green Party, especially its leader Daniel Cohn-Bendit, Christian Democratic Union (CDU) intellectual Heiner Geißler and groups within the Social Democratic Party (SPD) were early proponents of a multicultural society (Kraus and Schönwälder 2006; Faist 1994). The catchy abbreviation *multikulti*, which soon became popular, sounded fresh, modern and easy-going. Public appreciation of the concept tended to remain superficial, often folkloric, equating it with pizza and doner kebabs. Nowadays, *multikulti* and terms such as 'dreams/dreamers', 'illusion' or 'naïve' are frequently mentioned in the same breath, signifying its bad reputation.

Although current usage of 'multicultural' or *multikulti* signals the problems that Germany's multiculturalism is faced with, the term is seldom explicitly at the centre of public debates over relevant issues. Three key areas of debate can be identified (although they are closely interwoven): (1) immigration to Germany; (2) the multicultural reality in Germany – perceptions and assessments of positive and, mostly, negative aspects of ethnic diversity; and (3) ideas about how to deal with this multicultural reality.

The first step in adopting multiculturalism as a way to accom- modate diversity is to recognize the fact of cultural pluralism in a society. In Germany, official political discourse for decades not only ignored but denied the fact that cultural diversity was here to stay. In particular, the right-of-centre parties CDU and CSU continued until the 1990s to insist that Germany was 'not an immigration country'. At the same time, restricting immigration was a central political concern. At the end of the 1980s and during the early 1990s when Germany faced very large immigration flows (with high proportions of refugees and asylum seekers), there were two camps in the German debate on immigration. One, which included the governing Conservatives and the tabloid press, claimed that Germany was approaching breaking point, the limit of what it could absorb, conveyed by the slogan 'The boat is full'. The other camp, among them churches, trade unions, NGOs and the Greens, advanced humanitarian and human rights arguments (Wengeler 2006). The assertion that many asylum seekers were abusing the social assistance system of the German welfare state was emphasized by conservative parties and, even more so, by populist parties on the extreme right, such as the Republikaner. Asylum seekers were seen as problematic both because they are culturally different and because they represent economic competitors (Faist 1994).

Heated discussions marked the run-up to the asylum compromise of 1993, but more pragmatic economic considerations stressing the advantages of immigration for the functioning of the economy prevailed (Wengeler 2006). The idea of the foreign workforce as an economic factor that could be adjusted to fit the needs of German society had informed the rotation model of guestworker employment. More recently, immigration has again been seen as a necessity, but this time recruitment of high-skilled labour is the key consideration. Nevertheless, many Germans have trouble accepting immigration as a solution to the country's labour needs. The so-called Green Card initiative – a regulation allowing for work permits for highly qualified foreign workers in information and communication technology – was repudiated in 2000 by the then leading candidate of the CDU for the state government of Nord-Rhein Westphalia, Jürgen Rüttgers. He argued that Germany should invest in education and training instead of importing high-tech specialists from India, coining the slogan *Kinder statt Inder* ('children instead of Indians') – a mantra with which to stir up anti-foreigner sentiment. In 2011 Horst Seehofer, leader of the Bavarian Conservatives, called for a halt to immigration from 'alien cultures' on the grounds that Germany does not need any more Turkish or Arab immigrants because they do not integrate as well as others.

Seehofer's declaration leads us to an important thread in Germany's discourse on 'multiculturalism', reflecting the effects of the new ethnic diversity on society. On the one hand, concern has been expressed in the socio-economic realm about tensions resulting from the formation of a new lower class in society caused by migration. On the other hand, cultural differences are said to induce problems by undermining social capital and social cohesion. Over the last decades, cultural concerns appear to prevail, either because they are considered more urgent or because they are seen as the root cause of most of the other problems.

Today the debate focuses mainly on the failure of integration, illustrated by immigrants allegedly living in 'parallel societies', that is, closed off from the majority society, lacking German language skills and customs and obeying rules of their own. Especially with regard to Muslim immigrants, these rules are perceived as backward and narrow-minded, oriented towards traditional principles of honour and submission. The withdrawal into secluded ethnic communities is frequently considered the cause for the often poor educational achievement of immigrant children. Additionally, Muslim-dominated residential areas are suspected to be breeding grounds for violence and extremism (Kraus and Schönwälder 2006).

Ausländerkriminalität – literally foreigner criminality – has been a major topic of public debate for a long time. Wide support for the expulsion of criminal offenders born and raised in Germany has been illustrative of the majority's ethnic understanding of national belonging. Today, the high relevance attributed to religious-cultural factors, Islam in particular, is particularly significant. Since 9/11, Muslim fundamentalists have been seen as posing a serious terrorist threat. Outdated parenting styles in Muslim families are supposed to be the main reason for young male Muslims' (alleged) proneness to violence. In the tabloid press or readers' letters, incidents of 'honour killings' are cited as undisputable proof of the problematic nature of Islam in general.

The highly publicized incidents of 'honour killings', the practices of forced marriage described in bestselling books (such as Necla Kelek's *Die fremde Braut*, 2005) and debates about family violence and the Islamic headscarf have given rise to the gender dimension in Islam. Generally, it is Islam that has moved to the centre of public debates on multiculturalism. According to some opinion leaders, including Henryk M. Broder, Ralph Giordano, Necla Kelek and feminist Alice Schwarzer, Islam is inherently illiberal and anti-democratic, so it follows that pious Muslims constitute a threat to 'Western civilization' itself (O'Brien 2011).

The debate about the allegedly adverse economic and social effects of immigration on German society 'has become increasingly intense, shallow and aggressive', claimed Klaus J. Bade, a leading German researcher on immigration and one of the few dissenting voices to the pessimistic analysis of the situation, in a TV documentary.[1] A key reason for this is the impact of Thilo Sarrazin's *Germany Does Away With Itself*, in 2010. In it the author, a member at the time of the Social Democratic Party and of the Deutsche Bundesbank executive board, argued that Muslim immigrants were unwilling or unable to integrate. In blaming Muslims for all the problems of integration, Sarrazin went further than his predecessors by attributing cultural and social differences mainly to genetic disposition. According to Sarrazin, German society as a whole is inevitably becoming less intelligent because of the higher fertility rate among intellectually inferior Muslims.

The book evoked strong reactions. Most politicians immediately criticized it as racist, but it received massive public support among the German population. To the surprise of liberal intellectual circles in media and politics, respectable middle-class citizens shouted down Sarrazin's critics in public discussions and readings, and acclaimed Sarrazin as a hero for saying 'what everybody really thinks'. The book was seen as a taboo breaker and set off a wave of media coverage. Nearly all voices dismissed Sarrazin's 'genetic theory' as 'nonsense'. But the identifiable main opposing camps accused each other of denying the existence of serious problems because of blind political correctness or naivety and stirring up xenophobic tendencies with inappropriate generalizations and alarmism. One potential development arising from Sarrazin's success was the fostering of populist tendencies. As Habermas put it in an op ed article in *The New York Times* (2010), 'The usual stereotypes are being flushed out of the bars and onto the talk shows, and they are echoed by mainstream politicians who want to capture potential voters who are otherwise drifting off toward the right'.

The Sarrazin debate was typical of German discussions of multiculturalism in that it was the multicultural reality, not the multicultural concept or policies based on it, that was the main focus. As long as the facts of immigration and diversity were being officially denied, political discussions had largely been limited to repeated demands to implement *any* policy concerning these neglected areas. In the 1990s regulation of immigration was the central issue of public discourse while since then integration policy has become the centre of political attention (Heckmann 2010). There is a broad consensus on the general goal of 'integration', even if multiple definitions of it exist. Increasingly it is conceived as a process of adaptation lying primarily with immigrants, with the state providing necessary resources and structural supports. By contrast, appeals to the German majority to abandon prejudice against and create a welcoming atmosphere for immigrants so as to facilitate their integration have become less common (Wengeler 2006).

The degree of adaptation by immigrants to German society is highly contentious. Is it sufficient when immigrants accept the German constitution and acquire fundamental cultural, especially language, skills? Or are immigrants supposed to adopt the values and customs of the majority culture? The latter idea has repeatedly been the subject of political debates. In 2000 Friedrich Merz, then a leading Conservative politician, demanded that foreigners be prepared to integrate themselves into the German *Leitkultur*, or leading culture. This statement, giving German national identity priority over the 'multicultural society' advocated by the government of Social Democrats and Greens, came under fire, not least for implying some sort of German cultural supremacy. In 2006 the controversial concept of *Leitkultur* was re-introduced into the debate on the integration of immigrants by CDU politician Volker Kauder. In 2010 – after Sarrazin's book was published – the Christian Democrats adopted a resolution that Germany was based on a 'Judaeo-Christian heritage' which should be considered as the country's *Leitkultur*. The message was clear: *Leitkultur* should be understood primarily as a political tool in the struggle against Islam. Critics of the concept argue that the underlying idea of a distinct ethnically defined national identity, based on history, language, descent and culture, neither corresponds to social reality in modern societies, which are characterized by increasing pluralism, nor is the most effective basis of social cohesion. But alternative models – Habermas' 'constitutional patriotism' or human rights as the basis of an enlightened multiculturalism (Bielefeldt 2007) – are infrequently discussed in public.

Of particular concern over the last years has been the fact that relations between Germans and Turks have deteriorated. Repeated demands have been made by the right-wing political camp supported by an unlikely partner, groups concerned with women's rights, that Muslim immigrants should stop adhering to customs and traditions incompatible with modern Western culture. In turn, Turks have resented restrictive, exclusionary German policies, such as the language test taken abroad for immigrating spouses of Turks, as well as the current German government's opposition to Turkey's EU accession. Controversies about the building of mosques in German cities exacerbated this worsening of relations. Mosques are a visible sign of cultural diversity and of Muslims becoming an established part of German society. Consequently, when right-wing populist groups such as Pro-Cologne and Pro-NRW organize against the building of mosques and even win seats on local councils, this evokes a feeling of rejection within the local Muslim community. To be sure, public reactions to the building of mosques are mixed.

An additional factor affecting relations between Turks and Germans are the visits to Germany by Turkish Prime Minister Recep Tayyip Erdoğan. He urged Turkish immigrants to resist assimilation, which he called a crime against humanity, and to teach their children to speak and read Turkish before German (SpiegelOnline International 2011a, b). Many politicians criticized what they viewed as Erdogan's inflammatory rhetoric and his inaccurate description of Germany's integration policy. Many ordinary Germans watching television coverage of crowds of over 10,000 people waving Turkish flags and applauding Erdogan's speeches saw this as proof that Turkish immigrants and their descendants lacked a feeling of belonging to Germany and showed no willingness to integrate in the host society.

In November 2011 a series of murders committed by a Zwickau-based neo-Nazi terror cell calling itself the National Socialist Underground (NSU) was uncovered. Between 2000 and 2006 the killings of nine small business owners of Turkish and Greek origin, as well as a bomb attack in an immigrant neighbourhood in Cologne, shocked the German public. Authorities were accused of failing to take the threat from right-wing extremists seriously enough. The investigators, consistent with common prejudices, had assumed that the murders were motivated by family disputes or criminal gang rivalries. Learning that the murders were carried out by the NSU evoked a sense of collective shame. Chancellor Merkel described the serial murders as a 'disgrace for our country'. Media across the political spectrum published articles calling for tolerance and respect, asking whether xenophobic fears had been stirred up over the last decades, criticizing integration policies seeking to appeal to German voters and depicting immigrants as a security risk (SpiegelOnline International 2012). In contrast to the Sarrazin debate, the majority blamed itself and not immigrants for the affair.

Another factor that might have consequences for multiculturalism is the European debt crisis. The euro crisis distracted – at least for a time – public attention away from the challenges of cultural diversity. Many ordinary citizens in Germany were unhappy that their country had to pay the largest share of the bail-out of Greece. It is conceivable, therefore, that foreigners abroad may take on the role of scapegoats from the immigrants living within Germany. As the 'foreigners inside' are in several respects – as taxpayers, citizens potentially affected by social security cuts, and so on – in the same boat, lines of conflict may shift. Major changes to immigration and integration policies as a response to the European debt crisis seem unlikely. However, given the EU principle of the free movement of labour, a new migration wave from southern Europe can be expected. If the skills of these immigrants match the needs of Germany's economy, prospective immigrants from culturally distinct, non-EU countries may become disadvantaged.

Public opinion on multiculturalism

We cannot infer from public policy and public debate alone the reception accorded to immigrants and their descendants. Much depends on the views held by the majority population. In the remaining part of this chapter I examine public opinion on multiculturalism. The main questions addressed include how widespread attitudes are supporting multiculturalism today, and how these attitudes have changed in recent decades. Because of space constraints, I do not consider the issue of causal determinants of attitudes.

The analysis relies mainly on attitudinal data collected by the ALLBUS (Allgemeine Bevölkerungsumfrage der Sozialwissenschaften) survey programme (Koch and Wasmer 2004; Terwey 2000). ALLBUS is oriented toward academic users and sets very high methodological standards, especially with respect to sampling. It is based on repeated multi-thematic face-to-face surveys. Every two years since 1980, a representative cross-section of the population – the number of respondents varies between 3,000 and 3,500 – has been surveyed, using both constant and variable questions. In 1996 and 2006, ALLBUS included a topical module focusing on attitudes towards ethnic minorities. The survey thus allows us to compare people's views before and after the important changes of political practice in Germany initiated by the government of Social Democrats and Greens.

Based on an understanding of multiculturalism that combines the two key principles of social equality and participation, and cultural recognition I selected data for analysis concerning the following issues: (1) appreciation of cultural diversity; (2) support of state

Table 8.1 German views on cultural diversity in 1996 and 2006

		'Foreigners enrich German culture'		
		disagree	neutral	agree
'One feels like a stranger in one's own country because of foreigners'	disagree	Neither positive nor negative 1996: 41.1% 2006: 32.8%		Predominantly positive 1996: 30.0% 2006: 33.3%
	neutral			
	agree	Predominantly negative 1996: 22.6% 2006: 24.5%		Ambivalent 1996: 6.3% 2006: 9.4%

ALLBUS 1996 and 2006, own calculations. Note that n=3246 (1996) and n=3099 (2006).

action that promotes equal rights for foreigners and recognizes cultural diversity; (3) demands for cultural adaptation; and (4) social contacts with and social distance towards foreigners.[2]

Two items in ALLBUS 1996 and 2006 raise the issue of cultural diversity in general terms. One is formulated to place immigration-induced cultural diversity in a positive light. The proportion of German respondents[3] who agreed[4] that foreigners enrich German culture rose from 36 per cent in 1996 to 43 per cent in 2006. Paradoxically, when the issue is raised in negative terms, a similar increase can be observed, indicating the high degree of ambiguity in public opinion. In 2006 more interviewees agreed with the notion 'With so many foreigners in Germany, one feels increasingly like a stranger in one's own country' than in 1996. It seems as though Germans have developed more clear-cut attitudes towards cultural diversity. Whilst in the earlier data 41 per cent agreed neither with the positive item nor with the negative one, only 33 per cent did so in 2006 (see Table 8.1). One-third of the respondents held predominantly positive views on cultural diversity but approximately one out of four reported feelings of alienation, which were not counterbalanced by a positive valuation of cultural diversity.

If we turn the focus to equal rights (for a detailed analysis of the 1996 data, see Wasmer and Koch 2000), the German population makes clear distinctions between different groups of foreigners, and this is becoming increasingly the case. The statement that Turkish residents should have the same rights as Germans *in every respect* was supported by 37 per cent in 2006. By contrast, a clear majority of 59 per cent favours parity of treatment for Italians who, as EU citizens, already enjoy a far superior legal status anyway.

ALLBUS questions concerning concrete policy measures designed to promote particular forms of equality for foreigners living in Germany address the issue of social security (the same entitlement to welfare benefits and other social security benefits), opportunities for exercising political influence (the right to vote in local elections) and cultural issues (including the question 'Should there be Islamic religious instruction in state schools, should there only be Christian religious instruction or should there be no religious instruction at all in state schools?').[5] In 2006 between 43 and 48 per cent of German respondents expressed their willingness to grant parity of rights to immigrants (see Table 8.2).

The issue of Islamic religious education in public schools is a special case. In 2006 32 per cent stated that state schools should provide religious instruction for both Christian and Muslim children, while 33 per cent (mostly respondents from the eastern part of Germany) responded that they should provide no religious instruction at all. From an equal treatment perspective, one could therefore argue that a large majority shows no inclination to privilege the Christian religion. However, public schools in Germany actually do provide regular religious instruction for the main Christian religions, and it is not clear how interviewees who prefer no religious instruction at all would have answered a forced choice question with the other two response options. Thus, it seems appropriate to narrow the focus to those who do not entirely reject religious education. We find that about half of these respondents support Islamic religious education, slightly fewer in 2006 than in 1996.

An interesting result is the discrepancy between a generally positive attitude to equality of rights and attitudes towards equal treatment in specific spheres of life. Many of those who were strongly committed (scale points 6 or 7) to equal rights for Turkish residents *in every respect* nevertheless opposed specific rights. This holds true especially with respect to two concrete political measures which have been subjects under discussion: the local election voting right is opposed by 19 per cent of those who are generally strongly in favour of equality of rights; in turn, 22 per cent state that there should only be Christian religious instruction in state schools despite their strong agreement to 'equal rights in every respect'. This result is reminiscent of the 'principle-implementation-gap' described by Schuman et al.

Table 8.2 Public support in Germany for multiculturalism: 2006 compared to 1996

Concepts and Items (responses classified as multiculturalist position)	Responses in favour of multiculturalist positions Proportion in 2006 (%)	Responses in favour of multiculturalist positions Change since 1996 (percentage points)
Cultural diversity perception		
Cultural enrichment (agree)	42.8	+ 6.5
Stranger in own land (disagree)	52.6	− 4.4
General equal rights		
for Turks (agree)	36.7	+ 1.6
for Italians (agree)	59.2	+ 5.8
Policy support		
Same welfare benefits (agree)	47.4	+ 0.3
Local voting rights (agree)	42.5	+ 7.1
Religious instruction ('also Islamic', if any)*	47.6	− 3.5
Dual nationality (agree)	31.6	− 3.1
Demands for cultural adaptation		
Lifestyle adaptation (not agree)	19.9 (24.0 in 2010)	− 20.3
Lifestyle adaptation (not important as citizenship requirement)	9.8	− 12.1
German language (not very important as citizenship requirement)	18.7	− 27.1
Christian (not at all important as citizenship requirement)	48.4	− 9.3
Social distance		
Turks – neighbours (not unpleasant)	59.4	− 5.8
Italians – neighbours (not unpleasant)	94.3	+ 1.6
Contacts with foreigners		
Any contact ('yes')	71.9 (74.3 in 2010)	+ 5.8
Friendship ('yes')	48.8 (52.3 in 2010)	+ 5.1
n (2006 and 1996)	≈ 3100	≈ 3250

*n=2104 in 1996; n=2056 in 2006
ALLBUS 1996 and 2006, own calculations.

(1997) with regard to race relations in the US, and may be an indication that some respondents uphold the principle of equal rights only in a superficial way so as to resist giving up privileges.

Tolerance of dual citizenship is more compatible with

multiculturalism than with assimilationist views because the former accommodates transnational ties of immigrants while assimilationists seek to avoid 'divided loyalties' (Faist 2007). Thus, the finding that in 2006 less than a third of Germans – slightly fewer than in 1996 – agreed with the statement that foreigners should be able to acquire German citizenship without renouncing the citizenship they currently possess might be seen as an indicator for only weak support for multiculturalism.

Multiculturalism aims to foster equality and at the same time to promote the recognition of cultural plurality. If ethnic minorities were expected to assimilate into the host culture by abolishing their own cultures and traditions, this would be the opposite of a multicultural approach. Table 8.2 presents percentages of responses *not* demanding adaptation: they reveal a strong desire on the part of the German majority for immigrants' cultural adaptation. The most striking result is the dramatic increase in these demands.

Certainly, the items analyzed cannot be interpreted unequivocally as measuring attitudes towards multiculturalism. The ALLBUS questions represent demands for integration of immigrants into dominant values, culture and social behaviour that are contrary to multiculturalism to varying degrees. Therefore for each indicator it was important to distinguish which responses should be classified as 'in favour of multiculturalism'. Three of the indicators are based on the respondent's opinion on how important certain criteria should be in the decision regarding whether to grant German citizenship. Cultural preconditions for naturalization include: 'lifestyle adaptation', 'language ability' and 'church membership' (Diehl and Tucci 2011). The most exclusionary position would be to claim that 'whether the person belongs to a Christian denomination' should play a central role in becoming a German citizen.

In 1996 the majority stated that this ascriptive attribute should be not at all important (1 on a 7 point scale), and it dropped to 48 per cent in 2006. With respect to the importance of naturalization applicants being 'prepared to adapt to the German way of life', a decrease of a similar magnitude can be observed, but at a totally different level. Only a tiny minority of 10 per cent does *not* place high importance to this criterion in 2006. In turn, an inflated value placed on immigrants' German language skills stands for high barriers on nationality acquisition in cultural terms that contradict a multicultural approach. In tandem with policy priorities, survey results reveal an enormous increase in the proportion of respondents who feel that it is very important 'whether the person is fluent in German'. Correspondingly, in 2006 the proportion of Germans who were not insistent on this prerequisite more than halved from 1996.

The overall finding that Germans put increased emphasis on the cultural adaptation of immigrants is confirmed by the response to the softly formulated normative statement that immigrants 'should adapt their way of life a little more closely to the German way of life'. This question has been asked since 1980. Until 1994, the data had shown a slow but steady increase in those not agreeing with this demand, from nearly a third of (West) German respondents to about a half. Then the trend was reversed and the percentage dropped sharply to only one-fifth in 2006. The data from 2010 (24 per cent not agreeing with the statement) might indicate that this trend has come to an end. Up to the appearance of Sarrazin's book (when about 60 per cent of all interviews had been completed), 26 per cent did not expect foreigners to adapt a bit more to the German way of life, in contrast to 21 per cent of those interviewed later. This seems to reveal a short-term effect of the Sarrazin book.

Interpreting the results regarding cultural adaptation items is made difficult by the fact that there is no measure of demands for immigrants to eradicate their own culture. Some evidence is found in the International Social Survey Programme (ISSP) that can throw light on this issue.[6] When Germans are forced to choose whether it is better for a country that different racial and ethnic groups maintain their distinct customs and traditions or that they adapt and blend into the larger society, nearly two-thirds (64 per cent) chose adaptation in 2003. This was a far higher percentage than in 1995 (46 per cent), supporting the ALLBUS finding of an increasing inclination to a sceptical view of cultural diversity. Another clear indicator of the turn away from multiculturalism are ISSP results showing that the percentage of respondents disagreeing with the statement 'it is impossible for people who do not share Germany's customs and traditions to become fully German' (24 per cent in 2003) and the percentage agreeing that 'ethnic minorities should be given government assistance to preserve their customs and traditions' (33 per cent in 2003) have strongly declined, by 15 and 14 percentage points respectively, since 1995.

Let me supplement the results concerning public opinion on societal multiculturalism with indicators from ALLBUS on interethnic relationships at the personal level. After all, without interactions between the majority population and members of immigrant groups, recognition of cultural diversity could end up in separation and seg-regation instead of multiculturalism. Congruent with results for the equal rights items, Germans' 'feelings of social distance' vary greatly, depending on the immigrant group. Asked how pleasant or unpleas-ant it would be for the interviewee to have an Italian person as a neigh-bour, only a tiny minority of 6 per cent chose a negative scale point, compared to 41 per cent for a Turkish person. This gap has widened since 1996. The proportion of Germans who do *not* express negative feelings about a Turk as neighbour has even declined by 6 percentage points, a further indication that reservations about cultural diversity are to a large extent the result of anti-Muslim resentment.

ALLBUS data reaching back to 1980 point to a steady increase in contact between Germans and foreigners, and 2010 data substantiate this trend. Nearly three out of four respondents now report having some sort of personal contact with foreigners living in Germany, be that at work, in the neighbourhood, in their own family/family circle and/or among friends and acquaintances. Particularly noteworthy is that voluntary and more intimate contact – having foreign friends – continues to increase: about one half of the respondents state they have immigrant friends and acquaintances.

Overall, then, ALLBUS surveys show that the German public are divided in their view on multiculturalism. Only one of the attitudinal indicators in Table 8.1 – social distance towards Italians, not really a key indicator of multiculturalism – shows a clear majority of 60 per cent or more for the position labelled as 'in favour of multicul-turalism'. The picture is different if we look at the supporters of the only political party in Germany that has been committed to the idea of multiculturalism, the Greens. Most of the multicultural attitudes listed in Table 8.3 constitute a majority view.[7]

Especially in their evaluations of cultural diversity and the conten-tious issue of Islamic instruction, Green supporters have long been exceptional. But among them, too, a major shift towards demands for immigrants' adaptation and linguistic assimilation has taken place. Supporters of the two major political parties, the Christian Democrats and Social Democrats, also differ significantly from one another, with CDU supporters strongly opposed to multiculturalism. Yet again, attitudes are similar in both political camps with regard to the need for cultural adaptation of immigrants.

To sum up, some positive trends can be observed with respect to interethnic contacts and the majority's acceptance of equal political rights for immigrants. Some results may hint at a growing tendency to

Table 8.3 Support for multiculturalism in Germany according to voting
intentions: 2006 compared to 1996*

Concepts and Items	Responses in favour of multiculturalist positions 2006			Change since 1996 (percentage points)		
	CDU/ CSU (%)	SPD (%)	Greens (%)	CDU	SPD	Greens
Cultural diversity						
Cultural enrichment (agree)	37.5	46.7	70.4	+7.9	+8.0	+16.3
Stranger in own land (disagree)	49.8	56.8	75.4	−6.6	+0.1	+3.8
Rights and policies						
Equal rights for Turks (agree)	27.1	41.8	57.1	−0.7	+2.2	+3.5
Local voting rights (agree)	35.6	50.6	61.9	+7.8	+10.0	+6.0
Religious instruction ('also Islamic', if any)**	40.9	51.4	80.4	−4.5	−1.8	+12.9
Dual nationality (agree)	26.9	38.3	55.0	−0.4	−1.5	−3.2
Cultural adaptation						
Adapt way of life (not agree)	16.3	20.4	41.2	−16.3	−19.3	−20.6
Lifestyle adaptation (not important for naturalization)	7.6	9.0	24.6	−7.9	−14.8	−13.9
German language (not very important for naturalization)	17.1	15.1	32.2	−22.7	−34.2	−21.3
Christian (not at all important for naturalisation)	40.5	49.5	70.4	−8.0	−8.5	−2.0
Turk as neighbour (not unpleasant)	54.0	64.7	76.7	−3.8	−1.4	−4.6
n (2006 and 1996)	≈ 800	≈ 710	≈ 230	≈ 800	≈ 730	≈ 370

* For reasons of clarity, this table contains only items considered most meaningful and
respondents with the intention to vote for one of the major parties in Germany or for the
Greens.
** n=601 (CDU), 483 (SPD), 228 (Greens) in 1996; n=580 (CDU), 467 (SPD), 158 (Greens)
in 2006.

ALLBUS 1996 and 2006, own calculations.

Islamophobia. But the most striking result is the turnaround in public opinion that has taken place with regard to cultural adaptation. Many Germans nowadays prefer immigrants to adopt the German language and to conform to the German way of life, in accordance with the idea of a uniform *Leitkultur*. It is less clear whether the majority is expecting complete assimilation to German customs and norms or only conformity to some basic values and rules.

Conclusion

In Germany state actions as well as public discourses are regularly characterized by complexity and contradictions. There is no official national commitment to multiculturalism and no broad public support for multicultural ideas. So what about the questions posed in the introduction: Is there a common 'sceptical turn' against policies recognizing cultural diversity? Is Germany turning away from multiculturalism before actually having reached it?

I have described elite and public concerns about the negative effects of cultural diversity. To achieve the widely shared goal of socio-cultural integration of immigrants, a certain degree of acculturation, at a minimum linguistically, is considered vital, especially where Muslim immigrants are concerned. The challenge will be to accomplish integration without forcing immigrants to give up their own culture. A more differentiated and less biased view – especially on Muslims – will be required, acknowledging intracultural differences and avoiding insinuations about the general 'inferiority' of Islam. Sarrazin's book obviously was not helpful in this regard. On the other hand, the fact that Germany – in contrast to most of its neighbours – has no right-wing populist party with significant success at the polls gives reason to hope.

Radical cultural relativism is not an answer in cases of deep disagreements about values endangering social cohesion. In such cases – and not limited to intercultural differences – a solution acceptable to all may best be reached through deliberation. A deliberative accommodation of cultural diversity requires equality of opportunity and intercultural dialogue. In this sense, organizations such as the 'German Islam Conference' are a step in the right direction. But, since voting remains the usual method of decision in a democracy, extended voting rights for foreigners and/or lower barriers to citizenship are essential.

For many years, German politics has concentrated on promoting equal (or less unequal) access for immigrants to the educational system and the labour market. Research on the socio-economic integration of immigrants (Böcker and Thränhardt 2003; Koopmans 2003) comparing, for example, residential segregation and unemployment rates, has shown that Germany has been more successful in these areas than the multicultural pioneer that is the Netherlands. From an analysis of survey data on identification, language proficiency and use, religious observance and interethnic social contacts of Turkish immigrants in Germany, France and the Netherlands, Ersanilli and Koopmans (2011: 229) concluded that 'combating socio-economic disadvantages of immigrants is a more promising avenue to stimulate immigrants' socio-cultural integration than policies that focus on formal legal equality and cultural accommodation or assimilation'.

We might conclude, then, that Germany may neither celebrate cultural diversity nor strive for multiculturalism, but it nevertheless is able to promote equal opportunities and provide equal individual rights for immigrants. There are no signs that a policy of specific group rights could gain broad acceptance in the near future. But the state's commitment to provide equal opportunities for the individual's 'freedom of self-determination' recognized in the Convention of Human Rights – if understood as comprising cultural issues as a key area of personal choice – could be enough to secure that each immigrant can freely decide to what extent he or she adopts cultural elements of the host country and to what extent he or she maintains the culture of origin.

Notes

1. http://www.rbb-online.de/doku/titel_mit_s/sarrazins_deutschland.html
2. The terms used by the German public for both immigrants and their descendants have varied over time. The 1980s and 1990s term *Ausländer* (foreigners) gradually replaced the earlier term *Gastarbeiter* (guestworkers). New terms such as *Migranten* (migrants) are in the process of entering common use. *Ausländer* (since 1994) and *Gastarbeiter* are the terms used in ALLBUS questions (Blank and Wasmer 1996).
3. All analysis reported here is based on respondents holding German citizenship. Data have been weighted to correct the disproportional ALLBUS sample with unequal selection probabilities between western and eastern Germany.
4. If not otherwise stated, a response scale running from 1 = completely disagree to 7 = completely agree has been used.

5. For full question wording see ALLBUS questionnaires at http://www.
   gesis.org/allbus/recherche/frageboegen/
6. These are my calculations based on ISSP 1995: National Identity I and
   ISSP 2003: National Identity II.
7. The differences between supporters of the various parties are partly due
   to socio-structural composition, especially with respect to the variables
   of age and, more importantly, level of education. But multiple regres-
   sion analysis not provided here reveals that the effect of party affiliation
   remains highly significant after controlling for such variables.

References

Banting, K. and W. Kymlicka (2006), 'Introduction: Multiculturalism and
the welfare state: Setting the context', in K. Banting and W. Kymlicka (eds),
*Multiculturalism and the Welfare State. Recognition and Redistribution
in Contemporary Democracies*, Oxford: Oxford University Press.

Banting, K. and W. Kymlicka (2012), *Multiculturalism Policy Index*.
Available at http://www.queensu.ca/mcp/

Bender, S. and W. Seifert (2003), 'On the economic and social situations of
immigrant groups in Germany', in R. Alba, P. Schmidt and M. Wasmer
(eds), *Germans or Foreigners? Attitudes Toward Ethnic Minorities in
Post-Reunification Germany*, New York: Palgrave Macmillan.

Berghahn, S. (2009), 'Ein Quadratmeter Stoff als Projektionsfläche.
Gesetzliche Kopftuchverbote in Deutschland und anderen europäischen
Ländern'. Available at http://web.fu-berlin.de/gpo/pdf/berghahn/s_
berghahn_3_4.pdf

Bielefeldt, H. (2007), *Menschenrechte in der Einwanderungsgesellschaft.
Plädoyer für einen aufgeklärten Multikulturalismus*, Bielefeld: Transcript.

Blank, T. and M. Wasmer (1996), 'Gastarbeiter oder Ausländer? Ergebnisse
des Splits mit den reformulierten Gastarbeiterfragen im ALLBUS 1994',
ZUMA Nachrichten, 38 (May), pp. 45–69.

BMI (2012a), Federal Ministry of the Interior: Integration Courses Website.
Available at http://www.bmi.bund.de/EN/Themen/MigrationIntegration/
Integration/IntegrationCourses/Integration_courses_node.html

BMI (2012b) Federal Ministry of the Interior: Integration Website.
Available at http://www.bmi.bund.de/EN/Themen/MigrationIntegration/
Integration/integration_node.html

Böcker, A. and D. Thränhardt (2003), 'Erfolge und Misserfolge der
Integration – Deutschland und die Niederlande im Vergleich', *Aus Politik
und Zeitgeschichte. Beilage zur Wochenzeitung Das Parlament*, B 26, pp.
3–11.

Bundesministerium des Innern (ed.) (2011), *Migrationsbericht
des Bundesamtes für Migration und Flüchtlinge im Auftrag der
Bundesregierung. Migrationsbericht 2010*. Available at http://www.

bamf.de/SharedDocs/Anlagen/DE/Publikationen/Migrationsberichte/
migrationsbericht-2010.html

Castles, S. (2004), 'Migration, citizenship and education', in J. A. Banks
(ed.), *Diversity and citizenship education*, San Francisco, CA: Jossey-Bass.

Crepaz, M. (2006), '"If you are my brother, I may give you a dime!" Public
opinion on multiculturalism, trust, and the welfare state', in Banting and
Kymlicka (eds), *Multiculturalism and the Welfare State*.

Diehl, C. and I. Tucci (2011), 'Fremdenfeindlichkeit und Einstellungen zur
Einbürgerung', in 'Wer darf Deutsche/r werden?', *DIW Wochenbericht*,
31, pp. 3–8. Available at http://www.diw.de/documents/publikationen/
73/diw_01.c.376805.de/11-31.pdf

Ersanilli, E. and R. Koopmans (2011), 'Do immigrant integration policies
matter? A three-country comparison among Turkish immigrants', *West
European Politics*, 34 (2), pp. 208–34.

Faist, T. (1994), 'How to define a foreigner? The symbolic politics of
immigration in German partisan discourse, 1978–1992', *West European
Politics* 17 (2), pp. 50–71.

Faist, T. (2007), 'The fixed and porous boundaries of dual citizenship', in
T. Faist (ed.), *Dual Citizenship in Europe: From Nationhood to Societal
Integration*, Aldershot: Ashgate.

Federal Statistical Office (2011a), 'Wanderungen 2010: Deutlich mehr
Personen nach Deutschland zugezogen', Press release No. 180 (9
May). Available at https://www.destatis.de/DE/PresseService/Presse/
Pressemitteilungen/2011/05/PD11_180_12711.html

Federal Statistical Office (2011b), 'Wanderungen 2010: Ein Fünftel der
Bevölkerung in Deutschland hatte 2010 einen Migrationshintergrund',
Press release No. 355 (26 September). Available at https://www.destatis.
de/DE/PresseService/Presse/Pressemitteilungen/2011/09/PD11_355_122.
html

Habermas, J. (2010), 'Leadership and Leitkultur', *The New York Times*,
28 October.

Heckmann, F. (2010), 'Recent developments of integration policy in
Germany and Europe', European Forum for Migration Studies (EFMS),
paper 2010-4. Available at http://migration.ucdavis.edu/rs/files/2010/
heckmann-paper-recent-developments-of-integration-policy.pdf

Joppke, C. (2007), 'Beyond national models: Civic integration policies for
immigrants in Western Europe', *West European Politics*, 30 (1), pp. 1–22.

Joppke, C. and E. Morawska (2003), 'Integrating immigrants in liberal
nation-states: Policies and practices', in C. Joppke and E. Morawska
(eds), *Toward Assimilation and Citizenship: Immigrants in Liberal
Nation-States*, New York: Palgrave.

Joppke, C. and Z. Rosenhek (2002), 'Contesting ethnic immigration:
Germany and Israel compared', *European Journal of Sociology*, 43 (3),
pp. 301–35.

Koch, A. and M. Wasmer (2004), 'Der ALLBUS als Instrument zur Untersuchung sozialen Wandels: Eine Zwischenbilanz nach 20 Jahren', in R. Schmitt-Beck, M. Wasmer and A. Koch (eds), *Sozialer und politischer Wandel in Deutschland. Analysen mit ALLBUS-Daten aus zwei Jahrzehnten*, Wiesbaden: VS Verlag für Sozialwissenschaften.

Koopmans, R. (2007), 'Good intentions sometimes make bad policy. A comparison of Dutch and German integration policies', in *Migration, Multiculturalism, and Civil Society*, Berlin: Friedrich Ebert Stiftung.

Koopmans, R., P. Statham, M. Giugni and F. Pasy (2005), *Contested Citizenship: Immigration and Cultural Diversity in Europe*, Minneapolis, MN: University of Minnesota Press.

Kraus, P. A. and Schönwälder, K. (2006), 'Multiculturalism in Germany: Rhetoric, scattered experiments and future chances', in Banting and Kymlicka (eds), *Multiculturalism and the Welfare State*.

Kymlicka, W. (1995), *Multicultural Citizenship*, Oxford: Oxford University Press.

Münz, R. and R. Ulrich (2003), 'The ethnic and demographic structure of foreigners and immigrants in Germany', in R. Alba, P. Schmidt and M. Wasmer (eds), *Germans or Foreigners? Attitudes Toward Ethnic Minorities in Post-Reunification Germany*, New York: Palgrave Macmillan.

O'Brien, P. (2011), 'Immigration to Germany: past and present experience', Political Science Faculty Research Paper 2. Available at http://digital commons.trinity.edu/polysci_faculty/2

Peucker, M. (2010), 'Racism and ethnic discrimination in Germany. Update Report 2010', Bamberg: EFMS.

Schuman, H., C. Steeh, L. Bobo and M. Krysan (1997), *Racial Attitudes in America: Trends and Interpretations*, Cambridge, MA: Harvard University Press.

SpiegelOnline International (2011a), 'The world from Berlin: "Turkish Prime Minister Erdogan wants to be the father"', 3 January. Available at http://www.spiegel.de/international/germany/0,1518,748379,00.html

SpiegelOnline International (2011b), 'Erdogan urges Turks not to assimilate: "You are part of Germany, but also part of our great Turkey"', 23 February. Available at http://www.spiegel.de/international/europe/0,1518,748070,00.html

SpiegelOnline International (2012), 'The world from Berlin: "The shame must continue to burn in our hearts"', 24 February. Available at http://www.spiegel.de/international/germany/0,1518,817388,00.html

Terwey, M. (2000), 'ALLBUS: A German general social survey', Schmollers Jahrbuch. *Zeitschrift für Wirtschafts- und Sozialwissenschaften*, 120 (1), pp. 151–8.

Triadafilopoulos, P. (2012), *Becoming Multicultural: Immigration and the*

Politics of Membership in Canada and Germany, Vancouver: University of British Columbia Press.

Triadafilopoulos, T., A. Korteweg and P. Garcia Del Moral (2012), 'The benefits and limits of pragmatism: Immigrant integration policy and social cohesion in Germany', in P. Spoonley and E. Tolley (eds), *Diverse Nations, Diverse Responses: Approaches to Social Cohesion in Immigrant Societies*, Montreal and Kingston: McGill-Queen's University Press. Available at http://ebookbrowse.com/triadafilopoulos-korteweg-garcia-del-moral-the-benefits-and-limits-of-pragmatism-revised-14-09-11-pdf-d192042690.

Van Oers, R. (2010), 'Citizenship tests in the Netherlands, Germany and the UK', in R. Van Oers, E. Ersbøll and D. Kostakopoulou (eds), *A Re-Definition of Belonging? Language and Integration Tests in Europe*, Leiden: Brill Publishers.

Wasmer, M. and A. Koch (2000), 'Ausländer als Bürger 2. Klasse? Einstellungen zur rechtlichen Gleichstellung von Ausländern', in R. Alba, P. Schmidt and M. Wasmer (eds), *Deutsche und Ausländer: Freunde, Fremde oder Feinde?*, Opladen: Westdeutscher Verlag.

Wengeler, M. (2006), 'Zur historischen Kontinuität von Argumentationsmustern im Migrationsdiskurs', in C. Butterwegge and G. Hentges (eds), *Massenmedien, Migration und Integration*, Wiesbaden: VS Verlag für Sozialwissenschaften.

Zimmermann, K. F. (1999), 'Ethnic German migration since 1989 – results and perspectives/ Aussiedler seit 1989 – Bilanz und Perspektiven', IZA Discussion Papers 50, Bonn: Institute for the Study of Labour (IZA).

Chapter Nine

Danish Multiculturalism, Where Art Thou?

Nils Holtug

Introduction

It would be presumptuous to speak of a backlash against multicultural policies in Denmark because in Denmark such policies never gained much prominence in the first place. Thus, when Danish politicians and political commentators announce the end of multiculturalism, they seem to be expressing a desire that things should stay as they have been and perhaps a desire for more restrictive immigration and integration policies. An example is Søren Pind's (2011) denunciation of multiculturalism following his appointment as Minister of Integration in 2011. Pind echoed statements made by British Prime Minister David Cameron and German Chancellor Angela Merkel. But he also affirmed a statement he had made on his blog three years earlier: 'I really don't want to hear any more about integration. Please stop – the right word must be assimilation. There are so many cultures and people can go elsewhere and engage with them if this is what they want' (Pind 2008).

While multiculturalism may not have been on the Danish centre stage, political debates on immigration and integration have often addressed issues of how to tackle diversity. Such debates have been particularly heated in Denmark and, indeed, have resulted in particularly restrictive policies. Furthermore, it is noteworthy that while Denmark has some of the most restrictive immigration policies in Europe (Think Tank on Integration in Denmark 2004; Kærgård 2010b: 478), has had fierce debates over immigration and integration policies and is often perceived as being hostile to immigrants, a number of studies indicate that Danes are no more hostile or intolerant than other peoples in Europe. What is more, the trend line is that they are becoming more positive to immigrants. We might speak, then, of a 'Danish paradox', and in the present chapter I advance explanations for it.

At the outset, it is important to recognize that, to a large extent, Danish debates on immigration and integration tend to focus on Muslims – as, indeed, is the case elsewhere in Europe (Modood 2007: 4–5). At least in part, this reflects the fact that Muslims comprise by far the largest influx of immigrants from non-Western countries: it is estimated that there are 175,000–200,000 Muslims in Denmark, comprising up to 3.6 per cent of the population (Hussain 2011: 34).

I approach multiculturalism as a (normative) political doctrine that requires the accommodation of group differences in the public sphere, for example in laws, policies and state and municipal discourses, with the aim of reducing discrimination and hierarchy and securing inclusion and equality of opportunity (cf. Kymlicka 1995; Modood 2007; Parekh 2006; Phillips 2007; Young 1990). While the term 'accommodation of group differences' is somewhat vague, it is often associated with so-called group-differentiated rights – rights that are assigned to some but withheld from others, depending on their membership of cultural and religious groups (Holtug 2009: 81). By way of illustration, such rights may include an exemption for Sikh men from the legal requirement of wearing a safety helmet when working on construction sites so that they can wear a turban instead.

There are other ways of accommodating the concerns of cultural and religious groups and indeed other kinds of multicultural policies. For example, a traditional multicultural concern such as recognizing diversity within a common curriculum in schools does not differentiate the rights of school children but rather prescribes the same treatment for everyone (Banting et al. 2006: 87). Whether a particular concern for group difference is best captured by group-differentiated rights or, for example, by introducing new difference-blind rights may be an open question that multiculturalists will want to settle pragmatically.

This chapter begins with an overview of Danish immigration and integration policies, focusing especially on their (lack of) multicultural aspects. I then analyze the different discourses present in recent Danish debates on these issues, in response to which policies have been formed focusing on liberalism, active citizenship, liberal nationalism and conservative nationalism. I then turn to the attitudes of Danes with regard to multiculturalism, in part to determine to what extent policies have matched attitudes. Finally, I consider the Danish discussion of multiculturalism from a normative, political theory perspective, mainly to assess the strength of various common arguments against multiculturalism.

Policies on immigration and integration

Denmark is in many ways a very homogeneous society by international standards, in terms of both ethnicity and religion. In 2005 85 per cent of the Danish population were members of the State Lutheran Church, and Islam was the second largest religion with 3 per cent (Kærgård 2010b: 475). Nevertheless, like other European states, it has recently experienced increasing levels of immigration from non-Western countries, beginning with the arrival of guest workers in the 1960s and 1970s. In 1973 policies were implemented to halt immigration because of the recession, but the number of non-Western immigrants has nevertheless continued to rise for reasons of family reunification and asylum for refugees. Thus, whereas in 1980, 43,978 residents were born in non-Western countries, the number had risen to 227,296 by 2005 (Kærgård 2010a: 52).

As guest workers began to arrive, a pragmatic approach to integration was adopted (Hedetoft 2008: 47). The chief concern was that immigrants should fill gaps in the labour market, where they would experience the required level of integration until the time when they were expected to return to their countries of origin. However, the pragmatic approach was increasingly supplemented with policies that aimed at limiting immigration and integrating foreigners into what is perceived as the 'Danish way of life'. This development culminated with the election of a Liberal–Conservative coalition in 2001 that relied systematically for support on the votes of the nationalist Danish People's Party (DPP). The election of this coalition, as well as their victory in the two elections that followed, was heavily influenced by their increasingly restrictive policies on immigration and integration, including tightened immigration requirements (for example, to avoid Denmark becoming a 'refugee magnet'), reduced social benefits for immigrants and more restrictive rules for citizenship and permanent residence (including more difficult language and knowledge tests regarding Danish politics, history and culture). These measures were accompanied by a 'tougher' terminology to address the crime, educational underachievement, unemployment and (allegedly) illiberal practices of (some) immigrants and their descendants.

While this restrictive line was backed up by a parliamentary majority that sometimes included the Social Democrats until this party took power in 2011, it was also accompanied by fierce public debates. Particularly controversial was the so-called 'twenty-four-year rule' for family reunification of third-country nationals, requiring, amongst other things, that both spouses be at least twenty-four years old, more strongly attached to Denmark than to any other country and self-supporting, and that the prospective immigrant must pass a test showing basic knowledge of Danish language and society. The Liberal–Conservative government later applied this rule more selectively in order to attract qualified labour. Thus, applicants need a certain number of points to qualify with points being obtained in four categories: education, work experience, language qualifications and 'other'. For example, a doctoral or Master's degree from a Danish university or from a list of the world's top 50 universities will provide almost the necessary number of points even if the applicant is under twenty-four (Olwig et al. 2011).

Other controversial policies have included 'start help' (*starthjælp*), which gives immigrants a lower level of social benefits during the first seven years that they are in Denmark (Kærgård 2010a: 59), the increasingly strong language and knowledge requirements for citizenship and permanent residence and a policy of selecting quota refugees on the basis of their 'potential for integration', which has resulted in a significantly lower percentage of refugees from Muslim countries. Despite protests primarily from the left and the Social Liberal party (*Radikale Venstre*), the Liberal–Conservative government defended these restrictions as being 'tough but fair'.

After the Liberal–Conservative coalition lost power in September 2011 and an electoral coalition of Social Democrats, the Socialist People's Party and *Radikale Venstre* won the election, it was not clear how much of a difference this would make to existing policies. The new coalition abandoned 'start help' and sought to reintroduce the twenty-four-year rule in the original version (without the points system). However, it seemed doubtful that many of the restrictions imposed by the former government would be reversed.

In spite of these developments, the pragmatic approach has not been abandoned. In the 2011 Migrant Integration Policy Index, Denmark was ranked just above the EU average regarding the implementation of policies that are conducive to integration (MIPEX III 2011: 11). This overall score was based on both high and low performances in the different aspects of integration that were measured. Thus, Denmark does relatively well on labour market mobility, education, political participation and long-term residence, but poorly on anti-discrimination, access to nationality and especially family reunification.

At least two factors have played an important role in shaping restrictive Danish policies. The first is calculations indicating that non-Western immigrants are costly for the welfare state. They showed that while, in 2000, the typical profile of positive net transfers to the state was in the age interval of mid-twenties to early sixties, there was no age group in which non-Western immigrants on average had positive net transfers (Tranæs and Zimmermann 2004: 4; Wadensjö and Gerdes 2004: 334). Certainly, *descendants* of non-Western immigrants did not differ significantly from the typical profile of 'Danes' (Tranæs and Zimmermann 2004: 4). Economists and politicians worried that immigrants arriving in the country were undermining the basis of the Danish welfare state, with its high levels of social spending, even by European standards. The state response was to reduce the intake of asylum seekers and people seeking family reunification and to decrease social benefits for immigrants.

An assessment of the net costs of immigration suggested that in 2010 immigrants and descendants from 'less developed countries' cost the Danish state 4 billion and 11.7 billion DKK respectively. However, the group of descendants is relatively young which will both involve fewer costs and larger contributions later in their lives (Regeringens arbejdsgruppe 2011: 10).

A second factor making for a restrictive approach is growing Danish discontent with what have been viewed as too lenient policies. It resulted in support for the DPP and the Liberal–Conservative coalition. Of course, politicians may also have influenced public sentiments. Either way, popular support for restrictive policies has been a necessary condition for their implementation, and many Danes have genuinely been concerned about welfare costs, parallel societies, forced marriages, crime rates and the educational underachievement of immigrants and their descendants.

These developments have not produced a climate conducive to multicultural policies. Indeed, not only have scholars observed an apparent lack of such policies, but they have to some extent labelled existing policies assimilationist (Hedetoft 2010; Jensen 2010; cf. Mouritsen 2006). One bottom line is that in the index of multicultural policies (MCPs) for immigrants used by Banting et al., Denmark scores 0 out of a possible 8 (see Table 9.1).

194

Table 9.1 Multicultural Policy scores for selected countries

	Immigrant MCPs	*Indigenous MCPs*
Canada	7.5	7.5
Australia	7.0	3.5
UK	5.0	–
Netherlands	4.5	–
Belgium	3.5	–
Sweden	3.0	1.5
US	3.0	7.0
France	2.0	–
Italy	1.5	–
Denmark	0.0	6.0

Source: Banting et al. 2006, p. 86.

The multicultural policies identified by Banting et al. (2006: 56–7; cf. Vertovec and Wessendorf 2010: 3) include:

1. Constitutional, legislative or parliamentary affirmation of multi-culturalism, at the central and/or regional and municipal levels.
2. The adoption of multiculturalism in the school curriculum.
3. The inclusion of ethnic representation/sensitivity in the mandate of public media.
4. Exemptions from dress codes, Sunday closing legislation, and so on either by statute or by court cases.
5. Allowing dual citizenship.
6. The funding of ethnic group organizations to support cultural activities.
7. The funding of bilingual education or mother-tongue instruction.
8. Affirmative action for disadvantaged immigrant groups.

Multicultural policies of these kinds have played a limited role in Denmark but there are a few exceptions. Sikh men are exempted from the requirement of wearing a helmet when riding a motorbike. Liberal Danish rules for 'free schools' (*friskoler*), and the high level of financial support they receive, make it relatively easy for immigrants to form religious schools: in fact, Denmark has the highest number of Muslim free schools in Europe relative to country size (Jensen 2010: 194).

In some cases, however, multicultural policies have been retracted, such as the 2002 elimination of the requirement that municipalities provide mother-tongue instruction for immigrant children (Jensen

2010: 194). Nevertheless, municipalities may still choose to provide mother-tongue instruction, and generally it is easier to find examples of difference accommodation at the municipal level than at the level of the state (cf. Hedetoft 2010: 111). For example, the Municipality of Copenhagen has introduced a 'policy of inclusion' according to which 'diversity is a strength', and 'Copenhageners must be treated equally, but not necessarily identically' (Municipality of Copenhagen 2011: 6). Some schools with many Muslim children even choose to give children a day off for *Eid-al-fitr*.

There is one domain in which Denmark has implemented highly multicultural policies at the level of the state – on indigenous people in the Danish Commonwealth. Thus, Greenland and the Faroe Islands have been granted self-government rights in the Home Rule Government Acts, defining them as autonomous provinces (Adamo 2009: 210). Furthermore, Greenland and the Faroe Islands each have two seats set aside in the Danish Parliament. In the index of multicultural policies for indigenous peoples (see Table 9.1), Denmark scores 6.0 out of a possible 9 points.

Discourses on integration and social cohesion

A focal point in recent Danish debates on integration and immigration is the significance attached to social cohesion. This subject has played an increasingly important role since former Prime Minister Poul Nyrup Rasmussen (Social Democrat) began in the late 1990s to express a concern for 'cohesion' as the glue that holds society together. With the election of the Liberal–Conservative coalition in 2001 social cohesion became 'ethnicized', in the sense that ethnic and other forms of diversity became regarded as a threat to social cohesion. For example, in his Constitution Day speech in 2007, Prime Minister Anders Fogh Rasmussen stated that:

> if we are to maintain the high level of social cohesion that is so important for the progress and stability of Denmark, it is necessary that we continue to meet one another as human beings and citizens of Denmark in the public sphere – not as representatives of different religions. (quoted in Heinskou et al. 2007)

The suggestion that ethnic diversity drives down social cohesion has perhaps been most succinctly elaborated by former Minister of the Interior Karen Jespersen. She linked survey results indicating that Danes are the happiest people in the world and have the highest level of trust (Svendsen and Svendsen 2006: 88) with the fact that Denmark is an ethnoculturally homogeneous nation. This homogeneity and its positive effects, however, are perceived as being under threat (see Holtug 2010a and b):

> It is not about integration on the labour market or in the educational system, but about something more fundamental: the experience of being part of a *value-community* (*værdifællesskab*) in the society one inhabits.
>
> If such a community is missing, social cohesion withers away. The social capital that creates trust between citizens will be missing. Indeed, social scientists have shown that there is a relation between large ethnocultural differences and low levels of social trust in society. This has highly problematic consequences for the way society works and for the ability to work for common political goals. (Jespersen and Pittelkow 2005: 98–9)

One reason why social cohesion may play such a significant role in Danish debates is that this factor has been considered particularly important in a society committed to equality and high levels of social spending. Thus, the high Danish level of trust is often mentioned as a significant factor when explaining how it is possible for Denmark to be economically successful and competitive despite high taxes and social benefits – and therefore relatively low economic incentives to work (Svendsen and Svendsen 2006: 80–1).

Social cohesion is considered to be under threat but also necessary to avoid religious and political conflicts, parallel societies and crime, as well as to secure the level of solidarity required between citizens for maintaining the welfare state. This has resulted in a struggle over (1) which values are conducive to social and political stability; and (2) which values define what it means to be Danish; the assumption being that the answers to both questions are the same. A 'values commission' was established by the Liberal–Conservative government to identify which values are important for Danes (Ministry of Culture 2011); it was dropped when the Social Democratic-led coalition took power.

Let us call conceptions of what kinds of values are conducive to social cohesion 'community conceptions'. More precisely, a community conception can be usefully thought of as a set of (formal or informal) values regulating the conditions in which individuals interact in a group, including the distribution of political, social and cultural advantages, with the aim of securing social goods within that group, such as trust, cooperation, stability, belonging and solidarity.

What are the most important such conceptions in Danish policies and discourses?

Official policies often rely on what may be described as a traditional liberal approach that emphasizes the public-private sphere distinction (cf. Rawls 1993). Here, integration amounts to acknowledging or confirming a set of basic liberal values, and religion and other conceptions of the good are relegated to the private sphere. For example, in the Action Plan on Ethnic Equal Treatment and Respect for Individuals, the Liberal–Conservative government (2011: 1) stated that Danish society is based on fundamental values of personal and political liberty, respect for individuals, equality of opportunity and democracy. These are viewed as supportive of social cohesion (Government 2010: 2).

Increasingly, this liberal conception has been supplemented with Republican ideas about active or democratic citizenship (*medborgerskab*). Thus, in the Action Plan the former government (2011: 6) stressed the need for immigrants to become active citizens and supported citizenship classes in schools. In fact, active citizenship has become a buzzword, both at the level of the state and in municipalities (for example, Municipality of Copenhagen 2011). In part, this focus on active citizenship may be due to a strong tradition for civic participation in Denmark in the form of volunteering in civic organizations, where such participation is sometimes referred to as instrumental for the development of a high level of trust (Svendsen and Svendsen 2006: Ch. 3). However, while the rhetorical commitment to active citizenship is firm, especially as regards democratic participation, more often than not it is unclear what active citizenship is supposed to amount to. In other words, what is lacking is a specification of the particular civic virtues thought to uphold democratic institutions, solidarity and social cohesion (Laborde and Maynor 2008: 14–15).

Active or democratic citizenship has also become a popular community conception in academic circles (Korsgaard et al. 2007). Here, democratic citizenship is considered a more inclusive alternative to conservative nationalist community conceptions. It is sometimes claimed that democratic citizenship is more inclusive in that it does not presuppose a common identity based on common values (Christensen and Lindhardt 2007: 213). However, whatever the virtues of democratic citizenship are, this idea about the basis of inclusiveness is mistaken. Even democratic citizenship presupposes a joint commitment to liberal, democratic values and to a set of procedures for negotiating disagreements. Democratic citizenship is more inclusive than conservative nationalism in that the common identity it presupposes is less thick, and (partly for this reason) more accommodating towards difference.

While active citizenship has indeed become a buzzword amongst policymakers, this does not imply that all policies actually comply with this particular community conception. A former Minister of Culture in the Liberal–Conservative coalition, Brian Mikkelsen, commissioned a monocultural Danish Cultural Canon, consisting of selected Danish architecture, paintings, design, films, literature, music, theatre and artworks for children, to strengthen communal values by referring to a common Danish heritage (Ministry of Culture 2006). Mikkelsen (2004) described Danish authors as the 'voice of the nation' securing a Danish identity and sense of history. This community conception seems more in line with that of conservative nationalism than with active citizenship – a conception that focuses on political rather than cultural values. Likewise, the current Danish citizenship test includes questions not just about Danish political institutions, but also about Danish history and culture; the 2010 test included questions about Danish authors, painters and athletes.

Furthermore, the very policy documents that invoke active citizenship as the basis for Danish integration policies sometimes display a cultural or religious bias. The Action Plan referred to above expresses a concern for anti-discrimination and emphasizes the need to fight anti-Semitism (Government 2010: 2–3, 7), yet it does not mention discrimination against other ethnic or religious groups, including Muslims.

While some policies and influential discourses thus deviate from liberalism and/or Republican ideas about active citizenship, others assume particular interpretations. Some discourses, for example, lean towards liberal nationalism where a common national identity or culture is necessary for – or at least conducive to – maintaining the stability and cohesion of liberal institutions (Miller 1995). For example, Karen Jespersen holds that the liberal Danish welfare state relies on a common set of traditional liberal values, but also on a feeling of being Danish, rooted in a common history and cultural background and in the Danish language (Jespersen and Pittelkow 2005: 25; see also Holtug 2005). As pointed out above, she sees ethnic diversity – and especially the immigration of Muslims – as a threat to these values and so to social cohesion.

Another example of a liberal nationalist discourse pertains to the Lutheran justification of liberal neutrality endorsed by sections of the Liberal Party (*Venstre*) in the preceding Liberal–Conservative coalition governments. While former Prime Minister Anders Fogh Rasmussen's statement that there should be less religion in the public sphere was reminiscent of a French Republican conception of *laïcité*, his justification rested on a Lutheran conception of the separation of religious and worldly affairs. Indeed, on the same occasion, he stressed that Denmark is a Christian country and that the Queen needs to be a member of the Lutheran Established Church because she symbolizes national unity and therefore the foundation of Danish society (Bjergager and Hoffmann-Hansen 2006).

A further dominant discourse in Danish integration debates is that of conservative nationalism. Where liberal nationalists are concerned with the basis for securing liberal institutions and human rights, and only accept means for securing them that are compatible with liberalism, conservative nationalists believe that 'integration' requires assimilation to an entire culture or way of life. Søren Krarup, a priest and former MP for the DPP, holds that being Danish 'is not an idea, an ideology, a point of view. To be Danish is to be a Dane – that is, a child of Denmark's history, of the Danish language, of the Danish people's life and life-history' (Krarup 2001: 15). On this basis, he is sceptical of liberal approaches to integration because they imply equal treatment, rather than a policy of 'Denmark for the Danes' (Krarup 2001: 46). He is critical of liberal human rights which, echoing Burke, he finds ideological – abstract claims that have no foundation in the concrete (national) history and lives of actual people (Krarup 2001: 46; see also Holtug 2005).

Like other community conceptions described, conservative nationalism harbours distinct ideas about what factors are conducive to social cohesion. Kasper Støvring (2010), a Danish academic and public intellectual, argues that cohesiveness, including trust, presupposes a national culture encompassing a common Danish history, Danish language, a common (Protestant) religion and virtues such as politeness, honesty, dependability and parsimony (which, according to Støvring, are specifically Danish virtues). Thus, in a spectrum going from thick to thin community conceptions, conservative nationalism is at the thick end (see Figure 9.1).

The DPP has particularly targeted Muslims and expressed general doubts about the compatibility of Islam and liberal values.

thick			thin
conservative	liberal	active	liberalism
nationalism	nationalism	citizenship	
conservatism	nationalism	citizenship	liberalism

Figure 9.1 Conceptions of community: from thick to thin

It has labelled Islam an aggressive, oppressive, sexist, expansionist ideology. Pia Kjærsgaard, party leader, suggested that 'Islam is, in essence . . . a religion that cherishes violence'. Muslim symbols such as headscarves are considered sexist and 'un-Danish' – a term that has spread from the nationalist right to mainstream Danish politics. Both Kjærsgaard and Søren Krarup have compared the Muslim headscarf – as a symbol of Islam – to a swastika. Unsurprisingly, then, both conservative and liberal nationalists have been highly critical of multiculturalism (Jespersen and Pittelkow 2005; Krarup 2001). Krarup (2001: 114) even associates multiculturalism with a loss of identity and 'contempt for human beings and rape of the people'.

Interestingly, a process of 'liberalization' has been taking place in Danish integration debates: policies that are initially conceived on the nationalist right travel into mainstream Danish politics, but they undergo a transformation where the justification for the policy is elaborated in more liberal terms. A case in point is a 2009 law that renders it impermissible for Danish judges to wear religious symbols in courts of law. While the ideas behind the law were originally put forward by the DPP in terms of concerns about sexism and the alleged totalitarian connotations of Muslim headscarves, and while the debate that preceded the law focused almost exclusively on headscarves, it was ultimately justified in terms of a concern for state neutrality and the impartiality of courts, and ruled out religious symbols of all kinds (Holtug 2011).

While conservative and liberal nationalists differ in their value commitments, they have often employed similar rhetorical strategies. Thus, they often refer to the effort to promote more restrictive policies as a 'value war' (*værdikamp*) or 'culture war' (*kulturkamp*), and emphasize their courage in breaking taboos and silence, and to counter political correctness. In this respect the Danish debate seems similar to those in the Netherlands (Prins and Saharso 2010: 74). A contrast is often made to Sweden, which is perceived as being politically correct and repressive towards people who dare speak the truth about the problems of immigration. Furthermore, this value war is considered non-elitist and opposed to the soft liberal and multicultural sentiments of academic leftists and social liberals. Kærgård (2010b: 483) notes that the debate has been so fierce that the divide it has caused between ethnic Danes may be a larger threat to social cohesion than non-Western immigrants are.

Multiculturalist discourses, then, have played a relatively small role in Denmark in recent times, at least in national political debates. One reason may be that the discursive climate has pushed liberal critics of existing policies into defensive positions, where it becomes more important to fend off new restrictions than to propose new (politically unrealistic) policies to accommodate difference. Given that some surveys show limited support for multiculturalism, this may make mainstream political parties think twice before they propose multicultural policies.

Danish attitudes

In a survey of twenty-seven countries carried out in 2003 by the International Social Survey Program (ISSP), Denmark came out as the country most opposed to multiculturalism: 77 per cent believed that it is best for a country if different races and ethnic groups adapt and blend into the society that surrounds them, whereas 11 per cent responded that it is best for a country if these groups maintain their distinctive customs and traditions (see Table 9.2). Ironically Sweden, which generally self-identifies as multicultural (see Chapter 7), was the country that immediately followed Denmark: here 73 per cent supported adjustment (Larsen 2008: 29). Denmark was also the country with the highest percentage of people (54 per cent) who completely or partly disagreed that ethnic minorities should receive public support to maintain their customs and traditions (Larsen 2008: 32).

Eurobarometer 2000 survey results painted a different picture. Only 25 per cent of Danes responded that in order to become fully accepted members of society, people belonging to minority groups must give up their own culture; 69 per cent disagreed. The two sets of questions were formulated differently and interpreting results as commitments to multiculturalism or assimilationism/monoculturalism was problematic. For example, ISSP 2003 may have represented a commitment to 'integration' rather than 'assimilation'. Indeed, much depends on whether the norms that people think minorities should

Table 9.2 Danish attitudes to multiculturalism, 2000–11

Eurobarometer 2000
In order to become fully accepted members of the Danish society, people belonging to minority groups must give up their culture.
Agree: 25%
Disagree: 69%
(Source: Thalhammer et al. 2001: 48)

ISSP 2003
It is better for a country if different racial and ethnic groups maintain their distinct customs and traditions: 11%
It is better if these groups adapt and blend into the larger society: 77%
(Source: Larsen 2008: 27–9)

European Values Study 2008
It is best for society if immigrants:
  – maintain their distinct customs and traditions: (1999) 19% (2008) 16%
  – do not maintain their distinct customs and
    traditions but adopt Danish customs: (1999) 63% (2008) 49%
(Source: Borre 2011: 125)

TNS Gallup A/S 2011
Do you basically support:
  – a monocultural society: 29%
  – a multicultural society: 54%

Source: TNS Gallup A/S 2011.

conform to are cultural or just political – pertaining to, for example, paying one's taxes and obeying the law. A 1996 survey lends support to this view: 85 per cent of Danes agreed that immigrants should be allowed to keep up their language and culture (Togeby 1998: 1,147).

If Denmark has an above average proportion who agree that minority groups must give up their own culture (among EU-15 Denmark is fifth after Belgium, Greece, the Netherlands and France), it also has an above average proportion who disagree with this statement. This indicates that Danes are particularly polarized on issues of integration which is confirmed by more thorough analysis of Eurobarometer 2000 and ISSP 2003 surveys (Larsen 2008: Ch. 7; cf. Andersen 2002: 15). Thus, in a typology of people according to their attitudes towards minority groups (Thalhammer et al. 2001: 25), Denmark had the third highest percentage of intolerants (20 per cent) in EU-15 but also had the highest percentage of actively tolerant people, together with Sweden (33 per cent).

On the theme of multiculturalism, Eurobarometer 2000 revealed that Danes gave the highest support in EU-15 for the claim that diversity in terms of race, religion and culture add to a country's strengths (58 per cent); for promoting the understanding of different cultures and lifestyles (57 per cent); and for encouraging the participation of people in minority groups in political life (40 per cent) – the last finding being consistent with an ideal of active citizenship (Thalhammer et al. 2001: 29–30, 45). In turn the European Values Study in 2008 found that 16 per cent of Danish respondents said that it is best for society if immigrants maintain their own customs; 49 per cent said that it is best if they conform to Danish traditions. The respective figures for 1999 were 19 and 63 per cent. This showed there was no major fall in support for multiculturalism. But again, we should be careful when interpreting these results as commitments to multiculturalism or assimilationism.

Finally, a poll following Søren Pind's denunciation of multiculturalism indicated that 54 per cent favoured a multicultural society and 29 per cent supported a monocultural one. This was the case even though 58 per cent agreed that multiculturalism had pushed back Danish culture and 45 per cent agreed that a multicultural society meant more oppression of women and violence against children. Furthermore, 60 per cent responded that Denmark should aim to integrate immigrants, whereas 29 per cent responded that Denmark should aim to assimilate.

The body of evidence presented is, therefore, mixed. It does not lead us to an unambiguous conclusion about Danish commitments to multiculturalism, integration or assimilation. Moreover, the findings do not suggest that Danes are more hostile or intolerant towards immigrants than people in most other European or Western countries. Perhaps this is not surprising. According to a standard account of the exclusion of ethnic minorities, Ethnic Competition Theory, ethnic exclusionism may be affected by competition reinforcing mechanisms of social identification and contra-identification (Coenders et al. 2003: 9). In Denmark and many European countries, immigration of non-Westerners primarily increases competition amongst relatively poor, low-skilled workers who are also threatened by other effects of globalization such as outsourcing. Denmark follows the general trend in having these groups highly over-represented in opposing immigration (Andersen 2002: 16; Borre 2011; Larsen 2008). However, Denmark has relatively few non-Western immigrants compared to other European receiving societies. It also has high levels of social security. These two factors may decrease competition and mitigate negative effects on low-skilled Danes compared to their counterparts elsewhere in Europe.

The received view amongst social scientists working on attitudes to immigrants in Denmark is that Danes are no more hostile or intolerant than other peoples in Europe (Andersen 2002: 15; Larsen 2008: 64; Nielsen 2004: Ch. 9). Indeed, over the last three decades, they have been getting less hostile and more tolerant (Andersen 2002: 8–11; Borre 2011: 124–8; Gundelach 2011: 22; Togeby 1998).

A few results may illustrate these points. In Eurobarometer 2000, Danes were above the EU-15 average in endorsing an outlawing of discrimination against minority groups; encouraging the creation of organizations that bring together people from different races, religions and cultures; encouraging trade unions and churches to do more against racism; accepting people from Muslim countries who wish to work in the EU; accepting people fleeing from countries where there is serious internal conflict; and accepting people suffering from human rights violations in their country who are seeking political asylum (Thalhammer 2001).

The ISSP from 2003 did indeed indicate that Danes are particularly polarized on issues of immigration and integration – second among twenty-seven countries to the French (Larsen 2008: 71). But if, in general, they are no more hostile or intolerant than other peoples in Europe, why has the Danish debate been particularly heated and why have policies tended to be particularly restrictive? This is what I labelled the 'Danish paradox'. In part, polarization in Denmark may provide an explanation. It has meant that significant numbers of voters have shifted support from the Social Democrats and other parties on the left to the DPP. This populist party has made it easier for voters to make this move by combining restrictive immigration and integration policies with largely Social Democratic views on the welfare state. This has shifted the majority to the right, where the Liberal–Conservative coalition in power in the period 2001–11 needed to accommodate some of the wishes of the DPP to maintain their parliamentary majority, but also increased their own votes by attracting voters from the left who were dissatisfied with what they considered overly permissive policies.

The allegation that Danes are becoming more hostile and intolerant (Nielsen 2004) cannot be confirmed by surveys. While the percentage that held that the government should allow entry for anyone who wants to come to Denmark had dropped from 7 per cent in

1999 to 5 per cent in 2008, the percentage that held that the government should let in immigrants as long as there are jobs had risen from 24 per cent to 39 per cent (Borre 2011: 125). In their studies Togeby (1998: 1,151–2; cf. Gaasholt and Togeby 1995: Ch. 5) concluded both that Danes have never been as tolerant as their reputation may have suggested, and that intolerance has not risen but has instead decreased slightly since 1970, thus puncturing the 'myth of a tolerant people's gradual decline'.

Focusing on the issues that Danes find problematic regarding immigrants, many of these involve worries about respect for the law and the health of the welfare state (Nielsen 2004: 225). In a recent poll, 59 per cent of respondents supported a proposal according to which immigrants need to earn the right to certain social benefits, for example a full package of public health care (Bonde and Steensbeck 2011). The perceived threat to the welfare state is visible in survey results showing that 84 and 79 per cent agree that Denmark should allow more high-skilled workers from Western and non-Western countries to immigrate respectively. By contrast, only 31 per cent and 28 per cent agree that low-skilled Western and non-Western immigrants should be allowed entry (Dinesen et al. 2011: 10).

These survey results suggest that Danes are more worried about threats to the economy and the welfare state than about threats to Danish culture. Thus, even though they are not particularly proud of their nation, the aspects they are most proud of, relative to other peoples, relate to the welfare state and to democracy. In ISSP 2003, Danes came out prouder of their welfare state than any other people, whereas Swedes and Norwegians figured much lower down the list (Larsen 2008: 41). This suggests that Danish national identity relies heavily on a commitment to the welfare state that, perhaps, becomes more assertive when threats to it are perceived.

Even attitudes to multiculturalism may be affected by worries about social cohesion and thus, ultimately, the welfare state. However, not much is known about the effects of multicultural policies on the welfare state and, in fact, some studies suggest that public spending does not suffer from them (Banting et al. 2006). More generally, Denmark has one of the highest levels of trust in the world and this level has risen over the last twenty years even as immigration has increased from non-Western countries (Torpe 2010). In fact, such immigrants have far greater levels of trust than people in their countries of origin (Svendsen and Svendsen 2006: 174).

Negative views regarding immigrants are of course not restricted to concerns about law and order and the welfare state. Large minorities agreed in 1993 that there is reason to fear that Muslims will come to completely dominate Denmark (36 per cent) and that they don't like the increase in people of colour in the country (38 per cent) (Gaasholt and Togeby 1995: 40). According to a more recent poll, 53 per cent hold that Muslims are to blame if they are criticized in Denmark (Nannestad 2011: 1–4); 68 per cent of respondents who expressed an opinion disagreed that Islam, as a religion, is a threat to Denmark; 90 per cent stated that they don't care whether their neighbour is a Muslim or, for example, a Christian. And while 90 per cent of Danes have trust in people in their neighbourhood, only 55 per cent have trust in Muslims in Denmark (Christensen 2010: 155). Finally, 28 per cent would disapprove if a colleague of theirs wore a Muslim headscarf (Christensen 2010: 151). There is little doubt that many Danes are sceptical about Islam and in particular what is perceived as its 'illiberal' tenets. Nevertheless, these attitudes do not necessarily translate into strong anti-immigrant preferences; in Nannestad's survey 68 per cent of respondents said they would not mind if their son or daughter married a Muslim.

Concerns about the welfare state may, at least in part, explain the lack of multicultural policies in the country. People may be worried about the impact of multicultural policies on social cohesion, as well as about making Denmark too 'hospitable' and therefore attractive for refugees and other potentially 'expensive' immigrants. This is consistent with Will Kymlicka's (2010: 46) suggestion that where immigrants are considered net burdens to the welfare state, multicultural policies are more likely to suffer a backlash.

Another condition mentioned by Kymlicka (2010: 46) as detrimental to multicultural policies is the perception of immigrants as being illiberal, and there is little doubt that many Danes are worried about the liberal credentials of Islam. The further the majority goes in the direction of what Joppke (2009: 561) has dubbed militant (or illiberal) liberalism, the more it will be inclined to see minority cultures as threatening to liberalism and, presumably, the less it will incline towards multiculturalism. A case in point is the often-heard argument that Muslim requests for shower curtains in schools be rejected because they do not reflect Danish liberal-mindedness.

Apart from concerns about the welfare state and illiberal practices, a further explanatory factor may be that Denmark is still a relatively homogeneous society. Some evidence from social psychology suggests that majority groups tend to favour the assimilation of minority groups into a single culture – a way in which the majority may preserve its privileges. Minority groups tend to favour a multiculturalism that encompasses both their distinct identities and a common superordinate identity (Dovido et al. 2010). On this assumption, we should expect to find less support for multiculturalism in homogeneous societies, everything else being equal.

While Danes have been pushing for more restrictive immigration and integration policies, there is now evidence that they are content with the present level of restrictions. Thus, in 2011, only 34 per cent thought that immigration and integration laws should be tightened. Furthermore, support for these laws has dropped from 60 per cent in 2008 to 51 per cent in 2011 (TNS Gallup 2011). Indeed, in a survey from 2010, 63 per cent agreed with the Social Democrats' leader, Helle Thorning-Schmidt, that immigration policies are now tight enough (Berlingske Tidende 2010). Issues of immigration and integration played less of a role in the 2011 general election than they did in the previous three elections, and there is little doubt that the change of focus from such issues to the economic crisis helped the coalition of Socialists, Social Democrats and Social Liberals win.

This shift in attitudes may be related to a change in immigration policies designed to prioritize labour market needs. As a result, immigrants and descendants are experiencing higher levels of employment (Kærgård 2010a: 41; Ministry of Refugee, Immigration and Integration Affairs 2011). They are also becoming better educated (Jacobsen and Liversage 2010) and commit less crime (Andersen and Tranæs 2011: 11–16). A majority of Danes now say they prefer multiculturalism to monoculturalism (TNS Gallup 2011). However one should not underestimate the possibility that specific events – consider for examples the publication of twelve controversial Muhammed cartoons in 2005 – may reverse this trend.

Liberal theory and the Danish debate on multiculturalism

I conclude this chapter with a discussion of Danish debates on multiculturalism from a normative, political theory perspective. Political theorists who are attracted to multiculturalism often defend their claims on the basis of a liberal concern for equality of opportunity, suggesting that such equality requires sensitivity to the distinct cultural and religious interests of different individuals or groups (Cohen

1999; Holtug 2009; Kymlicka 1995; Modood 2007; Parekh 2006). Thus, specific options may have different values for people depending on their cultural and religious affiliation, such as the option of going to (a Protestant) church, or celebrating Christmas; and equality of opportunity requires equalizing the value of the options available to people (Holtug 2009).

A criticism often raised against multiculturalism in Denmark pertains to this egalitarian ideal. It consists in labelling group-differentiated rights (and even difference-blind minority accommodation) 'special rights' (*særrettigheder*), thus implicitly suggesting that minorities receive special – and especially good – treatment. In other words, the charge is that such rights involve discrimination. However, what the liberal argument suggests is that minorities should sometimes be accommodated insofar as this is necessary in order for them to obtain *equal* opportunities, not *better* opportunities. Therefore, insofar as such accommodation would in fact give minorities better opportunities than the majority, it would not be justified by the argument.

It should also be pointed out that while this objection to multiculturalism gains rhetorical appeal from the label *special* rights, highlighting how these rights are granted only to some, *all* rights are in fact special in this sense. For example, minors are not granted the right to vote, people who have jobs are not granted unemployment benefits, the healthy are not offered publicly funded medical treatments and so on. Arguably, what makes it just to restrict unemployment benefits to the unemployed is that this contributes to equality of opportunity. And, to the extent that multicultural accommodation is justified, the argument presented above suggests that this is for exactly the same reason.

Often, political rejection of multiculturalism in Denmark is also based on claims about how multiculturalism facilitates the emergence of parallel societies, school segregation, crime and the deterioration of the welfare state. However, the causal mechanisms assumed in these linkages are rarely spelled out and, indeed, are more difficult to establish than is acknowledged by critics (Kymlicka 2010; Vertovec and Wessendorf 2010). No doubt some kinds of multicultural policies may promote parallel societies, but this does not imply that all will.

In a recent influential Danish book, Jens-Martin Eriksen and Frederik Stjernfelt raise two further objections to multiculturalism. The first is that multiculturalism shares with conservative nationalism a series of dubious 'culturalist' assumptions, including the following: there are no impartial values on the basis of which differences between cultures can be normatively assessed; all cultures are entitled to tolerance or recognition; cultures are unified, organic entities in which the importance of each part can only be understood in relation to the whole; once individuals have been formed by their culture they become incapable of adopting other cultural perspectives on the world; each culture possesses a form of dignity that demands our respect (Eriksen and Stjernfelt 2008).

I support Eriksen's and Stjernfelt's reservations about many of these culturalist claims. However, the argument presented above relies on none of them. The only relation assumed between cultures and their members is that the value an option has for an individual depends on his or her cultural affiliation. For example, having a holiday at Christmas (or at Eid) may have a different value depending on one's religion.

The second criticism raised by Eriksen and Stjernfelt (2008: 190) is that group-differentiated rights may conflict with individual rights. For example, a right to affirmative action in universities may conflict with the right to be admitted on the basis of merit. However, not all group-differentiated rights give rise to a conflict of rights in this manner. Thus, even if Sikhs are exempted from a requirement to wear a helmet, this does not seem to *conflict* with other people's rights or interests. In addition, it is a general feature of rights that they may conflict with other rights; this has nothing in particular to do with group-differentiated multicultural rights. Thus, social rights may conflict with liberty rights but unless we are libertarians, this will not discourage us from endorsing social rights. Finally, the solution in cases of conflict is to weigh up the different considerations, in this particular case a meritocratic principle against a concern for equality of opportunity. This is not to prejudge how these particular values should be weighed in cases of conflict, but merely to point out that such weighing is a general aspect of rights.

What many of the objections raised here have in common is that they ascribe problems to multiculturalism that are in fact general aspects of theories of justice. Examples include the claim that group-differentiated rights are special rights, and that such rights may come into conflict with other rights. Thus, the case made against multiculturalism in Danish debates does not challenge multiculturalism in its strongest version. Whether such a multiculturalism is ultimately persuasive is a question for continuing examination.

References

Adamo, Silvia (2009), *Citizenship Law and the Challenge of Multiculturalism*, PhD dissertation, Faculty of Law, University of Copenhagen.

Andersen, Jørgen Goul (2002), *Danskernes holdninger til indvandrere. En oversigt*, AMID Working Papers 17/2002. Available at http://www.amid.dk/pub/papers/AMID_17-2002_Goul_Andersen.pdf

Andersen, Lars Højsgaard and Torben Tranæs (2011), *Etniske minoriteters overrepræsentation i strafferetlige domme*, Odense: Syddansk Universitetsforlag.

Banting, Keith, Richard Johnston, Will Kymlicka and Stuart Soroka (2006), 'Do multicultural policies erode the welfare state? An empirical analysis', in Keith Banting and Will Kymlicka (eds), *Multiculturalism and the Welfare State*, Oxford: Oxford University Press.

Berlingske Tidende (2010), 'Danskerne: Der er strammet nok', *Berlingske Tidende* 25 November. Available at http://www.b.dk/politik/danskerne-der-er-strammet-nok-0

Bjergager, Erik and Henrik Hoffmann-Hansen (2006), 'Religionen i Foghs private rum', *Kristeligt Dagblad*, 30 June.

Bonde, Annette and Bjarne Steensbeck (2011), 'Flertal: Udlændinge skal selv betale velfærd', *Berlingske*, 31 March. Available at http://www.b.dk/politiko/flertal-udlaendinge-skal-selv-betale-velfaerd

Borre, Ole (2011), 'De politiske værdiers udvikling', in Peter Gundelach (ed.), *Små og store forandringer. Danskernes værdier siden 1981*, Copenhagen: Hans Reitzels Forlag.

Christensen, Bjørg and Eva Lindhardt (2007), 'Medborgerskab og samfundets sammenhængskraft', in Camilla Sløk and Anne-Mette Nortvig Willesen (eds), *Kristendomskundskab, livsoplysning og medborgerskab*, Copenhagen: Forlaget Samfundslitteratur.

Christensen, Geert Laier (2010), *Tørklæder, tillid og tørre tal – en undersøgelse af indvandring og integration i Danmark*, Copenhagen: Forlaget Center for Politiske Studier.

Coenders, Marcel, Marcel Lubbers and Peer Scheepers (2003), *Majority Populations Attitudes Towards Migrants and Minorities. Report for the European Monitoring Centre on Racism and Xenophobia*, Ref. no. 2003/04/01. Available at http://fra.europa.eu/fraWebsite/attachments/Report-1.pdf

Cohen, Gerald A. (1999), 'Expensive tastes and multiculturalism', in Rajeev Bhargava, Amiya Kumar Bagchi and R. Sudarshan (eds), *Multiculturalism, Liberalism and Democracy*, New Delhi: Oxford University Press.

Dinesen, Peter Thisted, Robert Klemmensen and Asbjørn Sonne Nørgaard (2011), 'Attitudes towards immigration: The role of personal predispositions', paper prepared for the 34th Annual Scientific Meeting of the International Society of Political Psychology, 9–12 July, Istanbul.

Dovido, John F., Samuel L. Gaertner and Tamar Saguy (2010), 'Another view of "we": Majority and minority group perspectives on a common ingroup identity', *European Review of Social Psychology*, 18 (1), pp. 296–330.

Eriksen, Hans-Martin and Frederik Stjernfelt (2008), *Adskillelsens politik. Multikulturalisme – ideologi og virkelighed*, Copenhagen: Lindhardt & Ringhof.

Gaasholt, Øystein and Lise Togeby (1995), *I syv sind. Danskernes holdninger til flygtninge og indvandrere*, Århus: Politica.

Government (2010), *Handlingsplan om etnisk ligebehandling og respekt for den enkelte*, Copenhagen: Regeringen. Available at http://www.nyi danmark.dk/NR/rdonlyres/20BA8169-7806-416F-B412-48DA175 799DB/0/handlingsplan_etnisk_ligebehandling_2010.pdf

Gundelach, Peter (2011), 'Stabilitet og forandringer', in Peter Gundelach (ed.), *Små og store forandringer. Danskernes værdier siden 1981*, Copenhagen: Hans Reitzels Forlag.

Hedetoft, Ulf (2008), 'Social cohesion, belonging and ethnic diversity', paper presented at the 12th International Metropolis Conference, Melbourne: Monash Institute for the Study of Global Movements.

Hedetoft, Ulf (2010), 'Denmark versus multiculturalism', in Vertovec and Wessendorf (eds), *The Multiculturalism Backlash*.

Heinskou, Nilas Nordberg, Tanja Parker Astrup and Jakob Sorgenfri Kjær (2007), 'Grundlovsdag: Debat om værdier: Taler med tørklæde i mund', *Politiken*, 6 June.

Holtug, Nils (2005), 'Multikulturalisme', in Anna Paldam Folker, Kirsten Hansen and Sigurd Lauridsen (eds), *Bag den politiske retorik – essays i værdikampen*, Copenhagen: Tiderne Skifter.

Holtug, Nils (2009), 'Equality and difference-blind rights', in Nils Holtug, Kasper Lippert-Rasmussen and Sune Lægaard (eds), *Nationalism and Multiculturalism in a World of Immigration*, Basingstoke: Palgrave Macmillan.

Holtug, Nils (2010a), 'Immigration: Er der en konflikt mellem frihed og lighed?', in Kasper Lippert-Rasmussen and Nils Holtug (eds), *Kulturel diversitet: Muligheder og begrænsninger*, Odense: Syddansk Universitetsforlag.

Holtug, Nils (2010b), 'Immigration and the politics of social cohesion', *Ethnicities*, 10 (4), pp. 435–51.

Holtug, Nils (2011), 'Nationalism, secularism and liberal neutrality: The Danish case of judges and religious symbols', *Les Ateliers de l'Éthique*, 6 (2), pp. 107–25.

Hussain, Mustafa (2011), *Muslims in Copenhagen*, New York: Open Society Foundations.

Jacobsen, Vibeke and Anika Liversage (2010), *Køn og etnicitet i uddannelsessystemet*, Copenhagen: SFI.

Jensen, Tina Gudrun (2010), '"Making room": Encompassing diversity in Denmark', in Alessandro Silj (ed.), *European Multiculturalism Revisited*, London: Zed Books.

Jespersen, Karen and Ralf Pittelkow (2005), *De lykkelige danskere. En bog om sammenhængskraft*, Copenhagen: Gyldendal.

Joppke, Christian (2009), 'Is religion the problem?', *Ethnicities*, 9 (4), pp. 560–6.

Korsgaard, Ove, Lakshmi Sigurdsson and Keld Skovmand (eds) (2007), *Medborgerskab – et nyt dannelsesideal*, Frederiksberg: Religionspædagogisk Forlag.

Krarup, Søren (2001), *Kristendom og danskhed*, Højbjerg: Hovedland.

Kymlicka, Will (1995), *Multicultural Citizenship*, Oxford: Oxford University Press.

Kymlicka, Will (2010), 'The rise and fall of multiculturalism? New debates on inclusion and accommodation in diverse societies', in Vertovec and Wessendorf (eds), *The Multiculturalism Backlash*.

Kærgård, Niels (2010a), 'Etik og dilemmaer i indvandrerpolitikken', in Torkild Bak, Mette Bock and Jens Holger Schjørring (eds), *Grænser for solidaritet*, Copenhagen: Forlaget Anis.

Kærgård, Niels (2010b), 'Social cohesion and the transformation from ethnic to multicultural society: The case of Denmark', *Ethnicities*, 10 (4), pp. 470–87.

Laborde, Cécile and John Maynor (2008), 'The Republican contribution to contemporary political theory', in Cécile Laborde and John Maynor (eds), *Republicanism and Political Theory*, Oxford: Blackwell Publishing Ltd.

Larsen, Christian Albrekt (2008), *Danskernes nationale forestillinger*, Aalborg: Aalborg Universitetsforlag.

Mikkelsen, Brian (2004), 'Vi skal værne om vores historiefortællere', *Berlingske Tidende*, 26 August.

Miller, David (1995), *On Nationality*, Oxford: Oxford University Press.

Ministry of Culture (2006), *Danish Cultural Canon*. Available at http://kulturkanon.kum.dk/en/

Ministry of Culture (2011), 'Værdikommission er nedsat'. Available at http://kum.dk/Nyheder-og-Presse/Pressemeddelelser/2011/Februar/Vardikommissionen-er-nedsat/

Ministry of Refugee, Immigration and Integration Affairs (2011), 'Pressemeddelelse: Udlæningepolitikken sparer årligt staten for mia. af kroner'. Available at http://www.nyidanmark.dk/da-dk/Nyheder/Pressemeddelelser/Integrationsministeriet/2011/April/udlaendingepolitikken_sparer_aarligt_staten_for_mia.htm

MIPEX III (2011), *Migrant Integration Policy Index III*, Brussels: British Council and Migration Policy Group.

Modood, Tariq (2007), *Multiculturalism. A Civic Idea*, Cambridge: Polity Press.

Mouritsen, Per (2006), 'The particular universalism of a Nordic civic nation: Common values, state religion and Islam in Danish political culture', in Tariq Modood, Anna Triandafyllidou and Ricard Zapata-Barrero (eds), *Multiculturalism, Muslims and Citizenship*, London: Routledge.

Municipality of Copenhagen (2011), 'Get involved in the city. Citizenship + inclusion. Copenhagen's integration policy 2011–2014', City of Copenhagen. Available at http://www.kk.dk/Borger/Integration/Inklusion spolitik.aspx

Nannestad, Peter (2011), 'The Danes, Islam and Muslims', unpublished paper.

Nielsen, Hans Jørgen (2004), *Er danskerne fremmedfjendske?*, Aarhus: Aarhus Universitetsforlag.

Olwig, Karen Fog, Anders H. Stefansson, Jytte Agergaard Larsen, Nils Holtug, Allan Krasnik and Margit Warburg (2011), 'The point(s) of integration. A multi-disciplinary analysis of family reunification and selective immigration policy in Denmark', manuscript.

Parekh, Bhiku (2006), *Rethinking Multiculturalism. Cultural Diversity and Political Theory*, 2nd edition, Basingstoke: Palgrave Macmillan.

Phillips, Anne (2007), *Multiculturalism without Culture*, Princeton, NJ: Princeton University Press.

Pind, Søren (2008), 'Åh Danmark'. Available at http://www.soren-pind.dk/index.php?mod=weblog&cat=42

Pind, Søren (2011), 'Ordet skal føre kulturkampen', *Berlingske Tidende*, 12 March. Available at http://www.b.dk/kronikker/ordet-skal-foere-kulturkampen

Prins, Bauke and Sawitri Saharso (2010), 'From toleration to repression. The Dutch backlash against multiculturalism', in Vertovec and Wessendorf (eds), *The Multiculturalism Backlash*.

Rawls, John (1993), *Political Liberalism*, New York: Columbia University Press.

Regeringens arbejdsgruppe om udredning af indvandringens økonomiske konsekvenser (2011), *Indvandringens økonomiske konsekvenser*. Available at http://www.nyidanmark.dk/da-dk/Nyheder/Pressemeddelelser/Integr ationsministeriet/2011/April/udlaendingepolitikken_sparer_aarligt_ staten_for_mia.htm

Støvring, Kasper (2010), *Sammenhængskraft*, Copenhagen: Gyldendal.

Svendsen, Gert Tinggaard and Gunnar Lind Haase Svendsen (2006), *Social kapital. En introduktion*, Copenhagen: Hans Reitzels Forlag.

Thalhammer, Eva, Vlasta Zucha, Edith Enzenhofer, Brigitte Salfinger and Günther Ogris (2001), *Attitudes Towards Minority Groups in the European Union. A Special Analysis of the Eurobarometer 2000 Survey*, Vienna: European Monitoring Centre on Racism and Xenophobia.

Available at http://ec.europa.eu/public_opinion/archives/ebs/ebs_138_analysis.pdf

Think Tank on Integration in Denmark (2004), *Immigration and Integration Policies in Denmark and Selected Countries*, Copenhagen: Ministry of Refugee, Immigration and Integration Affairs.

TNS Gallup A/S (2011), *Lyngallup om Søren Pind*, TNS Gallup A/S and Berlingske Tidende, 11 March. Available at http://photosnap.dk/itu/wp-content/uploads/2011/05/DMK-online-version.pdf

Togeby, Lise (1998), 'Prejudice and tolerance in a period of increasing ethnic diversity and growing unemployment: Denmark since 1970', *Ethnic and Racial Studies*, 21 (6), pp. 1,137–54.

Torpe, Lars (2010), 'Sammenhængskraft, diversitet og etnicitet', unpublished paper.

Tranæs, Torben and Klaus F. Zimmermann (2004), 'Nyt', in Tranæs and Zimmermann (eds), *Migrants, Work and the Welfare State*, Odense: University Press of Southern Denmark and the Rockwool Foundation Research Unit, pp. 3–8.

Vertovec, Steven and Susanne Wessendorf (2010), 'Introduction: Assessing the backlash against multiculturalism in Europe', in Steven Vertovec and Susanne Wessendorf (eds), *The Multiculturalism Backlash*, Oxford: Routledge.

Wadensjö, Eskil and Christer Gerdes (2004), 'Immigrants and the public sector in Denmark and Germany', in Torben Tranæs and Klaus F. Zimmerman (eds), *Migrants, Work, and the Welfare State*, Odense: University Press of Southern Denmark.

Young, Iris Marion (1990), *Justice and the Politics of Difference*, Princeton, NJ: Princeton University Press.

Chapter Ten

Multiculturalism Italian Style:
Soft or Weak Recognition?

Tiziana Caponio

Introduction

Throughout the 1980s and 1990s theories of immigrants' integration – whether resting on the premises of multiculturalism, assimilation or universalist inclusion – did not spark much public debate in Italy. Instead the focus was control of borders, illegal immigration and criminality (Sciortino and Colombo 2004). This changed at the turn of the new millennium, when the radicalizing anti-immigrant discourse of the Northern League, together with such dramatic events as terrorist attacks in the US, London and Madrid, provoked a heated debate on the risks of multiculturalism in the context of a supposedly weak Italian identity among intellectuals, religious elites and politicians. Multiculturalism has entered the political agenda and public debate, then, as 'something to avoid', notwithstanding the fact that principles of group recognition were discernible in 1990s Italian integration policies at both a national and a local level.

In order to make sense of this apparent paradox, in this chapter I undertake an analysis of immigrant integration policies at different levels of government – national, regional and local – in Italy to find out how group recognition has been understood and framed in these different policymaking contexts. In the first section I look at the 1986 Italian immigration law and then at the 1998 reform, which attempted to strike a balance between groups' recognition and universal inclusion. The social actors and political parties supporting such a stance will be identified, as well as those endorsing a more assimilationist approach.

The second section deals with the new culturalist turn that emerged in Italian immigrants' integration policies at the beginning of the 2000s and which has led to the adoption in 2009 of the so-called Integration Agreement. The 'discovery' of Italian Greek-Roman and Christian-Judaic roots has, ironically, gone hand in hand with a growing disenchantment towards policies of group recognition. Yet attitudinal survey data show how immigrants' different cultures do not seem to represent a concern for Italian respondents.

The third section considers how cultural difference has been addressed in local level policymaking on immigrant integration. Whereas centre-left majorities give greater attention to issues of cultural accommodation than centre-right ones, concrete policies and local implementation practices suggest a similar approach which comprises two parts: (1) a preference for initiatives of intercultural dialogue and exchange, targeting in particular school education and second generations; (2) a functional conception of cultural competence in service delivery, that is, a concern to make the administrative machine work and reach immigrant users.

In the final section I identify the main characteristics of the Italian approach to the recognition of migrants' different cultures and its limits.

The 1980s and 1990s: between group recognition and universal inclusion

The first migration flows into Italy started at the end of the 1960s in the context of various *migratory systems* (Castles and Miller 2003), in other words as a consequence of colonial, cultural and commercial relations between Italy and certain sending countries (Colombo and Sciortino 2004). This is the case of the first foreign domestic workers who arrived in two waves: as domestic personnel accompanying the families of Italian colonial officials in the Horn of Africa (Eritrea, Ethiopia and Somalia) who were returning home after the Second World War; and as full-time, principally female domestic workers in the late 1960s for well-off Italian families who had contacts with Italian Catholic missions in countries such as Cape Verde and the Philippines.

An additional early migratory channel comprised foreign university students, many of them from the Middle East and Africa, who had been granted scholarships by the Italian government in the context of aid to developing countries. Also in the late 1960s a growing number of Tunisians migrated to Sicily, to be employed part time in the fishing industry where shortages of labour were becoming evident.

From this it is clear that Italy's immigrant population was from the very beginning characterized by great diversity in terms of countries of origin and cultural backgrounds. This might have been a positive sign for the implementing of multicultural policies. However the subject of integration entered the policy agenda only in the mid-1980s, and it did not evoke any public debate around the question of recognition (De Zwart 2005). The first immigration law, approved in 1986 behind closed doors, was enacted so as to comply with international obligations associated with the 1975 International Labour Organisation (ILO) Convention (n. 143) on the status of migrant workers. Italy had ratified and enthusiastically supported the Convention in 1980 in order to strengthen the protection of its emigrants abroad (Colombo and Sciortino 2004).

The law was characterized by a strong protectionist bias towards the Italian workforce (Zincone 2011: 262). It was also informed by a theory of integration shaped by the experience of past Italian emigrants abroad. In the law, native and EU citizens were assigned priority in access to employment. In addition, the hiring of workers from non-EU countries was discouraged by a complicated bureaucratic process and by a contribution tax that put aside resources for repatriation in the case of an emigant's dismissal from work. On the other hand, in terms of integration policy, 'regular non-EU workers' were extended the same rights as Italian workers, as well as a special right to the protection of their mother tongue and cultural background. This clearly reflected the perspective of an emigration country concerned with keeping ties with its emigrants abroad and encouraging their return (Bonifazi 2007). Italy's regional governments were entrusted with implementing cultural policies for immigrants, yet no financial resources were made available to them so that this part of the law existed only on paper.

A second immigration law, approved just four years later in 1990, did not stir any significant debate on immigrants' integration and cultural recognition. The main issues dividing political parties were entry controls, expulsions, inflow planning and the introduction of a new amnesty for illegal immigrants. The first mass amnesty had accompanied the 1986 law; before it, only a few limited amnesties had been introduced for foreign workers employed in specific sectors such as domestic and care services and fishing (Einaudi 2007).

The only political party that already in those early years of immigration regulation began to express scepticism about a 'multiethnic and multi-racial society' was the Northern League (Einaudi 2007: 149). As I discuss below, throughout the 1990s and 2000s this party built much of its electoral success on the politicization of the immigration issue, strongly opposing recognition of immigrants' cultural differences, especially those involving Muslim and Roma minorities.

The 1991 International Conference on Immigration organized by the Italian Presidency of the Council of Ministers and the Organisation for Economic Cooperation and Development (OECD) marked the start of a dialogue on integration issues in Italy between political leaders and academic experts. A preparatory study was commissioned to Poleis (*Centro di politica comparata*), an interdisciplinary research institute at Bocconi University in Milan composed of political scientists, legal experts and political philosophers. Poleis undertook an in-depth analysis of immigration controls and immigrants' integration laws in four European countries – France, the UK, the Netherlands and Germany – with the task of drawing recommendations for the Italian case. In recommending an integration policy, the research group suggested a balanced approach between recognition of immigrants' cultural difference and equal access to citizenship rights. This was thought to contribute in the long run to a common sense of belonging to the host country (Università Bocconi and Cnel 1991: 12).

Hence it is in the experts' debate of the early 1990s that the idea of an Italian 'third way' between the French assimilationist model and the Dutch multicultural one started to take shape. Cultural recognition was regarded essentially as an instrument to enforce substantive equality and avoid possible barriers in access to citizenship rights. This position also underpinned the work of the Commission for the Study of a Comprehensive Law on Immigration, established in 1993, by a centre-left government and composed almost exclusively of the same academic experts who had been involved in the previous Poleis study. Nevertheless, integration issues continued to have minor relevance in national-level political and public debate, which was monopolized by continuous emergencies such as Albanian mass arrivals in 1991, war refugees from the former Yugoslavia between 1992 and 1993 and new arrivals again from Albania in 1997 after the collapse of the so-called 'financial pyramid schemes'.

The situation was different at the local level where there was more apprehension about immigrants' reception and integration. In 1993 a then prominent political leader of the Northern League, Marco Formentini, was elected mayor of Milan on a political manifesto that presented immigration as a threat to public security. He was extremely critical towards the policies of the previous centre-left majority which had promoted various initiatives aimed at supporting immigrant associations and their representation (Caponio 2005). Countering Formentini's view, the Social Democratic Party in the 1995 local elections in Bologna – a traditional 'red' stronghold – championed immigrants' cultural differences and immigrant associations as a resource for the local society that should be included in policymaking processes (Però 2007).

Thus in the 1990s immigrant integration and recognition of cultural difference may have been absent from the national policy agenda but they represented hotly contested issues at a local level, where mayors were confronted with meeting immigrants' everyday needs and promoting harmonious interaction with the local population. This significant divide between national policies, which were primarily concerned with border control, entry regulations and inflow planning, and local attention to integration dilemmas was a challenge for the centre-left government led by Romano Prodi and elected in 1996. The government therefore undertook a comprehensive re-evaluation of existing legislation on immigration.

The preamble of Law no. 40/1998, known also as the Turco-Napolitano law after the names of the then Ministers of Social Affairs and Home Affairs, had introduced the concept of 'reasonable integration', signifying both nationals' and immigrants' physical and psychological well-being on the one hand, and positive interaction between the different groups on the other (Zincone 2000). On the basis of these two principles, a number of policy measures aimed at fostering individual equality and promoting intercultural relations was devised in all crucial spheres of immigrant incorporation – employment, health, education and professional training, housing and civic participation. In order to make reform measures effective, a National Fund for Immigrant Policy was introduced and allocated to the regions on the basis of programmes agreed upon with the municipalities.

The 'reasonable integration model' marked a move away from framing current immigrants in Italy as past Italian emigrants elsewhere. In line with the Poleis study, as well as with the work of the 1993 Commission, it considered cultural recognition as part of a broader strategy aimed at fostering immigrants' inclusion in citizenship rights and ensuring peaceful cohabitation. Such a principle of 'soft recognition' was agreed upon and supported by the Social Democratic party, the left-wing Catholics of the Popular Party, as well as other leftist parties such as the Communist Re-foundation (*Rifondazione Comunista*), the Italian Communists (*Comunisti Italiani*) and the Greens.

On the other side of the political spectrum, the most vocal oppo-sition came from the Northern League, denouncing during the Parliamentary debate the 'lack of attention to *our people*' and the risk of cultural and religious clashes (Einaudi 2007: 226). Other centre-right parties joined in the attack. One was *Forza Italia*, the centre-right party founded by Silvio Berlusconi in 1994. The other was the National Alliance party, emerging in that same period from the ashes of the Italian Social Movement with the intention of break-ing with its fascist tradition. These parties expressed their concern about illegal entry into Italy.

Multiculturalism was not a crucial issue in the 1997 Parliamentary debate of the Turco-Napolitano law. The attempt of the centre-left Prodi government to strike a balance between cultural recognition and universal inclusion reflected the standpoint of moderate centre parties, and in particular that of Catholic ones. The Centre Catholic Party, part of the centre-right opposition, had openly declared its concurrence with the centre-left government integration policy.

Once again, implementation was left to the regional and local tiers of government. The former, in particular, were assigned a central role in the planning of immigrant integration measures and, there-fore, in the choice of the integration approach to be pursued. A feder-alist reform coming into effect in 2002 strengthened the autonomy of regional authorities in matters of social policy, including immigrant integration. In this new institutional context, regions receive a share of the general Social Policy Fund and can decide whether to allocate funding for immigrant integration policy at all, and which measures to adopt.

To sum up, if the first two Italian immigration laws envisaged a sort of *weak recognition*, since immigrants' cultural backgrounds were appreciated in theory but no resources were devoted to develop concrete policies, the 1998 immigration law seemed more oriented to the enforcing of a principle of soft recognition (Caponio 2010: 60). This took into account the relevance of cultural difference in access to social services and social resources without explicitly acknowledging or institutionalizing group differences.

The 2000s: (re)discovered Italian culture first

If throughout the 1990s the public debate on immigration had centred around controlling illegal entry into Italy and criminal-ity, at the turn of the century a shift of focus occurred highlighting immigrants' cultural and religious diversity. Particular emphasis was given to the Muslim religion (Zincone 2001: 35). Two parallel developments underpinned such a change: a re-alignment of right-wing political parties on immigration, with the Northern League emerging as the main political entrepreneur of anti-immigrant feelings; and the start of a debate on Italian and European cultural identity.

On the first subject, we saw how the Northern League expressed its alarm at the cultural threat posed by 'uncontrolled' immigration during the Parliamentary debate on the Turco-Napolitano law. In the 1996 national elections, however, this party's radical positions formed part of a broader political strategy aimed at breaking its alliance with other centre-right parties. The Northern League warned of the possible secession of Northern Italy from the rest of the country and it emphasized the distinct identity of the *Padania* nation (Diamanti 2003: 74–9). According to the 1998 publication 'Padania, identity and the multiracial society', Padania people had the right to protect their identity from the 'contamination' of foreigners' different cultures (Guolo 2003: 61). The anti-immigrant discourse of the Northern League hit in particular at Muslim migrants and Roma people. Northern League mayors opposed the building of mosques in their towns; the case of Lodi, near Varese, was especially dramatic (Saint-Blancat and Schmidt di Friedberg 2005; Triandafyllidou 2006). Many Northern League mayors also opposed setting up transient campgrounds for Roma (Vitale 2009).

This radicalization of the Northern League took place at a time when a national debate arose over the Christian roots of Europe and Italy. It was essentially concerned with religious differences arising from the more visible presence of Islam in Europe and Italy. Leading conservative bishops such as Cardinal Maggiolini of Como and Cardinal Biffi of Bologna started to question the inter-religious dialogue pursued by Catholic grassroots organizations such as Caritas and promoted also by Pope John Paul II (Guolo 2003: 87–92). Cardinal Biffi argued that Muslim migrants were resolute in maintaining their difference, while Italians showed far less conviction about their Christian identity. It even led to a risk of Islamic conversion.

Public intellectuals in Italy, such as Giovanni Sartori, a political scientist, and Oriana Fallaci, a well-known writer, denounced the weakness of Italian liberal culture *vis-à-vis* Muslims' religious integralism. In a book published in 2000, Sartori expressed his approval of 'the good liberal society' that accepts diversity but requires assimilation to democratic values and lay principles. Enhancing cultural difference would lead to the fragmentation of society and its 'Balkanization', Sartori believed. He attributed the misguided policy to 'the bad consequences of multiculturalism' (Sartori 2000: 112). This view was radicalized further in a pamphlet published by *Corriere della Sera* immediately after the 9/11 terror attacks. Fallaci warned about the 'cowardice of Italian people' in not facing up to the Muslim threat to liberal democracy (Fallaci 2001).

Curiously, this culturalist discourse of the early 2000s did not seem to reverberate in the public opinion of the time. At least two indicators show a contradictory situation. First, electoral support for the Northern League, which reached its peak (10 per cent) in the 1996 national political elections, fell after the break-up of the centre-right alliance to just over 4 per cent in the 1999 European elections, and to barely 4 per cent in the 2001 Parliamentary elections (Diamanti 2003). The aggressive anti-immigrant and anti-Islam discourse of this party had either had no effect or had been counterproductive. At the same time, opinion polls carried out by the Fondazione Nord-Est (Bordignon 2008; Bordignon and Ceccarini 2007) from 1999 onwards on a representative sample of Italian citizens indicated that immigrants were primarily perceived as a threat to public order and people's safety, and far less to the country's 'culture, identity and religion'. However, as Table 10.1 indicates, cultural issues took a more prominent place in Italians' attitudes towards immigration in 2007.

The moderate character of Italian public opinion seems to reflect the ideas informing the 2002 immigration law, where centrist Catholic parties played a crucial role in toning down the initially bellicose rhetoric of the Northern League (Zincone 2011; Colombo and Sciortino 2003). This new law did not touch upon issues of immigrants' integration with the exception of access to public housing, which was limited to immigrants who had had a residence permit for two years or more. Yet, the new centre-right government which was elected in 2001 did not go ahead with implementing the above-mentioned 'reasonable integration' model. Hence this government did not explicitly address the issue of immigrant integration, although it was clear it did not share the idea of striking a balance between universal inclusion and group recognition.

The main innovation of the 2002 law was the so-called 'stay contract' which linked entry and stay in Italy to the possession of a job contract. It also permitted just six months for job searching in cases

Table 10.1 Attitudes towards migration in Italy: trends from 1999 to 2007

	October 2007	July 2005	April 2004	January 2002	October 1999
Immigrants pose a threat to public order and people's safety	50.7	39.2	37.2	39.7	46.1
Immigrants pose a threat to employment	36.7	35.1	35.5	29.2	32.2
Immigrants are a danger for our culture, our identity and our religion	35.1	26.6	30.2	23.9	27.3

Question: 'I am going to read you a list of statements concerning topical issues. Could you please tell me whether you strongly agree, agree, slightly disagree or strongly disagree?' The table combines percentages of those who 'agree' and who 'strongly agree'.

Sources: for 2007 Demos-LaPolis for Intesa San Paolo (in Bordignon 2008: 8); for other years Demos and Pi for Coop (in Bordignon and Ceccarini 2007).

where an immigrant had lost his job (instead of the previous one-year period). The law took a strictly functional conception of integration (Caponio and Graziano 2011). Immigrants were regarded as just 'workers' and were allowed to stay in the country only as long as they were considered 'useful' to the national economy.

Opposition towards multiculturalism and, with it, Islam – the two were increasingly interconnected ideas – resurfaced in the public debate of the mid-2000s. It followed the bombings in Madrid (March 2004) and London (July 2005); the murder of Theo Van Gogh, a Dutch filmmaker, in Amsterdam (November 2004); and the Danish cartoon crisis (September 2005). Some politicians became notorious for their radical positions: thus Roberto Calderoli, Northern League Minister for Administrative Simplification and Devolution, displayed a T-shirt reproducing one of the Danish cartoons during a national TV programme in 2006, and explained it was a demonstration of freedom of expression in Europe. The Minister's actions led to violent protests in front of the Italian consulate in Bengazi, Libya, which caused eleven deaths. The Minister was forced to resign.

Some important political leaders came out in favour of the nationalistic positions of the intellectuals and Catholic bishops described earlier. They emphasized the distinctiveness of Italian identity: Marcello Pera, *Forza Italia* President of the Senate, contended that Italy's identity lay in its Greek-Roman and Judaic-Christian heritage.

The Minister of Education, Letizia Moratti, known for her positions favouring preserving Catholic traditions in public schools, such as Christmas celebrations and the presence of crucifixes in classrooms, faced protests from Muslim but also lay parents denouncing the violation of the principle of freedom of religion (Guolo 2003: 125).

The *Lautsi* v. *Italy* case, initiated by a Finnish woman opposed to Catholic symbols in public schools, is the best-known legal challenge to the view that Italy's historic identity requires contemporary public displays of Catholic symbols. The case reached the European Court of Human Rights which, in an initial judgement handed down in 2009, ruled that this practice was not in conformity with Italy's own constitution which had been secular since 1985 when 'the confessional character of the state had been explicitly abandoned'. But in 2011 an appeal by Italy to the Grand Chamber of the Court succeeded in reversing the Court's original judgement in November 2009. The Chamber's rationale was that the display of the crucifix did not amount to 'indoctrination' and was therefore permissible. Secular critics pointed to an 'unholy alliance' bringing together Catholic and Eastern Orthodox interests which were able to change the ruling.

A new centre-left majority government was elected in 2006 but it no longer attempted to restore the 'reasonable integration model'. Instead it adhered to the newly emphasized cultural definition of Italian identity while trying at the same time to downplay the most radical and explicitly anti-Muslim positions of the Northern League. That summer a new controversy around Islam emerged. The Union of Islamic Communities in Italy (UCOII), a confederation bringing together some 104 local Muslim associations which was viewed by some observers as pushing radical positions, published an advertisement in the major Italian newspapers which compared Israeli repression in the Palestinian territories to the Nazi-organized Holocaust. The Union of Hebrew Communities in Italy vigorously protested this analogy and its condemnation was echoed by centre-right MPs, who launched warnings against the potential disloyalty of Muslims to democratic values. In this highly politicized climate, then Home Office Minister Giuliano Amato announced his intention to promote the drafting of a Charter of Values, Citizenship and Integration (*Carta dei valori, della cittadinanza e dell'integrazione*), which would identify a set of principles agreeable to and signed by new religious organizations in Italy. To carry out this task, a scientific committee composed of experts on religious issues and Islam in particular was appointed.

Given the initial narrow focus on Islamic communities, the scientific committee and Minister Amato gradually enlarged the scope of the proposed Charter. This development, I contend, marked the emergence of a new framing of immigrant integration in Italy (Caponio and Zincone 2011). According to the Scientific Committee, the Charter had as its goal the establishing of 'a clear integration path leading to citizenship [...] [similar] to the French *Contrat d'Accueil*', which required 'learning the Italian language, the basic notions of the Italian history and culture, as well as the sharing of the principles regulating our society' (Ministero dell'Interno 2007: 1–2). Contrary to the 'reasonable integration model', the new culturalist turn clearly put Italian civic culture first, while requiring some degree of assimilation of immigrants into the receiving society.

Such an approach to immigrant integration was reinforced by the ensuing fourth Berlusconi government, elected in 2008. It decided to combine the new culturalist discourse with repeated slogans framing immigrants as would-be criminals and threats to public security. It was in this context that a series of criminal cases between 2007 and 2008 involving Romanian and, in some cases, Roma immigrants shocked the public. They inflamed anti-Roma sentiments and stirred up criticism of the former Prodi government for not having introduced restrictions on entry of Romanian and Bulgarian citizens to Italy after these countries joined the EU in 2007. That was not an entirely justified criticism as Prodi's government had announced a moratorium on such in-migration, but it did not apply to low-skilled occupations – construction, tourist services, home care and domestic services – in which Romanian immigrants were traditionally employed in Italy.

Linking immigration with threats to public security and criminality was central to the Northern League's electoral campaign. It doubled its vote to over 8 per cent in the next election. Already in mid-2008, Northern League Home Affairs Minister Roberto Maroni presented a bill to the Senate called the Security Law, which essentially focused on adding new restrictions against undocumented immigrants as well as new measures facilitating their expulsion. It would even apply to citizens of the EU, specifically those from Romania.

The Security Law was approved in 2009 after a contentious Parliamentary debate. It institutionalized the migration-security link that had characterized Northern League political discourse since the early 1990s (Caponio and Graziano 2011). At the same time, this law also formally affirmed the new Italian culturalist approach on integration, defined as the 'process aimed at promoting civility (*convivenza*) between Italian and foreign citizens on the basis of the respect of the Italian Constitution'.

The law introduced the so-called Integration Agreement (IA) that was to be signed by the immigrant at the time of the issuing of the first residence permit. The IA commits the immigrant to achieve specific integration goals within a time span of two years: a sufficient level of knowledge of the spoken Italian language (level A2), as well as of the fundamental principles of the Italian Constitution and institutions and of Italian civic life (labour market functioning, fiscal obligations and so on). In essence, immigrants' different cultural backgrounds were treated as of subordinate relevance in the making of Italian society.

According to the official document, 'Integration and security programme: Identity and encounter' (*Piano per l'integrazione nella sicurezza. Identità e incontro*), approved by the government in 2010, an 'open identity' model of integration (*Modello dell'identità aperta*) should be pursued, based on 'the understanding and the respect of who we are, to be reciprocated by the natural curiosity towards others' cultures and traditions' (Ministero del Lavoro e delle Politiche Sociali 2010: 5). The respect for 'who we are', that is for 'our cultural identity', was defined, in a way similar to the Charter of Values, Citizenship and Integration, as 'an original combination of Judaeo-Christian and Roman-Greek cultures' (2010: 4). This is regarded as an essential pre-condition for starting on a path of integration based on 'rights and obligations, responsibilities and opportunities'. Immigrant cultures are regarded as a source of 'natural curiosity' – not as a resource for society as a whole.

Notwithstanding this culturalist turn, opinion polls carried out as part of the 2011 Transatlantic Trends: Immigration Survey showed a certain optimism in Italian public attitudes towards immigrant integration (Transatlantic Trends 2011: 14). Thus, 59 per cent of interviewees considered immigrants as 'very well' or 'well' integrated; the figure reached 77 per cent in the case of second-generation immigrants. Yet a certain distrust towards Muslim migrants also emerged, considered 'well' or 'very well' integrated by only 41 per cent of Italian respondents. Significantly, this negative attitude did not extend to second-generation Muslims, who were regarded as positively integrated by 66 per cent of Italian respondents. The survey found that the main concern continued to be illegal immigration, which was identified in Italy by 80 per cent of respondents compared to a European average of 67 per cent. Hence, public security rather than cultural identity appears to be the main concern of Italian respondents.

If Islam in Italy has served as the catalyst for the culturalist (re) definition of Italian identity as 'Roman-Greek and Christian-Judaic', undocumented immigrants are the trigger for discourse on public security. Depending on which period is considered, different nationalities have been identified by the mass-media and right-wing parties with the 'undocumented': Moroccans in the 1980s, Albanians in the 1990s, Romanians in the 2000s. In the latter case, the presence of a Roma minority has often led to an overlap of security and cultural arguments. An example was the decision of Northern League Home Office Minister Roberto Maroni to carry out a census of Roma living in the camps by fingerprinting people of all ages including children. This was intended to discourage the 'cultural practice' of employing them in begging (for a reconstruction see Ambrosini and Caneva 2012: 221–3).

Prejudice towards Roma has deep historical roots since they were already established in Italy in the fifteenth century (Piasere 2004). In fact, more than half of the estimated 120,000–150,000 Roma living in the country have Italian citizenship. Their condition of subalternity and marginalization is clearly reflected in today's attitudes towards this group. A 2008 opinion poll showed that 81 per cent of respondents did not like Roma very much or at all, while barely 7 per cent liked them (Arrigoni and Vitale 2008). In turn, according to a Eurobarometer survey carried out in the same period, 47 per cent of Italians interviewed would consider it 'bad' to have a Roma neighbour, against a European mean of 24 per cent (Eurobarometer 2008). This negative image can only be reinforced by discursive practices associating stigmatized Roma cultural practices such as nomadism with immigrant criminality and security threats. It leads to a racialization of 'the other' whose difference is constructed as dangerous and threatening (Maneri 2011). If in the case of the Muslim community the threat is identified with the weakening of Italian – in practice, Christian – cultural identity, in that of Roma it is citizens' security that is regarded as at stake.

The local level: a functional approach to group recognition

Regional and local authorities have always played a central role in the implementation of integration policies. Many of these were actually bottom-up initiatives dating from the late 1980s, reflecting initiatives taken by local NGOs and/or municipal administrations – even in the absence of national funding and of national guidelines. As mentioned earlier, since the early 1990s local political majorities have been developing different discourses on immigrant integration: whereas centre-left coalitions have framed immigration as a resource for the cultural enrichment of the local society, centre-right majorities have stressed issues of local security and public order, and have considered integration as closely linked to participation in the labour market (Caponio 2005).

Despite these differences in discourses on immigrant integration, many studies on local-level policies and policymaking in Italy (Caponio 2005; Campomori 2005) agree on the emergence of similar strategies in the treatment of issues related to immigrants' cultural difference. Municipalities privilege a conception of cultural recognition as strictly functional connected to service delivery, in other words, as an instrument to improve access to existing welfare provisions rather than as an instrument for enhancing immigrants' political participation. A case in point is cultural mediation carried out in municipal immigration offices: so-called 'link workers' made up of different nationalities are hired by local administrations in order to interact with end users of immigrant origin and provide information to culturally different clienteles. As I have noted, in a study comparing Bologna, Naples and Milan (Caponio 2010), cultural mediation can be part of a broader public discourse open to cultural recognition – as occurs in the first two cities – or it can be an informal practice undertaken by public officials in order to overcome obstacles in the delivery of services to immigrants – as in Milan. Significantly, in this city public officials do not use the label 'link workers' but prefer to speak of 'interpreters'. Yet the functions performed by foreign workers in immigration offices are similar in all three cases: to meet fellow nationals and discuss their needs; to provide them with information on existing services; to assist them in filling out forms in order to have access to specific resources (such as public housing); and to help them get orientated in the local society.

At the same time, however, Italian cities appear reluctant to recognize explicitly cultural difference. This is the case not only of the centre-right majority that governed Milan throughout the 1990s and 2000s, but also of centre-left administrations. Two kinds of policies can be mentioned in this respect: the recognition of immigrant associations and the visibility of different cultural and religious minorities in the public space. As far as immigrant associations are concerned, pioneer cities such as Bologna and Turin in the mid-1990s promoted specific policies aimed at favouring immigrant groups' representation in policymaking. But in the 2000s they reverted to a vaguer and softer 'intercultural approach' addressed to second generations in particular, which were regarded as more malleable and open to cultural dialogue than their parents (on the case of Bologna, see Ponzo 2009; on Turin, see Ricucci 2009).

On the other hand, with regard to the public visibility of immigrant minorities, this has been regularly contested, from opposition to the building of mosques to the forced eviction of Roma camps or opposition to their relocation (Ambrosini and Caneva 2012). If centre-right majorities have been particularly outspoken on these issues, centre-left administrations have acted in a similar way. In Bologna, notwithstanding the positive results of a public participatory process promoted by the local administration in order to overcome opposition to the building of a mosque on land to be granted by the municipality in the San Donato district, the centre-left majority led by ex-trade union leader Sergio Cofferati withdrew its offer, fearing at the last minute electoral consequences (Ponzo 2009). In turn, evictions and relocations of Roma camps have been systematically carried out in centre-left governed cities such as Bologna, Turin and Rome during the Veltroni (Democratic Party) administration.

Hence, the culturalist turn in national integration policy, as evidenced in the Integration Agreement described earlier, has been accompanied at a regional and local level by contradictory processes. On the one hand, service delivery continues largely to operate according to the 'reasonable integration' model, and it incorporates some principles of soft recognition, which translates into practices of pragmatic accommodation (De Zwart 2005), such as cultural mediation in the cities' immigration offices. On the other hand, far more problematic is the recognition of immigrant associations as well as of cultural difference in the public space. A vague intercultural discourse prevails, yet the visibility of both Muslim and Roma minorities in Italian cities seems to be systematically ignored. A sort of 'multiculturalism of convenience' emerges, since cultural difference is acknowledged when deemed necessary and useful for the regular functioning of services, but avoided when it poses electoral dangers to political actors.

Conclusion

The analysis of Italian immigrant integration policies underscores an oscillation between two conceptions of multiculturalism: the soft recognition approach underlying the 1998 Turco-Napolitano immigration law, which considered the recognition of immigrant cultures as a means to ensure immigrants' equal access to social services; and the weak recognition approach, which does not pursue any consistent integration goal but is primarily a bottom-up process initiated by policy practitioners so as to overcome obstacles they face when dealing on a daily basis with immigrant users. This latter approach characterized the first period of reception and settlement policies in Italy since the 1986 immigration law had just proclaimed the right to the protection of immigrants' cultural background without providing concrete implementation instruments; the responsibility to undertake such policies was left to local levels of government. Similarly, after the abandonment of the 'reasonable integration' model and the introduction of the Integration Agreement, cultural recognition has again entailed ad hoc pragmatic accommodation carried out at a local level in order to smooth service delivery.

Both soft and weak recognition treat cultural recognition as limited in two ways. First, they do not imply any inclusion or participation of immigrant associations in policymaking or, at a local level, in service delivery. Second, they do not explicitly allow for the expression of cultural difference in the public space. Multiculturalism Italian style has always avoided taking immigrant cultures too seriously into account, hoping instead that local administrations have the capacity to pragmatically accommodate immigrants' requests or, as under the recent intercultural approach, set the conditions for the gradual fading away of cultural difference.

Nevertheless the battles for recognition, especially at a local level, are not limited to access to social services but include such electorally hot issues as the building of mosques and the creation of Roma camps. The NIMBY ('not in my back yard') syndrome is as likely to come into play as accommodative policy positions are. Consequently, in the 2000s multiculturalism has come to be regarded as synonymous with separation between different groups and cultural conflict, evoking more or less explicitly the risks for public security linked to the behaviours of 'deviant' groups' (such as the Roma) and their religion (i.e. Muslim groups' international terrorism). The (re)discovery of the Greek-Roman and Christian-Judaic roots of Italian national identity clearly points out the need to define 'who we are' *vis-à-vis* newcomers, or at least in opposition to those among them who are perceived as having a stronger potentially divisive cultural identity.

Public opinion reflects these contradictory trends in Italian immigrant integration policy. Even though immigrant cultures are not considered as representing a threat to Italian cultural identity, a certain distrust towards first-generation Muslims emerges, as do particularly negative attitudes towards Roma. The conflation in the mass media and political discourse of security and identity arguments has contributed to a sharpening of such negative images and stereotypes of some groups' cultural differences – even framing them as 'intractable' differences.

The radicalization of the Northern League and the general political climate work against restoring a 'reasonable integration' model or some form of mediation in the realm of official policy. Informal practices of accommodation appear the only way out of the contradictions of the weak recognition approach, especially when these practices touch upon issues of group representation and public visibility. Such practices have recorded notable successes: pilot projects undertaken in particularly disadvantaged districts, such as San Salvario and Porta Palazzo in Turin or near the railway station in Reggio Emilia, are rated as 'best practices' by international fora such as the Intercultural Cities Programme of the Council of Europe and European Commission, or the Cities for Local Integration Project network funded by the European Foundation for the Improvement of Living and Working Conditions (Wood 2009; Lüken-Klaßen and Heckmann 2010). To what extent these grassroots practices will in the long run develop into an alternative model to today's sometimes radicalized discourse on immigrant groups' difference remains an open question.

References

Ambrosini, M. and E. Caneva (2012), 'Italy', in R. Zapata-Barrero and A. Triandafyllidou (eds), *Addressing Tolerance and Diversity Discourses in Europe. A Comparative Overview of 16 European Countries*, Barcelona: Cidob, pp. 207–30.

Arrigoni, P. and T. Vitale (2008), 'Quale legalità? Rom e gagi a confronto', *Aggiornamenti sociali*, 3, pp. 182–94. Available at http://www.aggiornamentisociali.it/download/0803ArrigoniVitale.pdf

Bonifazi, C. (2007), *L'immigrazione straniera in Italia*, Bologna: Il Mulino.

Bordignon, F. (2008), 'Ritorno alla penisola della paura', in *Demos & Pi* (6 October), *IV Rapporto su immigrazione e cittadinanza in Europa*. Available at http://www.demos.it/2008/pdf/dossier_immigrazione_2008.pdf

Bordignon, F. and L. Ceccarini (2007), 'Gli italiani e l'immigrazione', in *Demos & Pi* (April), *XIII Osservatorio sul capitale sociale degli italiani – Gli Italiani e l'immigrazione*. Available at http://www.demos.it/2007/pdf/capitale_sociale_13.pdf

Campomori, F. (2005), 'Integrare l'immigrato? Politiche di accoglienza a Vicenza, Prato e Caserta', in T. Caponio and A. Colombo (eds), *Stranieri in Italia. Migrazioni globali, integrazioni locali*, Bologna: Il Mulino, pp. 235–66.

Caponio, T. (2005), 'Policy networks and immigrants' associations in Italy. The cases of Milan, Bologna and Naples', *Journal of Ethnic and Migration Studies*, 31 (5), pp. 931–50.

Caponio, T. (2010), 'Grassroots multiculturalism in Italy: Milan, Bologna and Naples compared', in T. Caponio and M. Borkert (eds), *The Local Dimension of Migration Policymaking*, Amsterdam, Amsterdam University Press, IMISCOE Report Series, pp. 57–88.

Caponio, T. and P. R. Graziano (2011), 'Towards a security-oriented migration policy model? Evidence from the Italian case', in E. Carmel, A. Cerami and T. Papadopoulos (eds), *Migration and Welfare in the New Europe. Social Protection and the Challenges of Integration*, Bristol: Policy Press, pp. 105–20.

Caponio, T. and G. Zincone (2011), 'The National Policy Frame for the Integration of Newcomers in Italy', Research paper for the PROSINT (Promoting Sustainable Policies for Integration) Project (November). Available at http://research.icmpd.org/fileadmin/Research-Website/Project_material/PROSINT/Reports/IT_WP2_Final.pdf

Castles, S. and M. Miller (2003), *The Age of Migration* (3rd edn), Basingstoke: Palgrave Macmillan.

Colombo, A. and G. Sciortino (2003), 'The Bossi-Fini Law: explicit fanaticism, implicit moderation and poisoned fruits', in J. Blondel and P. Segatti (eds), *Italian Politics 2003*, Oxford: Berg, pp. 162–80.

Colombo, A. and G. Sciortino (2004), *Gli immigrati in Italia*, Bologna, Il Mulino.

De Zwart, F. (2005), 'The dilemma of recognition: administrative categories and cultural diversity', *Theory and Society*, 34 (2), pp. 137–69.

Diamanti, I. (2003), *Mappe dell'Italia politica. Bianco, rosso, verde, azzurro . . . e tricolore*, Bologna: Il Mulino.

Einaudi, L. (2007), *Le politiche dell'immigrazione in Italia dall'Unità a oggi*, Roma-Bari: Laterza.

Eurobarometer (2008), *Discrimination in the European Union*, Special issue no 296, Brussels: Eurobarometer.

Fallaci, O. (2001), 'La rabbia e l'orgoglio', *Corriere della Sera*, 29 September.

Guolo, R. (2003), *Xenofobi e xenofili. Gli italiani e l'Islam*, Roma-Bari: Laterza.

Lüken-Klaßen, D. and F. Heckmann (2010), *Intercultural Policies in European Cities*, Dublin: Eurofound.

Maneri, M. (2011), 'Media discourse on immigration. The translation of control practices into the language we live by', in S. Palidda (ed.), *Racial Criminalization of Migrants in the 21st Century*, Farnham: Ashgate, pp. 77–93.

Ministero dell'Interno (2007), *Carta dei valori, della cittadinanza e dell'integrazione*. Available at http://www.interno.it/mininterno/export/sites/default/it/sezioni/sala_stampa/notizie/immigrazione/2007_04_23_app_Carta_dei_Valori.html

Ministero del Lavoro e delle Politiche Sociali (2010), *Piano per l' integrazione nella sicurezza. Identità e incontro*. Available at http://www.lavoro.gov.it/NR/rdonlyres/02A1BA64-6AF8-4EC2-ADD3-EF601C360D34/0/pianointegrazione_web.pdf

Però, D. (2007), *Inclusionary Rhetoric, Exclusionary Practices. Leftwing Politics and Migrants in Italy*, Oxford: Berghahn Books.

Piasere, L. (2004), *I rom d'Europa*, Bari-Roma: Laterza.

Ponzo, I. (2009), 'Intercultural policies and intergroup relations – Case study: Bologna, Italy, CLIP', Eurofound. Available at http://www.eurofound.europa.eu/pubdocs/2010/386/en/1/EF10386EN.pdf

Ricucci, R. (2009), 'Intercultural policies and intergroup relations – Case study: Turin, Italy, CLIP', Eurofound.

Saint-Blancat, C. and O. Schmidt di Friedberg (2005), 'Why are mosques a problem? Local politics and fear of Islam in northern Italy', *Journal of Ethnic and Migration Studies*, 31 (6), pp. 1,083–104.

Sartori, G. (2000), *Pluralismo, multiculturalismo e estranei. Saggio sulla società multietnica*, Milan: Rizzoli Editore.

Sciortino, G. and A. Colombo (2004), 'The flows and the flood: the public discourse on immigration in Italy, 1969–2001', *Journal of Modern Italian Studies*, 9 (1), pp. 94–113.

Transatlantic Trends (2011), *Transatlantic Trends: Immigration*, German Marshall Fund (US), Compagnia di San Paolo, Barrow Cadbury Trust and Fundación BBVA. Available at www.transatlantictrends.org

Triandafyllidou, A. (2006), 'Religious diversity and multiculturalism in Southern Europe: The Italian mosque debate', in T. Modood, A. Triandafyllidou and R. Zapata-Barrero (eds), *Multiculturalism, Muslims and Citizenship. A European Approach*, New York: Routledge, pp. 117–42.

Università Bocconi and Cnel (eds) (1991), *Immigrazione e diritti di cittadinanza*, Rome: Editalia.

Vitale, T. (ed.) (2009), *Politiche possibili. Abitare le città con i rom e i sinti*, Rome: Carocci.

Wood, P. (ed.) (2009), *Intercultural Cities. Towards a Model for Intercultural Integration*, Strasbourg: Council of Europe Publishing.

Zincone, G. (ed.) (2000). *Primo rapporto sull'integrazione degli immigrati in Italia*, Bologna: Il Mulino.

Zincone, G. (ed.) (2001), *Secondo rapporto sull'integrazione degli immigrati in Italia*, Bologna: Il Mulino.

Zincone, G. (2011), 'The case of Italy', in G. Zincone, R. Penninx and M. Borkert (eds), *Migration Policymaking in Europe. The Dynamics of Actors and Contexts in Past and Present*, Amsterdam: Amsterdam University Press, IMISCOE Series, pp. 247–90.

Chapter Eleven

Redefining a (Mono)cultural Nation: Political Discourse against Multiculturalism in Contemporary France

Florent Villard and Pascal-Yan Sayegh

Introduction

In the last decade, discourse on the failure of multiculturalism has made its way into mainstream political discourse in many established nation-states in Europe. The case of France is no exception. With the election of Nicolas Sarkozy as President of the Republic in 2007, this discourse, accompanied by claims about the failure of the French model of integration, was institutionalized. It is an open question how much Sarkozy's loss to Socialist Party candidate François Hollande in 2012 can be attributed to this discourse stressing multiculturalism's failure; after all, the 'French model' is not traditionally associated with multiculturalism, at least in the normative, ideological sense. This does not mean that French society is not phenomenologically multicultural, but even in its descriptive meaning the term 'multiculturalism' has only recently entered political and academic discourses in France (Constant 2000: 17). The terms 'cultural diversity' (*la diversité culturelle*) or simply 'diversity' (*la diversité*) have traditionally been preferred to 'multiculturalism'.

This preference points to the underlying ideological distinction between the 'politics of indifference' (Kukathas 2003: 15; see also Chapter 3 in this book) centred on *individual* rights, and 'politics of recognition,' centred on *group* rights. This differentialist interpretation is what multiculturalism is normally understood to be in France (Taylor and Gutmann 1992). Since the political tradition of the French Republic has apparently nothing to do with multicultural politics, the idea of the 'failure of multiculturalism' appears to be a strange assertion in the French context. Indeed, some commentators have even argued that the multiculturalist ideal appears as the absolute counter-example of the French Republican model (Birnbaum 2004: 427).

From a phenomenological viewpoint, contemporary French

society is, without doubt, a multicultural society. But a normative definition of multiculturalism – the ethical dimensions of multi-culturalism and the idea of a multicultural society as a norm – has always been far from popular, especially among the political elite. As Banting and Kymlicka recount in their comparative work on multi-cultural policy in developed countries, France exemplifies what they call a 'weak policy' in favour of territorial minorities and migrants (in Doytcheva 2011: 63).

It was therefore puzzling, given France's distance from the notion of normative multiculturalism, that Sarkozy should have been asked in a prime-time talk show on the private television channel TF1 in February 2011 whether he thought 'multiculturalism is a failure and the source of many of society's problems'. Given that he replied unequivocally, 'Clearly my answer is yes, it is a failure', we are bound to ask: what exactly did multiculturalism mean to Sarkozy and how had it failed? In other words, what is the meaning of this new terminology in mainstream political (and media) discourse?

Framing the question of multiculturalism is especially important in France given the particular tradition of the French Republican model. The nature of the consequences of the change in political dis-course can have a profound effect on politics in the Fifth Republic. We therefore first present a theoretical and historical overview of the French Republican model. Second, we focus on more recent develop-ments related to integration and diversity in France before analyzing the discursive practices in question; a special focus is identifying how the discourse on the failure of multiculturalism combines with the nationalist identity politics enacted during Sarkozy's term in office (2007–12). We consider this relationship in the light of the financial and economic crises that have unfolded since 2008. In aligning these perspectives, we conclude by examining how the new terminology is representative of the political endeavour to redefine France as a monocultural society.

The French Republican model: an overview

France shall be an indivisible, secular, democratic and social Republic. It shall ensure the equality of all citizens before the law, without distinction of origin, race or religion. It shall respect all beliefs.

Article 1, French Constitution of 1958

The moral universalism of the 'Rights of Man' is derived from Enlightenment philosophies and is expressed in the first article of

The Declaration of the Rights of Man and of the Citizen, Approved by the National Assembly of France on 26 August 1789, but also in Thomas Jefferson's statement in the Declaration of Independence on 4 July 1776, and in the United Nations' Universal Declaration of Human Rights from 10 December 1948. This first part of the chapter accordingly describes the interpretation of these common Republican principles that the French Republican model represents, providing an historical overview of the traditional opposition of French political thought to ideological multiculturalism.

As stressed in our introduction, the French Republican model is often presented as the counter-example of the multicultural model. While the latter is based on recognition of group rights, the French Republican model is founded on national unity (van Zanten 1997). The theoretical origins of this model are to be found in the ideals of Enlightenment philosophies which themselves directly inspired the political imaginings of the French Revolution. The revolutionary definition of the nation was contractual and civic, representing universal values and progress. There were many interpretations for further defining this 'civic nationalism', but the Jacobin version discussed below has consistently remained the dominant interpretation in French Republican institutions, which are characterized by a rigorous political and ideological centralism.

In the French Republican model, the nation is conceived as an association of equal citizens. They are equal in rights and in treatment. Their equality is thus expressed in regard to the common law, defined as the core of the *res publica*, literally the public affair. This is the first point where, in theory, the Republican model differs from the multicultural model, as its basic logic necessarily implies that all citizens be treated individually and not collectively, otherwise there would be no universal attribute. If groups or communities smaller than the nation have distinctive sets of rights, there is no common law and the entire Republican institution collapses because the rights of individuals are the norm upon which the institution is built (Gauchet 1989: 78).

To prevent such a possibility, the Republic is defined as indivisible. In principle, this applies to the territory, the sovereignty and the people of the Republic, meaning, for instance, that the Republic cannot in theory become a federalist state. Thus, beyond the opposition to the 'old regime', the radical application of this principle fits well with the Jacobin tendency to oppose the reactionary, and most of all, revolutionary federalist trends. While the Republic is indivisible and its citizens – the nation – are united in equality, society itself is divided into the private and public spheres. In this conception, the line of difference between the two spheres is in the first instance defined on a basis of liberal toleration: in brief, anything that does not disturb the social order instituted by the law of the Republic is a private affair. This is in theory, of course, since such basic principles of universality are themselves performed by the Jacobin state. As a state, it is the warden of the social order, and its role consists in protecting individuals from the power of social groups (expressed, for instance, by the individual right to form and leave associations).

The construction of the unity of the French nation through the conscious project of erasing cultural and linguistic differences provides a further example of why the French Republican model appears as the absolute counter-example of the multicultural model. This project derives from a cultural interpretation of what Abbé Sieyès called the *adunation* or 'the act of writing, of connecting unassembled fragments into one whole' (Baecque 1997: 97). It translates into defiance against the expression and recognition of any form of regional or local cultures, and language in particular. The unification of the territory of the French Republican state was based on such cultural policy. With the steady rise of nationalism throughout the course of the nineteenth century, monolingualism became the norm of European modernity: it effectively created national languages and their respective high cultures. The linguistic element is one of the first *practical* cultural elements that defined nationality (Certeau et al. 1975).

Through this process of internal colonialism (Hechter 1975), the logic of which is at the basis of the 'civilizing mission' of the wider colonial enterprise (Bancel et al. 2005), regional and local cultures were seen as backward and reactionary, and, in consequence, their destiny had to be subsumed into the universal and modern Republican nation. This opposition between the practices of minority cultures and so-called progressive universal values and norms is recurrent in today's discourses concerning multiculturalism in France.

Thus, we can already observe how the French revolutionary version of the nation imagined political identity in opposition to the politics of identity implied in the idea of multiculturalism. Officially, and from a theoretical point of view, we could say that the French Republican state does not recognize any form of 'particularisms' as the citizens who make up the nation have, in theory, neither 'race', religion, ethnicity, class nor culture; this is what the politics of indifference implies. Nevertheless, in its historical application, the French revolutionary Republican model has recurrently been associated with assimilationist discourses and policies, not least through the French colonial enterprise.

The Jacobin revolutionary version of the nation continues to have strong support in contemporary French politics. Orthodox interpretations of Jacobin Republicanism are frequently expressed by both left-wing and right-wing politicians. Many invoke the principle of secularity – arguably a more nuanced rendering of *la laïcité* than secularism – as the core value of the Republic. Secularity emerged as the political solution to the relationship between church and state, and church and society during the French Revolution. But it was only during the Third Republic, at the end of the nineteenth century, that the secularity of the Republic would be institutionalized and defined the way it is today. The 1905 law on the separation of church and state can be considered the conclusive act of a series of measures that have made this institutionalization effective (Levillain 2005). It is also during the Third Republic that a 'national identity' started to be defined by state institutions, through a national language, a national geography, a national history, and so on; in sum, a national culture. (Noiriel 2007).

Over the long term the debates on secularity have led, across different nation states, to a separation of power between, to employ old-fashioned categories, the temporal and the spiritual. This has reduced the political power of religious institutions and granted a form of autonomy to political, temporal institutions. This follows from the Weberian idea that the state strives for cultural monopoly in a similar way as it strives for the monopoly on violence. It also shows the importance of religion in the traditional debates on diversity. The political and institutional answers to religious questions have taken the form of a secularization of society, based on the ideas of tolerance and the recognition of freedom of conscience and association.

In the French context, the principle of *laïcité* frames and limits the liberal principle of tolerance. In its orthodox interpretation, often supported by centre to left-wing political parties, it signifies the strict neutrality of the Republic by the exclusion of religious discourses and practices from the public sphere. In practice, this fine line is constantly being negotiated, which partly explains why in France the question of multiculturalism is often directly linked to religion.

In contemporary French politics, one of the politicians who

most clearly represents this purist Republican tradition is Jean-Luc Mélenchon, leader of a new leftist party (*Front de gauche*) and former member of the Socialist party. Commenting on Sarkozy's statement on multiculturalism, he posted a blog entry: 'The only identity of France is the Republic and the political contract it implies: it cannot be "cultural"' (Mélenchon 2011). The problem is that this cultural neutrality has always been an idealist myth and the equality to which it pertains is not effective in real life. Mélenchon placed a strong fourth in the first round of the 2012 presidential elections with 11 per cent of the overall vote.

If there were to exist a French version of multiculturalism, a search for it might begin with the work of Jean-Loup Amselle (2003). This French anthropologist argues that assimilation always presupposes a pluri-ethnic national community. He gives examples of discriminatory policies towards colonized populations, and state policies of tolerance or discrimination involving minorities in France even before the Revolution (especially in the case of the Jewish community). His thesis is that the political process of Jacobin homogenization that we have described implies the existence of various minorities – earlier in history these were regional cultural minorities and then later, from the end of the nineteenth century, immigrant minorities initially from Europe but subsequently from the former colonies after they gained their independence. Before assimilation can occur, Amselle argues, there has to be a 'racialization' of society through recognition. After all, assimilation implies that minority cultures blend into the majority. He adds that the recognition of minority groups or cultures does not necessarily lead to assimilation – it is always possible that a particular group will be impossible to assimilate. In this convoluted way, Amselle describes this as the French version of multiculturalism.

Assimilation, integration and the multicultural turn

Before analyzing contemporary political discourses relating to multicultural issues, we review the principal developments in integration and diversity policy in contemporary France. First, it is important to note that it was only in the 1990s that multiculturalism began to appear as a research theme in academia with pioneering works by Patrick Weil on what was termed the 'immigrant question' (1991). Other innovative scholarly research was carried out by Michel Wieviorka and François Dubet (1997) and Alain Touraine (1995).

Prior to this, multiculturalism was seldom a subject of scholarly inquiry.

More recently, a new generation of sociologists and historians has been engaged in research on postcolonial immigration from the perspective of identity politics and postcolonial studies (Blanchard 2005; N'Diaye 2006). This particular evolution of a research agenda is symptomatic of the more general difficulties in French society of dealing with its colonial past. This ambivalence on how to deal with the colonial past was revealed in 2005 when the Conservative majority in the French Parliament voted for a bill that would have inserted in the national education curriculum an official history of the 'positive role of the French presence abroad' and the positive values of French colonization (Law 2005-158 of 23 February 2005, *Journal officiel*, 24 February 2005). The Constitutional Council rejected this bill in 2006.

On the state level, the new official policy of 'integration' was first implemented during the 1980s, replacing the old project of assimilation. Integration implied a more subtle, interactive and subjective process for the immigrant in his or her identification with the values and norms of society (Weil 2005). Its objectives are not necessarily the total acculturation of the individual, as is more the case with assimilation. Although there is no mention of multiculturalism, or of the recognition of particular group rights, with an integration policy came a commitment to respect cultural diversity and to struggle actively against territorial discrimination and exclusion. The extension to foreigners of the right to form associations in 1981 was the first step in this new policy of integration.

It is also during this period that the *politique de la ville*, or urban policy, was developed (Garbaye 2011: 99). It consisted of public action to promote the economic and social integration of underprivileged communities, most of them ghettoized immigrant populations on the urban peripheries, the *banlieues* (Kepel 2012). These policies, which are still in effect today, include the development of social housing estates and their renewal, the economic development of designated 'zones', as well as the promotion of equal opportunities through education (Donzelot 2006). Despite these efforts, many observers have judged these policies to be insufficient and at times inconsistent since they have failed to address the general state of exclusion of the *banlieues* (Paquot 2007). These policies exemplify the 'politics of redistribution', which in academic debates on multiculturalism have been contrasted with the 'politics of recognition'

(Barry 2001; Fraser and Honneth 2003). Addressing socio-economic inequality, the *politique de la ville* failed to tackle the wider issue of the inequality of status of postcolonial communities.

In the wake of the antiracist movements of the 1980s and the first social unrest in the *banlieues*, a number of new civil organizations set up to fight discrimination and promote the rights of minorities emerged. The most prominent were two organizations created by the so-called *Beur* movement (*beur* is an argot word that means Arab): *SOS Racisme* and *France Plus*. Initiated by young people of postcolonial descent and supported by leftist political forces, notably François Mitterrand's Socialist Party, the movement made wider civil society realize that France had an important population of colonial origin, many of whom were living in difficult social and economic conditions. While fighting against 'racial' discrimination, such organizations as *SOS Racisme* subscribed to the Republican tradition on equal rights and *laïcité*; there was no direct reference to the multiculturalist idea of recognition (Garbaye 2011: 97–102).

More recently, in the aftermath of the violent riots in the *banlieues* in November 2005, new initiatives advocating a clearer multiculturalist orientation have emerged. Such is the case for *Indigènes de la République* (literally 'Natives of the Republic'). The use of the term *indigènes* is a direct reference to the colonial past, as it traditionally refers to colonized populations. Founded in December 2005, the organization not only combats discrimination and racism; it demands genuine recognition of the specific identities and historical trajectories of postcolonial immigrants and their descendants, constructing in this way a continuity between the colonial past and the specific situations of ethnocultural minorities today. Indeed, *Indigènes de la République* is very much concerned with questions relating to memories and narratives of the past. In this vein, one of their main objectives is to 'denationalize the history of France'. Less polemical, the founding in November 2005 of the Council of Black Associations of France (CRAN – *Conseil représentatif des associations noires de France*), reflecting the model of CRIF (*Conseil représentatif des institutions juives de France*), the Jewish Council, is also representative of the emergence of a multiculturalist ethic within French society. Similarly, its objectives are to fight against discrimination and for true equality.

Over the last twenty years, an evolution of the political discourse has taken place on the make-up of French society. Neither left-wing nor right-wing parties deny that France is an ethnically hybrid and mixed society. Even Sarkozy, as grandson of a Hungarian immigrant, insisted in his speeches on the idea of a *France métissée* (mixed-race France). Before his election as President, Sarkozy often appeared to be an advocate of multiculturalism, stating in 2003 that 'France has become a multicultural country' (Fassin 2011). Following this logic, during his first term as Minister of the Interior (2002–4) he supported the formation in 2003 of the French Council of the Muslim Religion (CFCM – *Conseil français du culte musulman*).

While this 'multiculturalist turn' is significant, it is still circumscribed by the Republican tradition, and many difficulties remain for the official recognition of the diversity of French society. For example, in 2008 the French Senate voted by a large majority against the recognition in the French Constitution of regional languages as part of the nation's heritage. The French Academy went even further in stating that this recognition would have threatened 'French identity'. The legal status of 'exogenous' languages was not even mentioned in this debate. This furnishes an example of contemporary practices that reproduces the idea of *adunation* cited earlier.

Beyond the question of languages, there are many laws that restrict multiculturalism in France. The 2004 law against 'visible religious signs' in schools is another significant example. It is the product of the Bernard Stasi report commissioned by President Jacques Chirac in 2003 on the application of the principle of *laïcité* in the Republic, and culminated a decade-long debate centred on the question of the Muslim veil. In 2010 another law was passed against concealing one's face in a public space, this time targeting the niqab. The fact that the law was promoted by Communist Member of Parliament André Guérin shows how the traditional themes of the far right associated with orthodox interpretations of secularity have reconfigured the French political scene in recent years. It also shows clearly that these issues, which are historically linked to the sensitive theme of *laïcité*, are able today to transcend traditional political divides.

The strong opposition to the use of 'ethnic statistics' in France further exemplifies how Republican principles limit the implementation of policies of recognition, in spite of the creation in December 2004 of a government body dedicated to the fight against discrimination, the High Authority for the Fight against Discrimination and for Equality (HALDE – *Haute autorité de lutte contre les discriminations et pour l'égalité*).

In accordance with the set of Republican principles, the state has to ensure equality of treatment. We have shown how, in France, these principles translate into a politics of indifference which, to avoid any form of discrimination, does not make use of categories that could recognize particular forms of belonging. Thus, the official statistics do not include 'sensitive questions' related to ethnicity, 'race' and religion as these aspects are not part of the public sphere, at least *de jure*. We can note that this approach hampers implementation of policies of positive discrimination of the type associated with multicultural politics, although in the past decade there has been an increase in the attention given in the media and in politics to the so-called 'visible minorities'.

The categories used for gathering statistics in France are based on the distinction between nationals and foreigners, and take into account elements such as the place of birth and the different ways of obtaining nationality. In this set of categories, an immigrant is a national born abroad or a foreigner and, conversely, a foreigner is simply defined as a non-national even if born in France. It leads to the paradoxical result that a national can be considered an immigrant, that is, if born abroad as a non-national and having obtained nationality later. In addition, such distinctions are often blurred by media and political discourse, even when referring to official statistics. This often results in a widespread confusion between these categories, which allows for an ideologically driven utilization amalgamating foreigners and immigrants, as well as French citizens of foreign origin.

Immigration as a 'threat' to national identity

The amalgamations and blurring of categories can be observed in the recent development of political discourse under Sarkozy's presidency. Having identified 'national identity and immigration' as a core political issue during the presidential campaign of 2007, President Sarkozy and numerous government officials repeatedly referenced the above categories and related statistics in their speeches. The 2012 presidential elections were also punctuated by references to immigrants and foreigners in France, above all by Sarkozy and Marine Le Pen, leader of the far-right *Front National* (FN). As a core political issue, the relationship between national identity and immigration has also triggered debates in the academic community (Noiriel 2007) as it appropriates traditional FN discourse in particular (Sayegh 2008).

After his election as President of the Republic, Sarkozy

institutionalized the controversial relationship between national identity and immigration by creating in May 2007 a Minister for Immigration, Integration, National identity and Co-development. Most of the prerogatives of the newly created ministry were previously part of the Ministry of the Interior which Sarkozy had headed on two occasions (2002–4 and 2005–7). The new ministry was absorbed back into the Ministry of the Interior in November 2010, suggesting the failure of combining national identity with immigration in particular. It was just such a formulation, which until then was not common in mainstream political discourse, that led to statements on the failure of multiculturalism and the integration system in France as well as to attacks on 'unwanted' and 'uncontrolled' immigration.

This imagined pressure arising from immigration was presented as the reason behind the cultural and economic problems faced by French society. The main explanation for this systemic failure, according to Sarkozy, was to be found in the lenient immigration policies of his predecessors and in the lack of a vigorous promotion of French national identity. In a campaign video from 2007 on national identity, Sarkozy concluded that:

> If we do not tell newcomers and people who want to become French what France is, how can they be integrated? The failure of the French integration system is due to the fact that we have forgotten to talk about France. Myself, I do not want to forget France, because France is at the heart of my manifesto.

It is significant that in February 2012, during his first campaign meeting as official candidate for the presidential elections, Sarkozy returned to the theme of his 2007 campaign: 'Today, I have come to talk about France. We don't talk enough about France, as if it were old-fashioned to talk about France.'

The first Minister of the newly founded and short-lived Ministry, Brice Hortefeux (2007–9), had elaborated on Sarkozy's thinking. In a 2007 press conference he declared:

> First of all, let's confront the truth: the French integration system has failed. The proof is the much-too-high concentrations of populations of foreign origin living in just three regions out of twenty-two: 60 per cent of foreigners live in Ile-de-France, Rhône-Alpes or in PACA [Provence-Alpes-Côte d'Azur], sometimes in real urban ghettos. More proof is the average unemployment rate of foreigners that stands at above 20 per cent, which is more than twice the national average. In certain *banlieues*, this

rate reaches 40 per cent. We must therefore tell the French people the truth: our integration system is no longer a model. And to successfully integrate, immigration must firstly be controlled.

This statement shows a confusing and arcane use of categories. 'Population of foreign origin', for instance, can refer to a vast array of people of different status. The statistical data on this category only tell us that most of the people of foreign origin live in three of the main French urban centres. It is unclear whether such oversimplified arguments, associated with sometimes unverifiable statistics, qualify as 'proof' of the failure of the integration system. When a discourse on unemployment and foreigners is combined with 'populations of foreign origin', it can reflect stigmatization and fuel further marginalization of already marginalized groups in French society. The reference to the *banlieues* is of particular importance as this imagery had been recurrent in Sarkozy's discourse since his term as Minister of the Interior; it was a way of creating and designating an internal other. Essentially, the use of statistics in this context serves the purpose of formulating pseudo-rational arguments that evade more complex debate and denote a tendency to stigmatize foreigners and postcolonial communities by portraying them as a risk and a threat to the well-being and integrity of French society. Symbolically, it results in a spurious division of French society between the newcomers and the hosts. The restructuring of the policies accompanying this discourse, such as with the implementation of 'target figure' policies, notably for asylum seekers and for the expulsion of illegal immigrants, can be ascribed to a xenophobic governmental practice (Valluy 2009).

Michel Feher, president of the organization *Cette France-là* ('This France') whose major objectives were to audit immigration policy under Sarkozy's presidency, concluded that Hortefeux's Ministry was the first of three stages in toughening up discourses and policies on immigration and national identity (Feher 2011). Its main rallying cry was the same as the one promoted by Sarkozy during the presidential campaign: the theme of 'unwanted' immigration and the promotion of a policy of 'chosen immigration' (*immigration choisie*) which would be carried out through the target figure policies.

The second stage was marked by the economic crisis of 2008 and the appointment of a new minister and former member of the Socialist Party, Eric Besson (2009–10). His policies and discourse emulated those of his predecessor while enhancing the image of immigrants as representing social risk. An example of this inherent threat caused by immigration was Besson's reference in November 2009 to 'grey marriages' – marriages in name only where the French spouse is manipulated into believing it is a true marriage. In Besson's words, it was 'sentimental fraud for a migratory goal'. It was also under Besson's patronage that the debate on national identity Sarkozy had called for during the presidential campaign was organized. The debate was unpopular and highly criticized by actors in civil society due to its political underpinnings and was closed down quickly (Noiriel 2007).

The third and ongoing stage referred to by Feher was initiated after the jurisdiction of the controversial ministry had been reintegrated into the Ministry of the Interior in late 2010. The newly appointed Minister of the Interior, Claude Guéant, announced new objectives for the reduction of *legal* immigration, where Hortefeux had focused on fighting *illegal* immigration. If the reasons for more explicit anti-immigration discourse are not altogether clear other than political and electoral considerations, it is nonetheless important to note that since the 2008 economic crisis began, the stigmatization of immigrants and French citizens of foreign origin – Muslims in particular, but also socio-economic categories which until then had generally been seen in a more positive light – has increased. As one example, procedures for foreign students to acquire work permits and visas have become more expensive and more restrictive since an Interior Ministry circular on 31 May 2011.

Guéant provided an excellent example of the tendency to stigmatize foreigners when in May 2011 he misinterpreted official statistics while claiming that two-thirds of children failing in the education system are children of immigrants. The National Institute for Statistics and Economic Studies (INSEE – *Institut national de la statistique et des études économiques*), which usually refrains from commenting on how official statistics are used, issued a communiqué the next month correcting Guéant's interpretation of the study in question (INSEE 2005): the study estimated the percentage of children leaving the secondary education system without qualifications who are the children of immigrants was 16 per cent.

This example of the political utilization of statistics formed part of a common practice under Sarkozy's presidency. In January 2012 Guéant gave a press conference presenting the achievements of the previous year's immigration policy. Its success, he contended, could be measured by a series of statistics highlighting how initial 'target figures' had been surpassed: thus, in 2011 there had been 32,912 expulsions of foreigners, exceeding the target number of 28,000. Guéant also pointed to the reduction of legal immigration to show how effective the restrictive policies had been; he spoke in the context of the law on immigration passed in June 2011. The accuracy of many of these figures remains obscure, notably as the expulsion statistics included Romanian citizens who, under European law, have the right to freedom of movement. This did not prevent Guéant from arguing in January 2012 in favour of the 2011 immigration law. He did this by using many of his predecessors' arguments and framing the policy as integral to the Republican tradition:

> The sense of our policy is a certain conception of France and of French society. We want France to remain faithful to its values, its great Republican principles, such as *laïcité* and equality between men and women. We refuse communitarianisms and the secluded life of ethnic or religious communities that follow their own rules, which are neither the rules of the Republic nor of France. It is for that reason that the foreigners we welcome must integrate. It is they who must integrate and not the other way round.

This assertion displays how Guéant, following in the footsteps of Sarkozy, Hortefeux and Besson, draws a clear line between 'a certain conception of France', supposedly shared by a national community, and those who are welcomed by this community, although this second group is opaque as it also includes communities that are already part of French society. This mechanism was used by Sarkozy during the talk show when he declared that multiculturalism had been a failure (TF1, 10 February 2011):

> The truth is that in all our democracies we have been too concerned about the identity of those who come and not enough about the identity of those who welcome. A person coming to France must be ready to blend into one single community, which is the national community.

This discourse implies the creation of two categories of people in French society while calling into question the central Republican principle of equal rights. The same applies to an earlier speech made by Sarkozy in Grenoble in July 2010 just after a week of riots in which police officers had been shot at. The President suggested that naturalized French citizens who have been French for less than ten years should be stripped of their nationality if they 'willingly attempt to kill a police officer'. This oblique hint to revise the law on citizenship, which had originally been part of the 2011 law on immigration and would have legally created two kinds of citizens, was considered anti-constitutional and was subsequently rejected by the Senate.

Sarkozy's 2011 statement also pointed to the reappearance of an assimilationist discourse that underlines the monocultural redefinition of national identity. Nationality or citizenship is not limited to a political identity: becoming French is a process of blending into the French community, in other words 'acculturation'. During the talk show in February 2011, the characteristics of Sarkozy's French national identity were defined with a clear and simplistic Islamophobic subtext:

> The French national community does not want to change its way of life, its style of life, the equality between men and women, the liberty for little girls to go to school, so that some Imans can preach violence or change the calendar.

This negative definition of identity includes multiple aspects. The 'way of life' referred to suggests an anthropological definition of 'culture' but then, making use of arguments related to discourses for the recognition of particular rights, Sarkozy takes up themes that are of a legal nature. The line drawn between two categories of citizenship represents a definitive step away from the Republican principles of civic national unity.

Conclusion

The conception of France that emerged from the discourses of Guéant or Sarkozy is often vague. In many instances, it is defined negatively, through xenophobic and often Islamophobic stigmatization. In all cases, it suggests the fixity of an essential eternal French national identity, under assault from endless immigration imagined as embodying anti-French sentiment. In February 2012, Guéant triggered yet another controversy by declaring at a meeting of a right-wing students' union that 'our civilization needs to be protected' and that 'all civilizations are not equal' – a veiled attack on the supposed relativism of the Socialist Party. Guéant's reference was to French civilization rather than Western civilization in general.

If we look for the affirmative elements – what France is rather than what it is not – in this conception of France, we find that Sarkozy repeatedly asserted that the roots of France are 'essentially Christian'. This could simply be an effect of the return of the religious element in political affairs – a global trend – or part of electoral politics. The many speeches by Sarkozy referring to Joan of Arc may nevertheless appear to be more than a mere hijacking of a figure dear to the FN: it was an embrace of this 'certain conception of France'. The line drawn between those who are coming and those who are welcoming is thus defined in the subtext as a cultural line. In this way, it is also a step back to assimilationist discourses pointing to a 'monocultural' redefinition of national identity based on a relativist and differentialist definition of culture and identity, perhaps resulting from the increase in acceptability of far-right cultural racism (Lentin 2005).

On another level, this imagined line of differentiation also denotes a reversal of the secular principle of the French Republic. While affirming the validity of the principle of *laïcité*, Sarkozy was promoting what he called in his 2007 speech at the Lateran Palace in Rome 'positive secularity'. Nevertheless, how to apply this idea has been unclear and ambiguous. In some instances, we have seen how it resulted in discourses and policies that could be described as multicultural. In other instances, and more so as Sarkozy's presidency was coming to an end, the principle of *laïcité* became used as a cover for pursuing nationalist identity politics.

Between 2007 and 2012 the Sarkozy presidency and the government he appointed promoted a form of French national communitarianism. Ironically, this conception mirrors the differentialist multicultural policies that are conventionally juxtaposed with the French model. It therefore suggests more than a mere failure of the integration system. If it had failed, different accounts were presented of its failure, depending on how national identity was understood. Sarkozy's conception suggested a failure of government policies – and their ideological underpinnings. Faced with complex international and global phenomena, they privileged short-term results in the form of division, restriction and exclusion. From this perspective, we wonder whether the nationalist identity politics of the Sarkozy regime clouded its failure to address larger issues, some induced by long-standing traditions, others by recent developments of a global nature. It may be that there are no answers to such challenges that are simply national.

It is difficult to assess the long-term impact of Sarkozy's one-term presidency on issues related to *laïcité* and diversity in France. Both the 2012 presidential and legislative elections – which were decided victories for the French left – are perhaps illuminating in this respect. First, the results hint at a general polarization of the political debate, with space opening to the left of the Socialist Party (PS) and, simultaneously, record high support for the FN on the far-right (Marine Le Pen received 18 per cent of the presidential vote even though her party subsequently gained just two legislative seats). In comparison to the FN, the mixed success of Mélenchon (11 per cent for the presidential candidate of the *Front de Gauche*, but ten elected parliamentary deputies from the party) may be partly ascribed to the trauma of the 2002 presidential election when Jacques Chirac, the right-wing candidate, faced off against Jean-Marie Le Pen of the FN in the runoff round. A large proportion of the 2012 electorate may have cast their vote based on a logic of 'never again' in relation to the 2002 scenario – in effect, voting against Sarkozy in both rounds to secure the victory of the more consensual PS candidate, François Hollande.

Second, Hollande's victory over Sarkozy signifies a return to the Republican frame of reference that we described in the first section of this chapter. The consensual reaffirmation of the Republican tradition operated by Hollande is not surprising since under his secretariat (1997–2008), the PS represented more consensual positions associated with social democracy rather than socialism per se. This is further illustrated in the frame within which Hollande picked up themes long heralded by Sarkozy, such as immigration control, but framed in socio-economic rather than xenophobic and culturally stigmatizing terms.

Finally, Sarkozy's defeat reflected the failure of the electoral game played by his party with the far right. It has de facto participated in the consolidation of the FN as a force to be reckoned with. Sarkozy's failure will also lead, in the medium term, to a reconfiguration of right-wing political forces. Given the extended floor given to far-right arguments under Sarkozy's presidency and his ensuing electoral defeat, it would not be surprising to observe the right wing reforming around the ideological premises of the FN.

References

Amselle, J.-L. (2003), *Affirmative Exclusion, Cultural Pluralism and the Rule of Custom in France*, Ithaca, NY: Cornell University Press.

Baecque, A. de (1997), *The Body Politic: Corporeal Metaphor in Revolutionary France: 1770–1800*, Stanford, CA: Stanford University Press.

Bancel, N., P. Blanchard and S. Lemaire (eds) (2005), *La fracture coloniale. La société française au prisme de l'héritage colonial*, Paris: La Découverte.

Barry, B. (2001), *Culture and Equality: An Egalitarian Critique of Multiculturalism*, Cambridge, MA: Harvard University Press.

Birnbaum, P. (2004), 'Entre universalisme et multiculturalisme: le modèle français dans la théorie politique contemporaine', in A. Dieckhoff (ed.), *La constellation des appartenances: Nationalism, libéralisme et pluralisme*, Paris: Presses de Sciences Po.

Blanchard, P. (2005). 'La France entre deux immigrations', in P. Blanchard, N. Bancel and S. Lemaire (eds), *La fracture coloniale: La société française au prisme de l'héritage colonial*. Paris: La Decouverte.

Certeau, M. de, D. Julia and J. Revel (1975), *Une politique de la langue, la révolution française et les patois: L'enquête de Grégoire*, Paris: Gallimard.

Constant, F. (2000), *Le multiculturalisme*, Paris: Flammarion.

Donzelot, J. (2006), *Quand la ville se défait: Quelle politique face à la crise des banlieues*, Paris: Éditions du Seuil.

Doytcheva, M. (2011), *Le multiculturalisme*, Paris: La Découverte.

Fassin, E. (2011), 'Nicolas Sarkozy en marche vers le "monoculturalisme"', *Le Monde*, 25 février.

Feher, M. (2011), 'Ces propos profitent davantage au FN qu'à Nicolas Sarkozy (Interview)', *Libération*, 29 November.

Fraser, N. and A. Honneth (2003), *Redistribution or Recognition? A Political-Philosophical Exchange*, London: Verso.

Garbaye, R. (2011), *Emeutes vs Intégration: comparaisons franco-britanniques*, Paris: Presses de Sciences Po.

Gauchet M. (1989), *La Révolution des droits de l'Homme*, Paris: Gallimard.

Hechter, M. (1975), *Internal Colonialism: The Celtic Fringe in British National Development*, Berkeley, CA: University of California Press.

INSEE (2005), *Les immigrés en France*, Collection Insee-Référence. Available at http://www.insee.fr/fr/publications-et-services/sommaire. asp?id=104&reg_id=0

Kepel, G. (ed.) (2012), *Banlieue de la République: Société, politique et religion à Clichy-sous-Bois et Montfermeil*, Paris: Gallimard.

Kukathas, C. (2003), *The Liberal Archipelago: A Theory of Diversity and Freedom*, Oxford: Oxford University Press.

Lentin, A. (2005), 'Replacing "race", historicizing "culture" in multiculturalism', *Patterns of Prejudice*, 39 (4), pp. 379–96.

Levillain, P. (2005), 'Les débats au début de la IIIe République', *La laïcité: des débats, une histoire, un avenir (1789–2005)*, Actes du colloque organisé sous le haut patronage de M. Christian Poncelet, Président du Sénat, en partenariat avec le Comité d'Histoire Parlementaire et Politique, le vendredi 4 février 2005, Paris: Palais du Luxembourg.

Mélenchon, J.-L. (2011), 'Le boulot du travail: Un extra-terrestre nous a parlé, une interview coulée, le multiculturalisme', *Le Blog de Jean-Luc*

Mélenchon, 23 February. Available at http://www.jean-luc-melenchon. fr/2011/02/23/le-boulot-du-travail/

N'Diaye, Tidiane (2006), *L'Eclipse des Dieux: Ou grandeur et désespérance des peuples noirs*, Paris: Éditions du Rocher.

Noiriel, G. (2007), *A quoi sert 'l'identité nationale'*, Marseille: Agone.

Paquot, T. (2007), 'Politiques de la ville', *Projet*, 4 (299), pp. 16–23.

Sayegh, P.-Y. (2008), 'Discursive elements in the (de)banalization of nationalism. A study of speeches by Gordon Brown and Nicolas Sarkozy', *CFE Working Papers Series* No. 35, Lund: Centre for European Studies, Lund University.

Taylor, C. and A. Gutmann (eds) (1992), *Multiculturalism and the Politics of Recognition: An Essay*, Princeton, NJ: Princeton University Press.

Touraine, A. (1995), *Pourrons-nous vivre ensemble ? Egaux et différents*, Paris: Fayard.

Valluy, J. (2009), *Rejet des exilés: Le grand retournement du droit de l'asile*, Paris: Éditions du Croquant.

Van Zanten, A. (1997), 'Le traitement des différences liées à l'origine immigrée à l'école française', in N. Marouf and C. Carpentier (eds), *Langue, école, identités*, Paris: L'Harmattan, pp. 149–68.

Weil, P. (1991), *La France et ses étrangers: l'aventure d'une politique de l'immigration, 1938–1991*, Paris: Calmann-Levy.

Weil, P. (2005), *La France et ses étrangers. L'aventure d'une politique de l'immigration de 1938 à nos jours*, Paris: Gallimard.

Wievorka, M. and F. Dubet (1997), *Une société fragmentée: le multiculturalisme en débat*, Paris: La Découverte.

Part IV

Multiculturalism's Future Converts?

Chapter Twelve

Poland: Multiculturalism in the Making?

Renata Włoch

Introduction

My working assumption is straightforward: there has been no articulated ideology or politics of multiculturalism in Poland. Even academic reflection on multiculturalism is scarce, as is multicultural discourse in the media (Grzymała-Kazłowska 2009; Weinar 2009). The explanation is simple: Poland is a notable exception in the set of nation states in representing a state made up of one nation. The 2002 census showed just 1.4 per cent of ethnic or national minorities in the country's total population of 38 million. According to 2007 Eurostat estimates there are under 0.1 per cent of foreigners in the country. This paints a picture of one of the most homogeneous societies in the world.

Yet after 1989 the make-up of Polish society began to change in the mix of processes of democratization and globalization. Cultural differences became more visible with the growing assertiveness of the autochthon minorities, as well as the arrival of growing numbers of legal and illegal immigrants. The Polish state Europeanized its politics towards minorities and immigrants and introduced measures safeguarding the rights of its culturally different citizens and residents. Polish people began to get used to diversity, though not always without encountering problems.

This chapter describes the multicultural past of the Polish state and the politics on cultural pluralism during the communist period. It then examines the ethnic, national and religious landscape of contemporary Polish society. The third part identifies the incipient legal and institutional provisions safeguarding cultural pluralism. I then review the changes in attitudes of Poles on ethnic, national and religious difference. I conclude with an assessment of the future of cultural pluralism in Poland.

Multiculturalism in Polish history

The homogeneity of Polish society is a relatively recent phenomenon. At the peak of its power in the sixteenth century, ethnic and religious diversity was a defining feature of the Gentry Republic made up of the Kingdom of Poland and the Great Duchy of Lithuania. Poles, Ruthenians, Lithuanians, Jews – invited by King Kazimierz the Great in the fourteenth century after they had been expelled from Western European countries – Tartars, Armenians, Germans, Scots, Karaites and Protestant refugees from Czech lands, France and the Netherlands lived in relative harmony. Poland experienced no religious wars, there was (mostly) peaceful cooperation between Catholic, Protestant and Orthodox gentry and no religious harassment was discernible. Poland was regarded as the state without stakes.

Yet in the late eighteenth century this multicultural state plunged into anarchy and was partitioned by its stronger neighbours. Poland was to regain independence only in 1918. In 1931 ethnic Poles constituted 65 per cent of the population, Ukrainians 16 per cent, Jews 10 per cent, Byelorussians 6 per cent and Germans 3 per cent. Unfortunately, in most cases because of unresolved territorial disputes, relations between the Polish majority and the minorities were strained. The interwar period was also marred by growing anti-Semitism.

World War II radically changed the multi-ethnic and multi-religious landscape of the Polish state. Nazi atrocities dramatically reduced the size of the Jewish minority. Most of the survivors, hastened by several post-war pogroms, decided to emigrate to Israel. During conferences in Yalta and Potsdam the great powers agreed with the proposal of Joseph Stalin, a self-appointed 'expert' on the national question, to change the borders of the Polish state. Poland lost considerable territory in the east to Belarus, Ukraine and Lithuania. In return it gained territories in the west and north (Warmia and Masuria) at the expense of defeated Germany. They were named the 'Regained Lands', although their connection with the Polish state was already dubious in the twelfth century.

The 1946 census – the last one of the twentieth century that posed the nationality question – showed the Polish population was comprised of 10 per cent ethnic and national minorities. These data quickly lost their validity due to the centrally organized politics of resettling the German minority. The former German cities of Breslau and Stettin became populated by Poles forced out of Lvov and Vilnius. In 1948 the authorities carried out a brutal mass relocation of Ukrainians and Lemkos from the south-eastern part of the country to the Regained Lands, where they were dispersed and put under strict supervision for being 'dangerous elements' (Drozd and Halczak 2010: 91–112).

From 1945 to 1989 the communist regime ideologically sustained the illusion of Poland as a homogeneous, one-nation country. Denial of ethnic and national diversity was considered crucial to sustaining the unity of artificially reconstructed territory. Official propaganda maintained that the Poles were the main victims of the Nazis, while official atheism muted the question of religious diversity. Remaining 'problematic' minorities were encouraged or forced to migrate: this was the case of the population of Masuria and Silesia of ambivalent national identity that left for Germany in the 1960s and 1970s, and of the Jews who left Poland after the 1968 political witch hunt. Another problematic minority, the Roma, were forced to give up their traditional yet, in the eyes of the communist authorities, 'unproductive' nomadic style of life. Other minorities were granted limited rights to preserve their different identities provided that they did not bring them into the public sphere.

This hidden ethnic pluralism was solidified by weakly institutionalized policy that linked elements of the politics of difference on the local level (in the form of folkloric culture) with a denationalizing of discrimination on the national level (Łodziński 2010: 21). Even if there was no state-organized forced assimilation, it was on the way thanks to modernization, migration of the younger members of rural communities to cities and the spread of dominant Polish culture via television. The walled-in communist state did not welcome immigrants. From the 1970s academic centres began to attract students mainly from other communist countries, but their numbers were negligible.

The year 1989 marked a watershed in the approach of Polish authorities to ethnic and national minorities. New political elites began to perceive the recognition of their existence as tangible proof of democratization. The ethnic and national pluralism of Polish society was emphasized by the first non-communist Prime Minister, Tadeusz Mazowiecki. Parliament appointed a Committee of National and Ethnic Minorities composed of legislators of minority backgrounds or from regions inhabited by minorities. The financing of minorities' organizations and education was transferred from the Ministry of Home Affairs to the Ministry of Culture and Art, which symbolically marked the shift from control to support.

During the first decade of post-communist independence the issue of rights of national and ethnic minorities did not trigger any major squabbles between political parties. The immigrant theme did not appear at all, not even in the discourse of far-right parties. Authorities had to develop policies towards minorities from scratch as there were no ready internal institutional scripts. But external models were available: political elites with the support of the over-whelming majority of society had adopted the goal of joining the organizational structures of Western Europe, such as the Council of Europe, NATO and the European Union. Poland readily adopted European solutions in the area of treatment of minorities in order to authenticate its claim to the status of a truly European country. Polish politics toward minorities was 'Europeanized' from the outset and followed the post-Cold War pattern of highlighting 'minority rights' (Łodziński 2005).

Ethnic, national and religious pluralism

AUTOCHTHON MINORITIES

Poland's ethnic, national and religious landscape can be charted with the use of the 2002 census, the first in fifty years to include the question of nationality. It found that 96 per cent of citizens were ethnically Polish, 2 per cent did not declare their nationality and 1.2 per cent declared themselves to be of another nationality. Among these were (in thousands): Silesians (173), Germans (152.8), Byelorussians (48.7), Ukrainians (30.9), Roma (12.8), Russians (6), Lemkos (5.8), Lithuanians (5.8), Kashubians (5) and Slovaks (2) (GUS 2010a). In most cases ethnic or national diversity coincides with religious difference, and the two dimensions of otherness tend to be mutually reinforcing. Of these nationalities only the Slovaks, Lithuanians and Roma are Roman Catholic, like the majority of the Poles. Most Byelorussians, Ukrainians and Lemkos are Orthodox or Greek Catholics, while the Germans are in large part Protestant. A tiny indigenous Muslim community is represented by the Tatars. Most minorities are regionally concentrated: nearly all the Silesians and Germans inhabit two provinces (Śląskie and Opolskie); 95 per cent of Byelorussians and 90 per cent of Lithuanians live in Podlaskie (GUS 2010a).

After 1989 most minorities experienced a renaissance in their ethnic, national and religious awareness and some even an institutionalization of cultural identity. This was particularly the case of the German minority whose existence was either denied or was treated as an expression of false consciousness during communist rule. Growing integration of Poland with Western Europe meant easier contact with countrymen across the border which, in turn, translated into financial and organizational support for the German community. In the 1999 regional reform Germans, thanks to their assertiveness and the diplomatic efforts of the German government, defended the administrative autonomy of Opolskie province where 70 per cent of them lived.

The 2005 Act on Ethnic and National Minorities (see below) did not take into account the most populous minority according to the 2002 census – the Silesians, an indigenous population inhabiting the historical land of Silesia. Over time they were shaped by German, Czech and Polish political and cultural influences which contributed to their ambiguous, multidimensional and fluid identity. Some Silesians consider themselves German, some accentuate their Polish nationality and Silesian regional or ethnic difference, based mainly on Silesian dialect, but some assert a separate Silesian identity and demand to be recognized as a separate nation. Communist authorities had carried out 're-Polonization' efforts which were counterproductive: they shaped a defensive identity among some Silesians, consistent with the process described by Manuel Castells as 'exclusion of the excluding by the excluded' (Castells 2008).

Sociologists have interpreted the 'Silesian nation option' as a sign of popular disillusionment with both German appropriation of the Silesian identity as one of the elements of the ethnic make-up of the German nation and, simultaneously, the dismissive attitude of the Polish government (Dolińska 2010: 344). One major association, the Movement for Silesian Autonomy, has called for sweeping fiscal and economic autonomy for Silesia and the eventual transformation of the unitary Polish state into a federation. The more radical Association of People of Silesian Nationality demands official registration which Polish authorities refuse to do as it would be tantamount to recognition of a Silesian nation; the stance of the Polish authorities was upheld by the European Court of Human Rights in 2004. In December 2011, however, the regional court in Opole registered the Association of People of Silesian Nationality, which may be a sign of the changing attitude of the Polish government. The Silesian language was not recognized as a regional language by the 2005 Act and is not taught in schools.

The Kashubians are another autochthon community living in the Pomeranian region, and they were more successful in gaining state recognition: they have worked out a standardized version of their language. This community underlines its Kashubian ethnicity, usually without negating its Polish nationality. Kashubians' pragmatic approach won them the status of a minority using a regional language – the only one recognized in Polish law. This means that Kashubian may be used as an auxiliary language in municipalities where Kashubians constitute more than 20 per cent of the population. In 2009 more than 10,000 children learnt Kashubian at school (Obracht-Prondzyński 2010: 392).

The Roma are the most notable of the remaining autochthon minorities. Together with their physiognomic features, their culture and language is remarkably different from those of the rest of society. During communist rule the Roma were forced to abandon their nomadic lifestyle. Poland's systemic transformation after 1989 was catastrophic for many of them: their living conditions deteriorated because of unemployment and some Roma communities became impoverished ghettos. The practice of early marriages among the Roma sparked some controversy but, surprisingly, Polish courts discreetly recognized the specificity of Roma culture in this area, for example, handing down a suspended sentence to a husband accused of paedophilic behaviour in marrying an underage girl. The most pressing problem concerns the educational performance of Roma children.

Immigrant communities

In the communist era Poland was a country of virtually zero immigration. The few incomers were typically students from 'ideologically friendly' countries like Vietnam. In the 1980s, particularly after the introduction of martial law, many Poles chose emigration on political or economic grounds. The emigration trend continued in the 1990s and intensified after Poland joined the EU.

So far Poland has not become a country of immigration: in 2009 there were about 100,000 regular migrants. The number of irregular migrants has been estimated to be anywhere from several thousand to as many as 450,000 (Godlewska 2010; Stefańska et al. 2011). Zero immigration is coming to an end as each year the Polish labour market attracts more foreigners. In 2010 the Labour Offices registered 55,000 working foreigners; in the first half of 2011 there were over 86,000 applications to hire a foreign worker (MPiPS 2012). Moreover the character of migration is slowly but inexorably changing from temporary to permanent.

Immigrants fall into four general categories: citizens of the EU and other highly developed countries; economic immigrants from the former USSR, Asia and Africa; refugees; and repatriates. Immigration is mainly economic in character; there are only 17,000 foreign students at Polish universities. The profile of immigrants coming to Poland is somewhat different from that in other European countries. They are usually well-educated (36 per cent of them claim higher education); most of them are of a productive age (20–59 years). Their median age is slightly higher than that of the Polish population (Eurostat 2010). Migrants rarely bring their families with them, which is not surprising given that Poland is not yet considered a settlement country.

The most populous immigrant groups are the Ukrainians and the Vietnamese (Grzymała-Kazłowska 2008). The peak in Vietnamese migration to Poland was in the second half of the 1980s and today there are between 25,000 and 40,000 Vietnamese in the country, most of them illegally. They form a somewhat isolated, self-contained, well-organized and economically successful mercantile community. But as they value educational achievement, they send their children to Polish schools. The second generation has begun to mingle with Poles, often to the dismay of their parents who worry about having 'banana kids' (yellow on the outside, white on the inside).

No precise data are available on the number of Ukrainians in Poland, although some sources estimate it to be as high as 700,000. They come to Poland to work in construction and agriculture as well as in services such as childcare, domestic service and hospice care. The insignificant cultural distance between Ukrainians and Poles and the existence of the autochthon Ukrainian minority facilitates their social integration, including in the form of intermarriage.

Most of the other migrants come from either former Soviet Republics: Belarus, Russia, Armenia, Moldova and, recently, Georgia; or from advanced economies such as Germany, the US, France and Britain. One in three migrants comes from a neighbouring country but there is a growing number of Turks and people from Africa.

In 2011 around 3,000 refugees lived in Poland, about half of whom were settled in thirteen refugee centres. Several thousand held the status of a tolerated stay (UDSC 2010). The overwhelming majority (up to 90 per cent) in both categories were Chechen. The Chechens began to come to Poland after the first and second Chechen war, but usually quickly left for Western Europe. In 2004 Poland accepted the Dublin Convention and became a country with the obligation to take care of refugees making their first contact with Europe. Polish authorities reluctantly granted Chechens formal refugee status, though they formally remain citizens of the Russian Federation. No more than 8 per cent of asylum applications annually are given a positive decision. The rest are granted 'tolerated status' which means that they can stay in refugee centres but are not entitled to unemployment benefits and cannot leave Poland. The absence of a coherent integration programme in Poland contributes to growing anomie among those living in the refugee centres. Over time, the initial sympathy extended towards the Chechens as victims of Russian brutality is giving way to growing aversion and conflicts between them and local communities.

Religious difference

Despite the quickened pace of secularization (EVS 2008), Polish society retains its deeply religious traits. Nearly 90 per cent of Poles are Catholic, more than half of them attend mass once a week and the Catholic Church has traditionally and formally been recognized as having privileged status in public life (CBOS 2009). Among other religious affiliations, 1.3 per cent is Orthodox, 0.4 per cent Protestant, 0.3 per cent Jehovah's Witnesses (about 130,000) and 0.01 per cent Muslim and Buddhist (GUS 2010b).

In contrast with the situation of many Western countries the Muslim community in Poland is not regarded as problematic, mainly because of its minuscule size but also thanks to the 600-year-old tradition of coexistence with well-assimilated Tatars. Yet there are signs of growing disparities between assimilated, ethnic and folkloric Tatar Islam and the more universalistic Islam of recent immigrants. In the case of Chechens, religious difference (they usually profess the more fundamentalist Wahhabi version of Islam) is concomitant with a sense of exclusion and discrimination. When Poland becomes home for hundreds of Afghani translators and servicemen who will accompany returning Polish troops, this may sharpen the issue of Islam. As the Polish Muslim community becomes larger and better organized, it may articulate religious-based demands that will prove a challenge to Polish authorities (Włoch 2009).

Legal and institutional conditions of cultural pluralism

I shall now review the ways in which cultural pluralism in Poland has been reflected in the evolution of legal and institutional frameworks.

FUNDAMENTAL LEGAL ACTS

After regaining political independence in 1989 Poland adopted international standards for minority protection developed by the Council of Europe, the Organization for Security and Cooperation in Europe (OSCE), the UN and the EU. These included signing the European Convention of Human Rights (in 1994), the Framework Convention for the Protection of National Minorities (which entered into force in 2001) and, after many years of delay, the European Charter of Regional and Minority Languages (signed in 2009). As an EU member state Poland became involved in European cooperation in the area of immigrant policy; this trend was solidified after Poland entered the Schengen Agreement in 2007. Accordingly policies towards members of ethnic and national minorities and immigrants were modelled on the European experience.

One of the distinguishing features of the Polish model is the recognition and special status granted to select ethnic and national communities. The constitution adopted in 1997 (article 35) gave Polish citizens belonging to national or ethnic minorities the freedom to preserve and develop their own language, to protect customs and tradition and to develop their own culture. The constitution underlined the rights of the minorities to establish educational, cultural and religious institutions and to participate in the resolution of matters connected with their cultural identity. It is worth noting that the constitution linked the individual and group aspects of protection for minorities.

After a prolonged process of consultation and deliberation, in 2005 Parliament passed the Act on Regional Language, National and Ethnic Minorities. The unique Polish aspect of the law lay in a strictly defined concept of a national and ethnic minority. A national minority was defined as a community smaller in number than the rest of the population of the Republic of Poland; essentially distinguished from the rest of the citizens by its own language, culture or tradition; willing to safeguard its language, culture or tradition; conscious of its individual historical ethnic community and interested in its expression and protection; whose ancestors have resided within the present territory of the Republic of Poland for at least one hundred years; and identifying itself with the nation found in its own country. The definition of an ethnic minority was identical save for the last condition. On this basis the Act identified nine national minorities – Byelorussian, Czech, Lithuanian, German, Armenian, Russian, Slovak, Ukrainian and Jewish – and four ethnic minorities – Karaites, Lemkos, Roma and Tartars. Additionally, the Act recognized Kashubians as a community using a regional language. Only these communities received special rights and state support.

Members of these communities were granted the right to use and spell their first names and surnames in concordance with the spelling of their native languages, particularly on marriage certificates and identity cards. The recognized minorities could use their language as auxiliary in those municipalities where they numbered at least 20 per cent of inhabitants; here they could introduce bilingual names of places, objects and streets. As of November 2011 this right had been exercised in 787 cases (324 German names; 397 Kashubian; 30 Lithuanian; 27 Byelorussian and 9 Lemko) (MSWiA 2011).

Additionally, these recognized communities were entitled to influence legislation on minorities as well as the distribution of financial resources for safeguarding their identity and language through the Joint Commission of Government and Ethnic and National Minorities. The more numerous minorities (Germans, Kashubians, Byelorussians, Ukrainians, Roma, Lithuanians and Lemkos) have two representatives and the rest one each. The Commission includes a special working team for the Roma, the minority in the worst socio-economic position.

Hence, the Act introduced strict differentiation between the status of the recognized minorities whose culture and tradition were deemed worth supporting and safeguarding, and the rest of the minorities. The condition of one-hundred-year settlement on the territory of the Polish state excluded more recent immigrant communities, such as Vietnamese. The condition of 'essential distinction' from the rest of the citizens was subject to discretionary interpretation: despite reservations held by linguists, the Kashubians were granted the status of a community using a regional language, while the important Silesian community was not even mentioned in the Act.

POLITICAL RIGHTS

Access to political rights is different for members of recognized ethnic or national communities, for EU nationals and for third-country nationals. According to the Electoral Code, electoral committees set up by candidates of national and ethnic minorities do not have to reach the 5 per cent electoral threshold to get their candidates into Parliament. Since 1991 only the German minority has elected deputies (seven Members of Parliament in 1991, two in 1997–2005 and one after 2007). Some minority representatives (Byelorussian and Ukrainian) are elected to Parliament as candidates of the main political parties.

In terms of political rights for third-country nationals Poland was ranked second to last in the 2010 MIPEX index. The MIPEX report (2010) described the situation in Poland as 'seriously unfavourable', since foreigners have no voting rights and cannot join political parties or associations. They may join NGOs, trade unions or social organizations, but cannot establish them. There is no consultative body representing immigrant interests attached to the government. Poland did not ratify the 1992 Convention on the Participation of Foreigners in Public Life at the Local Level.

CITIZENSHIP REGIME

Theories of citizenship indicate that the choice of citizenship regime depends on the idea of a nation that is adopted (Brubaker 1992). In the case of Poland, nation making reflected a political pattern not dissimilar to that of France and Britain. After the partitions, nation building was anchored in culture.

The preamble of the 1997 constitution defines the Polish nation as a political one ('We, the Polish Nation, all citizens of the Republic'). A member of the Polish nation is a person holding citizenship of the Polish state. Yet Poland has adopted a *jus sanguinis* regime, which means that a person born in Poland to foreign parents does not automatically become a Polish citizen. The 2000 Act on Repatriation facilitates the path to citizenship for people of Polish descent living in the new independent post-Soviet countries. This points, therefore, to an ethnic definition of the nation state.

Up to 2009 granting of citizenship was a prerogative of the President. Naturalization was entirely discretionary, making access to nationality difficult and uncertain as an application could be rejected on nebulous grounds (Górny and Pudzianowska 2010). In 2009 Parliament passed a new Citizenship Bill which smoothed the path to citizenship by giving broader competences to provincial governors. It came into effect in 2012, only after the Constitutional Court dismissed the presidential veto lodged by the late President Lech Kaczyński and sustained by his successor Bronisław Komorowski.

The Court ruled that there are two non-conflicting modes of acquiring Polish citizenship: the discretionary granting of citizenship by the President, and obligatory administrative recognition of citizenship if the candidate has fulfilled the stipulated basic conditions (for example, if he or she is a stateless person or a refugee; has been married to a Polish citizen for three years; was granted permission for residence because of his or her Polish background; and has lived in Poland for two years). The Court emphasized that the new regulation expresses an 'open vision of Polish citizenship'.

EDUCATION

The Polish state guarantees basic multicultural rights in education (Głowacka-Grajper 2009). The 1991 Educational Act stipulates that public schools should enable children to preserve their national, ethnic, linguistic or religious identity. Children of minorities recognized by the 2005 Act may choose one of the following options: they can learn all subjects in their native language apart from Polish language and the history and geography of Poland (the option chosen by Lithuanians); schools can be bilingual; or the native language may be taught as a separate school subject (chosen by most minorities). If the minority is dispersed (Ukrainians) interschool bodies can be established.

Special strategies of educational development have been developed for the Lithuanian and German communities prepared by the Ministry of Education in cooperation with minority associations and local authorities. In addition, in 2012 the Tatars received government funding for the translation of a primer and lesson book in Tatar for children. Only the Karaites (who are too few) and Russians (because Russian is popularly taught as a second language in schools) do not use state-guaranteed opportunities to promote their culture and language. In the school year 2009–10 minority languages were taught in over 1,000 schools (MEN 2010).

The state guarantees the right to education for immigrant children. There are about 4,000 foreign pupils in Polish schools. In 2010 the Ministry of Education issued a directive emphasizing the right of migrant children to learn Polish as well as their own language, and extending the right to free education up to eighteen years of age. Yet the MIPEX report notes a gap between legal provisions and the reality of Polish schools: the intercultural elements of education are absent from school curricula, staff are not prepared to meet the needs of migrant children and the support system is insufficient.

The most acute problem concerns the underprivileged status of Roma children at school. As they often do not read and write Polish fluently, they are often classified as developmentally retarded and sent to special status schools or to separate classes. It must be said that traditional Roma culture does not attach high value to educational achievement and even resents institutional education, seeing it as a threat to Roma identity. This translates into diminished opportunities on the labour market, and resulting exclusion and social marginalization of the Roma community (Zawicki 2010).

ACCESS TO THE LABOUR MARKET

Data show growing demand for immigrant labour in Poland despite an overall high level of unemployment. After EU accession in 2004 a widening gap in legal status between EU citizens and third-country nationals was observable. In 2006–8 a series of decrees from the Ministry of Labour opened up the Polish labour market for seasonal workers. But as the MIPEX report (2010) states, the 'non-EU newcomers with the right to work are simultaneously encouraged to integrate into the labour market and discouraged from integrating into it'. For example, they can use training and public employment services, but they also need legal permission to change jobs. In 2007 Parliament adopted the Polish Charter that grants special privileges to people of Polish descent living in countries that formerly made up the USSR: they may work without legal permission or establish companies on the same basis as Polish citizens.

ANTI-DISCRIMINATION MEASURES

Some provisions against discrimination on the basis of race, ethnic background, nationality and religion were introduced in the Labour Code in 2009. Ethnic crimes are punished according to the 1997 Penal Code. But it took a long time and a lawsuit, filed by the European Commission in the International Court of Justice, before

Poland introduced a separate anti-discrimination Act incorporating European directives into the Polish legal system. It came into effect in January 2011 and penalized unequal treatment on the basis of gender, race, ethnic background, nationality, religion, world view, disability, age or sexual orientation. In contrast to other European countries, Poland did not establish a separate institution to investigate cases of discrimination, which may seriously impede the effectiveness of the new regulation.

The only minority provided with special protection against discrimination and further marginalization is the Roma. Since 2001 the Ministry of Home Affairs has carried out a programme for local governments and Roma associations involving support of activities in the areas of education, life conditions, health, unemployment, increasing knowledge of the Roma community, and cultural and civic education about Roma.

RELIGIOUS RIGHTS

The 1989 law on freedom of belief and religion, together with the 1997 constitution, stipulate that the Polish state is secular and neutral in all matters concerning religion. The relations between the state and fifteen religions are regulated by separate legal acts. Religious associations and churches may register with the Ministry of Home Affairs and Administration in order to gain full rights provided for by the state. Many areas of 'reasonable accommodation' of religious practices have been designated; for example, Muslims are exempt from regulations concerning slaughter. There are no Islamic schools in Poland, but since 1989 the Ministry of Education has allowed Muslims to use school classrooms during the weekends for religious education purposes. The Catholic Church holds a privileged position in many areas of public life yet, as Fetzer and Soper argued (2005), the formalized place of religion in public life can serve as an opportunity structure for integrating immigrants whose culture involves a strong religious aspect, for example Muslims.

Immigration and integration policy

Analysis of government documents and state laws shows how Poland has not yet adopted a comprehensive immigration doctrine although it applies many European measures in this area. Strategic governmental documents such as the 'Poland 2030' report refer to immigration in passing, for example as a possible future solution to deal with an ageing society (Szymanderski 2010; Łotocki 2009). In 2007 the government appointed an Interdepartmental Group on Migration Issues attached to the Ministry of Home Affairs and Administration, but its work is still at an early stage. Immigration is not seen as an urgent problem that requires immediate action.

Similarly, Poland has not as yet worked out a complex strategy of immigrant integration (MIPEX 2010). In 2005 the governmental European Committee presented a document entitled 'Proposal of activities towards creating a complex policy of integration of foreigners in Poland'. The document identified four areas of future policy – political, legal, institutional and substantive – but did not suggest any specific integration measures to be taken. For the time being the sole elements of integration policy are those in the Individual Integration Programmes made available to refugees (and since 2008 to persons with a permit for 'tolerated stay'), which originated in the 2004 law on social assistance. The refugee is provided with financial support, health insurance, social guidance, help with job searching, vocational training and courses, but it is stipulated that the success of integration depends on his or her own effort. In 2007 only 231 people took part in the programme. In 2008 the Ministry of Labour and Social Policy emphasized that there were no plans for its expansion because 'the inflow of immigrants is a new phenomenon and up until now there has been no need to undertake integration of other groups of foreigners'.

On the other hand, the issue of integration of immigrants and refugees is being addressed by non-governmental organizations. Poland is participating in the European Fund for the Integration of Third Country Nationals for 2007–13. The financing enables academic and non-governmental institutions to analyze the position of foreigners in Poland and to produce detailed reports that may serve as the basis for future policies. The Catholic Church's NGO Caritas and representatives of local authorities, NGOs, migrant associations and academic institutes have formed a special Expert Group Monitoring Progress in Integration Policy, which furnishes information to the Ministry of Labour and Social Policy.

Social attitudes towards cultural and religious pluralism

Attitudinal surveys reveal a surprisingly high level of acceptance of ethnic, racial and religious difference among Polish respondents. In

2007, 70–80 per cent stated that they supported admitting a person of different ethnicity or nationality into Poland, granting that person Polish citizenship, working with him or her, making friends and living in the same neighbourhood. One in five declared maximum openness, and only 4 per cent wanted no contact (Jasińska-Kania and Łodziński 2009). Poles would more readily accept a person of a different religion or ethnicity to the highest political office (this happened when Jerzy Buzek, a Lutheran, served as Prime Minister between 1997 and 2001; he went on in 2009 to become President of the European Parliament) or simply as a neighbour than the average European (Eurobarometer 2009).

The 2008 European Values Survey (EVS) noted how only 12 per cent of Poles would not like to have people of a different race as neighbours, 17 per cent would not like immigrants, foreign workers or Jews, one in three would protest against Roma and one in four against Muslims as neighbours (EVS 2008). In her analysis of processes of exclusion, Jasińska-Kania (2009: 42–3) highlighted changes in conditions allowing for full participation of persons of another nationality in the life of the Polish national community. After joining the EU Poles began to attach more significance to the institutional and cultural aspects of inclusion, and less significance to psychological and ideological factors. Good knowledge of the Polish language, having Polish citizenship, being a permanent resident and following the Polish way of life were now deemed more important than the subjective feeling of being Polish or – which may appear surprising – being a Catholic. This was confirmed by the results of the 2011 elections, when two apparently well-assimilated 'Afro-Poles' were elected to Parliament.

In a 2011 survey on attitudes towards other nations, Poles identified Czechs, Italians, French, Spanish, Slovaks and English as their favourite nations; the least favourite were Romanians, Arabs and Roma. Poles usually expressed warmer feelings towards Western nations, which is understandable in light of the Western ambitions and connections prevailing in society. The less developed nations from Eastern Europe serve as a negative point of reference, but there has been a steady rise in sympathy towards all nations, particularly Ukrainians and Lithuanians (CBOS 2012). As Jasińska-Kania and Łodzinski (2008) put it, the alien 'others' were becoming 'the different among us'.

The fact is that attitudes about cultural pluralism remain on the abstract level. In fact, most Poles rarely encounter examples of cultural, racial, ethnic, national or religious difference in their everyday lives (Klaus and Wencel 2010). Only one in four Poles has a friend or knows somebody of a different ethnic background who lives in Poland; the EU average is 57 per cent (Eurobarometer 2009). Only recently have celebrities from a distinctly non-Polish background appeared, from naturalized soccer players to TV presenters. Still they are treated as an exotic novelty, far removed from everyday experience. Ethnic, national or religious difference is no longer taboo in public life, but many Poles are surprised when they learn that their iconic ski jumper Adam Małysz is Lutheran, as well as former Prime Minister and European Parliament President Buzek.

Only one-third of Poles agree that discrimination on ethnic grounds is frequent in Poland, in comparison to two-thirds across the EU (Eurobarometer 2009). There are few reported cases of crimes involving a racial or ethnic angle. According to the Helsinki Foundation the most frequent crimes of this kind are hate speech and beatings, usually perpetrated by groups of young men (Fagasiński 2010). Two serious and in some ways interconnected social pathologies are anti-Semitism and so-called 'phantom Islamophobia'. Anti-Semitic discourse is common in the far-right media; the controversial Catholic station 'Radio Maryja' has been criticized by both the Vatican and the European Parliament for anti-Semitic discourse. Jews are also the most common target of hate speech on the Internet (FWL 2011).

Surveys suggest that many Poles do not like Muslims and they fear Islam: 46 per cent of respondents declared a negative attitude toward Muslims in 2006 compared to 38 per cent of French and 23 per cent of British respondents. This aversion had been higher: in 2005 it had been around 30 per cent of Polish respondents. Only in Spain was the rise in aversion to Muslims more pronounced, from 37 per cent in 2005 to 60 per cent in 2006 (Pew Global Attitudes Project 2006). In Poland there is little cultural contact with Muslims plus the historical experience with the Islamic world has been generally positive, so this dislike seems unjustified and irrational (Górak-Sosnowska 2006). What can be termed a 'platonic' Islamophobia was probably contracted via media coverage of conflicts centring on Islam in Western Europe: the hijab wars in France, mosque building in Switzerland and Italy. It was reinforced by a fear of fundamentalist Islamic terrorism. Islamophobia may merely be the new face of old racism and xenophobia, a convenient tool for the exclusion of strangers.

Conclusion

Multiculturalism as it is understood in Western political practices, media reporting and academic discourse is in Poland considered as a Western European invention responding to specific Western European problems and deeply rooted in the colonial past. As Sławomir Łodziński, a leading Polish researcher in the field, has argued, in the case of Poland the very category of multiculturalism seems inadequate. A much better match are the conceptions of the 'politics of equal recognition' and the 'politics of difference' outlined by Charles Taylor (Łodziński 2005). On the one hand, the Polish state is gradually constructing an anti-discrimination system that will ensure access to identical rights for everyone. On the other hand, the state has introduced specific systems of rights for select minorities. The analysis of the legal and institutional measures taken over the last two decades may lead to the initial conclusion that they have evolved in accordance with the trends characteristic of other liberal democratic states – integration of already present minorities, exclusion of immigrants.

We can say, then, that Poland remains a country of 'folkloric cultural pluralism'. Autochthon minorities seem well rooted and the only occasional controversy involves the question of whether a Silesian nation exists. It is resurrected from time to time by former Prime Minister Jarosław Kaczyński, leader of the opposition nationalist party, who believes Silesians' struggle for recognition is a 'hidden German option'. Some commotion arose over planning the 2011 census when a number of minorities (Silesians, Ukrainians and Lemkos) criticized the methodology used in the 2002 census. It asked questions that required 'either-or' answers regarding the respondent's nationality; in other words, a respondent had to declare whether he or she was Polish or Silesian. Some people answered no nationality (2 per cent). In reality the source of the complaints was that census figures indicating the size of particular ethnic and national communities were markedly lower than the inflated estimates provided by their leaders. A compromise on the 2011 questionnaire was reached: it would contain questions about one's nationality (understood as ethnic or national belonging, not citizenship); identification with another nation or ethnic community; language used at home; and mother tongue. The results of the census were to be published in late 2012.

What differentiates Poland from Western European countries is the fact that immigration and immigrants are not perceived as important issues. They do not constitute an important part of public debate and have not become political issues, even for far right parties. Only 13 per cent of 700 candidates standing in the 2011 parliamentary elections found it necessary to address immigration and integration questions in their political programme (Szajkowska 2011).

Yet this situation is bound to change. Poland's steady economic growth has made it a more attractive country for potential immigrants to search for work or to settle with their families. At the same time, the deepening demographic crisis caused by one of the lowest fertility rates in Europe and a greying society means that – notwithstanding recent economic successes – Poland will have to cope with the same dilemmas that Western Europe faced in the 1960s and 1970s which led to policies encouraging immigration. Polish authorities will soon need to give higher priority to formulating an integration policy. Undoubtedly, the recent rocky experiences of Western models of diversity will shape thinking on this matter.

The ethnocultural homogeneity of Polish society and the resilience of traditional national identity may incline policymakers to draw more extensively from the French model of assimilation and what is seen as its steadfast rejection of negotiating over the cultural values deemed fundamental to the character of the nation. The liberal British model of parallel identities seems a less plausible alternative in the Polish context. It seems that the most probable path of evolution of the incipient Polish model of 'vanilla multiculturalism' is a gradual extension of its framework of recognition to include more minorities, including immigration-based ones. A political decision that may signal such change was the amnesty announced at the end of 2011 for illegal economic migrants and unsuccessful asylum seekers in Poland; from January 2012 they would receive a residence permit valid for two years allowing them to work legally in Poland.

REFERENCES

Brubaker, Rogers (1992), *Citizenship and Nationhood in France and Germany*, Cambridge, MA: Harvard University Press.
Castells, Manuel (2008), *Siła tożsamości* [*The Power of Identity*], Warsaw: Wydawnictwo Naukowe PWN.
CBOS (Centrum Badania Opinii Społecznej) (2009), *Dwie dekady przemian religijności w Polsce*, BS/120/2009.
CBOS (Centrum Badania Opinii Społecznej) (2012), *Stosunek Polaków do innych narodów*, BS/02/2012.
Dolińska, Katarzyna (2010), 'Ślązacy', in Stefan Dudra and Bernadetta

Nitschke (eds), *Mniejszości narodowe i etniczne w Polsce po II wojnie światowej*, Krakow: Nomos, pp. 338–55.

Drozd, Roman and Bohdan Halczak (2010), *Dzieje Ukraińców w Polsce w latach 1921–1989*, Warsaw: Tyrsa.

Eurobarometer (2009), 'Discrimination in the European Union. Perceptions, experiences and attitudes'. Available at http://ec.europa.eu/public_opinion/archives/ebs/ebs_296_en.pdf

Eurostat (2010), 'Population of foreign citizens in the EU27 in 2009'. Available at http://epp.eurostat.ec.europa.eu/cache/ITY_PUBLIC/3-07092010-AP/EN/3-07092010-AP-EN.PDF

EVS (European Values Study (2008). Available at http://www.european valuesstudy.eu/evs/surveys/longitudinal-file-1981-2008.html

Fagasiński, Maciej (2010), 'Racism and discriminatory practices in Poland', ENAR (European Network Against Racism) Shadow Report 2009/2010. Available at http://cms.horus.be/files/99935/MediaArchive/publications/shadow%20report%202010-11/20.%20Poland.pdf

Fetzer, Joel S. and J. Christopher Soper (2005), *Muslims and the State in Britain, France and Germany*, Cambridge: Cambridge University Press.

FWL (Fundacja Wiedzy Lokalnej) (2011), *Raport mniejszości*. Available at www.raportmniejszosci.pl

Głowacka-Grajper, Małgorzata (2009), *Mniejszościowe grupy etniczne wobec polskiego systemu oświaty. Przekaz kulturowy a więź etniczna*, Warsaw: Wydawnictwa Uniwersytetu Warszawskiego.

Godlewska, Justyna (2010), 'Migracje i imigranci w Polsce – skala, podstawy prawne, polityka'. Available at http://www.eapn.org.pl/expert/files/Migracje%20i%20imigranci%20w%20Polsce-skala,%20podstawy%20prawne,%20polityka.pdf

Górak-Sosnowska, Katarzyna (2006), 'Platoniczna islamofobia'. Available at www.arabia.pl/content/view/282077/2/

Górny, Agata and Dorota Pudzianowska (2010), 'Country Report: Poland', EUDO Citizenship Observatory. Available at http://eudo-citizenship.eu/docs/CountryReports/Poland.pdf

Grzymała-Kazłowska, Aleksandra (ed.) (2008), 'Między jednością a wielością. Integracja odmiennych grup i kategorii imigrantów w Polsce', Warsaw: Ośrodek Badań nad Migracjami WNE UW.

Grzymała-Kazłowska, Aleksandra (2009), 'Clashes of discourses: The representations of immigrants in Poland', *Journal of Migration and Refugee Studies*, 7 (1) (April), pp. 58–81.

GUS (Główny Urząd Statystyczny) (2010a), 'Wyniki Narodowego Spisu Powszechnego Ludności i Mieszkań 2002 w zakresie deklarowanej narodowości oraz języka używanego w domu'. Available at http://www.stat.gov.pl/gus/8185_PLK_HTML.htm

GUS (Główny Urząd Statystyczny) (2010b), 'Wyznania religijne.

Stowarzyszenia narodowe i etniczne 2006–2008'. Available at http://www.stat.gov.pl/cps/rde/xbcr/gus/PUBL_oz_wyzn_rel_stow_nar_i_etn_w_pol_2006-2008.pdf

Jasińska-Kania, Aleksandra (2009), 'Wykluczanie z narodu: dystanse społeczne wobec mniejszości narodowych i migrantów', in Aleksandra Jasińska-Kania and Sławomir Łodziński, *Obszary i formy wykluczenia etnicznego w Polsce. Mniejszości narodowe, imigranci, uchodźcy*, Warsaw: Wydawnictwo Naukowe Scholar, pp. 39–57.

Klaus, Witold and Katarzyna Wencel (2010), 'Dyskryminacja cudzoziemców w Polsce 2008–2010', in Klaus Witold (ed.), *Sąsiedzi czy intruzi. O dyskryminacji cudzoziemców w Polsce*, Warsaw: Instytut Spraw Publicznych, pp. 42–132.

Łodziński, Sławomir (2005), *Równość i różnica: mniejszości narodowe w porządku demokratycznym w Polsce po 1989 r.*, Warsaw: Wydawnictwo Naukowe Scholar.

Łodziński, Sławomir (2010), 'Polityka wobec mniejszości narodowych i etnicznych w Polsce w latach 1945–2008', in Stefan Dudra and Bernadetta Nitschke (eds), *Mniejszości narodowe i etniczne w Polsce po II wojnie światowej*, Krakow: Nomos, pp. 13–34.

Łotocki, Łukasz (2009) *Integracja i dyskryminacja – krajobraz 2009*, Warszawa: Instytut Spraw Publicznych.

MEN (Ministerstwo Edukacji Narodowej) (2010), 'Odpowiedź sekretarza stanu w Ministerstwie Edukacji Narodowej z upoważnienia ministra na zapytanie nr 7853 w sprawie języka nauczania w szkołach mniejszości narodowych w Polsce'. Available at http://orka2.sejm.gov.pl/IZ6.nsf/main/192408A4

MIPEX (Migrant Integration Policy Index III, Poland) (2010). Available at http://www.mipex.eu/poland

MPiPS (Ministerstwo Pracy i Polityki Społecznej) (2012), 'Cudzoziemcy pracujący w Polsce – statystyki'. Available at http://www.mpips.gov.pl/analizy-i-raporty/cudzoziemcy-pracujacy-w-polsce-statystyki/

MSWiA (Ministerstwo Spraw Wewnętrznych i Administracji) (2011), 'Urzędowy Rejestr Gmin, w których używany jest język pomocniczy'. Available at http://msw.gov.pl/portal/pl/178/2958/Ustawa_o_mniejszosciach_narodowych_i_etnicznych_oraz_o_jezyku_regionalnym.html

Obracht-Prondzyński, Cezary (2010), 'Społeczność kaszubska', in Stefan Dudra and Bernadetta Nitschke (eds), *Mniejszości narodowe i etniczne w Polsce po II wojnie światowej*, Krakow: Nomos, pp. 356–93.

Pew Global Attitudes Project, Public Opinion Survey (2006), 'The great divide: How Westerners and Muslims view each other'. Available at http://www.pewglobal.org/2006/06/22/the-great-divide-how-westerners-and-muslims-view-each-other/

Stefańska, Renata (2011), 'Migration and Integration Policy', in Paweł Kaczmarczyk (ed.), *Recent Trends in International Migration in Poland.*

The 2010 SOPEMI report, CMR Working Paper, no. 51 (109), section 2, pp. 10–17.

Szajkowska, Klaudia (2011), *Polska krajem przyjaznym imigrantom czy wprost przeciwnie? Co deklarują kandydaci?*, press note on the research by MamyPrawoWiedzieć. Available at http://wiadomosci.ngo.pl/wiadomosci/687354.html

Szymanderski, Jacek (2010), 'Stan faktyczny i kierunki rozwoju integracji cudzoziemców w Polsce', Warsaw: Stowarzyszenie Wolnego Słowa.

UDSC (Urząd do Spraw Cudzoziemców) (2010). Available at http://www.udsc.gov.pl/Statystyki,229.html

Weinar, Agnieszka (2009), 'Multiculturalism debates in Poland', in *Emilie. A European Approach to Multicultural Citizenship: Legal, Political and Educational Challenges. Poland*, Warsaw: Centre for International Relations.

Włoch, Renata (2009), 'Islam in Poland. Between ethnicity and universal umma', *International Journal of Sociology*, 39 (3) (Fall), pp. 58–67.

Zawicki, Marcin (2010), 'Polityka wobec mniejszości romskiej w Polsce w latach 2000–2009', in Stanisław Mazur (ed.), *Krajowe i wspólnotowe polityki publiczne wobec mniejszości romskiej*, Krakow: Małopolska Szkoła Administracji Publicznej Uniwersytetu Ekonomicznego w Krakowie, pp. 115–34.

Chapter Thirteen

Multinationalism, Mononationalism or Transnationalism in Russia?

Sergey Akopov

How multiculturalism and multinationalism have been theorized in Russia

Some may claim that since multiculturalism has never been adopted as an official policy in Russia, the Russian case has no right to be presented in a cross-national book on multiculturalism. In this chapter I would like to show, however, that Russian historic experience of ethnic diversity management is unique and can be of great importance to a comparative analysis of multiculturalism. In addition, Russian society and Russian identity today are facing challenges similar to those found in other European – and Western – countries: economic and cultural globalization; massive migration; weakening of citizens' exclusive attachment to one nation state; the danger of nationalism; and the rise of extremists. Russia may not have immigration-based multiculturalism if immigration is restricted to the movement of peoples between sovereign states. But it does have a growing multiculturalism based in internal migration across an extraordinarily diverse and expansive territory.

The echo of 'the collapse of multiculturalism' announced by a number of European politicians was distinctly heard in Russian media and public life throughout 2010 and 2011 and, particularly, during the 2012 presidential election campaign. In fact it was the critique of multiculturalism that became the starting point for Vladimir Putin's article entitled 'Russia: The National Question' published in *Nezavisimaya Gazeta* (23 January 2012); it bore the subtitle 'Self-Determination of the Russian People: A Multiethnic Civilization Sealed with a Russian Core'. According to Putin:

> [the] failure of the multicultural project is caused by the crisis of the 'nation state' – namely, the state that has historically been built exclusively on the basis of ethnic identity. And it is a challenge to be faced not only by Europe, but many other regions in the world'. (Putin 2012:1)

Tariq Modood describes multiculturalism as 'the recognition of group differences within the public sphere of laws, policies, democratic discourses and the terms of a shared citizenship and national identity' (Modood 2007: 2). Whether we agree or not with the implications stemming from Putin's article – itself an interesting object for in-depth discourse analysis – in the case of the Russian Federation the public sphere of laws, policies, democratic discourses and national identity are understood in a very different way from how they are in the European Union or the United States. There are historical and cultural reasons for Russia being different that are familiar to the Russian specialist. Here I wish to apply Modood's definition of multiculturalism to the case of Russia.

When considering the public sphere of laws and policies one has to remember that historically Russia emerged as an extremely diverse federative state with a controversial imperial heritage and a very sophisticated federal structure. The political relationships between the centre and regions of Russia became even more problematic during the period of its Soviet history. The current Russian Federation possesses an enormous territory covering eleven time zones and a population composed of over 160 ethnic groups that speak 100 languages and dialects and representing all major world religions. Therefore it may be more appropriate to view the Russian Federation not as a *multicultural* but as a *multinational* entity.

The complexity of relations between federal and regional authorities was worsened by economic problems after the fall of the USSR, as well as the absence of strong democratic and parliamentary traditions in the imperial and Soviet histories of the country. These deficits created significant objective difficulties for the development of multicultural policies in the public sphere. On the one hand, the federal government has to guarantee autonomy and decentralization for Russian regions; on the other it is obliged by the constitution to keep Russia's 'diversity within unity' across its vast and underpopulated (particularly by Asian standards) territory.

From a historical perspective the Russian Empire annexed most of its regions before the 1917 revolution. After the abdication of the Tsar and collapse of the Russian Empire new symbols of state identity and nation building were embedded in the Soviet ideology of Marxism-Leninism. The USSR was held up as a vanguard of international working-class solidarity. This was the ideology that largely held Russia's regions together until 1991. However by the end of perestroika, and encouraged in part by Gorbachev's policy of glasnost, resentment of Moscow's domination over far-flung regions promoted a further growth of regional nationalism and separatism. After the fall of the USSR national antagonisms that had built up over several centuries inside the Russian Empire started to act like 'delayed land mines'. The model of cultural and ethnic assimilation, and later integration of regional minorities, into *homo sovieticus* – an ideological template obliterating difference – suddenly ceased to exist. Several former regions of the Russian Empire and of the Soviet Union drifted away from the nascent Commonwealth of Independent States (CIS) to subsequently join NATO and the more economically promising EU.

The legal aspect of Russia's multinationalism is to a large degree defined by the Russian Constitution and Russian Constitutional Law. At the end of the 1990s the Russian federal government faced the problem of keeping separate regional elites and their Republics – for example, the special cases of Tatarstan and Chechnya – within one state. In 2000, in order to strengthen territorial unity and increase 'vertical' federal power over all the Russian regions, seven federal districts were created, each to be administered by an envoy appointed by the President. This signalled the end of the 'Russia of regions' that had existed for a brief period in the 1990s. The heads of the seven federal districts serve as 'liaisons' between regions and the federal government and are primarily responsible for overseeing the compliance of the regions with federal laws.

The restructuring of the Russian regions also involved a reduction in the number of 'subjects of the Russian Federation' from eighty-nine (as identified in the 1993 Constitution) to the current eighty-three; this was carried out through the merging of a number of regions between 2003 and 2007. Moreover, from 2004 the governors of Russian regions – including the twenty-one national or ethnic Republics – were no longer elected but were instead appointed by the President. A more detailed analysis of the dynamics of Russian federalism can be found in the work of Natalya Pankevich. She defines three stages of the evolution of Russia's federal structure after the fall of the USSR: the first stage was overcoming the 'secessionist model' (1990–2); the second comprised the formation of a dualistic model (1993–8); and the final stage involved the restoration of an all-inclusive federal model (from 1999) (Pankevich 2008: 117–78). All these processes led inevitably to further centralization of the Russian federal state. In January 2012, just two months before Putin's return to the presidency, President Dmitry Medvedev tried to reverse this course by introducing a bill that would have reinstated the procedure of direct elections of the governors.

Today Russia remains probably the most constitutionally complex, ethnically multifarious and numerically multiple federation in the world. In legal terms Russia is an 'asymmetric' federation: although all eighty-three Russian regions have equal representation (two delegates each) in the Upper Chamber of the Russian Parliament – the Federation Council – they differ and are asymmetric in terms of the degree of political autonomy they exercise. For example, the twenty-one 'Republics' enjoy the most autonomy among all the 'subjects of the Federation' as each has its own constitution, Parliament and, until 2011, President (in that year the title of 'President' was replaced by that of 'Head of Republic'). These Republics are allowed to establish their own official language alongside Russian and they have their own symbols of sovereignty – flag, emblem, anthem and capital city. Article 5 of the Russian Federal Constitution even defines Republics as 'states'; in practice, they are represented by the federal government in Russia's international affairs.

Other tiers of the federal system are ostensibly purely territorial and administrative, but as we can see from the account below recognition of ethnic and cultural difference is never far from the surface. Besides the twenty-one Republics there are forty-six 'oblasts' (provinces) – the most common type of federal 'subjects'. Unlike the Republics, oblasts are not national but territorially based entities. Accordingly they merit less political autonomy. Many oblasts are located around the largest Russian cities, for example Nizhni Novgorod Oblast and Sverdlovsk Oblast, located near the city of Yekaterinburg. Another tier in the federal structure is made up of nine 'krai' – territories whose designation is mostly historic: the name 'krai' was originally given to frontier territories of the Russian Empire such as Krasnodar Krai which, with the Rostov Oblast, constitute the historic homelands of the Cossacks. Four 'autonomous okrugs' (districts) were initially autonomous entities within 'oblasts' and 'krais' that were created for ethnic minorities. Their status was elevated to that of federal subjects in the 1990s after the break-up of the USSR; a notable example is the Yamalo-Nenets Autonomous Okrug in northwestern Siberia. One autonomous oblast – the Jewish Autonomous Oblast – was established by Joseph Stalin in 1934 'in order to allow the Jews of the Soviet Union to receive a territory in which to pursue Yiddish cultural heritage within a socialist framework' (see Akopov and Razumeyko 2011: 9). Finally among the eighty-three subjects of the Russian Federation are two federal metropolises, Moscow and St Petersburg, which, significantly, experience the most migration and multicultural development in Russia today.

An additional component of Modood's definition of multiculturalism involves the question of national identity. In this respect we observe that alongside the evolution of Russian federalism, the country has also undergone significant changes in the theoretical understanding of what a nation is. During the Soviet era Stalin's 'primordial' theory of the nation dominated thinking. Primordialism, or essentialism, is the argument that nations are ancient and natural phenomena. The assumption was that the community would have a fixed, unmalleable nature over time. In 1912 Stalin, the future head of the People's Commissariat of Nationalities, contended that 'the nation is a historically stable community of people that emerged on the basis of common language, territory, economic life and mentality, manifested in commonality of culture' (Stalin 1946: 296).

Primordialism, however, became the target of massive criticism in the West after World War II. Influenced in particular by the works of Ernest Gellner and Benedict Anderson, many scholars have come to treat the nation as a community constructed by the technologies and politics of modernity. Nevertheless, the primordial conception continued to dominate Soviet policies and discourses. This approach was widely accepted by Soviet scholars, in particular by the director of the influential Institute of Ethnography of the USSR Academy of Sciences and notable Russian historian Lev Gumiliev. The prevailing philosophy in the USSR about nations could be generally characterized as assuming that individual nations, nationalities and ethnicities were defined in similar categories and all of them were controlled by the centralized Soviet state.

Today scholars and officials in Russia are slowly moving away from primordial understandings of the nation towards a constructivist approach in their explanations of the nature of national identity. For Olga Malinova, identity is a very effective mechanism for political mobilization and it is regularly used to shape collective political claims. Yet, once we attribute identity to a group, there is a risk that this identity will be transformed into some innate objective reality – in other words, it undergoes a process of reification – which often becomes cluttered with myths (especially about 'national character'). In fact those myths are the result of competition between different narratives of identity (Malinova 2005: 13). The latter can be dangerous and can lead to separatist nationalism inside a country.

An attempt to position nations as existing naturally and eternally often enables elites to capitalize on xenophobic moods, making enemies out of immigrants and ethnic minorities. That has been an argument advanced by Valerii Tishkov (2007), director of the Institute of Ethnology and Anthropology of the Russian Academy of Sciences. His concern has been to stop 'the race for regional identities' and instead promote them by way of one strong identity of 'Rossiyanin' – a citizen of multicultural Russia. (The best translation of 'Rossiyanin' would probably be the German *Russländer*.) According to Tishkov this implicit stress on a multicultural experience would best help preserve both the unity and diversity of contemporary Russia. In many ways this model resembles the French conception of *'le citoyen avec l'identité civique'*.

Since the 'invention' of the doctrine of 'sovereign democracy' in 2006, the idea of strengthening the sovereignty and unity of Russia and rebuilding its status as a great civilization has been paramount in official discourse. The consolidation of Russia's general identity rather than privileging separate multicultural identities within the state is the predominant objective. So, in this respect, Putin's article 'on the national question' reshapes the doctrine of 'sovereign democracy' by attempting to toe a fine line between preventing both Russian nationalism and anti-Russian nationalism, each of which has the potential to be a destructive force. 'I am deeply convinced that attempts to expound on the idea of building a Russian "national", mono-ethnic state is contrary to the whole of our thousand-year history,' Putin wrote. 'Moreover, it is the shortest path to the destruction of the Russian people and Russian statehood and any viable sovereign state on our land'. By the same token, Putin also noted the danger of excessive pandering to individual ethnic groups – the danger of multiculturalism. He advocated that all Russians should espouse a 'civic patriotism' and conform to a 'single cultural code' (Putin 2012: 1). He also cautioned against the growth of regional national parties which he viewed as susceptible to separatist agendas.

In the case of Russia the transformation to *le citoyen* has been considerably delayed and questions remain unanswered. For example, how can we strengthen the development of 'Rossiyanin identity' without suppressing long-standing Russian regionalism? How can we cement 'civic patriotism' in conditions of global migration? Finally, what does all this tell us about the future of multicultural theories and the liberal values they rest on (see Chapter 3) in Russia?

Before offering answers to these challenging questions let us review empirical evidence bearing on the issue of multiculturalism.

Empirical evidence on multiculturalism in contemporary Russia

In accordance with governmental order No. 1074 of the Russian Federation from 23 December 2009 the All-Russia population census was conducted in October 2010. Although the official results of the census 'on national composition' were only finalized in June 2012, the Department of Federal State Statistics published preliminary results (Table 13.1) enabling us to observe key trends in the dynamics of the Russian Federation's ethnic configuration. Since the Russian Constitution grants citizens the right of free choice in terms of their national belonging, the data were based on respondents' self-evaluation. The 2010 census also provided information on the language skills of the respondents.

Although the overall population of Russia decreased from 145 million in 2002 to 142 million in 2010, Russians who are Russian Orthodox have remained the preponderant majority, at 81 per cent both in 2002 and 2010. Many believe that this fact justifies describing Russia as a mono-national (mono-ethnic) state and, as such, it creates difficulties for establishing an equal dialogue between Russians and other ethnic groups. We have to take into account, however, the fact that the Russian population is spread around the territory unevenly. For example, in the Republic of Tatarstan the Russian population is barely 40 per cent, with Tatars representing 53 per cent of the total population. In the Chuvash Republic Russians are an even smaller minority (27 per cent) with Chuvash making up 68 per cent. In two Russian Federation Republics in the Caucasus, the minoritarian status of Russians is dramatic: 2 per cent in Chechnya (compared to 95 per cent ethnically Chechen) and 0.8 per cent in the Republic of Ingushetia (Federal Department of State Statistics Report 2011).

Since the mid-2000s the demographics of the migration flow to Russia have been changing. The share of labour migrants from Ukraine and China is declining while the independent states in Central Asia (in particular, Uzbekistan and Tajikistan) and the Caucasus region are now the leading sending countries. According to the 2010 census the largest diaspora living in the territory of Russia is from Uzbekistan (131,000 compared to only 71,000 in 2002). The Ukrainian diaspora has decreased from 231,000 (in 2002) to only

Table 13.1 The largest self-identified ethnic groups in Russia and their language abilities

Ethnic groups and languages	2002 All-Russia Census (millions) / % from total population	2010 All-Russia Census (millions) / % from total population	2010 All-Russia Census % of respondents speaking languages
Russian(s)	115.89 (80.64%)	111.02 (80.90%)	99.41%
Tatar(s)	5.55 (3.87%)	5.31 (3.87%)	3.09%
Ukrainian(s)	2.94 (2.05%)	1.93 (1.41%)	0.82%
Bashkir(s)	1.67 (1.16%)	1.58 (1.15%)	0.83%
Chuvash(s)	1.64 (1.14%)	1.44 (1.05%)	0.75%
Chechen(s)	1.36 (0.95%)	1.43 (1.04%)	0.98%
Armenian(s)	1.13 (0.79%)	1.18 (0.86%)	0.48%
English	insignificant (0.00%)	insignificant (0.00%)	5.48% (7,574,303)
German(s)	0.597 (0.41%)	0.394 (0.29%)	1.50% (2,069,949)
French	insignificant (0.00%)	insignificant (0.00%)	0.45% (616,394)
Spanish	insignificant (0.00%)	insignificant (0.00%)	0.11% (152,147)
Chinese	0.034 (0.02%)	0.028 (0.02%)	0.05% (70,722)

Source: *Rossiiskaya gazeta* 2011, p. 14 and *Federal Department of State Statistics Report 2011*.

93,000 (in 2010), while the Tajikistani diaspora has increased from 64,000 to 87,000 (*Rossiiskaya gazeta* 2011: 14).

The religious composition of migrants is also changing: about 41 per cent are Muslim or come from Muslim countries. Nowadays 70 per cent of migrant workers come from small towns and villages rather than large cities and capitals. The educational level of migrants is rapidly decreasing: half of the newcomers have no professional qualifications and the percentage of workers who speak Russian at a basic level is also declining. Many Russian scholars argue that the preconditions for ethnic conflicts in Russia are now rooted not so much in economic competition as in the sphere of sociocultural differences. The situation of growing ethnic imbalances and lack of integration mechanisms for migrants results in a rise in the level of xenophobia. But unlike the situation in Germany or France, Russian residents demonstrate a negative attitude towards not just immigrants from outside Russia (Central Asia, Moldova, China, Vietnam, the Caucasus and so on), but also towards their fellow Russian citizens coming from other parts of the same country (especially from the North Caucasus region) simply because they are perceived as 'visible minorities'. According to public opinion polls, visible minorities evoke a strongly negative attitude towards newcomers in Russia generally and the cities of St Petersburg and Moscow in particular (see Akopov and Rozanova 2010: 78–9).

In December 2010 thousands of youth representing football fans of Spartak-Moscow and chanting nationalist slogans held a rally at Manezhnaya Square in Moscow which turned violent. It resulted in rioting and ethnically motivated violence across Moscow and made the square's name synonymous in the media with the growth of nationalist sentiments in Russia. According to the Russian Public Opinion Research Center (VCIOM)[1], 65 per cent of those aware of the ethnic conflict in Manezhnaya Square responded that they did not support the participants. This attitude was spread across the supporters of political parties: 68 per cent of both United Russia and A Just Russia expressed opposition to the troublemakers. The numbers were not much different for other demographic groups: elderly citizens (74 per cent), residents of medium-sized cities (71 per cent) and of rural areas (69 per cent). The majority of respondents (79 per cent) replied that they would not take part in such actions. This was the response of supporters of United Russia (83 per cent), the elderly (87 per cent), citizens educated to post-secondary level (81 per cent) and the population of the north-west of Russia (87 per cent).

By contrast, a more supportive attitude to the rioters was expressed by 18 per cent of the survey sample among whom were followers of the Liberal Democratic Party LDPR (41 per cent), inhabitants of large agglomerations (St Petersburg and Moscow at 27 per cent) and young people under thirty-four (22–4 per cent). Moreover, 11 per cent of respondents replied that they might take part in such violent actions: LDPR (32 per cent), young people under thirty-four (16 per cent), the less educated (14 per cent), people from the Far East (15 per cent), from the Urals and the central parts of Russia (14 per cent), from the North Caucuses (13 per cent) and from the south of Russia (12 per cent).

Other public opinion polls directly and indirectly confirm these tendencies. For example, a survey conducted by VCIOM on 'Russians' attitude towards international marriages'[2] vividly illustrated how the most favoured marriages are those between Russians (70 per cent). More 'neutral' attitudes were found regarding marriages between Russians, Ukrainians and Byelorussians (45 per cent), Slavs or Europeans (44 per cent), citizens of the Baltic States (43 per cent) and Americans (41 per cent). As hostile attitudes we can classify reactions to marriages between Russians and Chechens (65 per cent), Arabs (63 per cent), people from Central Asia (60 per cent), Caucasians (54 per cent) and Jews (46 per cent).

In another survey[3] Russian citizens were asked: 'Please name the nations and peoples that make you feel irritation or resentment'. Most often, respondents' negative emotions were directed at Caucasian peoples (29 per cent). The next most negative choice, with a much lower percentage, was people from Central Asia (6 per cent). Only 3 per cent of respondents – a surprisingly low proportion – stated that they did not like Chinese or Jews. One respondent in two could not name specific reasons for rejecting other peoples and nations. Those who could come up with such a reason often expressed their concerns about the threat of terrorist attacks (13 per cent) and the reluctance of newcomers to take into account the norms and practices followed in Russia (11 per cent).

Poll results published by VCIOM in 2012 (24 January) were based on surveys conducted among the residents of Moscow and St Petersburg. They confirmed that among the ethnic groups that evoke most resentment were all the people of Caucasian origin (31 per cent of negative answers in Moscow and 28 per cent in St Petersburg). The second most negatively regarded group were people from Tajikistan (23 per cent of negative answers in Moscow and 24 per cent in St Petersburg). Ranked next in terms of negative attitudes expressed were those targeting Azerbaijans (17 per cent in Moscow) and Uzbeks (18 per cent in St Petersburg).[4]

In February 2012 VCIOM released the results of their poll on reactions to Putin's suggestions that stricter immigration laws be adopted and criminal liability be assigned to violators of such rules and regulations regarding migrant registration. It turned out that 77 per cent of Russians supported this idea while 79 per cent endorsed Putin's idea about preventing closed national enclaves from appearing on the political map of the Russian Federation.[5] These attitudes did not represent ripe conditions for the spread of liberal, multicultural values.

Normative implications

What are the normative implications of the apparent decline in multiculturalism for liberal values in Russia? The question takes on greater importance given the absence of liberal political parties in the State Duma since 2003; these parties are generally considered to be the Russian United Democratic Party (Yabloko) and the Union of the Right Forces. Or is it the case that an inverse relationship exists: multiculturalism is not very popular in Russia because of the lack of wide support for liberal values?

Meeting in St Petersburg in April 2011, the Russian Association of Political Sciences held a round table discussion on 'the role of the St Petersburg political science epistemic communities in an era of crisis of multiculturalism in Europe'.[6] The proceedings indicated that even within the academic community the attitude towards the future of multiculturalism in Russia could be characterized as very cautious. The circumspect approach towards multiculturalism in Russia is reflected in a number of works. In his paper entitled 'Why should Russia have multiculturalism?' Vladimir Malakhov, a specialist in nationalism and citizenship studies at the European University in St Petersburg, expressed

> concerns about the policy of cultural pluralism (multiculturalism) caused by the forms in which multiculturalism was implemented in some Western states, namely the ethnocentrism of such policies. Since the term 'multiculturalism' is now firmly associated with ethnically and religiously motivated isolationism, it seems inappropriate to try to release this term from its negative connotations and give it a new civic-democratic sense. (Malakhov 2002: 57)

For Yekaterinburg academic Victor Martyanov, multicultural-ism has failed to solve the problem of the coexistence of different identities and interests within a framework of competition and hierarchy. In practice multiculturalism therefore turns into an eth-nonationalism while the demands for cultural equality, pluralism and tolerance remain only abstract imperatives. Instead of integra-tion of group interests on the basis of universal transnational values and institutions, multiculturalism has helped set in motion processes of diffusion of sovereignty and nation-state identity (Martyanov 2007: 267).

As we can infer, both Malakhov and Martyanov do not argue against the philosophy of multiculturalism as such. They recognize the emergence of multicultural communities even in the absence of corresponding values. Thus, Malakhov notes how

> today the major Russian cities, in their ethnic, linguistic, religious and life-style diversity, more and more resemble the mega-cities of the West. There is no doubt that the cultural diversity of the Russian people under the influence of migration will only increase. In this situation to hold on to the monocultural ideals would mean to stay dreadfully deaf ... Therefore, the question is not whether to encourage or not to encourage, promote or not to promote cultural diversity, but what forms should be promoted. (Malakhov 2002: 58)

In considering the normative implications of weak multiculturalism in Russia, it may be constructive to consider changing the philosophy of multinationalism or of mononational civic patriotism in Russia in the direction of transnationalism. I suggest that the concept of transnationalism and the values it embodies might be the appropri-ate way to explain how we can override a fear of foreigners, the challenges of migration and in general the neo-Schmittian paradigm of politics. Raymond Taras has provided the following definition of the term:

> *Transnationalism* – a condition where national interests are subordinated to wider ones involving promotion of a national common good – is a term that meets with widespread approval in the EU ... The assump-tion of most theories of transnationalism is that citizens have multiple, nested, situational and fluid identities – not a single fixed one. Moreover transformative political processes have challenged traditional, restric-tive notions of national citizenship. Economic and cultural globalization has further weakened citizens' exclusive attachment to the nation-state ... The paradigmatic form of transnationalism today is Europeanness. (Taras 2009: 69–70)

European nations, Taras points out, are not what they used to be: with the integration of millions of non-Europeans, host societies have been substantially transformed. Rather than using the terms assimilation or integration, Taras supports the proposal made by the European Commission against Racism and Intolerance to use the category 'integrated society'. Hence he refers to successful integration as a two-way process, one of mutual recognition and inclusion of majority and minority groups. Many people are also increasingly involved in transnational politics through their discourse, networks, commerce and organizations. In the process, they have developed identities of a supranational kind (Taras 2009: 70).

Describing the same transformations in Europe, Spanish academic Luis Moreño notes that at the beginning of the twenty-first century, national state identities are openly questioned and have become problematic. A parallel development to this is a noticeable strengthening of sub- and supra-state identities. In plural polities, decentralization, federalization and subsidiarity seek to provide an institutional response to the stimuli of their internal diversity (Moreño 2006: 2). Following Moreño, I suggest that parts of his typology can be applied to an analysis of pluralism in contemporary Russia. The notions of 'dual' or 'compound' identity – or perhaps 'shared citizenship' from Modood's definition – can help explain the process of devolution and decentralization not only in Britain and Spain (reflecting the Scottish and Catalan cases respectively), but also in Russia regarding the historically complex cases of regional identities.

We can perhaps even apply Moreño's terminology (2006) of 'cosmopolitan localism' to Russian agglomerations such as Moscow and St Petersburg. When employing the term transnational community, I consciously distinguish it from postnationality, which presumes the complete erosion of nationality-anchored identity. I agree with Taras that postnational values spread unevenly – more so in the Western part of Europe where it utterly challenges the *raison d'être* of the nation state. Accordingly, in the case of European Russia it is not postnationalism but transnationalism that seems a more balanced and appropriate principle governing identity construction than nationalism and xenophobia.

Many scholars have stressed the negative effects of globalization, claiming that the interests and agendas of transnational corporations, major banks and financial institutions, and media organizations result in a market-driven globalism that crushes cultural diversity and turns the citizen into a mere consumer. This perspective is often replicated in media coverage (see Petersson 2006). However, Paul Hopper has persuasively argued that globalizing processes contribute to a more profound cosmopolitanism by affording us the opportunity to experience a greater range of cultural influences and traditions to mix and match in the process of self-constitution (Hopper 2006: 65). In this respect Russia's 'opening up' to the West is always a trade-off for elites but is also an inevitable and constructive process promoting the educational and economic interests of Russian citizens.

Negotiations aimed at abolishing visa regimes between Russia and the EU, and Russia and the US, is incontrovertible evidence that Russia is a far more transnational society than it used to be – or appears to be. Although the results of the 2012 Russian presidential elections show that the vast majority of the population (64 per cent) supports Putin's philosophy of geopolitics, it is of great significance that the runner-up in Moscow (with 20 per cent) and St Petersburg (16 per cent) was Mikhail Prokhorov. In his election programme Prokhorov emphasized the need to 'develop and launch strategies to integrate the EU and Russian Federation into a single geoeconomic area with common economic and visa regulations, a common currency based on the euro and the ruble, and compatible legal systems'. On the subject of multiculturalism, Prokhorov called for an elimination of 'the existing division of Russia's federal districts and, after a referendum, the implementation of a programme of consolidation of the Russian Federation to create between twenty-five and thirty units, each with its own strong economic and historical identity' (Prokhorov 2012). This consolidation could have the effect of institutionalizing pluralism in a more effective and rational way which, in turn, could at some point produce twenty-five to thirty embryonic multicultural regions in Russia.

Missionary zeal of a chosen nation, and as a result a deep-seated and widespread nationalism, seems characteristic of many former empires, including Russia. However, Marlene Laruelle writes that:

> as paradoxical as it may at first seem, the Kremlin interprets nationalism as an instrument in the service of Russia's triple goal: modernization, normalization and Westernization . . . even if this is achieved by military or totalitarian means, as once occurred under Peter the Great. (Laruelle 2009: 203)

Or, as Russell Bova concisely puts it, 'no one in China, India or the Arab world, to take but a few examples, would ask whether they were Europeans, let alone state as unequivocally as did Gorbachev and Putin . . . that "we are Europeans"' (Bova 2010: 37). As a result, contemporary Russia's path should lead not to an 'enemy'-based militarized patriotism or 'enlightened conservatism' but rather to 'cosmopolitan patriotism' – at least claiming European heritage.

My normative preference for the development of a cosmopolitan patriotism that subsumes Western liberal and multicultural experiences reflects ideas found in Martha Nussbaum's *desiderata* for the US system of education:

> As students here grow up, is it sufficient for them to learn that they are above all the citizens of the United States but they ought to respect the basic human rights of citizens of India, Bolivia, Nigeria, and Norway? Or should they – as I think – in addition to giving special attention to the history and current situation of their own nation, learn a good deal more then they frequently do about the rest of the world in which they live, about India and Bolivia and Nigeria and their histories, problems and comparative successes? Should they learn only that citizens of India have equal basic human rights, or should they also learn about the problems of hunger and pollution in India, and the implication of these problems for the larger issues of global hunger and global ecology? Most important, should they be taught that they are, above all, citizens of the United States, or should they instead be taught that they are, above all, citizens of the world of human beings, and that, while they happen to be situated in the United States, they have to share this world with citizens from other countries? I suggest . . . arguments for the second concept of education, which I call cosmopolitan education. (Nussbaum 1996: 6)

Actors in contemporary international politics, Martyanov observes, 'usually prefer boxing to chess, and situational tactical pragmatism to long-term normative strategy. Therefore the world is experiencing a deficit of normative politics, in other words, a lack of widely-accepted long-term goals and values' (Martyanov 2007: 282). The politics of fear based almost exclusively on power exposes the absence of both political trust and transparency. World politics today is carried out 'behind closed doors'. The situation in contemporary international relations is similar to the one in Russian domestic politics described by Michael Urban – a lack of communicative space for the opposition. He argues that such opposition must be part of or 'loyal' to some entity greater than either itself or that which it opposes (Urban 2010: 187). I conclude, then, that we need space for loyal opposition and political trust transcending images of the 'enemy' – whether projected on the international arena or at home targeting ethnic minorities (see Akopov 2010).

Storytelling is a universal anthropological phenomenon for conveying meaning. While humankind is a storytelling creature, not all professional storytellers provide 'good case narratives'. For better or for worse, today's media as well as blogospheres make the narratives spun by public intellectuals more widespread and influential than ever before. Some narratives promote intercultural understanding and dialogue, others conflict and cultural wars. Intellectuals on the edge of multiple national cultures and boundaries, that is, intellectuals with transnational identities and values, can bridge political 'walls' and raise 'curtains' that divide cultures.

Transnational intellectuals are equipped to transcend the nationalism of their nation states. But – of special importance at a time of a supposed retreat from multiculturalism – they can also narrate an alternative to old-style multiculturalism – understood negatively as the triumph of relativism and diversity over human universality. The dialectics between the global and the local – 'the paradox of our times', in David Held's apposite phrase – involve a grappling with collective issues that are increasingly global yet using means to resolve them that remain national and local, weak and incomplete (Held 2010: 143). Multicultural theories seem, therefore, inadequate in addressing global issues, including those of international migration, that are best resolved by translocal or transnational actors.

Notes

1. Survey by VCIOM, 18–19 December 2010; 1,600 respondents from 138 towns in 46 regions of Russia. More details on data are available at http://wciom.ru/index.php?id=268&uid=111221
2. VCIOM, 3–4 July 2010; 1,600 people in 140 towns in 42 regions of Russia. See http://wciom.ru/index.php?id=268&uid=13774
3. VCIOM, 1–2 May 2010; 1,600 respondents from 140 towns in 42 regions of Russia. See http://wciom.ru/index.php?id=268&uid=13515
4. VCIOM, 14–24 November 2011; 1,200 respondents from Moscow and St Petersburg. See http://wciom.ru/index.php?id=459&uid=112356
5. VCIOM, 28–29 January 2012; 1,600 respondents from 138 towns in 46 regions of Russia. See http://wciom.ru/index.php?id=459&uid=112370
6. The report on this seminar is available at http://rapn.ru/?grup=595&doc=3656

References

Akopov, S. (2010), 'Communication without the "enemy": Transnational intellectuals and narratives of reconciliation', *Russian Journal of Communication*, 3 (1/2), pp. 97–122.

Akopov, S. and N. Razumeyko (2011), 'Imagined communities in the unimaginable state?', *Regional Insights*, 2 (1) (spring), pp. 9–12.

Akopov, S. and M. Rozanova (2010), 'Migration processes in contemporary St. Petersburg', *NISPAcee Journal of Public Administration and Public Policy*, III (1) (summer), pp. 77–92.

Bova, R. (2010), 'Russia and Europe after the Cold War', in K. Engelbrekt and B. Nygren (eds), *Russia and Europe: Building Bridges, Digging Trenches*, London and New York: Routledge, pp. 19–38.

Federal Department of State Statistics Report (2011), 'The results of the 2010 census in the regions of Russia'. Available at http://www.gks.ru/free_doc/new_site/perepis2010/perepis_itogi1612.htm

Held, D. (2010), *Cosmopolitanism. Ideals and Realities*, Cambridge: Polity Press.

Hopper, P. (2006), *Living with Globalization*, New York: Berg.

Laruelle, M. (2009), *In the Name of the Nation. Nationalism and Politics in Contemporary Russia*, New York: Palgrave Macmillan.

Malakhov, V. (ed.) and V. Tishkov (co-ed.) (2002), *Multiculturalism and the Transformation of Post-Soviet Societies*, Moscow: Russian Academy of Sciences, Institute of Ethnology and Anthropology.

Malinova, O. (2005), 'Identichnost kak kategoria praktiki i nauchnogo analisa: o razlichii podhodov', in O. Malinova and A. Sungurov (eds), *Prava cheloveka i problemi identichnosti Rossii v sovremennom mire*, St Petersburg: Norma.

Martyanov, V. (2007), *Metamorfozi Russkogo Moderna: vyzhivet li Rossiya v globalizuyushemya mire*, Ekaterinburg: Russian Academy of Sciences, Urals Branch.

Modood, T. (2007), *Multiculturalism*, Cambridge: Polity Press.

Moreño, L. (2006), 'Scotland, Catalonia, Europeanization and the "Moreno question"', *Scottish Affairs*, 54 (winter), pp. 1–21.

Nussbaum, M. (1996), *For Love of Country: Debating the Limits of Patriotism*, Boston, MA: Beacon Press.

Pankevich, N. (2008), *Modeli Federativnogo Ustroistva: Zakonomernosti politicheskoi transformatsii*, Ekaterinburg: Russian Academy of Sciences, Urals Branch.

Petersson, B. (2006), *Stories about Strangers: Swedish Media Constructions of Socio-Cultural Risk*, Lanham, MD: University Press of America.

Prokhorov, M. (2012), *A Real Future (Election Program)*, Official web site 'Mikhail Prokhorov', Russian Federation Presidential Candidate. Available at http://mdp2012.com/program/federation.html

Putin, V. (2012), 'Rossiya: Natsional'nii vopros', *Nezavisimaya Gazeta*, 23 January. Available at http://www.ng.ru/politics/2012-01-23/1_national. html

Stalin, J. (1946), 'Marxism and the national question', in J. Stalin, *Works*, 14 vols, Moscow: Progress Publishers, vol. 2, pp. 300–81.

Taras, R. (2009), *Europe Old and New*, Lanham, MD: Rowman & Littlefield.

Tishkov, V. (2007). 'Mezhetnicheskie otnosheniia i konflikty: perspektivy novogo tysiachiletiia', in V. Bocharov (ed.), *Antropologiya vlasti*, 2 vols, St Petersburg: St Petersburg University Press, vol. 2, pp. 482–93.

Urban, M. (2010), *Cultures of Power in Post-Communist Russia: An Analysis of Elite Political Discourse*, Cambridge: Cambridge University Press.

Chapter Fourteen

Multiculturalism and Minorities in Turkey

Ayhan Kaya

This chapter examines the management of ethnocultural diversity in Turkey, which has undergone enormous change since the turn of the new century. I distinguish between 'diversity as a phenomenon' and 'diversity as a discourse' in the Turkish context, and will claim that the state and various ethnic groups have generally employed discursive diversity. This has been to remain consonant with the prevailing discourse of unity in diversity within the European context which followed the Helsinki Summit of the European Union in December 1999. I then consider rising Euroscepticism and parochialism in Turkey which became discernible after accession negotiations about membership started with the EU in 2005. It has brought about a retreat in official discourse, I document, regarding recognition of the ethnocultural and political claims of various minority groups, such as Kurds, Alevis, Circassians, Lazis, Armenians, Greeks and others.

Diversity as a phenomenon and as a discourse

There are two alternative ways of comprehending diversity in the Turkish context: diversity as a phenomenon and diversity as a discourse. The former refers to the coexistence of different ethnocultural and religious groups in a historical process. It entails either a primordial phenomenon encompassing migration flows through Asia Minor, or a politically generated phenomenon as in the settlement of various ethnic groups in Central Anatolia by imperial (nineteenth-century) and Republican (twentieth-century) settlement laws (Kirişçi 2000; Dündar 2001; Çağaptay 2006; Şeker 2007; Ülker 2007). In either case diversity as a phenomenon was not necessarily valued by the ruling powers, and was sometimes even denied.

The nation-building process in Turkey that was initiated at the beginning of the twentieth century has developed in parallel with attempts to homogenize the nation by denying the diverse character of the Anatolian population. This process is characterized by a heterophobia resulting from the fear of losing the remaining parts of the Ottoman Empire. As in other examples of nation building, recent Turkish history is marked by homogenization. The persisting Sèvres Syndrome, derived from the Sèvres Peace Treaty signed by the Allied powers and the Ottoman Empire in 1920 and leading to the dissolution of the Ottoman Empire, still drives fear of a break-up of the Turkish state (Öniş 2004: 12).

Nevertheless, we can find recent signs of recognition of ethnic, religious and cultural differences by the Turkish state. Diversity as a discourse gained momentum in the last decade in the attempt to join the EU. The shift from homogenization to diversity discourse may seem to be a product of external factors such as EU norms. But it reflects more complex processes than that, subsuming both internal and external factors. The Kemalist rhetoric of homogenizing nationalism had involved a retrospective narrative emphasizing how the Muslim origins of the nation kept it together in the face of imperialist European powers. But Kemalist ideology encountered various challenges in the aftermath of the 1980 military coup originating from previous taboo phenomena – the ethnocultural and religious diversity comprised of Islam, Kurds, Alevis, Circassians, globalization, liberalization and Europeanization.

The historical context of multiculturalism in Turkey

Management of ethnocultural and religious diversity in the Ottoman Empire was mainly carried out on the basis of the ideology of multiculturalism, which was literally called the '*millet* system'. *Millet* is an Ottoman Turkish term referring to confessional communities in the Ottoman Empire; it comes from the Arabic word *millah* ('nation'). Subject populations such as the Christians were classified by their religious affiliations. Their civil concerns were settled by their own ecclesiastical authorities delegated to them by the Sultan. This was the way the government secured access to the non-Muslim populations (Mardin 1981: 192). With the *Tanzimat* reforms (1839–76) *millet* started to refer to legally protected religious minority groups other than the ruling Sunni Muslims (Mardin 1981: 196; Zürcher 2003: 66).

Beside the Muslim *millet*, the main *millets* in the Ottoman Empire were the Greek, Orthodox, Jewish, Armenian and Syrian Orthodox populations (Barkey 2007). The *millet* system worked efficiently until the age of nationalisms when the Ottoman Empire began to crack. Until then interaction between Muslims and non-Muslims had been circumscribed because of the ethnocultural and religious boundaries essentialized by the *millet* system. Moreover, non-Muslims, though they were allowed to maintain their own religious and cultural heritage, were subject to certain rules, including limits on intermarriage and special taxes in lieu of military service (Mardin 1981; Kymlicka 1992). Therefore, the acceptance of *millets* was dependent on their willingness to abide by the regulations of the Empire, which encouraged conformity. The political system did not perceive members of the *millets* as individuals but rather as a part of a collective non-Muslim identity. It nevertheless strictly applied the principle of equality during the *Tanzimat* era (Tunaya 1960).

Decision making was concentrated in the hands of a small political elite, at the centre of which stood the Sultan. His power was theoretically absolute, but in practice it was limited by the existence of three major power structures, the *Ulema* (religious intellectuals), the military and the bureaucracy (Szyliowicz 1966). The separation of the *khalifa*, as an ideal religious figure, and the Sultan, as the actual ruler, resulted in several unique social formations: this included the establishment of a group of military-religious rulers who emerged from sectarian elements, and the autonomous *ulema* who developed networks that brought together – under one religious and often also social-civilizational umbrella – varied ethnic and geopolitical groups, tribes, settled peasants and urban groups (Eisenstadt 2006: 447–9). Through their control of education, of the judiciary and of the administrative network, the *ulema* acted as agents of the state, and secured the state's control of societal life (Mardin 1981: 194). As a result, the *ulema* were the umbrella under which the *ummah* was able to convene, and together the two entities constituted an autonomous public sphere. This decoupling of an autonomous and vibrant public sphere from the political arena – more precisely, the realm of rulership – distinguished Turkey from Europe and constituted one of the distinctive characteristics of Muslim civilization (Eisenstadt 2006: 452).

Tolerating difference

Ottoman multiculturalism was usually coupled with the term 'tolerance', which has a long history in the Turkish context tracing back to the early days of the Ottoman Empire. It is also found in everyday popular usage in modern Turkey. Turks are generally proud of the *millet* system of the Ottoman Empire, which is often celebrated as the guarantor of tolerance and as respecting the boundaries between religious communities.

Official discourse celebrating tolerance is still discernible in contemporary Turkey, although it is little more than a myth. For instance, research conducted by Ali Çarkoğlu and Binnaz Toprak (2007) found that more than half of the Turkish population was intolerant of having gays and atheists as their neighbours. It also uncovered that 42 per cent of respondents were intolerant of having Greeks and Armenians as their neighbours and 28 per cent intolerant of Kurdish-origin neighbours (Çarkoğlu and Toprak 2006). The myth of tolerance has been functional in concealing mistreatment of ethnocultural and religious minorities other than the majority of Sunni-Muslim Turks.

Tolerance has been confined to the acceptance of Sunni Muslims and their secular counterparts under the banner of a Sunni-Muslim-Turkish nation; it does not embrace all different kinds of ethnocultural and religious minorities. As Karen Barkey (2008: 110) stated, tolerance in the Ottoman context as well as in other imperial contexts refers to the 'absence of persecution of people but not their acceptance into society as full and welcomed members of community'. Tolerance is actually nothing but a form of governmentality (Foucault 1979), designed to maintain peace and order in multi-ethnic and multidenominational contexts. The Ottoman imperial experience and the Turkish national experience have confirmed how tolerance of non-Muslims, non-Sunni Muslims and non-Turks was dependent on their not challenging the Sunni-Islam-Turkish order. If ethnocultural and religious minorities did transgress, their recognition could easily turn into suppression and persecution. I claim, therefore, that 'tolerance' is nothing but a myth in Turkey, as it is in other countries such as the Netherlands or the Balkans (Walzer 1997; Hayden 2002; Brown 2006).

The defining distinctiveness of the early Republic was Turkification policies that sought the dominance of Turkishness and Sunni Islam in every walk of life, from the language spoken in the public space to citizenship, national education, commerce, public-sector employment, industrial life and even settlement laws (Aktar 2000; Yıldız 2001). Inheriting an imperial legacy, many new laws set out to homogenize the entire nation without tolerance of difference. Moreover, it is highly probable that the ethnocultural diversity among the Muslim population of the Republic had been underestimated because of the use of the Ottoman *millet* system borrowed by the Republican state elite. The *millet* system did not consider ethnic differences among Muslims. All Muslims, regardless of their other differences, belonged to one and the same 'Muslim nation'. Paradoxically, the success of the Turkish rupture from the past lay in the continuity of the Ottoman notion of *millet*. Hence, the modern Turkish Republic became indifferent to ethnocultural differences.

Republican indifference towards diversity

Assimilationist and/or exclusionary policies of the Republic's elite sought both to erase social and cultural diversity and to assign a national identity based on Sunni Islam and Turkishness being the dominant role in social and political spheres. Diverse religious, ethnic and cultural values were frequently suppressed by homogenizing policies such as a nationalist Turkish history model initiated in 1932; a ban on the use of mother tongue and ethnic minority names; discriminatory settlement policies and discriminatory citizenship laws granting citizenship exclusively to migrants of Muslim origin; the imposition of a wealth tax in 1942 targeting non-Muslims; and the forced migration of Kurds in the east and south-east of Turkey (Ülker 2007; Kaya 2007).

Ethnocultural minorities adopted different means to cope with the state's homogenizing policies. Within the framework of majority nationalism, they chose to be involved in the construction of a homogeneous Turkish nation, disguising their ethnic identities in public and identifying themselves as a constitutive element of the Turkish nation. Thus, assimilationist and/or exclusionist state policies have shaped the ways in which ethnic groups have developed their identities and political participation strategies. One example is particularly vivid: Moiz Kohen Tekinalp, a Turkish nationalist of Jewish origin, in his 1928 work *Turkification* (*Türkleştirme*) listed the main incorporation strategies for non-Turkish ethnic minorities into the political system. He proposed ten commandments for Turkish-Jews:

1. Turkify your names
2. Speak Turkish
3. Pray in Turkish in synagogues
4. Turkify your schools
5. Send your children to Turkish schools

6. Get engaged in national issues
7. Stick together with Turks
8. Affiliate yourself with the community spirit
9. Fulfil your duties in the national economy
10. Be aware of your rights
    (cited in Landau 1996)

There is strong evidence that these commandments also applied to some Muslim communities such as Kurds and Circassians (Yıldız 2001).

Since the 1919 Turkish war of independence Kurds, Alevis and Circassians have insisted that they are constitutive elements of the nation. They opposed the idea of being a minority and underlined the fact that they also belong to the Muslim nation. They were not part of the official minorities programme of the Lausanne Treaty (1923), which identified Armenians, Jews and Greeks as official minority groups. The myth of being a 'constitutive element of the nation' persists to this day. It is remarkable that Kurds and Alevis denounced the term 'minority' applied to them by the European Commission in its 2005 Progress Report on Turkey. They accused the EU of trying to divide Turkey at a time of growing Euroscepticism.

Ethnocultural and religious diversity challenges

In the aftermath of the 1980 military coup Kemalist ideology was challenged by multiculturalist claims raised by ethnocultural and religious groups. As José Casanova (2006) put it, the project of constructing a nation state from above was bound to fail because it was too laicist for the Islamists, too Sunni for the Alevis and too Turkish for the Kurds, Circassians and Lazis. A Turkish state in which the collective identities and interests of groups constituting the majority of the population are unable to obtain public representation cannot be a representative democracy, even if it is established on modern secular Republican principles. Let us examine the different multicultural claims one by one.

ISLAMIST MULTICULTURALISM AS A CHALLENGE TO THE KEMALIST REGIME

The emergence of the Welfare Party (WP, *Refah Partisi*) with an Islamic social base and political agenda posed a profound challenge to the state-centric Republican and secular regime in both political and cultural terms. This party together with the broader Islamist movement sought to address the inequalities of the global system by transcending the state and mobilizing the marginalized and under-privileged social groups within an expanding Islamic civil society (*umma*) and the framing structure of identity politics. The WP tried to generate electoral support from a broad Islamist social network both by supporting socio-economic opportunity structures for the social integration of the Islamist forces into the growing liberal economy and competitive urban life, and by channelling their inter-ests and demands into national politics through political parties.

Like Islamist movements in other Middle Eastern countries, Islamist communities, Sufi orders (*tarikats*) and Islamic welfare associations provide a network for the marginalized classes that offers different social services: employment, religious and secular education, health services, food, clothing and energy supplies. The state failed to provide these in its unmanaged transition to the liberal economy (Hale and Özbudun 2009: 16–18).

Islamist political mobilization appealed to both the winners and the losers of the global and liberal economy. The newly emerging Islamic bourgeoisie, which was becoming integrated into the liberal system from the 1980s on, distributed to the poor the wealth it had accumulated from the publishing houses, private media chan-nels, university preparatory courses, Islamic banks and financial institutions and holding companies it ran (Hale and Özbudun 2009: 13). Through its connections with these Islamist communi-ties, the WP attracted the votes of the Islamic bourgeoisie, the upper middle class and the marginalized lower class and also stimulated political mobilization of the conservative and Islamist social forces, which dramatically challenged the Republican and secular segments.

The hostility of the dominant regime towards the Islamist forces led to a political crisis in 1997. The WP's challenge to the secular regime stemmed from its articulation of Islamic values in political life; specifically, it involved demands for the exercise of Islamic law, the segregation of the sexes in social life, religious education and the headscarf issue. WP demands for the incorporation of Islam into formal politics were designed to enable WP acquisition of state power and the formation of an Islamic social order; recognition of religious (Islamic) freedom and conscience and the protection of religious rights such as the wearing of the headscarf and religious clothing in public places were the tools to achieve these goals (Hale and Özbudun 2009: 7–9).

The military/bureaucratic state elite made it clear that the WP's Islamist demands could not be tolerated. In January 1998 a Constitutional Court decision ordered the WP to be closed down (Hale and Özbudun 2009: 4). The WP and the Islamist forces had constituted a religious and cultural challenge to the Republican and secular regime and sections of society. The WP had suggested adopting a legal framework allowing each legally recognized community to be governed in accordance with its own religious rules. In doing so, it had proposed a return to the *Medina Covenant* of Prophet Muhammad's time, the age of happiness (*asr-ı saadet*) in which a kind of multiculturalism based on religious differences was experienced (Hale and Özbudun 2009: 7–8).

The WP had also attempted to undermine the secular Western order and to incorporate movements stressing a religious and Islamic way of life in politics. Therefore, the party and Islamist forces had posed religious and cultural challenges both in encouraging the political participation of Islamist segments in the secular Republican order, and in striving to Islamize society and culture. The state elite and dominant secular interests reacted by purging them from the formal political sphere.

Alevi Revivalism since the 1990s

Another challenge to the Republican state and the myth of a homogeneous nation arose from the Alevi community. Since the sixteenth century, when Sunni Islamic traditions were imposed on other religious groups in Anatolia (Erman and Erdemir 2008), Alevis were compelled to adopt a defensive attitude towards their own community and identity by living in small social enclosures in rural areas. The *millet* system of the Ottoman Empire had recognized Islam as the main constitutive element and did not distinguish between Muslim subjects on the basis of ethnocultural differences (Yıldız 2001). Alevis were therefore imagined as integral subjects of the 'Sunni Muslim nation'.

In order to promote Kemalist modernization in the first decades of the twentieth century, Turkey's Republican elite implemented policies for the secularization of political and social life (Göle 1997). One of these policies was the elimination of religious communion and practice outside the mosques; it therefore ruled out the *Cemevis*, dervish lodges and special places for Alevi communion (Erman and Erdemir 2008). Through these means, Alevi communities were deprived of the places where they could be organized as a religious community separate from Sunni ones.

At the start of the new century state discourse called for accommodation by Sunni secularists of Alevi cultural and religious practices. But we can just as easily find cases of intolerance and conflict. As an ethno-class group, the Alevi community living in the shanty town of Gazi on the outskirts of Istanbul has emerged as a resistance group. It regards Alevi identity as superior to the Turkish national identity – in contrast to the groups of moderate Alevis that form a democratic, pluralistic and peaceful movement. The Alevi community of Gazi has displayed distrust of the bureaucracy, state authorities, politicians and municipal governments that ignored its grievances. 'Othering' of 'poor and different' Alevis has also deprived them of basic social services.

In March 1995 violent clashes broke out following attacks by a gunman on coffee houses in Gazi. The Alevi community became involved in an armed conflict with police forces which were late to intervene. Fifteen people were killed by the police. This outbreak of violence between security forces and marginalized Alevis revealed an embedded mutual intolerance and hatred between the Sunni-Muslim-Turkish majority and ethno-religious minorities such as the Alevis which surfaced when a catalyst appeared. The widening gap between rich and poor also played a part.

From the 1990s Alevis raised their cultural and religious claims, which revolved around four issues: (1) eliminating compulsory courses on religious culture and morality in primary and secondary school education, which were seen as promoting Sunni Islam; (2) seeking state recognition of Alevi communion houses (*Cemevi*) being equal to mosques as places of worship; (3) asking for equal treatment of Alevis in the allocation of resources by the Directorate of Religious Affairs attached to the Prime Minister's office (which employs all the Imams, hatips and muezzins in Turkey and abroad); and (4) combating negative stereotypes of Alevis mostly framed by extremist Sunnis. Some progress in meeting these demands has been recorded under the Justice and Development Party government.

KURDISH REVIVALISM

At the end of the 1980s political parties representing Kurdish identity and defending Kurdish cultural and political rights began to enter the formal political arena. The abolition of articles in the Turkish Penal Code that restricted freedom of expression laid the ground for the formation of legal ethnic and religious parties (Sahin 2008: 134). In addition, abandoning their alliances with the leftist parties of the 1970s, the Kurdish political and intellectual elite replaced old communist slogans and socialist economic programmes for an eventual independent Kurdistan with demands for the cultural rights of Kurds and a democratic consolidation of the Republic. During the 1990s the attempts of the Kurdish political elite to represent Kurdish cultural and political interests by participating in national politics through political parties were undermined by rulings of the Constitutional Court questioning the legitimacy of a party founded on a particular ethnic identity.

Since the establishment of the Turkish Republic, the state has never displayed tolerance towards the expression in the public sphere of Kurdish identity. The Kemalist elite regarded the Kurdish population as the most formidable threat to the nation state conceived as Republican, secular, modern and bureaucratic and anchored in a homogeneous Turkish national identity (Kaya and Tarhanlı 2008). First, as demonstrated in a series of Kurdish rebellions between 1925 and 1938, Kurdish tribal and religious leaders were rivals of central political authorities. Second, the Kurdish people were perceived as an obstacle to the Kemalist modernization project and Westernization. This was due to their purported 'backward, pre-modern and unprogressive' communal and primordial lifestyle based on Sufi orders (*tarikats*), tribes, sheikhs, landlords, warlords and rebels. An increasing affiliation of the Kurds with the Kurdish Workers Party (PKK, *Partia Kerkeran Kurdistan*) made them even more intolerable for the majority Turkish nation and the state (Kirişçi and Winrow 1997).

Since 1984 the PKK has led an armed struggle against the Turkish Armed Forces in south-eastern Turkey. In order to defend Turkish territorial integrity and national security, martial law had been introduced in 1987 in the eastern and south-eastern regions and was renewed fifty-seven times until it was finally abolished in 2002. Moreover, in 1985 the military adopted a strategy of arming village guards, who were recruited from some Kurdish tribes (Olson 2009).

The rise of Kurdish ethnic nationalism and the attempts to secure Kurdish representation in national politics was paired with an armed struggle and low-intensity warfare between the Kurdish minority and the Turkish state. The armed conflict has divided Kurds themselves and has cost them jobs (Kaya et al. 2009). Racism and institutional discrimination towards the Kurds in Turkey's large cities and in western Anatolia has grown. Since the mid-1980s the Kurds have been associated by the majority Turkish population with secession-ism, division, disintegration, terror, violence, drug trafficking, the informal economy and the arms trade.

Since the early 1990s it has become a recurring pattern that Turkish political leaders address the importance of the Kurdish ques-tion before embarking on democratization (Watts 2009). Süleyman Demirel was the first Prime Minister to publicly declare that the government recognized the 'Kurdish reality' (1992). Similarly, Recep Tayyip Erdoğan, Prime Minister from 2003, also stated that his government was aware of the 'Kurdish question' (2005). In August 2005 he gave a historic speech in Diyarbakır explaining that the cul-tural, religious and historical bonds between Turks and Kurds would provide solutions to the Kurdish question: 'The sun warms every-body and the rain is God's grace for everybody. Thus I address those asking, "What will happen to the Kurdish question?" The Kurdish problem is my problem . . . We will solve all the problems through democracy' (cited in Yavuz 2009: 189; see also Yavuz 2001).

Tezcür (2009: 10) examined the Islamic elements raised by Erdoğan in defining the bond between the Turks and the Kurds when he noted that 'there is a single nation (*millet*) in Turkey'. What the Prime Minister meant by a single nation appeared to be the nation of Islam, which has its roots in the Ottoman *millet* system. The Islamist polity shaped by Erdoğan's Justice and Development Party (AKP, *Adalet ve Kalkınma Partisi*) has also had a remarkable resonance among Kurds with Islamist orientations, including such groups as the Med-Zehra, Mazlum-Der and Mustazaf-Der (Tezcür 2009).

The ruling AKP's tolerant approach towards the Kurds has brought about several reforms regarding the recognition of Kurdish identity in a multiculturalist style. The AKP has taken steps to expand the cultural rights of the Kurds. Turkey's state-run radio and television network TRT's new TV channel, TRT 6, launched a 24-hour broadcast in the Kurdish language in January 2009. In addi-tion, a department of Kurdish language and letters was established at Mardin Artuklu University, located in south-eastern Turkey, in 2011. Kurdish language courses have also been provided by several universities in larger Turkish cities since 2009. These policy innova-tions reflect a changed mindset in the ruling political elite, indicating that they are willing to come to terms with the past and repair the damage caused by military force in the recent past.

Kurdish political claims reached new levels in the past few years with greater political mobilization in local and national politics. Kurdish nationalism took the form of civil disobedience initiated by a combination of Kurdish political actors and the PKK (Aslan 2009). Kurds have engaged in a process of reconciliation with the Turkish state that involves issues such as education in the mother tongue, civil rights, coming to terms with the past and unsolved killings and disappearances of people. Thus, since 2008 Kurds have taken legal action with respect to murders committed by paramilitary forces in order to identify and prosecute those responsible. The judiciary branch has become an important institution in the reconciliation process (Olson 2009: Chs 2 and 7; Ünver 2009).

Kurds have also become more assertive in such identity areas as renaming their children, their streets, villages, parks and urban quarters in accordance with Kurdish national mythology. Renaming has not taken place without controversy, highlighting how the formal nationalism of the state and minority nationalism mutually condition each other. Past interventions of the Turkish state to regulate and control the private lives of Kurds have politicized many forms of cultural expressions, such as Kurdish naming. Official discourse on Turkishness has influenced the ways in which Kurdish activists have imagined Kurdish identity and have pushed them to define it in more exclusivist political terms (Aslan 2009: 13). For example, the name of a Turkish military barracks was changed in 2011 because it bore the name of a Turkish general who had massacred thirty-three unarmed Kurdish villagers in 1943 (Barkey and Fuller 1998: 28; Özgen 2003). Similarly, a AKP deputy proposed changing the name of Sabiha Gökçen Airport in Istanbul because it was hurtful to Kurds; Sabiha Gökçen was the adopted daughter of Mustafa Kemal Atatürk and was the first female pilot believed to have dropped bombs on Kurds in Dersim in 1938. These claims have been amplified by the public apology issued by Prime Minister Tayyip Erdoğan in November 2011 for what had happened in Dersim.

The European integration process: quest for a multiculturalist state?

The EU perspective offered at the European Union Summit in December 1999 radically transformed the political establishment in Turkey, opening up new prospects for ethnic, religious, social and political rights. Kurds, Alevis, Islamists, Circassians, Armenians and a number of religious and ethnic groups in Turkey have subsequently become ardent supporters of the EU, interpreting the project of political union as an opportunity for peace and transnational integration. It is no longer the *retrospective past*, replete with ideological and political recriminations among various groups, that dominates social consciousness but rather the *prospective future* in which ethnic, religious and cultural differences are recognized and embraced in a democratic way. In short, the EU was the major catalyst in accelerating the process of democratization in Turkey in the early years of the new century.

The 1999 Helsinki Summit stimulated a series of reforms in Turkey. In fact, the country recorded more reforms in just over two years than during the whole of the previous decade. Several laws were passed in Turkey's National Parliament to fulfil the Copenhagen political criteria for EU candidature. These included the right to broadcast in one's mother tongue; freedom of association; the limitation of military influence on the judiciary; more civilian control over the military; transferring extra-budgetary funds to which the military had access to the general budget of the Defence Ministry; removing military members from the High Audio Visual Board (*Radyo ve Televizyon Üst Kurulu*, or RTÜK) and the Board of Higher Education (*Yükseköğretim Kurulu*, or YÖK); removing military judges from the State Security Courts (*Devlet Güvenlik Mahkemeleri*, or DGM) and, subsequently, the abolition of those Courts; the extension of civil rights to officially recognized minorities (Armenians, Jews and Greeks); reformation of the Penal Code; the abolition of the death penalty; the release of political prisoners; the abolition of torture by the security forces; and greater protection for the press. Furthermore, strict anti-inflationary economic policies were carried out in line with International Monetary Fund directives; institutional transparency and liberalism were accepted; both formal nationalism and minority nationalism were even-handedly discouraged; and socio-economic disparities between regions were targeted.

The EU perspective has also provided the Turkish public with an opportunity to come to terms with its own past (*Vergangenheitsbewältigung*). Widely discussed conferences entitled 'The Ottoman Armenians during the Demise of the Empire', 'The Assyrian Diaspora' and 'The Kurdish Question' were organized at Istanbul Bilgi University in 2005 and 2006. These conferences paved the way for public discussion of subjects that had hitherto been taboo in contemporary Turkish history. Legal and political changes underscored the transformation of Turkey in terms of recognizing diversity. This transformation corresponds to a discursive shift which officially recognizes Turkey as a multicultural country. That is to say, multiculturalism is no longer just a phenomenon in Turkey; it is also an officially recognized legal and political fact.

Furthermore, these far-reaching reforms reinforced human rights, and individual rights and liberties, by liberalizing the law on the freedom of association and demonstration; abolishing the death penalty and all means and practices of tortures by the security forces; revising the Penal Code; eliminating the term 'forbidden language' from the press law; permitting limited broadcasts in Kurdish on private radio and TV channels; introducing limited broadcasts in Arabic, Circassian and various dialects of Kurdish (such as Kurmançi and Zaza) on the national radio and TV channels; and allowing ethnic languages and dialects to be taught in private courses. As a result, the reform packages, which were adopted to raise social awareness, tolerance and acceptance of ethnocultural minorities, encouraged ethnocultural groups in turn to articulate their claims through legitimate political channels.

Since 2001 successive Turkish governments have taken initiatives to raise the status of the civil and cultural rights of non-Muslim minorities through a variety of legal amendments. In accordance with the Copenhagen political criteria, constitutional amendments extended individual rights and liberties to every citizen and over-hauled structures to promote democratic consolidation and the enhancement of the rule of law and human rights (Oran 2004). The EU reform packages gradually restored the civil and cultural rights given to the non-Muslim minorities by the Lausanne Agreement (Oran 2004).

The ban on establishing associations for the preservation and diffusion of languages and cultures other than Turkish and traditional to minorities was lifted. Use of the 'forbidden language' was re-legalized in the law on associations. Restrictions on learning and publishing in different languages and dialects other than Turkish were eliminated. The right to acquire property that had belonged to foundations set up by the non-Muslim minorities was restored. Limitations on the use of names other than Turkish were abolished through a change in the law on population. Furthermore, the EU General Secretariat in Ankara decided to drop the use of the term 'non-Muslims' in identifying officially recognized minorities in Turkey (Kaya 2009). Seeking to update the government's terminology in order to reflect the new reality, Turkey's chief negotiator for European Union affairs announced a decision to use the term 'different belief groups' instead of *gayrimüslim* (non-Muslim) in official EU correspondence. This decision was taken after the chief negotiator had received a letter from the vice-patriarch of the Ancient Syriac Orthodox Church, who pointed out that 'Muslim' means 'believer' in Aramaic – a north-west Semitic language used in ancient times as the everyday speech of Syria. The letter drew attention to the use of *gayrimüslim* – the preferred term for non-Muslims in Turkey – implying 'nonbelievers'.

Furthermore, the discursive shift from 'majority nationalism' to 'diversity as a discourse' fostered by the governing party created an incentive for adopting greater tolerance of the ethno-religious rights of non-Muslim minorities. The political elite, Turkish and Armenian intellectuals and civil society organizations were induced to open public discussion on the taboo subject of the Armenian 'genocide'. But not just that: there was now open debate in Turkey on Armenian ethnic minority rights, Armenian-Turkish diplomatic relations and the impact of the Armenian diaspora on issues related to Armenians living in Turkey.

Strikingly, the debates on the Armenian 'genocide' both at state and society levels furnished important examples of an increase in the level of tolerance and acceptance of Armenian ethnic and cultural rights. One case of such greater tolerance was the conference entitled 'Ottoman Armenians during the Demise of the Empire' held at Istanbul Bilgi University in 2005 (Kaya 2009). Although some Turkish ultranationalists brought a lawsuit against the organizers of the conference and the court ruled that their claims were in part justified and lawful, this conference became a barometer of eradicating biased views on the Armenian issue (Kaya 2009).

Conclusion: retreat from multiculturalist state discourse

Turkey experienced a profound social, political, economic and legal transformation in the first decade of the new century. It paved the way to official recognition of ethnocultural and religious diversity, which has always been the reality of this region of the world. However, this positive mood fundamentally changed after December 2004 when EU-level and national government leaders started negotiations with Turkey on its membership application. The start of negotiations together with various internal and external developments caused tensions to rise between nationalist, patriotic, statist, pro status-quo groups in Turkey on the one hand, and pro-EU groups on the other. This was the time that the virtuous cycle of the period between 1999 and 2005 was replaced with the vicious cycle starting from late 2005. A new nationalist wave swept the country, especially across middle- and upper middle-class groups. The electoral cycle of presidential and general elections was punctuated with militaristic, nationalist and Eurosceptic attitudes coupled with rising violence and terror in the country.

The fight between the Justice and Development Party and the other statist political parties, backed by the army, crystallized during the 2007 presidential election. The AKP had nominated then Minister of Foreign Affairs Abdullah Gül as presidential candidate but he did not meet the expectations of Turkey's traditional political and military establishment; he failed to reach the required two-thirds majority in the assembly vote. This failure resulted from the fact that the presidential post has symbolic importance in Turkey since it was first occupied by Mustafa Kemal Atatürk, founder of modern Turkey. However, the establishment argued that, as someone with pro-Islamist values and a wife who wears a headscarf, Gül was inappropriate for the office. The conflict even led to military intervention in politics in April 2007, an intervention notoriously labelled 'e-intervention' because of the way it was announced on the web page of the Chief of Staff. However, the nationalist and military alliance against the AKP was unsuccessful and in the general election held in July 2007 the party won a landslide victory, receiving 47 per cent of the votes cast. Following the elections, Abdullah Gül was elected to the presidential office.

Prior to the constitutional referendum in late 2010 minorities had become outspoken once again. They had become more receptive to the idea of creating a completely new democratic constitution that would be prepared in the new Parliament due to convene after the general elections of July 2011. The results consolidated the power of the AKP: this time it registered a landslide victory, gaining more than 50 per cent of the vote (Yılmaz 2011). Decisive in the consolidation of the AKP's power in Turkey were economic prosperity; growing Turkish 'Lira nationalism' (based on the currency); a strong commitment to weakening the traditional legacy of the Turkish army; the emergence of Turkey as an imposing 'soft power' in the region; the establishment of friendly relations with Middle Eastern countries, Russia, those in the Caucasus and North Africa; and the emergence of a political climate conducive to mediating the interests of different ethnocultural groups in the run-up to drafting a new constitution.

Minorities have today become more assertive about finalizing a more democratic and inclusive constitution. It would be prepared with the inclusion of all segments of society. Minorities have expressed their preference for a political system that grants rights to all communities in Turkey, with violence and racism excluded from the process. In meetings held by various ethnocultural and religious groups in different cities across Turkey between 2010 and 2012, there was general agreement that the constitution should be redrawn so as to more effectively guarantee individual rights and to remove any reference to ethnicity. Specifically, there was a desire to see a change in Article 66 of the Constitution which defines Turkish citizenship this way: 'Everyone bound to the Turkish state through the bond of citizenship is a Turk'. The other major demand by minorities has been to ensure that rights are granted on the basis of citizenship, not on ethnicity which favours the Sunni-Muslim Turks.

An optimistic conclusion can be that, instead of heeding nationalist and militaristic electoral messages which are based on parochial, anti-global and anti-European discourse aiming at 'nationalist closure', the Turks are opting for Europeanization, globalization, stability and progress. However, the EU no longer serves as a beacon for Turkey. In the absence of its influence, the political divide present at the top of the Turkish state is being turned into a social divide between moderate Islamists and secular fundamentalists, which bring into play broad constellations of political and non-political actors such as the political parties, Parliament, the judiciary, the army, academics, non-governmental organizations, the media and business circles.

REFERENCES

Aktar, Ayhan (2000), *Varlık Vergisi ve 'Türkleştirme' Politikaları*, Istanbul: İletişim Yayınları.
Aslan, Senem (2009), 'Incoherent state: The controversy over Kurdish naming in Turkey', *European Journal of Turkish Studies*, 10. Available at http://ejts.revues.org/index4142.html
Barkey, Henry J. and Graham E. Fuller (1998), *Turkey's Kurdish Question*. Lanham, MD: Rowman & Littlefield Publishers.
Barkey, Karen (2007), 'An Ottoman model of toleration: Constructing mechanisms of inter-religious, inter-ethnic peace', unpublished paper, Columbia University, New York.

Barkey, Karen (2008), *Empire of Difference: The Ottomans in Comparative Perspective*, Cambridge: Cambridge University Press.

Brown, Wendy (2006), *Regulating Aversion: Tolerance in the Age of Identity and Empire*, Princeton, NJ: Princeton University Press.

Çağaptay, Soner (2006), *Islam, Secularism and Nationalism in Modern Turkey*, London and New York: Routledge.

Çarkoğlu, Ali and Binnaz Toprak (2006), *Religion, Society and Politics in a Changing Turkey*, Istanbul: TESEV Publications.

Casanova, José (2006), 'The long, difficult, and tortuous journey of Turkey into Europe and the dilemmas of European civilization', *Constellations*, 13 (2), pp. 234–47.

Dündar, Fuat (2001), *İttihat ve Terakki'nin Müslümanları İskan Politikası (1913–1918)*, Istanbul: İletişim Yayınları.

Eisenstadt, Schmuel N. (2006), 'The public sphere in Muslim societies', in Nilüfer Göle and Ludwig Amman (eds), *Islam in Public: Turkey, Iran, and Europe*, Istanbul: Istanbul Bilgi University Press, pp. 443–60.

Erman, Tahire and Aykan Erdemir (2008), 'Aleviler ve Topluma Eklemlenme Sorunsalı', in Ayhan Kaya and Turgut Tarhanlı (eds), *Türkiye'de Çoğunluk ve Azınlık Politikaları*, Istanbul: Tesev Publications, pp. 20–54.

Foucault, Michel (1979), 'Governmentality', *Ideology and Consciousness* 6 (autumn), pp. 5–21.

Göle, Nilüfer (1997), 'Secularism and Islamism in Turkey: The making of elites and counterelites', *Middle East Journal*, 51 (1), pp. 46–58.

Hale, William and Ergun Özbudun (2009), *Islamism, Democracy and Liberalism in Turkey: the Rise of the AKP*, London: Routledge.

Hayden, Robert M. (2002), 'Antagonistic tolerance: competitive sharing of religious sites in South Asia and the Balkans', *Current Anthropology*, 43 (2) (April), pp. 205–31.

Kaya, Ayhan (2007), 'The impact of the Europeanization process on the perception of minorities in Turkey', *AJAMES, Annals of Japan Association for Middle Eastern Studies*, Tokyo, 22 (2).

Kaya, Ayhan (2009), 'Turkey-EU relations: The impact of Islam on Europe', in Samim Akgönül and Christian Moe (eds), *Islam in Europe*, Leiden: Brill.

Kaya, Ayhan and Turgut Tarhanlı (eds) (2005), *Türkiye'de Çoğunluk ve Azınlık Politikaları: AB Sürecinde Yurttaşlık Tartışmaları*, Istanbul: TESEV Publications.

Kaya, Ayhan et al. (2009), *Günümüz Türkiyesi'nde İç Göçler: Geri Dönüs mü, Entegrasyon mu?*, Istanbul: Istanbul Bilgi University Press.

Kirişçi, Kemal (2000), 'Disaggregating Turkish Citizenship and Immigration Practices', *Middle Eastern Studies*, 36 (3) (July), pp. 1–22.

Kirişçi, Kemal and Gareth Winrow (1997), *The Kurdish Question and Turkey: An Example of Trans-state Ethnic Conflict*, London: Frank Cass.

Kymlicka, Will (1992), 'Two models of pluralism and tolerance', *Analyse und Kritik*, 14 (1), pp. 33–56.

Landau, Jacob M. (1996), *Tekinalp: Bir Türk Yurtseveri (1883–1961)*, Istanbul: İletişim Yayınları.

Mardin, Serif (1981), 'Religion and secularism in Turkey', in Ali Kazancıgil and Ergun Özbudun (eds), *Atatürk: Founder of a Modern State*, London: C. Hurst & Co., pp. 191–220.

Olson, Robert (2009), *Blood, Beliefs and Ballots: The Management of Kurdish Nationalism in Turkey, 2007–2009*, Costa Mesa, CA: Mazda Publishers.

Öniş, Ziya (2004), 'Turkish modernization and challenges for the new Europe', *Perceptions: Journal of International Affairs*, 9 (3) (autumn), pp. 5–28.

Oran, Baskın (2004), *Türkiye'de Azınlıklar: Kavramlar, Teori, Lausanne, İç Mevzuat, İçtihat, Uygulama*, Istanbul: İletişim Publications.

Özgen, Neşe (2003), *Van-Özalp ve 33 Kurşun Olayı: Toplumsal Hafızanın Hatırlama ve Unutma Biçimleri*, Istanbul: Tüsdav Yayınları.

Sahin, Bahar (2008), 'Türkiye'nin Avrupa Birligi Uyum Süreci Baglamında Kürt Sorunu: Açılımlar ve Sınırlar', in Ayhan Kaya and Turgut Tarhanlı (eds), *Türkiye'de Çoğunlık ve Azınlık Politikaları: AB Sürecinde Yurttaslık Tartısmaları*. Istanbul: TESEV Publications, pp. 120–54.

Şeker, Nesim (2007), 'Demographic engineering in the late Ottoman Empire and the Armenians', *International Journal of Middle Eastern Studies*, 43 (3), pp. 461–74.

Szyliowicz, Joseph S. (1966), 'Political participation and modernization in Turkey', *The Western Political Quarterly*, 19 (2) (June), pp. 266–84.

Tezcür, Güneş Murat (2009), 'Kurdish nationalism and identity in Turkey: A conceptual reinterpretation', *European Journal of Turkish Studies*, 10. Available at http://ejts.revues.org/index4008.html

Tunaya, Tarık Zafer (1960), *Türkiyenin Siyasi Hayatında Batılılaşma Hareketleri*, Istanbul: Yedigün Matbaası.

Ülker, Erol (2007), 'Assimilation of the Muslim communities in the first decade of the Turkish Republic (1923–1934)', *European Journal of Turkish Studies*. Available at http://ejts.revues.org/index822.html

Ünver, H. Akın (2009), 'Turkey's "Deep State" and the Ergenekon conundrum', *The Middle East Institute Policy Brief*, 23 (April). Available at http://www.mei.edu

Walzer, Michael (1997), *On Toleration*, New Haven, CT: Yale University Press.

Watts, Nicole F. (2009), 'Re-considering state-society dynamics in Turkey's Kurdish southeast', *European Journal of Turkish Studies*, 10. Available at http://ejts.revues.org/index4196.html

Yavuz, Hakan (2001), 'Five stages of the construction of Kurdish nationalism in Turkey', *Nationalism and Ethnic Politics*, 7 (3) (August), pp. 1–24.

Yavuz, M. Hakan (2009), *Secularism and Muslim Democracy in Turkey*, Cambridge: Cambridge University Press.

Yıldız, Ahmet (2001), *Ne mutlu Türküm diyebilene: Türk ulusal kimliğinin etmo-seküler sınırları (1919–1938)*, Istanbul: Iletişim Yayınları.

Yılmaz, Gözde (2011), 'Is there a puzzle? Compliance with minority rights in Turkey (1999– 2010)', Working Paper 23, Kolleg-Forschergruppe, The Transformative Power of Europe, Berlin: Free University.

Zürcher, Erick Z. (2003), *Turkey: A Modern History*, London: I. B. Tauris.

Part V

Conclusion

Chapter Fifteen

Multiculturalism: Symptom, Cause or Solution?

Ulf Hedetoft

The conceptual paradox

'Multiculturalism' is a paradoxical notion, while 'multicultural' is not. The -ism part of the concept may connote ideology, policy or discourse, but in all cases it stands for an approach to a culturally diverse social reality informed by a normative objective to frame, control and steer developments in a particular direction. While 'multicultural' simply describes a state of affairs – a society composed of people representing different cultural and ethnic backgrounds and attachments – 'multiculturalism' more often than not is prescriptive or, when used by analysts, is meant to designate either a state committed to a social model viewing multiculturalism as in some way desirable or, more negatively, a state following worthwhile if objectionable motives.

This notion of multiculturalism is paradoxical (and hence difficult to handle in real terms), because it runs counter to the generic model and intellectual template on which nationalism is grounded. Empires are based on ideas and practices of diversity regimes and political models for managing geographically expansive units. Even post-imperial states in early-European modernity (following the Peace of Westphalia in 1648) were routinely 'multicultural', 'composite' or 'heterogeneous' in one way or another; examples include Denmark, Italy, Germany, France and Britain. But the nation state was from its inception, as notably Ernest Gellner (1983) has memorably described it, based on the (political) ideal of congruity between culture, territory, ethnicity and politics, between state and nation, and between citizenship, identity, language and belonging. In other words, the nation state from earliest times rested on cultural homogeneity – monoculturalism – in spite of the indisputable fact that reality, then as well as now, is frequently typified by cultural diversity, majority-minority tensions, linguistic hierarchies, regional disparities and religious conflict.

319

In this societal cauldron, political ambition and sociocultural reality are at a particular kind of loggerheads. The former increasingly, as time goes by, is shaping societies, citizens and cultural identities in their own image, honing them into shape and moulding people's perceptions of belonging to fit their national origin and ascriptive belonging. The template becomes reality, more or less successfully, more or less completely. But in all its manifestations it effects a marriage between identity and culture, private and public attachments, reason and emotion. The ideal-type end-product is the 'state of nature', where vertical and horizontal differences within societies are minimalized, whereas differences between one nation state and another – physically separated by visible or virtual borders – are aggrandized.

Although this may come across as a political game of power and domination, the process contains its own more or less calculated rationality – as many scholars of nationalism and modernity have pointed out. The modern nation state conforms to the integration of societies, markets and loyalties which is needed in order to make it functional in economic terms, manageable with regard to skills, communication and mobility, and governable as far as social inequalities, unrest and temporal change are concerned. In this sense, nationalism is a completely rational construction, since it welds particular interests together into the *volonté générale*, in turn translating into the affective dispositions of national identities (Hedetoft 1995).

It is on this background and within this context that multiculturalism pops up as a paradoxical creature, an alien intruding into the (ideally) close-knit compact between peoples and states. Here the point to observe is not that the ideal is, after all, no more than an ideal, constantly contravened by a muddied reality of less-than-monocultural social arrangements. This is true, but irrelevant. The real point is that multiculturalism presents itself to the national mindset as an uncomfortable ideological rival, a competing -ism, casting doubt on the hegemony of nationalist idealism and challenging the most basic *a priori* assumptions of the modernist nation state in Europe. Multiculturalism's presumed linkage between a political superstructure and a multifarious social and cultural fabric below, consisting of not only different but sometimes contradictory cultural attachments and beliefs, stands in stark contrast to the most fundamental ideas of European modernity and European nationalism. It revisits, but in oddly new ways, Europe's composite imperial past.

Conceptually, therefore, it is no wonder that reactions have been sceptical, often hostile, even though multiculturalist ideas and programmes are 'logically' embedded in novel global processes and contexts, to which they may seem properly suited. It is all the more wondrous, then, that despite this conceptual history, multiculturalism has managed over the past thirty-five years to make a notable impact across European states and to influence debates and to some extent policies of integration and social engineering in significant ways (this volume being one example out of many; see also, for example, Parekh 2000 and Vertovec and Wessendorf 2010). This 'success story' deserves a few analytical comments – first in a generic perspective, and then with regard to a representative comparative example at single-country level.

Recent historical background: the generic trajectory

Although these country-based experiences and reactions as regards the degree of assimilation of multiculturalist positions and policies diverge considerably, it is still possible to identify the generic sources underlying the relative success that 'multiculturalism' enjoyed across Europe for more than thirty years (from 1975 to 2006–7 approximately) and to some extent still does, and the environment that made it possible for its narrators to gain extensive recognition, political attention and media coverage. There are basically four such relevant sources and backgrounds.

1. The legacy of World War II

The disrepute into which Nazism's nationalist and racist narratives and practices cast nationalist ideology more generally led to a moral delegitimization of the classic European nation state and its regimented division between 'us' and 'the other'. Bolstered by the first steps towards European unification, it also produced a public questioning of national monoculturalism and impenetrable borders – primarily in states harshly impacted and/or morally denigrated by the war. In the course of this critical and self-searching process in which colonial attachments and ideas also came under fire, nationalist attitudes and practices underwent modification and mollification, preparing the ground for competing identifications and alternative worldviews.

2. New patterns of immigration into European countries

After World War II not only did Europe – Western Europe as it was then usually conceived and labelled – become an immigration destination on a large scale, but immigrants started to arrive from former or current colonies (India, Pakistan, Algeria, Morocco, Mozambique, the West Indies, Uganda, Chile, and so on) or, alternatively, from countries closer to Western Europe but which were still regarded as somewhat alien, backward and culturally or politically 'strange' (Yugoslavia, Hungary, Turkey, Iran). The Empire 'struck back', initially quite mildly, but gradually more vehemently and with notable effects on public debates, political agendas, decision-making processes and academic preoccupations. From the early 1960s onwards, therefore, debates across Europe about issues such as racism, discrimination, ethnic origin, citizenship, belonging, stereotypes and borders proliferated and made a tangible impact on Europeans' idea of themselves, their history and their political and social attitudes. The increasing presence of 'others' in 'our midst' in more and more countries throughout the 1960s and early 1970s challenged the new-found openness, tolerance and subdued nationalism of many Western European peoples and political actors. It generated vicious debates about national identities (as in Britain), more downplayed and accommodating debates about the economic or cultural benefits of newcomers (as in Sweden) or neutered debates about international morality and international conventions (such as those in Germany). In most (though not all) cases, however, it kept questions about national identity alive and prevented European nationalism from reverting to complacency about the blessings of the monoculturalist compact between state, territory and ethnicity – whether civil or sanguine.

3. Emergence of rights-based struggles of ethnic minorities

After World War II historical ethnic minorities outside the 'ethnic core' of national populations (Brubaker 1996) launched a struggle for national and international recognition of their rights. These nationalities had a long sedentary history of inhabiting the territory of the nation state: examples are the Sami in Norway, Romanians in Hungary, Roma in the Czech Republic, Finns in Sweden, Russians in Lithuania and Basques in Spain. This development is closely tied to the developments outlined under the first two points, which provide an environment conducive for the advances made and the visibility given by the media to these struggles. These were enhanced by UN- and EU-inspired support in terms of institutional acceptance and possibilities for taking cases involving infringement of collective or individual rights, racism or discrimination to court. This involves policies of identity and recognition by often vocal minorities, leading in many countries to a questioning of the monoculturalist social model by way of a pursuit of policies of minority representation and institutional flexibilities which accommodate multiple claims of multiculturalism, in any one of its many guises.

4. ADVOCACY OF THE MULTICULTURALIST CAUSE

Many vocal spokespeople of ethnic-minority backgrounds along with numerous academics from among the ethnic majority began to set out their vision of what was to develop into the multicultural model of organizing diversity in European societies. They generally expressed liberalist, globalist, tolerant or socialist sympathies, and today they see multiculturalism as either a means for prying open the closed compact and rigid borders of national societies, or as a way to restate a moral cause and ethical positions of intercultural toler-ance and understanding. Multiculturalism would be nothing without such people, since they personally spearhead and visibly embody a particular social trend, giving it both moral legitimacy and access to politics and the media. This is one of the major reasons – though far from the only one – why the discourse and practice of multicultural-ism hit home in Sweden from approximately the mid-1970s, while it never did in Denmark. Immigrant and minority communities were able to breed vocal advocates in Sweden, not in its neighbouring Nordic country, although historical and institutional path depend-encies might have predicted a similar outcome. This will be further addressed in the following section.

Historical background from single-country perspectives: a Danish–Swedish comparison

In spite of the fact that all European nation states, at one level of abstraction, conform to a common blueprint of monocultural state-people interaction and have all been impacted by the post-war proc-esses sketched above, it is still true that Europe's nation states have grown into modernity in different ways and have developed diverse political, administrative and institutional cultures in the course of history. In addition, the constitution of national consciousness and auto-perceptions has taken place against a background of different images of alterity and through nationally specific interactions between political and social mechanisms of inclusion and exclusion.

These facts co-determine the framing and reception of multiculturalist positions in different countries. The manner in which nation states talk about, legislate for and cope with ethnic and historical minorities differs, because states relate differently, culturally and politically, to the four generic sources of multiculturalism listed above. Nationalism was not evenly de-legitimized in all European countries – it was more devalued in loser nations, for instance, than in states that ended up on the winning side. Immigration patterns (size, origin, reasons and so on) vary markedly from one country to the next. In the UK immigration (from former or current colonies) came early, in Germany somewhat later and in Finland hardly at all. Some states possess large historical minorities, some smaller, and others none – and they enjoy very different political recognition. Finally, vocal advocates depend a lot on happenstance and coincidence, the levels of education in a society and the degree to which they encounter a propitious public climate and events suited to the message they want to convey.

For all these reasons, national integration regimes (Favell 2001; Spencer 2003) – by which I mean institutionalized configurations of closure and openness, pragmatism and idealism, political and economic interests in immigration and ethnic minorities – vary on important dimensions. These variations, in turn, are intimately linked to differences in frames for national identity perception and different models for active citizenship. Cases presented in this book have highlighted the role played by institutionalized configurations of closure and openness and the variations in models of diversity and citizenship that they have generated.

These reflections apply even to nation states that on crucial parameters appear to be similar, because they structurally represent the same type of social formation, comparable interactions between state and citizens, and analogous political and cultural histories. An obvious example is Sweden and Denmark – both Scandinavian welfare states with well-developed democratic structures, both old monarchies, both small states with a pronounced sense of social equality and just distribution across sections of the population and both nurturing a perception of 'the other' as Scandinavian kith and kin, with whom one feels culturally and socially connected. (For more thorough reflections on these and the following issues, see for example Hedetoft et al. 2006.)

In spite of such similarities, migration policies of the two countries have diverged significantly since the early 1970s, and public debates about these issues and the way they are perceived to be dealt with in the other country have frequently been at loggerheads (hence the case of Sweden is located in Part II of this book and that of Denmark in Part III). In crude terms, one may imagine Danish homogeneity facing Swedish multiculturalism by way of these binary contrasts: a closed, exclusionary regime encountering one that is open and inclusive; assimilation contrasting with official recognition of difference; ideas that frame 'others' as the problem confronting ideas framing the national society as a barrier to integration; welfare being variously projected as hindrance to or a path towards integration; 'others' being seen as victims of or responsible for their own destiny; institutional rigidity facing flexible adaptation of institutions to new groups; and demands for single, exclusive citizenship standing in opposition to possibilities for multiple citizenship. In this light, the two countries are worlds apart: Danish discourses of national self-sufficiency seem to collide with a Swedish regime driven by international morality and accountability, features that in Denmark are pejoratively cast as 'political correctness', preventing a free debate and open acknowledgement of how comprehensive the 'real problems' are.

A closer look at history provides us with a key to understanding these differences. In brief, Denmark's reluctance towards (politically recognized) multiculturalism stems partly from the success of its monocultural welfare model and the negative images associated with its former imperial status, and the history of loss and defeat that led to the country's present-day size, homogeneity and self-acclaimed 'littleness'. In addition, large-scale immigration came late (much later than in Sweden), and the 1970s ban on economic immigration never prepared the public for an acceptance of or a balanced debate about the pros and cons of immigration and cultural diversity. Instead migration soon came to be associated with cultural menace, economic burden and political risk. These voices of anxiety and romantic nationalism found outspoken political advocates from the mid-1990s onwards. Finally, political representation in Denmark only recognizes the historical minorities of Greenland and the Faroe Islands, not immigrant ethnic minorities.

Nevertheless, debates in both countries have undergone a gradual but noticeable change over the past decade and now less readily live up to these crude ideal-types. In Sweden, immigrants not infrequently become framed as a source of social problems today, no doubt partly under the influence of the Danish politicization of immigrants and integration since the mid-1990s. While it is undoubtedly still true that there are 'no votes for xenophobia in Sweden', as Fredrik Reinfeldt, the Swedish Prime Minister, once put it, public debates on these issues have noticeably become both franker and more polarized.

In Denmark on the other hand, parts of the Danish debate have been inspired by perceptions of Swedish tolerance and diversity talk. Now, moderating the Danish inclination toward assimilationism, one notes a growing acknowledgement among political actors, business representatives and the electorate too, that global challenges require more 'diversity management' in corporate Denmark, more institutional flexibility and less austere migration policies – not least, admittedly, because such altered positions can be argued pragmatically as being in the economic and demographic interests of a small nation in search of economic growth and adaptation to a fast-changing global context (Hedetoft 2010).

Historically, Sweden has thus evolved from paternalistic multiculturalism, through anti-discriminatory strategies, to a murkier position, where exclusionary strategies and integration demands based on the values of the host country can now also be articulated, though they are still in opposition to the dominant consensus. Denmark, on the other hand, has moved from conditional tolerance in the 1970s and 1980s, through demands on newcomers for acculturation and financial self-subsistence, into a more polarized debate. Exclusionary strategies and demands for integration on the conditions stipulated by the host country are being modified by a growing interest in cushioning the negative effects of institutional discrimination, more proactive immigration policies in the interest of economic sustenance and an incipient rejection of exclusionary practices and vote-catching strategies based on anti-immigrant rhetoric.

In all these senses we find traces of significant convergence between the two countries, a pattern representing a larger macro-trend in Europe. Elements of a convergence of approaches are identifiable in the case studies presented in this book. Nevertheless, as we can infer from these cases, there are limits to the extent and depth of the convergence trajectory. From my single-case perspective, I note, first, that the discursive relations of power are differently configured.

Multiculturalism is still official politics in Sweden and must be contrasted with the official Danish policy of ethnic homogeneity.

Second, the two national welfare systems (once generally referred to as 'the Nordic model') are constructed on the basis of two different pathways towards consensus and social success. The Swedish one is corporatist, basing itself on centralized institutions, political co-optation and top-down security for social and cultural interest groups. The Danish one is based on decentralized networks, acceptance of freely concluded labour-market contracts and an elastic and malleable 'flexicurity model' (Campbell et al. 2006). In cultural terms, the Swedish model is geared to attempts to engender consensus, whereas cultural and identity-seeking monoculturalism is the implicit precondition for the functionality of the Danish.

Third, in Denmark as well as Sweden it is eminently true that institutions matter. They tend to create their own path dependencies – handed-down patterns of thought, assessment and social practice – including in the management of ethnic and immigrant issues. It is no coincidence, for instance, that Sweden has nurtured an Ombudsman institution handling cases of ethnic discrimination, while Denmark has not (the idea has been rejected on several occasions); that Denmark has a liberal law allowing for the creation of government-sponsored civic (including ethnic and religious) associations; or that the Swedish Foreign Minister, in March 2006, was compelled to withdraw from her position due to a gauche and ambiguous handling of a ramification of the cartoon affair in Sweden, with quite unexpected consequences, while her Danish opposite number stayed steadfast in spite of severe international ramifications, confidently banking on even stronger domestic popular backing after the affair (Hedetoft et al. 2006).

At the same time, however, the cases also typify the general European pattern of value-based convergence around 'cohesion talk'. Although the Swedish Foreign Minister's faux pas was due to a 'multiculturalist' reaction intended to put a halt to the dissemination of the Mohammed cartoons in Sweden and thus prevent the tainting of Sweden's international image, the reason this act – which might well have gone unnoticed or even been publicly supported in the past – now ended in public disgrace was the very same principle that fanned the fires of public uproar in Denmark in the first place: the right of free speech interpreted as the freedom to speak openly and with no moral strings attached about ethnic minorities, particularly Muslims (Hedetoft et al. 2006).

From popularity to backlash: the vindication of nationalism

On a microscopic level, the Danish–Swedish duel encapsulates the current tide against multiculturalism, the vindication of European nationalism in the traditional ethnic format and the factual, though hardly theoretically understood, attempt to overcome the inherent paradoxes of the multiculturalist approach to societal cohesion. The tendency is understandable in historical perspective (see the previous section), but it raises three significant questions. Why return to exclusionary responses in a global age calling for, some might argue, diversity answers to questions of cohesiveness? How thoroughgoing is the 'backlash' really? And, perhaps most fundamentally, is multiculturalism really a model at all, and if it is not, what implications follow?

The response to the first of these questions is, briefly put, that popular and political reactions to imagined threats are not always guided by economically driven rationality, but by affective knee-jerk throwbacks to well-tried models and identity solutions. 'Globalization' is often viewed less as an opportunity than as a risk, and national-ethnic cohesion lends itself well as a safe and alluring haven in times of trouble. This reaction is visible not just in the domain of migration policies, but also in the way in which member states of the EU are developing walls of suspicion and reluctance toward full integrative membership. In this sense, we are witnessing the 'Decline of the West', or Oswald Spengler's (1991) *Untergang des Abendlandes*, take 2.

The political and normative backlash against ideas of multiculturalism encapsulates the twenty-first-century tragedy of the European continent, a region gradually becoming more marginalized on the global stage, looking more and more like a museum of past successes, and choosing on that background the defiant option to retreat willingly to past solutions rather than looking for and implementing radically new pathways ahead. This basically defeatist worldview spells resignation in the face of global challenges. Multiculturalism is, paradoxically, often cast in the role as cause and perpetrator of the tragedy of powerlessness, but it is no more than one representation out of many of the European inability to cope with global competition, climate challenges, ageing populations, security risks and new patterns of demographic mobility. The cultural backlash against diversity in favour of mono-ethnicity is really not about the application of this or that factual solution, but about the subtext of cultural despair and political surrender that this tide subtly reflects.

That said, it is relevant to enquire how thoroughgoing and deep-seated the backlash really is. There are two important perspectives to bear in mind when addressing this question. First, in what domains and to what extent has multiculturalism been a dominant and influential factor in shaping the European political and cultural landscape? And second, has multiculturalism ever been implemented and practised in any European country as a genuinely alternative social policy model?

As indicated in the section on the generic trajectory above, multiculturalism has been a relatively comprehensive and, some would argue, unexpected success in Europe since at least the early 1970s. But a closer look will reveal that this success has been primarily ideational, ideological and normative. Multiculturalism as an idea and a reflective frame for setting the stage for public debates about integration, egalitarianism and anti-discrimination has been able to make a significant impact on cultural and political environments, both as a means for promoting liberal attitudes to immigrants and for fulminating against them while supporting traditional national ethnic homogeneity. It has also, as already mentioned, been able to frame official government discourses about immigration and integration issues in a significant number of European nation states and has thus worked as a vehicle for manifesting the good will, good faith and internationalist attitudes of political actors in these countries, most of them boasting, for different reasons, of a history of cultural diversity and experience in handling ethnic differences.

Nevertheless, it is necessary to question the depth of multiculturalism's impact. An important part of the debates about the concept has focused on how to define and understand it. Scholars have proposed quite different, sometimes incompatible, interpretations, ranging from very 'thin' to very 'thick' versions of multiculturalism. Not only does this debate reveal the uncertainty of the central notion itself, it is a sign of a much more fundamental problem: that is, it is well-nigh impossible to ascertain to what extent multiculturalism is really a well-defined model in its own right and, for the same reason, whether it has been or is being practised (or has tangible impacts), politically or socially, even in countries usually designated as partial to multiculturalism.

So let me turn to the third and most central question posed above. Is multiculturalism a model at all? If one takes that concept seriously, might it not just be a politically convenient term that describes nationally specific bundles of historical preferences and experiences, useful for political rhetoric and displays of consistent political action, but in practice continuously compromised, negotiated and reinterpreted in the light of new developments, shifting national interests, political bargaining and globally convergent (learning) processes?

Probably not! A contextual point is that things often sound more pompous at higher levels of political discourse and theory than on the 'local' ground, where there is often more 'multiculturalism' than expected in highly 'monocultural' societies (such as France and Denmark), and less than would be expected in societies dominated by official commitments to diversity (as in the case of Britain and Sweden). As was wisely concluded in a recent volume, '[n]ormative multiculturalism seems out of reach in Western European countries, which are going through a multicultural crisis without having actually experienced any multicultural model' (Silj 2010: 237). Multiculturalism has rather, it is argued, become 'the synonym of a would-be "crisis" of migrant integration and citizenship' (Silj 2010: 237). Or, in other words, either multiculturalism is often blamed for the failures of national integration policies, or national integration models are blamed for the failure to adopt a workable multicultural solution. But 'models' are in fact frequently opaque and contradictory; they serve as rhetorical ploys rather than operational facts, are relative rather than absolute and remain open to different theoretical and practical interpretations.

This does not mean that models (whether multicultural or not) are no more than figments of the imagination with no impact on immigration policies and integration discourses in different countries (see Hedetoft 2010). As path-dependent cultural and institutional barriers to be managed and sometimes (increasingly) overcome, as philosophies of integration management, they are very real indeed. However, politicians are pragmatists and not easily bound by ideational statements and rhetorical commitments to theoretical social models if circumstances call for other measures or new practices. In addition, the global push towards policy convergence, for example, transmitted through trans-state learning processes, tends in the course of time to neutralize nationally divergent solutions grounded in political and cultural history.

At the end of the day the much-vaunted talk about the crisis of multicultural solutions and the backlash against diversity has little to do with failed models, abortive practices or problems deriving from cultural diversity in its own right. Multiculturalism in that perspective is little more than a straw man standing in for much more serious reasons underlying the European debacle. It symbolizes and legitimizes the political desire to champion value-based national cohesion within nation states increasingly exposed to global risks of fragmentation and cleavage, to recreate classic national-ethnic homogeneity, European style, in circumstances radically inimical to that ambition. In the process, it 'strengthens the incommensurability between empirical *reality* and public and political *narratives* on race, ethnicity and identity' (Silj 2010: 250). In that sense, 'multiculturalism' is a fall guy for the ongoing decline of statist control, and the cultural backlash against it – a quixotic struggle against windmills.

Groundhog Day in full sunshine: forward to the past?

Popular myth will have it that on 2 February, known as Groundhog Day, the groundhog comes out of winter hiding, surfaces from its burrow, probes the weather conditions and, if it is a sunny day, immediately takes cover again, for its instincts tell it that fine weather is an omen of many more cold days and weeks ahead. The prospects seem bright, but the groundhog is too cautious to take any chances, choosing instead to rely on well-tried reactions. Better safe than sorry!

European nation states display similar behaviour when it comes to dealing politically with cultural diversity and multi-ethnicity. At best they sometimes dare to look the animal in the face, ask it to enter the house for a short visit, even speaking politely to it and about it. But at the end of the day, when push comes to shove, they routinely obey knee-jerk reactions, raise their guard, ask it to leave and return to business as usual. Or try to. For business is really not what it used to be any more. Globalization is here to stay, ethnic mobility too, and nation states find themselves pursuing their interests and dealing with problems of sovereignty, economic growth and social well-being in circumstances continuously changing, challenging conventional solutions and handed-down wisdom. Standing firm on orthodox nationalism, monoculturalist policies, old-school sovereignty and 'secure borders' will in all likelihood – barring exceptionally fortunate circumstances – prove to be of very little help, as states attempting that route have already realized to their detriment.

This does not necessarily mean that 'practised multiculturalism' (or whatever term we may choose to employ) is the solution, or for that matter even part of the solution to the conundrum. The conceptual paradox is as real as the global challenges are daunting, and there is no easy fix, no magic panacea. The problem is not only that European nations, scared of their own shadow in sunny conditions because it seems too good to be true, instinctively and sometimes desperately grope for historical solutions to future challenges; this timidity is also the problem. There is clearly a need for social experiments – even identity experiments – in order to address questions of social solidarity and cultural belonging in ways that are in sync rather than at loggerheads with emerging conditions of global competition, flows of skills and people, as well as multiple forms and objects of attachment.

'Multiculturalism' in this context, therefore, should be regarded both as a symptom of the malaise and as an explicit sign that we face a fundamental problem waiting for new, thoroughgoing and future-oriented remedies that will help resolve the conceptual paradox and possibly even take us beyond multiculturalism. Such a highly complex toolbox still has to be constructed and deployed intelligently. What is certain beyond any doubt is that European nation states, with or without the EU in its current shape, will be able neither to devise convincing and legitimate societal cohesion nor to halt the decline from global status and influence as long as they insist on behaving like the mythical groundhog on a sunny day in February.

References

Brubaker, Rogers (1996), *Nationalism Reframed: Nationhood and the National Question in the New Europe*, Cambridge: Cambridge University Press.

Campbell, John L., John A. Hall and Ove K. Pedersen (eds) (2006), *National Identity and the Varieties of Capitalism: The Danish Experience*, Montreal and Kingston: McGill-Queen's University Press.

Favell, Adrian (2001), *Philosophies of Integration*, London: Palgrave.

Gellner, Ernest (1983), *Nations and Nationalism*, Ithaca, NY: Cornell University Press.

Hedetoft, Ulf (1995), *Signs of Nations*, Aldershot: Dartmouth.

—— (2006), 'Denmark's Cartoon Blowback', *openDemocracy*, 1 March. Available at www.openDemocracy.net

—— (2010), 'Between angels and demons: boundary symbols and symbolic politics in the Danish management of aliens', *Politik*, 13 (4), pp. 45–54.

Hedetoft, Ulf, Bo Petersson and Lina Sturfeldt (eds) (2006), *Bortom*

Stereotyperna: Invandrare och integration i Danmark och Sverige, Gothenburg: Makadam.

Parekh, Bhiku (2000), *Rethinking Multiculturalism*, Basingstoke: Macmillan.

Silj, Alessandro (ed.) (2010), *European Multiculturalism Revisited*, London: Zed Books.

Spencer, Sarah (ed.) (2003), *The Politics of Migration*, special issue of *The Political Quarterly*, London: Wiley-Blackwell.

Spengler, Oswald (1991), *The Decline of the West*, ed. Arthur Helps and Helmut Werner, New York: Oxford University Press [originally published in two volumes in German as *Der Untergang des Abendlandes*, vol. 1, Vienna: Verlag Braumüller, 1918; and *Welthistorische Perspektiven*, vol. 2, Munich: Verlag C. H. Beck, 1922].

Vertovec, Steven and Susanne Wessendorf (eds) (2010), *The Multiculturalism Backlash*, London: Palgrave.

Index

Note: page numbers in *italics* denote tables or figures

A Just Russia, 287
accommodation of differences
  cultural, 53–6, 67, 99, 149,
    305
  equality of opportunity,
    184–5
  laws and policies, 191
  left-/right-wing, 217
  and liberalism, 70
  municipal level, 196
  politics of, 16, 41, 43, 53
  pragmatic, 112, 113, 114,
    230–2
  religious, 67, 149, 169, 270,
    305
  social/political rights, 99, 209
  state models, 42
acculturation, 69, 184, 242,
  250, 326
ACOM, 110
Action Plan, Denmark, 198,
  199
Action Programme, EU, 32
Admission Law, Belgium,
  128–9
Advisory Committee on
  Minorities Research
  (ACOM), 110
affirmative action programmes,
  169, 210
Akopov, Sergey, 20–1, 294
AKP, 307, 308, 312
Albanian immigrants, 219, 228
Alevi community, 302, 304–5
Alibhai-Brown, Yasmin, 80
ALLBUS survey, 176–84
Amato, Giuliano, 225, 226
Amselle, Jean-Loup, 241
Amsterdam, 113
Amsterdam Treaty, 32
Anderson, Benedict, 283
Anthony, Andrew, 77
anti-discrimination, 32, 45,
  168, 269–70, 274

anti-immigration parties, 3,
  100, 105, 221, 222
anti-Islam discourse, 223, 225;
  see also Islamophobia
anti-paternalism, 65
anti-racism, 8–9, 84, 243
anti-Semitism, 7, 199, 258, 273
anti-terrorism approach, 76,
  87–90
Armenian genocide, 311
assimilation
  Denmark, 190, 326
  Flanders, 126
  France, xii, 15, 20, 35, 240
  and integration, 84, 204,
    241–5
  Italy, 216
  minority groups, 207–8
  Netherlands, 98, 104–6,
    112–14
  political membership, 52
  racialisation, 241
  resisted, 175, 180
  Sweden, 141
  Turkey, 301–2
assimilationism
  differentialism, 101
  and dual citizenship, 101,
    180
  integration, 39, 84, 115, 204,
    241–5
  liberal state, 56
  multiculturalism, 53, 99
  national identities, 28
  vs recognition of difference,
    325
  rise of, 112
Association of People of
  Silesian Nationality, 261–2
asylum seekers
  Belgium, 122, 124
  Denmark, 192, 194
  France, 247
  Germany, 165, 171

Poland, 275
Sweden, 145, 149
Atatürk, Mustafa Kemal, 308,
  312; *see also* Kemalist
  regime
Ausländerkriminalität, 172
autochthon minorities, 260–2,
  274; *see also* indigenous
  populations
autonomy
  Belgium, 120, 121, 128, 132,
    135
  collective, 16, 68
  culture, 59–62
  institutional, 240
  Italy, 221
  personal, 56, 58, 59, 64–5,
    68
  Polish provinces, 261
  Russian regions, 261, 280,
    282
Azerbaijan, 289

Bade, Klaus J., 172–3
banlieues, 242–3, 246–7
Banting, Keith, 5, 6, 9, 75, 85,
  194, *195*, 237
Barkey, Karen, 300
Barry, Brian, 75, 82
Basques, 58, 322
Belgian Nationality Law, 133–5
Belgium
  Admission Law, 128–9
  asylum seekers, 122, 124
  autonomy, 120, 121, 128,
    132, 135
  Centre for Equal
    Opportunities and
    Opposition to Racism, 125
  citizenship, 133
  Commission for Intercultural
    Dialogue, 130
  Equal Opportunities and
    Social Integration, 130–1

federalisation, 120, 121–2, 135–6
Flemings/Walloons, 18, 120–1, 125
immigrants, 11, 122–4
immigration policy, 120–1, 125–7
Interculturality Sessions, 130–1
labour migrants, 128–9
languages spoken, 121, 125
local elections, 136
Nationality Law, 133, *134*
naturalisation, 133
population composition, *124*
2010 elections, 127–35
work permits, *123*, 129
see also Brussels region; Flanders; Wallonia
Berlusconi, Silvio, 221, 226
Besson, Eric, 247–8
Beur movement, 243
Bevelander, Pieter, 11–12
Bhabha, Homi K., 10
Blair, Tony, 76, 81
Blommaert, Jan, 125, 126
Blunkett, David, 85
Bolkestein, Frederik (Frits), 103, 108
Bologna, 19, 229–30
border controls, 216, 220, 331
Borevi, Karin, 18
Bova, Russell, 292–3
Britain, 3, 8–9
citizenship test, 27–8
coalition government, 76
cultural exemptions, 150
EHRC, 32
faith schools, 80
immigrants, 11
integration, 76–7
multiculturalism, 15, 17, 75–6, 78
Muslims, 78, 88
national identities, 28, 322
Nationality, Immigration and Asylum Act, 27–8, 85–6
New Labour, 26–7
post-7/7 bomb attacks, 9
re-nationalisation, 26–7
British Commonwealth, 82–3
British Nationality Act (1958), 82–3
Broder, Henryk M., 172
Brown, Gordon, 76, 86
Brubaker, Rogers, 322
Brussels region, 123–4, 127, 129, 132
Bulgarian immigrants, 226
Buzek, Jerzy, 272, 273

Calderoli, Roberto, 224
Cameron, David, xv, 25, 78, 84, 190
Canada, 3–4, 10, 12–13, 40
Caponio, Tiziana, 19, 229
Caritas, 222
Çarkoğlu, Ali, 300
Casanova, José, 302
Castells, Manuel, 261
Castles, Stephen, 166
Catholic Church
Italy, 217, 220, 221, 222, 223, 225
Poland, 15, 258, 260, 264, 270, 271, 272
CDU, Germany, 170, 174, 182
Centre for Equal Opportunities and Opposition to Racism, Belgium, 125
CFCM, 244
Charter of Values, Citizenship and Integration, Italy, 225, 226
Chebel d'Appollonia, Ariane, 12
Chechnya, 264, 281, 285
Chirac, Jacques, 244
Choudhury, T., 86
Christian Democratic Union *see* CDU
Christian Social Union (CSU), 170
Christianity, 15, 30, 78, 178, 180; *see also* Catholic Church; Lutheran Church; Orthodox Church; Protestantism
Church of Sweden, 150
church/state, 53–4, 55, 240
Chuvash Republic, 285
Circassians, 302
Cities for Local Integration Project, 232
citizenisation, 131, 141
Citizens of the United Kingdom and Commonwealth (CUKC), 82, 83
citizenship, *38*
active, 198–9, 204
Belgium, 133
civil rights, 167
counterterrorism strategies, 87
democratic, 198–9
dual, 31, 101, 179–80
equality, 31, 44
France, xii, 248–9
Germany, 27, 165, 167, 180
identity, 33
liberal, 54–5
multiculturalism, 41, 44
Netherlands, 103

non-discrimination, 30, 31
normative models, 33–40
North American context, 38–9
open, 99
plural state, 36
Poland, 267–8
policies on, 11
probationary, 86
Roma community, 228
Russian Federation, 284
securitisation, 90–1
state, 33, 46–7, 58
Sweden, 140, 153–4
Turkey, 313
Citizenship Law, Germany, 27, 167
citizenship rights, 26, 140, 219
citizenship tests, 5, 11, 27–8, 85–6
civic thickening, 17, 75, 76
CMEB, 36–7, 41, 80–1
Cofferati, Sergio, 230
Cohen, Nick, 77
cohesion/equality/difference models, 36, 37, 38, 39, 41, 89–90
Cohn-Bendit, Daniel, 170
COIC, 89
colonialism, 239, 322
Commissariat Royal à la Politique des Immigrés (CRPI), 125
Commission for Intercultural Dialogue, Belgium, 130
Commission for Racial Equality, 77, 83
Commission for the Study of a Comprehensive Law on Immigration, 219
Commission on Discrimination, Sweden, 148–9
Commission on Immigration, Sweden, 143
Commission on Integration and Cohesion (COIC), 89
Commission on the Future of Multi-Ethnic Britain *see* CMEB
Committee of National and Ethnic Minorities, Poland, 259–60
Communist Re-foundation, Italy, 220
communitarianism, 58, 62, 65, 68, 251
communities, thick to thin, *201*
conservative nationalism, 200–1
Conservative Party, Sweden, 142, 144

Conservative–Liberal Democrat coalition, Britain, 76
Convention on the Participation of Foreigners in Public Life at the Local Level, 267
Copenhagen, 196
Corriere della Sera, 223
cosmopolitanism, 26, 39, 291, 292, 293
CRAN, 243
Crepaz, Markus, 164
CRIF, 243
CRPI , France, 125
CSU, Germany, 170
CUKC, 82, 83
cultural diversity, 176, *177*
  accommodation of, 53–6, 67, 99, 149, 305
  changing conceptions, 70
  France, 236
  Germany, 163
  globalisation, 331
  immigrants, 229
  Italy, 222
  public opinion, 181
  recognition, 166, 176, 229–30
  voluntarism, 65–8
cultural exemptions, 149–51, 191, 195, 210
cultural pluralism, 141–2
  Germany, 170–1, 180
  LO, 142–3
  Poland, 257, 265–70
  social attitudes, 271–3
  Sweden, 145
cultural turn, 58, 216–17, 227, 230
culture
  adaptation, 176–7
  autonomy, 59–62
  communitarianism, 65
  differentialism, 57–9, 68
  identity, 62–3, 261
  recognition, 62, 63–4, 219, 229–30
  re-discovered, 221–30
culture war, 201
Czech Republic, 322

Dagens Nyheter, 142
Danish cartoons, 208, 224, 327
Danish Commonwealth, 196
Danish Cultural Canon, 199
Danish People's Party (DPP), 192, 194, 201, 205
Day, Richard J. F., 9–10
DCLG, 83, 89, 90
De Voretz, Don, 11–12
De Zwart, Frank, 112
decolonisation, 100, 145

Demirel, Süleyman, 307
Democratic Party, Italy, 230
democratisation
  Poland, 257, 259–60
  Turkey, 307, 309
Denmark
  Action Plan, 198, 199
  assimilation, 190, 326
  asylum seekers, 192, 194
  attitudes to multiculturalism, 202–8
  citizenship tests, 27
  diversity management, 326
  exclusionary strategies, 326
  family reunification, 193, 194
  foreigners, 192
  free schools, 195
  guest worker approach, 192
  homogeneity, 192, 197, 207–8, 327
  immigration, 4, 190, 192–6
  integratiion, 190, 192–202
  Islamophobia, 206–7
  language requirements, 27
  Liberal–Conservative coalition, 192, 193, 194, 196, 198
  migration policy, 325
  MIPEX, 193–4
  monocultural society, 330
  mother-tongue instruction, 195–6
  Muslim immigrants, 191
  national identities, 28, 199
  and Netherlands, 201–2
  political parties, 193, 205
  refugees, 192
  religions, 192
  religious education, 195
  social cohesion, 196–202
  social security, 204
  special rights, 209
  start help, 193
  state policies, 19
  and Sweden, 202, 324–7
  values commission, 197
  welfare state, 194, 199, 206, 207, 325, 327
Department for Communities and Local Government *see* DCLG
Di Rupo, Elio, 135, 136
Diesen, Ingrid, 144
difference, 33, 42, 45–6, 274; *see also* diversity; group difference; Other; religious difference
differentialism, 54–7
  assimilationism, 101
  cultural, 57–9, 68

immigration policies, 100
Kymlicka, 68
  rights, 69
discrimination, 57, 69, 80, 89–90, 150–1
Discrimination Act (2008), Sweden, 150–1
diversity
  Britain, 3
  cultural, *34*
  equality, 82–5
  immigration, 3
  integration, 39
  liberalism, 52–3
  migration-related, *43*
  Quebec, 39
  Russian Federation, 20–1
  universalism, 82
  see also cultural diversity; ethnic diversity; ethnocultural diversity
diversity management, 12, 15, 132, 326
DPP *see* Danish People's Party
dress-codes, 150, 151
Dubet, François, 241
Dublin Convention, 264
Dutch language, 131; *see also* Netherlands; Duyvendak, Jan Willem, 109, 111, 113, 114–15

economic factors, 4, 10–11, 172–3, 247
education
  anti-racist, 84
  Catholic Church, 225
  cosmopolitanism, 293
  Germany, 169, 178, 185
  Poland, 268–9
  Sweden, 144
  USA, 293
  see also religious education
Education Act, Sweden, 151
EHRC, 32, 78, 83
Employment Directive, 32
English Defence League, 77
English for Speakers of Other Languages (ESOL), 28, 85–6
Enlightenment philosophies, 237, 238
Entzinger, Han, 114
Equal Opportunities and Social Integration, Belgium, 130–1
Equality Acts, Britain, 83, 89
Equality and Human Rights Commission *see* EHRC
equality of opportunity, 33, 45, 184–5, 208–9
equality/diversity, 82–5

Erdoğan, Recep Tayyip, 175, 307, 308
Eriksen, Jens-Martin, 209–10
ESOL (English for Speakers of Other Languages), 28, 85–6
Ethnic and National Minorities Act, Poland, 261
ethnic diversity, 27, 81, 170, 204, 258–9
  backlash against, 328–9
  Germany, 171–2
  Italy, 217–18
  management of, 279–80
  social cohesion, 196–7, 199
  Turkey, 297–8
ethnic minorities
  assimilation resisted, 180
  desecuritisation, 139
  hybrid identities, 61
  identity, 279
  inclusion, 78
  monitoring, 80–1
  post-immigrant, 81–2
  rights-based struggles, 322–3
  riots, 100
  Turkey, 21
Ethnic Minorities Policy, Netherlands, 101–2, 106, 108, 110
ethnocultural diversity, 21, 79, 297, 300–1, 302–8, 312–13
Eurobarometer 2000 survey, 202–3, 204, 205
Europe
  anti-immigration parties, 3
  imperial past, 320
  multiculturalism, xii, 3, 6, 21–2
  nationalism, 328–31
  re-nationalisation, 26, 28–9
  Westphalia, Peace of, 319
European Charter of Regional and Minority Languages, 265
European Convention of Human Rights, 265
European Court of Human Rights, 30, 261
European Foundation for the Improvement of Living and Working Conditions, 232
European Union
  Action Programme, 32
  Anti-discrimination Directives, 168
  debt crisis, 175–6
  free movement of labour, 176
  integration, 308–9

Pact on Immigration and Asylum, 27
  rights of ethnic minorities, 322
  Turkish membership proposed, 311–12
European Values Study (EVS), 203, 272
Europeanness, 290, 292–3
Euroscepticism, 297
EVS, 203, 272
exclusion, 7, 204, 242–3, 272, 301–2, 324, 326
exit option, 67–8

Faas, Daniel, 75
Faist, Thomas, 79
faith schools, 80
Fallaci, Oriana, 222–3
family reunification
  Denmark, 193, 194
  Germany, 165
  immigration, 7, 123–4, 168
Faroe Islands, 196, 325
Favell, Adrian, 124
federation of communities, 34, 35, 36
Feher, Michel, 247, 248
Fekete, Liz, 90
feminist approach, 13–14
Fernández, Christian, xv, 16–17
Fetzer, Joel S., 270
Finnish people, in Sweden, 143, 322
Flanders, 121–2, 123
  assimilationism, 126
  citizenisation, 131
  cultural homogeneity, 125–6
  Dutch language, 131
  integration, 127, 130, 131, 132, 135
  Kulturnation, 125
  labour migrants, 127
  and Nationality Law, 133
  NVA party, 128, 136
  work permits, 123–4, 129
Flemings, 18, 120–1, 125, 126
FN, France, 245, 252
Fondazione Nord-Est, 223
forced marriage, 168, 172, 194
foreigners
  attitude to, 288
  Denmark, 192
  France, 242, 245, 246–7, 248–9
  Germany, 164–6, 174, 176, 177–8, 179, 180–2, 184, 185n2
  Italy, 222
  Poland, 257, 263, 267, 271

right to form associations, 242, 267
  Russia, 290
  stigmatisation, 248
  unemployment, 247
  see also immigrants
Formentini, Marco, 219–20
Fortuyn, Pim, 104, 108, 115
Forza Italia, 221, 224
Foucault, Michel, 300
Framework Convention for the Protection of National Minorities, 265
France
  antiracist movements, 243
  assimilationism, xii, 15, 20, 35, 240
  asylum seekers, 247
  banlieues, 242–3, 246–7
  citizenship, xii, 248–9
  communitarianism, 251
  Constitution, 237
  CRAN, 243
  cultural diversity, 236
  electoral cards, xii
  foreigners, 242, 245, 246–7, 248–9
  Front National, 245, 252
  immigrants, 11
  integration, 242, 246–7
  Jacobin state, 238, 239, 240
  laïcité principle, 151, 200, 240, 244, 248, 251
  migration research, 7
  monocultural society, 330
  multiculturalism, 19–20, 236, 237
  national identities, 245–50
  nationalism, 20
  naturalisation, 248–9
  religious clothing, 244
  secularism, 240
  Socialist Party, xii, 243, 252
  urban policy, 242–3
France Plus, 243
free schools, Denmark, 195
freedom of association, 66–7
freedom of choice, 144–5
freedom of expression, 224, 306, 327
freedom of movement, 82–3, 176
freedom of religion, 225
Freedom Party, Netherlands, 105
French Academy, 244
French Council of the Muslim Religion (CFCM), 244
French languages, 40, 132, 244
French Republican model, xii, 20, 35, 126, 236, 237–41, 240

Front de gauche, 241, 252
Front National (FN), 245, 252
The Future of Multi-Ethnic Britain (CMEB), 80

Gagnon, Alain, 39–40, 41
Gastarbeiter (guestworkers), 164–5
Geißler, Heiner, 170
Gellner, Ernest, 283, 319
gender discrimination, 57
Geneva Convention, 11
Gentry Republic, 258
German General Social Survey, 164
German Islam Conference, 168, 169, 184
German language, 168–9, 180–1
Germans in Poland, 260, 261
Germany
  asylum seekers, 165, 171
  citizenship, 165, 167, 180
  Citizenship Law, 27
  cultural diversity management, 163
  cultural pluralism, 170–1, 180
  education, 169, 178, 185
  ethnic diversity, 171–2
  federalism, 166
  foreigners, 164–6, 174, 176, 177–8, 179, 180–2, 184, 185n2
  Green Card initiative, 171
  Green Party, 170, 182
  immigrants, 11, 164–5, 165–6
  immigration, 18–19, 164, 170–1
  integration, 27, 168, 169–70, 173–4
  Islam, 169, 178
  labour migrants, 164–5
  Leitkultur, 26, 27, 29, 174, 184
  MIPEX, 163
  multicultural model, 163–4, 166–70
  national identities, 28, 174
  naturalisation, 165, 167, 180
  populist political parties, 175
  public opinion on multiculturalism, 176–84
  refugees, 165
  Social Democrats, 170, 182
  Turks, 165–6, 167, 174–5, 177–8, 182
Gerteis, Joseph, 39, 41
Giordano, Ralph, 172

globalisation, 4, 328, 331
  cultural, 279, 290
  negative effects, 291–2
  outsourcing, 204
  Poland, 20, 257
  Turkey, 298, 313
Goodhart, David, 78
Gorbachev, Mikhail, 280–1
Gove, Michael, 77
Greater London Council, 84
Greece, 30, 176
Green Card initiative, 171
Green Party, Germany, 170, 182
Green Party, Italy, 220
Greenland, 196, 325
group differences, 79, 191
  recognition, 217, 218, 219, 228–30, 280
Guéant, Claude, 248–9, 250
guest worker approach, 164–5, 87, 171, 185n2, 192
Guiraudon, Virginie, 111–12
Gül, Abdullah, 312
Gumiliev, Lev, 283

Habermas, Jürgen, 173, 174
Hagendoorn, L., 97–8
  When Ways of Life Collide, 110
Hague, William, 81
Halbertal, Moshe, 62, 64
HALDE, 32, 244
Hammar, Tomas, 143
Hannerz, Ulf, 146
harm principle, 64
Hartmann, Douglas, 39, 41
Hedetoft, Ulf, 21–2, 320, 325, 326, 327
Hegel, Georg Wilhelm Friedrich, 62
Heinskou, Nilas Nordberg, 196
Held, David, 294
Helsinki Foundation, 273
Helsinki Summit, 21, 297, 309
Herder, Johann, 62
High Authority for the Fight against Discrimination and for Equality (HALDE), 32, 244
Hobolth, Mogens, 10–11
Holland *see* Netherlands
Hollande, François, 252
Holtug, Nils, 19
homosexuality, 64
Honneth, Axel, 62
honour crimes, 150, 172
Hopper, Paul, 292
Horn of Africa migrants, 217
Hortefeux, Brice, 246–7
human rights, 145, 238
Hungary, 322

Iacovino, Raffaele, 39–40, 41
identity
  Christianity, 30
  citizenship, 33
  culture, 62–3, 261
  dual/compound, 291
  group, 66
  hybrid, 61
  integration, 100
  personal, 62, 64
  supranational, 291
identity politics, 239
IMER, 6
IMISCOE, 7–8
Immigrant Minority Language and Culture classes, 101–2
immigrants
  Belgium, 11, 122–4
  cultural diversity, 229
  deficit perspective, 168
  educational levels, 123
  France, 11
  Germany, 164–5
  illegal, 216, 221–2, 227–8, 262–3
  integration, 97, 98
  Poland, 262–4
  protection policies, 11, 218
  Sweden, 11, 143–4, 145–6, 147–8, 154–5
  unemployment, 4, 112, 148
  Wallonia, 122–3, 126
  see also integration; labour migrants
immigration
  Belgium, 120–1, 125–7
  colonialism, 322
  Denmark, 4, 190, 192–6
  differentialism, 100
  diversity, 3
  economics, 4, 10–11, 172–3, 247
  family reunification, 7, 123–4, 168
  Germany, 18–19, 164, 170–1
  intercultural approach, 230
  Italian laws, 223–4
  national identities, 245–50
  Netherlands, 4, 100–1
  Northern League, 218–19
  politicised, 18
  postcolonialism, 242
  post-World War II, 322
  refugees, 6, 7
  research, 219, 229
Immigration, Asylum and Nationality Act, Britain, 85–6
Immigration Act, Germany, 167
Immigration Board, Sweden, 143

Imoual, A., 89
IMPALA, 10–11
inclusion, 7, 44, 216, 217–21, 324
indifference, politics of, 236, 240, 245
Indigènes de la République, 243
indigenous populations, 3, 20, 61–2, 79, *195*, 196, 260; *see also* autochthon minorities
Individual Integration Programmes, 271
Ingushetia, Republic of, 285
INSEE (National Institute for Statistics and Economic Studies), 248
integrated society concept, 291
integration
    assimilation, 39, 84, 115, 204, 241–5
    Belgium, 125–7, 132
    Britain, 76–7
    civic, 5, 79, 105, 168
    civil-cultural, 129–32
    Denmark, 190, 192–202
    diversity, 39
    European Union, 308–9
    failure, 172, 236
    Flanders, 127, 130, 131, 132, 135
    France, 242, 246–7
    Germany, 27, 168, 169–70, 173–4
    identity, 100
    immigrants, 97, 98
    Italy, 19, 216, 231
    labour migrants, 7
    liberalisation, 201
    Muslims, 5, 29
    nation state, 320
    national regimes, 324
    nationality, 133–5
    Netherlands, 100–1, 102–3, *107*, 114–15
    philosophies of, 127
    Poland, 270–1
    social, 28, 39
    socio-economic, 129–32, 185
    Sweden, 18, 147–8, 153, 325
Integration Agreement, Italy, 216–17, 227, 230, 231
integration courses, 167–8
intellectuals, 294, 311
Intercultural Cities Programme, 232
interculturalism, 40, 41, 230
Interculturality Sessions, Belgium, 130–1
interethnic relationships, 181–3

International Conference on Immigration, 219
International Labour Organisation Convention, 218
international migration and ethnic relations (IMER), 6
International Social Survey Program *see* ISSP
Islam
    Chechens, 264
    Denmark, 192
    education, 178, 182
    fundamentalism, 19, 150
    Germany, 166, 169, 178
    and liberal values, 201, 207
    Turkey, 303–4
    and Western civilisation, 172
    see also Muslims
Islam Conference, 168, 169, 184
Islamist multiculturalism, 302–4
Islamophobia, 88, 184, 206–7, 250, 273
ISSP, 202, *203*, 205, 206
Italian residents, Germany, 165–6, 178, 182
Italian Social Movement, 221
Italy
    Albanian immigrants, 228
    assimilation, 216
    attitudes to immigration, *224*
    autonomy, 221
    Bulgarian immigrants, 226
    Catholic Church, 217, 220, 221, 222, 223, 225
    Charter of Values, Citizenship and Integration, 225, 226
    Communists, 220
    cultural diversity, 222
    cultural turn, 221–8, 230
    Democratic Party, 230
    emigrants to Germany, 165–6
    ethnic diversity, 217–18
    foreigners, 222
    Green Party, 220
    immigration laws, 223–4
    integration, 19, 216, 231
    Integration Agreement, 216–17, 227, 230, 231
    labour migrants, 224
    national identity, 216, 228, 231–2
    Popular Party, 220
    protectionism, 218
    public opinion on immigration, 232
    religious diversity, 222–3

Roma community, 19, 219, 226, 228, 232
Romanian immigrants, 226
Security Law, 226–7
Social Democratic Party, 220
Social Policy Fund, 221
stay contract, 223–4
third way approach, 219
Union of Hebrew Communities, 225

Jacobin state, 238, 239, 240
Jacobsson, Bengt, 143
Jasińska-Kania, Aleksandra, 272
Jefferson, Thomas, 238
Jenkins, Roy, 84
Jespersen, Karen, 196–7, 199, 201
Jewish Autonomous Oblast, 282
Jewish Council (CRIF), 243
Jews
    deported, 110
    France, 241, 243
    Ottoman Empire, 35
    Poland, 258, 259, 266, 272, 273
    religious clothing, 151
    Russia, 282, 288
    in seclusion, 62, 64
    Turkey, 298, 301–2, 309
    Ultra-Orthodox, 64, 65
    see also anti-Semitism
John Paul II, Pope, 222
Joint Commission of Government and Ethnic and National Minorities, 266
Joppke, Christian, 29–31, 75, 79, 83, 207
jus sanguinis, 30, 165, 267
jus soli, 27, 133, 167
Justice and Development Party, Turkey *see* AKP

Kaczyński, Jarosław, 274
Kaczyński, Lech, 267–8
Kashubians, 262, 266
Kauder, Volker, 174
Kaya, Ayhan, 21
Kazimierz the Great, 258
Kelek, Necla: *Die fremde Braut*, 172
Kelly, Ruth, 90
Kemalist regime, 298, 302–4, 306
Kepel, Gilles, 77
Kivisto, Peter, 75, 79
Kjærsgaard, Pia, 201
Komorowski, Bronisław, 267–8

Koopmans, Ruud, 38, 97, 110, 112, 163, 166
krai, 282
Krarup, Søren, 200–1
Kukhatas, Chandran, 65–8
Kulturnation, Flanders, 125
Kurdish Workers Party (PKK), 306
Kurds, 301, 302, 305–8, 310
Kymlicka, Will
  accommodation of cultural differences, 99
  British multiculturalism, 75
  civic integration, 5
  cross-national studies, 9, 237
  cultural rights, 60–1, 64
  differential treatment, 68
  diversity policy, 5, 6
  immigrants as illiberal, 207
  liberal multiculturalism, 4, 41
  minority rights, 83
  multiculturalism, 75, 85, 138, 139, 154
  welfare state factors, 207
Kærgård, Niels, 202

Labour Government, 87; *see also* New Labour
labour migrants, 208
  Belgium, 128–9
  Flanders, 127
  Germany, 164–5
  integration, 7
  Italy, 224
  Poland, 263, 269
  qualifications, 193
  Russian Federation, 285, 287
  Sweden, 140
laïcité principle, 151, 200, 240, 244, 248, 251
language requirements, 27, 153
language tests, 11, 168, 174
Laruelle, Marlene, 292
Lausanne Treaty, 302, 310
Lawrence, Stephen, 81
Le Pen, Marine, 245, 252
Lefèvre, Théo, 120
Leijon, Anna-Greta, 145
Lester, Anthony, 82
Liberal Democratic Party, Russian Federation, 288
Liberal Party, Sweden, 151, 153–4
Liberal–Conservative coalition, Denmark, 192, 193, 194, 196, 198
liberalism
  accommodation, 70
  challenged, 22
  culturalism, 57–9
  Denmark, 208–10

differentialism, 54–7
diversity, 52–3
  and Islam, 201, 207
  Joppke on, 29
  non-discrimination, 30
  public/private spheres, 198
  religious liberty, 53–4
  repressive, 168
  society, 68–9
  universalist, 30
Lijphart, Arend, 97
link workers, 229
Lithuania, 322
LO, 140, 142–3
local authorities, 84–5
Localism Act, 84
Locke, John, 57
Łodzinski, Sławomir, 272, 274
London 7/7 bombings, 77, 87, 89, 224
Lutheran Church, 192, 200

McGhee, Derek, 86–7
Mackey, Eva, 10
Madrid bombings, 224
Malakhov, Vladimir, 289, 290
Malik, Kenan, 82
Malinova, Olga, 283
Malmö Institute (MIM), 7
managed migration points system, 86–7
Mansouri, Fethi, 75
Margalit, Avishal, 62, 63, 64
marginalisation, 64, 228, 270
Maroni, Roberto, 226, 228
marriage
  arranged, 69
  Belgium, 133
  forced, 168, 172, 194
  grey, 248
  international, 288
  Roma, 262
  Russia, 288
  Sweden, 150
  Turkey, 299
  Ukrainians/Poles, 248
Marshall, Thomas Humphrey, 32
Martiniello, Marco, 18, 120, 125
Martyanov, Victor, 290, 293
Marxism-Leninism, 280
Maussen, Marcel, 111
May, Theresa, 90
Mazowiecki, Tadeusz, 259–60
Medina Covenant, 304
Medvedev, Dmitry, 281–2
Meer, Nasar, 5, 16, 17, 75–6, 85
European Multiculturalisms, 9

'The multicultural states we are in', 76
Mélenchon, Jean-Luc, 241, 252
Merkel, Angela, xv, 25, 163, 175, 190
Merz, Friedrich, 174
Metropolis network, 7
migrant labour *see* labour migrants
migration, 5, 6–8, 111–12, 113–14, 325; *see also* immigration
Mikkelsen, Brian, 199
Mill, John Stuart, 54, 64
millet system, 35, 298–9, 300, 301, 304–5
MIM (Malmö Institute), 7
MINAB, 88
Minorities Memorandum, 101, 102
minority groups
  assimilation, 207–8
  attitudes to, 203
  cultures, 66, 78, 154
  identity, 47, 61
  languages, 61
  rights, 83, 145, 154
minority schools, 144
MIPEX (Multiculturalism Policy Index), 5–6
  Denmark, 193–4
  Germany, 163
  Poland, 267, 269, 271
Mitterrand, François, 243
Moderate Party, Sweden, 153
Modood, Tariq, xv
  British multiculturalism, 8, 17, 75–6, 78
  European Multiculturalisms, 9
  Multicultural Politics, 8–9
  'The multicultural states we are in', 76
  on multiculturalism, 3, 5, 16, 280, 283
  Plural State, 41
  revised multiculturalism, 85
  state/citizenship, 33–8
  types of state, 33, 34, 35–6, 37
monoculturalism, 319, 323, 330
Moratti, Letizia, 225
Moreño, Luis, 291
Moroccans, 113, 228
Moscow, 283, 287–8
Mosques and Imams National Advisory Board (MINAB), 88
mother-tongue learning, 102, 143, 144, 195–6, 262, 268
Mouritsen, Per, 30

multiculturalism, 139
  advocacy of, 323
  assimilationism, 53, 99
  backlash against, 328–31
  as challenge, 52, 69–70
  citizenship, 41, 44
  as conceptual paradox,
    319–21, 331–2
  dangers of, 284
  in decline, xv, 25, 289–94
  expansion, 6
  failure of, 236, 279
  impact in Europe, 21–2,
    329–31
  as normative concept, 26, 44,
    191–2, 330
  path-dependency, 111–12,
    114, 166
  policies, 166–70, 194, 195
  political, 52–3, 76, 79, 80,
    139–40
  postcolonialism, 14
  post-immigration, 79
  re-balancing, 76, 85
  research on, 241–2
  resilience, 40–5
  retreat from, 75–6, 78–9,
    138, 145–9, 155
Multiculturalism Policy Index
  see MIPEX
Muslim headscarf, 30, 151,
  169, 172, 201, 244, 303–4
Muslims
  in Britain, 9, 78, 90–1
  in Denmark, 191
  in France, 248
  in Germany, 163, 166, 169,
    172, 173
  integration, 5, 29
  in Italy, 219, 222–3, 227–8
  in Poland, 264–5, 270
  radicalism, 28, 90–1
  in Russia, 287
  Sunni, 300, 304–5
  Tatars, 260, 264
  Turkish, 299, 300–1
  see also Islam

nation state, 279, 319, 320,
  323–4
National Alliance, Italy, 221
national identities
  assimilationism, 28
  Britain, 322
  citizenship, 26
  Denmark, 28, 199
  emphasis on, 33, 34, 45
  Europe, 27, 28
  France, 245–50
  Germany, 28, 174
  immigration, 245–50
  inclusive, 76

Italy, 216, 228, 231–2
  Joppke, 29–30
  Poland, 260–2, 274
  Russian Federation, 279, 283
  Sarkozy, 20, 245–6, 248
  Sweden, 152
  Turkey, 301
  updating, 44
National Institute for Statistics
  and Economic Studies
  (INSEE), 248
National Minorities Debate,
  103
National Socialist Underground
  (NSU), 175
nationalism, 20, 200–1, 283,
  324, 328–31
Nationality, Immigration and
  Asylum Act, UK, 27–8,
  85–6
Nationality Law, Belgium, 133
nationhood, 283
naturalisation, 11–12
  Belgium, 133
  France, 248–9
  Germany, 165, 167, 180
  Poland, 267–8
Nazism, 259, 321
'Near Neighbours' strategy, 91
Neighbourhood Policies, 105
Netherlands
  academics on
    multiculturalism model,
    110–11
  anti-immigration parties, 100
  assimilation, 98, 104–6,
    112–14
  citizenship, 103
  civic integration
    programmes, 105
  and Denmark, compared,
    201–2
  Ethnic Minorities Policy,
    101–2, 106, 108
  ethnic riots, 100
  Immigrant Minority
    Language and Culture
    classes, 101–2
  immigration, 4, 100–1
  integration, 100–1, 102–3,
    107, 114–15
  Jews, deported, 110
  multicultural model
    deconstructed, 106–13
  multiculturalism, 4, 15,
    17–18, 97–102
  National Minorities Debate,
    103
  new realism, 108
  pillarism, 97, 110–11, 112
  populist political parties, 115
  terrorist acts, 100

neutrality, 33
  contentlessness, 44
  cultural, 241
  in German schools, 169
  as goal, 46
  Joppke, 31
  liberal, 41
  state, 16, 55–6, 65–7, 69
New Labour, 26–7, 81, 84, 91
New Opportunities for
  Research Funding Agency
  Co-operation in Europe
  (NORFACE), 8
New York Times, 173
Nezavisimaya Gazeta, 279
NIMBY syndrome, 231
non-discrimination, 30, 31
NORFACE, 8
Northern League, 216, 218–19,
  221, 222–3, 225, 232
Norway, 11
NSU, 175
Nussbaum, Martha, 293
NVA party, Flanders, 128,
  136

Öberg, Kjell, 143
oblasts, 282
oil crises, 100
Okin, Susan Moller, 13–14
Orthodox Church, 260; see
  also Russian Orthodox
  Church; Syrian Orthodox
  Church
Other, 13, 321
Ottoman Empire, 35, 298,
  299–300
Oudkerk, Rob, 113
Ouseley Report, 85
outsourcing, 204

Padania nation, 222
Palestine cause, 91, 225
Pankevich, Natalya, 281
Parekh, Bhikhu, 36–7, 75,
  80, 99
  Rethinking Multiculturalism,
    8
parochialism, 21, 297
partnership goal, 8, 143, 144
path-dependency, 111–12, 114,
  166, 327, 330
Pera, Marcello, 224
PET (Preventing Extremism
  Together), 87–90
Pfaff, William, 77
Phillips, Melanie, 77
Phillips, Trevor, 78
Pietsch, Juliet, 75
pillarism, 97, 110–11, 112
Pind, Søren, 190, 204
Pittelkow, Ralf, 197, 199, 201

PKK (Kurdish Workers Party),
306, 308
pluralism, 8–9, 10, 38, 39,
41, 260–4, 274; *see also*
cultural pluralism
Poland
anti-discrimination, 269–70
asylum seekers, 275
autochthon minorities,
260–2
border changes, 258
Catholic Church, 15, 258,
260, 264, 270, 271, 272
citizenship, 267–8
Committee of National and
Ethnic Minorities, 259–60
democratisation, 259–60
education, 268–9
emigrants to Germany,
165–6
Ethnic and National
Minorities Act, 261
ethnic composition, 258–9,
260–2
Europeanisation, 257, 260
foreigners, 257, 263, 267,
271
Germans in, 260, 261
globalisation, 20, 257
homogeneity, 20, 257, 275
immigrants, 262–4
integration, 270–1
Islamophobia, 273
Jews, 258, 259, 266, 272,
273
labour migrants, 263, 269
MIPEX, 267, 269, 271
mother-tongue instruction,
268
multiculturalism, 15–16,
258–60
Muslims, 264–5, 270
national identities, 260–2,
274
national minorities, 266
naturalisation, 267–8
Orthodox Church, 260
pluralism, 257, 265–70, 274
political rights, 267
Protestantism, 260
provinces, 261
refugees, 264
Regional Language, National
and Ethnic Minorities Act,
265–6
religious differences, 264–5,
270
Repatriation Act, 267
Roma community, 20, 259,
262, 266
secularisation, 264
'Poland 2020' report, 270–1

Poleis institute, 219
Polish Charter, 269
Poppelaars, Caelesta, 112
Popular Party, Italy, 220
populist political parties, 97,
104, 108–9, 115, 175
postcolonialism, 14, 242, 243,
247
post-immigration, 26, 33,
79, 81
Potsdam conference, 258
Prevent agenda, New Labour,
91
Preventing Extremism Together
(PET), 87–90
primordialism, 283
Prins, Baukje, 108, 109
Pro-Cologne, 175
Prodi, Romano, 220, 226
Prokhorov, Mikhail, 292
Pro-NRW, 175
protection policies, 11, 218
Protestantism, 15, 97, 111,
200, 258, 260, 264
PS *see* Socialist Party, France
Putin, Vladimir, 279, 284, 289,
292

Quebec, 39, 40

Race Directive, 32
race equality legislation, 82
race relations, 178–9
Race Relations Acts, Britain,
17, 83–4
racism, 251, 306–7, 322
Rasmussen, Anders Fogh, 196,
200
Rasmussen, Poul Nyrup, 196
Rath, Jan, 110, 111
Rawls, John, 54–5, 198
Raz, Joseph, 58, 63
reception policies, 231
recognition, 220, 221, 231
vs assimilation, 325
cultural rights, 65
culture, 62, 63–4, 219,
229–30
group differences, 217, 218,
219, 228–30, 280
religious differences, 303–4
recognition, politics of, 236,
242–3, 274
refugees, 6, 7, 11
Denmark, 192
Germany, 165
Poland, 264
Sweden, 149
Regained Lands, 258–9
Regional Language, National
and Ethnic Minorities Act,
Poland, 265–6

Reinfeldt, Fredrik, 326
religious clothing
France, 244
Muslim headscarf, 30, 151,
169, 172, 201
Turkey, 304
see also Sikhs
religious differences
belief groups, 311
Denmark, 192, 195
Italy, 222–3
Jews, 65
liberalism, 53–4
Poland, 264–5, 270
recognition of, 303–4
secluded minorities, 62
social attitudes, 271–3
state, 299
Turkey, 302–4
religious education, 80, 178,
195
re-nationalisation, 26–7, 28–9
Repatriation Act, Poland, 267
Republic ideal, 34, 35, 198
Republikaner, Germany, 171
rights
citizenship, 26, 140, 219
civil, 167
cultural, 60–1, 64, 65, 154
differentialism, 69
equal, 176–9
ethnic minorities, 322–3
group-differentiated, 209,
210, 236
individual, 236, 237–8
migrants, 10
minority groups, 83, 145,
154
public/private, 33, 46
social/political, 99, 209, 267
special, 209
see also human rights
riots
Britain, 77, 85
France, 243, 249
Netherlands, 100
Russia, 287–8
ritual slaughter, 150
Rodriguez-Garcia, Dan, 75
Roggeband, Conny, 109
Roma community
children's education, 268
Czech Republic, 322
forced eviction, 230
Italy, 19, 219, 226, 228, 232
marginalisation, 64, 228,
270
Poland, 20, 259, 262, 266
Sweden, 141
Romanian immigrants, 226,
322
Runnymede Trust, 80, 82

Russian Association of Political Sciences, 289
Russian Empire, 280, 281
Russian Federation, 15–16
  census, 285
  centralisation, 281–2
  citizenship, 284
  Constitution, 281
  diversity, 20–1
  ethnic composition, 285–6
  ethnic/language groupings, 286
  Europeanness, 292–3
  foreigners, 288, 290
  Jews, 282, 288
  labour migrants, 285, 287
  Liberal Democrats, 288
  and Lithuania, 322
  multinationalism, 279–85
  Muslims, 287
  national identities, 279, 283
  normative implications, 289–94
  regional autonomy, 261, 280, 282
  riots, 287–8
  transnational approach, 21
Russian Orthodox Church, 285
Russian Public Opinion Research Center (VCIOM), 287–9
Russian United Democratic Party, 289
Rutte, Mark, 105
Rüttgers, Jürgen, 171

Sabiha Gökçen Airport, 308
St Petersburg, 283, 287, 289
Sámi population, 145, 322
Sarkozy, Nicolas
  defeated, 252
  election of, 236
  immigrant grandfather, 244
  on immigration, 247
  Islam, 250
  on Joan of Arc, 251
  monocultural turn, 20
  on multiculturalism, xv, 25, 237, 241
  national identity, 20, 245–6, 248
Sarrazin, Thilo, 184
  Germany Does Away with Itself, 163, 172–3
Sartori, Giovanni, 222–3
Sayegh, Pascal-Yan, 19–20
Scheffer, Paul, 97, 108, 114
Scheffer debate, 104
Schengen Agreement, 265
Scholars Roadshow, 88
Scholten, Peter, 17–18, 99, 111
Schuman, Howard, 178

Schwarz, David, 142
Schwarzer, Alice, 172
Scientific Committee, 226
Scotland, 77, 79
Scruton, Roger, 75
secularism, 240, 251, 264
securitisation, 87–91
Security Law, Italy, 226–7
Seehofer, Horst, 171
segregation, 19, 38, 47, 97, 185, 209, 303
separatism, 41, 55
settlement policies, 76, 231, 301
Sèvres Peace Treaty, 298
Sicily, 217
Sieyès, Abbé, 239
Sikhs, 150, 191, 195, 210
Silesians, 261–2, 266, 274
Silj, Alessandro, 331
  European Multiculturalism Revisited, 9
Smith, Jacqui, 86
Sniderman, Paul M., 97–8
  When Ways of Life Collide, 110
social cohesion, 79, 84–5, 196–202, 206–7
Social Democratic Party, Germany, 170, 182
Social Democratic Party, Italy, 220
Social Democrats, Denmark, 193
Social Democrats, Sweden, 140–1, 142–3, 144, 146, 154
social distance, 177, 182
Social Liberal party, Denmark, 193
Social Policy Fund, Italy, 221
social security, 204
socialist party, Wallonia, 128
Socialist Party (PS), France, xii, 243, 252
society
  categories, 248
  cultures, 60–1, 287
  fragmentation of, 25, 223
  liberalism, 68–9
  public/private spheres, 239
Soper, J. Christopher, 270
SOS Racisme, 243
SOU, 144
South Korea, 14
sovereign democracy, 284
Spain, 30, 322
Spalek, Basla, 89
Spengler, Oswald, 328
Staatnation, 125
Stalin, Joseph, 258, 282, 283
start help, Denmark, 193

Stasi, Bernard, 244
state
  church, 53–4, 55, 240
  citizenship, 33, 46–7, 58
  decentred, 33
  difference, 42
  liberal, 35, 36, 56
  neutrality, 55–6, 65–7, 69
  religion, 299
  separatist, 38
  see also nation state
Statham, Paul, 97
stay contract, Italy, 223–4
Stjernfelt, Frederik, 209–10
Stotijn, Rosanne, 112
Støvring, Kasper, 200
Sunni-Muslims, 300, 304–5
Surinam, 100
Swann, Michael, 85
Sweden
  abuse ignored, 150
  assimilation, 141
  asylum seekers, 145, 149
  citizenship, 140, 153–4
  Commission on Discrimination, 148–9
  Commission on Immigration, 143
  Conservative Party, 142, 144
  cultural exemptions, 149–51
  cultural pluralism, 142, 145
  and Denmark, 202, 324–7
  Discrimination Act, 150–1
  Education Act, 151
  ethnic discrimination Ombudsman, 327
  Finnish people, 322
  immigrant and minority policy, 11, 143–4, 145–6, 147–8, 154–5
  Immigration Board, 143
  integration policy, 18, 147–8, 153, 325
  Liberal Party, 151, 153–4
  LO, 140, 142–3
  migrant labour, 140
  migration policy, 7, 325
  Moderate Party, 153
  multiculturalism, 15, 138–45, 326
  national identities, 152
  refugees, 149
  retreat from multiculturalism, 145–9, 155
  Roma community, 141
  Social Democrats, 140–1, 142–3, 144, 146, 154
  Sweden Democrats, 152, 154, 155
  welfare state, 141, 144, 154, 327

Sweden Democrats, 152, 154, 155
Swedish Citizenship Commttee, 153
Swedish Trade Union Confederation (LO), 140
Switzerland, 11
Syriac Orthodox Church, 311

Tajikistan, 287, 288–9
Tanzimat era, 298–9
Taras, Raymond, 290–1
Tatars, 260, 264, 268
Tatarstan, 281, 285
Taylor, Charles, 4, 62–3, 64, 68, 274
Tekinalp, Moiz Kohen: *Turkification*, 301–2
terrorist acts, 9, 100, 216; *see also* London 7/7 bombings
Tezcür, Güneş, 307
Thatcher, Margaret, 84
Thielemann, Eiko, 10–11
Thomas, Paul, 76
Thorning-Schmidt, Helle, 208
TNS Gallup A/S 2011, *203*, 208
tolerance, 66, 299–300
Toprak, Binnaz, 300
Touraine, Alain, 241
Transatlantic Trends: Immigration Survey, 227–8
transnationalism, 290, 291, 294
Triadafilopoulos, Phil, 169
Triandafyllidou, Anna: *European Multiculturalisms*, 9
trust, 197, 206–7
Tunisians in Sicily, 217
Turco-Napolitano law, 220, 221, 222, 231
Turkey, 21
  assimilationism, 301–2
  church/state, 299
  citizenship, 313
  Constitution, 313
  democratisation, 307, 309
  ethnic diversity, 297–8
  ethnocultural diversity, 297, 300–1, 302–8, 312–13

  and European Union, 311–12
  exclusionist policies, 301–2
  freedom of expression, 306
  globalisation, 298, 313
  historic multiculturalism, 298–9
  IMF, 309
  Jews, 298, 301–2, 309
  millet system, 35, 298–9, 300, 301, 304–5
  multiculturalism, 15–16
  Muslims, 299
  national identities, 301
  non-Muslim minorities, 299, 310–11
  racism, 306–7
  religious diversity, 302–4
  ultranationalists, 311
  WP, 302–4
Turks in Germany, 165–6, 167, 174–5, 177–8, 182

UCOII, 225
Uitermark, Justus, 112–13
Ukrainians, 263, 285, 287
unemployment, 4, 112, 127, 148, 204, 246–7
Union of Hebrew Communities, Italy, 225
Union of Islamic Communities in Italy (UCOII), 225
Union of Right Forces, 289
United Nations, 185, 238, 322
United Russia, 287
United States of America, 293
Universal Declaration of Human Rights, 238
universalism, 30, 82, 237–8
Urban, Michael, 293
urban policy, 105, 242–3
USSR, 280, 281, 283
Uzbekistan, 285, 287, 289

Van Gogh, Theo, 224
VCIOM, 287–9
Venstre, 200
Verdonk, Rita, 104
Vermeulen, Floris, 112
Verschueren, Jef, 125, 126

Vertovec, Steven, 99, 150, 195
  Multiculturalism Backlash, 9
Vietnamese, 263, 266
Villard, Florent, 19–20
Vink, Maarten, 111
Vliegenthart, Rens, 109
voluntarism, 65–8
voluntary associations, 57–8
Vranken, Jan, 125

Wallonia
  assimilation in history, 126
  diversity management, 132
  Flemish, 126
  French language, 132
  French model, 126
  immigrants, 122–3, 126
  socialist party, 128
  unemployment, 127
  Walloons, 18, 120–1, 125
  work permits, 123–4, 129
Walzer, Michael, 55
Wasmer, Martina, 18–19
Weil, Patrick, 241
Welfare Party (WP), Turkey, 302–4
welfare state
  Denmark, 194, 199, 206, 207, 325, 327
  refugees, 11
  Sweden, 141, 144, 154
Wessendorf, Susanne, 150, 195
  Multiculturalism Backlash, 9
Westphalia, Peace of, 319
Wievorka, Michel, 241
Wilders, Geert, 108–9, 115
Włoch, Renata, 20
Wolf, Martin, 77
World War II aftermath, 321
WP, Turkey, 302–4
WRR Report, 102, 103, 108

xenophobia, 173, 284, 287

Yalta conference, 258
Yishkov, Valerii, 284
Yugoslavia, former, 148, 165–6, 219

Žižek, Slavoj, 13